How the World Compares

Series Editor

Rodney Tiffen, University of Sydney, Sydney, NSW, Australia

How the World Compares provides an encylopaedic examination of social indicators from 18 economically advanced, stable liberal democracies. It offers important points of reference for political science researchers and students, and it presents a unique and accessible perspective for anyone interested in comparative politics. In nearly all countries, most public controversies and policy debates are conducted with a solely domestic focus, either ignoring international experience or using it opportunistically and selectively. People in many countries have beliefs about their own uniqueness – for better and worse – that are largely uninformed by deep knowledge of other countries. How the World Compares provides a much-needed backdrop to such debates, bringing together reliable data on the most relevant social indicators and comparing them across relevant countries. The core of these books offers data drawn from international organisations (especially the OECD but also from sources such as agencies of the United Nations and World Bank) and analysis, concentrating on the 18 affluent democracies that have the most in common. There is an examination of global distributions, as well as emerging global trends between the major powers in key areas such as population, economics, energy use, and so forth. Finally there is national data concentrating on the specified country alone. The first country to be analysed is the Unites States. The books cover as many aspects of social life as possible, from taxation to traffic accidents, homicide rates to health expenditure, and interest rates to internet usage. The discussion focuses on changes over time and comparisons between countries, looking at how the data relate to national debates about policies, performance and prospects, especially if these have been conducted in a vacuum.

More information about this series at http://www.springer.com/series/15592

Rodney Tiffen • Anika Gauja •
Brendon O'Connor •
Ross Gittins • David Smith

How America Compares

Rodney Tiffen
University of Sydney
Sydney, NSW, Australia

Anika Gauja
University of Sydney
Sydney, NSW, Australia

Brendon O'Connor
University of Sydney
Sydney, NSW, Australia

Ross Gittins
Sydney Morning Herald
Sydney, NSW, Australia

David Smith
University of Sydney
Sydney, NSW, Australia

ISSN 2522-5340 ISSN 2522-5359 (electronic)
How the World Compares
ISBN 978-981-13-9581-9 ISBN 978-981-13-9582-6 (eBook)
https://doi.org/10.1007/978-981-13-9582-6

© Springer Nature Singapore Pte Ltd. 2020
This work is subject to copyright. All rights are reserved by the Publisher, whether the whole or part of the material is concerned, specifically the rights of translation, reprinting, reuse of illustrations, recitation, broadcasting, reproduction on microfilms or in any other physical way, and transmission or information storage and retrieval, electronic adaptation, computer software, or by similar or dissimilar methodology now known or hereafter developed.
The use of general descriptive names, registered names, trademarks, service marks, etc. in this publication does not imply, even in the absence of a specific statement, that such names are exempt from the relevant protective laws and regulations and therefore free for general use.
The publisher, the authors and the editors are safe to assume that the advice and information in this book are believed to be true and accurate at the date of publication. Neither the publisher nor the authors or the editors give a warranty, expressed or implied, with respect to the material contained herein or for any errors or omissions that may have been made. The publisher remains neutral with regard to jurisdictional claims in published maps and institutional affiliations.

This Springer imprint is published by the registered company Springer Nature Singapore Pte Ltd.
The registered company address is: 152 Beach Road, #21-01/04 Gateway East, Singapore 189721, Singapore

Contents

1	**People and Life Expectancy**		1
	1.1	Global Population	1
	1.2	Population Growth	3
	1.3	Urbanisation	4
	1.4	The Ageing Society	6
2	**Government and Politics**		9
	2.1	Constitutional History	9
	2.2	Heads of State and Heads of Government	11
	2.3	Federalism	12
	2.4	Legislative Structures	13
	2.5	Governments, Executives and Legislatures	15
	2.6	Electoral Systems	16
	2.7	Party Systems and Electoral Choice	18
	2.8	Political Participation	19
	2.9	The Judiciary	21
	2.10	Political Finance	22
	2.11	Electoral Integrity	24
	2.12	Corruption	26
	2.13	Assessing Democracy	27
3	**Economics**		29
	3.1	Contemporary Economic Income and Growth	29
	3.2	Long-Term Economic Development	30
	3.3	Inflation and Interest Rates	31
	3.4	Changing Economic Structures	33
	3.5	International Trade	34
	3.6	Globalising Economies	36
	3.7	Exchange Rates	38
	3.8	Productivity	39
	3.9	Global Competitiveness and Economic Freedom	40
	3.10	Human Development Index	42
4	**Work and Labour**		45
	4.1	Labour Force Participation and the Ageing Society	45
	4.2	Unemployment	47
	4.3	Part-Time Work and Working Hours	48
	4.4	Underemployment, Unsatisfactory and Vulnerable Work	50
	4.5	Trade Unions	51
	4.6	Industrial Disputes	53

5 Government Taxes and Spending ... 55
- 5.1 Government Taxes and Spending ... 55
- 5.2 Government Debt and Budget Balances ... 56
- 5.3 Structure of Government Spending ... 58

6 Health ... 61
- 6.1 Health Expenditure ... 61
- 6.2 Financing Health Care ... 62
- 6.3 Healthcare Services ... 64
- 6.4 Healthcare Personnel ... 66
- 6.5 Gender and Mortality ... 67
- 6.6 Mortality and Causes of Death ... 69
- 6.7 Cancer ... 71
- 6.8 Non-medical Determinants of Health ... 72

7 Education ... 75
- 7.1 Educational Attainment ... 75
- 7.2 Education Spending ... 77
- 7.3 Maths, Science and Reading Skills ... 78
- 7.4 Education and Equity ... 80
- 7.5 Schools' Resources and Learning Environments ... 81
- 7.6 Primary Students' Learning Skills ... 83
- 7.7 Pre-primary Education ... 85
- 7.8 Adult Competencies ... 86

8 Inequality and Social Welfare ... 89
- 8.1 Income Inequality ... 89
- 8.2 Wealth Inequality ... 90
- 8.3 Poverty ... 91
- 8.4 Disability ... 93
- 8.5 Poverty and the Ageing Society ... 95
- 8.6 Government Social Spending and Redistribution ... 96
- 8.7 Child Poverty and Social Mobility ... 98

9 Immigration and Refugees ... 101
- 9.1 Immigration Flows ... 101
- 9.2 Settlement of Immigrants ... 103
- 9.3 Refugees ... 105
- 9.4 Asylum Seekers ... 107

10 Gender ... 109
- 10.1 Women and Work ... 109
- 10.2 Gender and Education ... 111
- 10.3 Glass Ceilings and Equity Issues ... 112
- 10.4 Women in Public Life ... 113
- 10.5 Global Gender Gap ... 115

11 International Relations ... 117
- 11.1 Military Spending and Foreign Aid ... 117
- 11.2 America's International Standing ... 118
- 11.3 Terrorism ... 120
- 11.4 Globalisation ... 122

12 Environment ... 125
- 12.1 Biodiversity ... 125
- 12.2 Global Warming ... 127

	12.3	Greenhouse Gas Emissions	129
	12.4	Energy	130
	12.5	Policies and Pollution	132
	12.6	Environmental Performance and Health	134
13	**Science, Technology and the Digital Revolution**		137
	13.1	Inputs	137
	13.2	Outputs	138
	13.3	The Digital Revolution	140
	13.4	Digital Divides	142
	13.5	Online and Automated Activities	143
14	**Media**		147
	14.1	Newspapers and Online News	147
	14.2	Television and Public Broadcasting	149
	14.3	Worlds of Journalism	150
	14.4	Public Responses and Attitudes	152
	14.5	Press Freedom	153
	14.6	Cinema and Cultural Industries	155
15	**Family**		157
	15.1	Marriage	157
	15.2	Children	159
	15.3	Households	160
	15.4	Mothers and Employment	161
	15.5	Family Policy	163
	15.6	Childcare and Early Education	164
	15.7	Abortion	166
16	**Lifestyles and Consumption**		169
	16.1	Housing	169
	16.2	Food	171
	16.3	Alcohol	172
	16.4	Eating and Drinking Habits	174
	16.5	Urban Mobility and Transport	175
	16.6	Most Liveable Cities	177
	16.7	Happiness and Social Capital	178
17	**Crime and Social Problems**		181
	17.1	Measuring Crime Trends	181
	17.2	Homicides and Firearms	182
	17.3	Law and Justice	184
	17.4	Imprisonment and Capital Punishment	186
	17.5	Suicide	187
	17.6	Motor Vehicle Deaths	188
18	**Religion**		191
	18.1	Religion	191

Introduction

America—the good, the bad and the average

We are surely blessed to be citizens of the greatest nation on earth.
President Obama, Democratic Party Convention speech 2012

... our pride and gratitude in the United States of America, the greatest, freest nation in the world—the last, best hope of man on Earth.
Ronald Reagan, a farewell speech, January 1989

Leaders of all countries find ways to celebrate their patriotism. Perhaps Americans reach greater heights of grandiloquence than most, but all countries nurture myths about their own uniqueness. Political leaders often use superlatives as a rhetorical invocation, but these are normally an expression of emotional attachment rather than an attempt at serious comparison.

Much of America's pride in its self-proclaimed exceptionalism grows out of its history, beginning with the foundation of colonies believed to be inspired by divine providence, the War of Independence, and the framing of what is the world's oldest surviving democratic constitution. For the next century or more, it was able to make favourable comparisons with Europe. Its lack of aristocracy meant that social mobility was more possible. The frontier society gave a sense of a land of opportunity, where both national economic growth and personal advancement seemed achievable. The large migrations from Europe created a dynamic society and a sense of people building new and better lives.

Of course, there is also a darker underside to this oft-repeated historical narrative of exceptionalism. But our concern here is how it affects contemporary understandings, whether the celebration of a rich heritage becomes a means of avoiding today's challenges and whether exceptionalist rhetoric is an obstacle to learning from others.

Patriotism can be deployed as a means of ignoring unwelcome evidence. In 2012, when the Affordable Care Act (sometimes called Obamacare) was under debate, Republican leaders voiced their opposition with comparative claims: John Boehner thought the United States has 'the best healthcare delivery system in the world', and his colleague Mitch McConnell put it in almost the same patriotic formula: the USA has the 'finest healthcare system in the world'. Unlike the general invocations of patriotism above, this is a claim that can be examined empirically, even if the makers of the claim never do so.

Similarly, the celebration can easily slide into boastfulness. President Trump told a political rally in August 2018:

> I want clean air. I want crystal clean water. And we've got it. We've got the cleanest country in the planet right now. There's nobody cleaner than us, and it's getting better and better.

Again, this is a comparative claim but one that shows scant regard for the available comparative evidence. But with the advent of Trump and the idea that America has to restore its greatness, another narrative of patriotic victimhood has become more prominent. On several occasions, Trump claimed that Americans were 'the highest taxed nation in the world'.

How America Compares makes comparison, and especially bounded comparison, its central purpose. If we compare the United States with Uganda, the Ukraine or United Arab Emirates, the differences are so overwhelming that few lessons can be learned. Rather in bounded comparison, we are comparing the United States with the 17 countries with which it has most in common. This of course does not mean these countries are identical with America. (It is a common fallacy for people to say two situations are not comparable when they mean they are not identical.) Rather, it means that these 18 countries have sufficiently similar political, economic and social characteristics to make comparison illuminating.

The selected countries have conquered—at least for the overwhelming majority of their populations—the basic struggle for life, so that their average life expectancy is close to 80. The bulk of their populations has access to good nutrition, safe drinking water and adequate shelter. All have close to universal basic literacy. All are among the most affluent societies in the world. All have capitalist mixed economies, with a strong public sector. All have been stable liberal democracies since at least the late 1940s, with constitutionally governed, largely non-violent political competition and different parties alternating in power while central institutions remain stable, and where the government is by some minimal standard representative and publicly accountable. In addition, a further condition of minimum size was imposed—that the countries have populations of at least four million. This criterion excluded Iceland and Luxembourg, which otherwise would have been included.

The aim is to compare these countries on a wide range of social, economic and political phenomena, to provide a sourcebook, where an encyclopaedic range of measures are brought together in one volume. President Trump's claim that Americans are the most highly taxed people in the world is easily disposed of. Similarly, measures of the cleanliness of air and water can be fairly easily agreed. Many claims are more complicated: How do you measure 'generosity' or the 'best' health care? However, as this book shows, a range of comparative indicators can anchor such discussions with evidence.

While the focus of comparison is often on the contrasts, just as illuminating are the commonalities, particularly when countries share long-term trends, such as the ageing society and the changing roles of women. There is an industry of politicians, journalists and market analysts devoted to intensively reporting short-term changes and sometimes exaggerating their significance. There is much less public effort devoted to analysing the medium and long term. So whenever possible, we not only offer snapshot comparisons, but seek to trace common or contrasting trajectories—whether all these countries are experiencing greater unemployment, increased health spending, rising crime rates, etc.

Such a procedure allows us more perspective on the extent (and sometimes the limits) of the change we have already experienced. More cautiously it gives us some, although a very imperfect, basis for considering future developments. The future is rarely a simple extrapolation from the past, but charting secular trends is one tool for projecting future scenarios, and hence for planning, and making policy decisions to give societies a greater mastery of their destiny.

Why compare? Comparison serves three major purposes. Firstly, it helps us to see ourselves more clearly. As Rudyard Kipling wrote a century ago—albeit in a somewhat different spirit—what do they know of England, who only England know? In social science terms, it allows us to delineate the individual case more precisely, to make explicit what might otherwise have remained unexamined. What we imagine to be unique may be common to many societies, while what we take for granted as the natural or only way of doing things may in fact be unusual or even unique.

Secondly, comparison expands our universe of possibilities. It increases our knowledge that there are alternatives—alternative policies, different institutional arrangements, contrasting cultural assumptions. Most policy discussions take place within a restricted frame of reference. Domestic contention tends to focus upon our hopeless politicians, obstructive trade unions or rapacious corporations, looking only inward when looking outwards can suggest policy and social alternatives beyond the framework within which domestic politicians are casting the problem. Equally, while the focus of comparison tends to concentrate on differences and contrasts, commonalities are often just as important and interesting. When trends and problems are broadly shared among a number of countries, the causes are unlikely to be solely home-grown.

Thirdly, comparison is the social scientist's substitute for the experiment. We cannot subject whole societies to experimental testing, so disciplined comparison is one means for testing generalisations. The study of commonalities and contrasts allows us to be more disciplined in ascribing explanations and examining relationships. By charting similarities and differences, we can be more precise in our descriptions and more discriminating in our analyses.

While the potential value of comparative work is great, so unfortunately are the obstacles confronting it. One problem, common to all social science research, is particularly pronounced: many of the most interesting and subtle aspects of sociopolitical life defy quantification or the construction of valid indicators to summarise simply their trends and differences. There is often truth in the charge that comparative measures are too crude to be meaningful. We do not claim that the tables in the following pages exhaust all there is to say about the quality of social and political life in these countries, but they offer data that provides parameters in which such qualitative discussions can proceed in a more informed way.

Sometimes, comparing whole countries may not be illuminating. A single measure of transport does not take account of differences between metropolitan and rural areas, and average real estate prices will not show if particular cities are becoming unaffordable. In a federal system, states may have different election laws or taxes. A single measure of pollution will not pinpoint local problems. So, we need to note where internal variations—due to region, or class, or race—mean that a single national measure is not revealing.

The greatest problem in comparative work is equivalence. Different countries may measure the same concept in different ways, or what may seem to be the same indicator has a different meaning when put in its larger social context. To address these issues, we have, whenever possible relied on the work of international organisations whose professionals have made extensive and informed attempts to harmonise the data from different countries. The single greatest organisational source of data has been the Organisation for Economic Cooperation and Development (OECD), to which all 18 countries belong.

We have also made use of international bodies, such as the World Bank, the IMF and the many agencies of the United Nations, especially when we have sought to also include a global perspective. In recent times, there has also been a range of commercial and professional organisations and academic research institutes which have produced valuable data. In this book, we are the beneficiaries of the expertise and professionalism that all these groups have brought to their task.

When international organisations publish compendia of statistical information, they are often constrained by diplomatic considerations to present their data in a neutral and non-controversial way. Sometimes, they are not reader-friendly. Sometimes, they make little effort to explain for the non-specialist the value and limits of the measures they are reporting.

In contrast, in this book, we have very deliberately exercised an editorial hand in the presentation of data. We have been selective not comprehensive about the years for which data is presented (trying to keep tables clear and making judgements about when added detail would add more clutter rather than extra meaning). Rather than invariably presenting tables with countries in alphabetical order, we have often listed them in hierarchical order according to the phenomenon being studied, so that the main ordering and differences between countries are more quickly apparent. (In such 'league tables', most people focus on rankings and differences, but as indicated earlier, what is often at least as important is how they have moved in common.)

Most importantly, this is not just a book of tables, but rather each page of tables is accompanied by a commentary about the meaning of the data, including sometimes a discussion of its limits. In this way, we have sought to provide the reader not only with reliable and pertinent data, but with some discussion of its interpretation and significance.

Each page puts America in an international context. Sometimes, this will confirm those who view America as the best. Sometimes, it confirms the counter-narrative of America as the worst, and just as often as these two extremes, it often puts America in the middle.

Abbreviations

H	hours
NYT	*New York Times*
OECD	Organisation for Economic Cooperation and Development
S	Section
T	Table
WP	*Washington Post*

All other abbreviations are explained on the page on which they are used.

List of Tables

Table 1.1	Global population milestones	2
Table 1.2	National population sizes	2
Table 1.3	Population growth rates	3
Table 1.4	Changing populations	3
Table 1.5	Fastest growing countries globally	4
Table 1.6	Most sharply declining populations globally	4
Table 1.7	Area and population density	4
Table 1.8	Urbanisation	5
Table 1.9	Biggest city	5
Table 1.10	Trends in life expectancy	6
Table 1.11	Fertility rates	7
Table 1.12	Old-age dependency ratio	7
Table 2.1	Constitutional history	10
Table 2.2	Male suffrage	10
Table 2.3	Women's suffrage	10
Table 2.4	Heads of state	11
Table 2.5	Federal and unitary state structures	12
Table 2.6	Taxation by level of government	13
Table 2.7	Legislative structures	14
Table 2.8	Governments, executives and legislatures	16
Table 2.9	Electoral systems	17
Table 2.10	Number of national elections	17
Table 2.11	Party systems	18
Table 2.12	Electoral choice and government formation	19
Table 2.13	Electoral participation	19
Table 2.14	Political participation beyond elections	19
Table 2.15	Bills of rights and judicial review of government decisions	20
Table 2.16	Method and length of judicial appointments	21
Table 2.17	Political donations and expenditure	23
Table 2.18	Public funding to political parties	23
Table 2.19	Electoral integrity 2012–2017	24
Table 2.20	Electoral integrity—United States	25
Table 2.21	Corruption perception index	25
Table 2.22	Bribe payers' index	25
Table 2.23	Index of public integrity	26
Table 2.24	Freedom scores 2018	27
Table 2.25	Trust in institutions	28
Table 3.1	GDP per capita	30
Table 3.2	Contemporary economic growth	30
Table 3.3	World's 20 biggest economies	30
Table 3.4	Income per capita 1870–1998	31

Table 3.5	Economic growth 1820–1998	31
Table 3.6	Inflation	32
Table 3.7	Long-term interest rates	33
Table 3.8	Employment in agriculture	33
Table 3.9	Employment in industry	33
Table 3.10	Employment in services	34
Table 3.11	GDP by sector	34
Table 3.12	Exports	35
Table 3.13	Imports	35
Table 3.14	Current account balance	35
Table 3.15	Trade in services	36
Table 3.16	Outward foreign direct investment	36
Table 3.17	Inward foreign direct investment	37
Table 3.18	Import penetration	37
Table 3.19	Global value chains	38
Table 3.20	Exchange rates	38
Table 3.21	Big Mac index	39
Table 3.22	Growth in labour productivity	39
Table 3.23	Contributions to GDP growth	40
Table 3.24	Investment in intellectual property products	40
Table 3.25	Global competitiveness index	41
Table 3.26	Economic freedom	41
Table 3.27	Human development index	42
Table 4.1	Labour force participation	46
Table 4.2	Labour force participation among older people	46
Table 4.3	Employment rates of older people	46
Table 4.4	Life expectancy at 65	46
Table 4.5	Unemployment	47
Table 4.6	Youth unemployment	47
Table 4.7	Long-term unemployment	48
Table 4.8	Part-time employment	48
Table 4.9	Female part-time employment	49
Table 4.10	Annual hours worked	49
Table 4.11	Employees working very long hours	50
Table 4.12	Low-income work	50
Table 4.13	Involuntary part-time employment	51
Table 4.14	Job strain	51
Table 4.15	Risks from automation	51
Table 4.16	Trade union membership	52
Table 4.17	Trade union membership in public and private sectors	52
Table 4.18	Collective bargaining systems	53
Table 4.19	Industrial disputes	53
Table 4.20	Quality of labour relations	54
Table 4.21	Public trust in trade unions	54
Table 5.1	Government spending	56
Table 5.2	Total tax	56
Table 5.3	Government deficits and surpluses	56
Table 5.4	Government debt	57
Table 5.5	Financial net worth of government	57
Table 5.6	Structure of government spending	58
Table 6.1	Health expenditure and GDP	62
Table 6.2	Health expenditure per person	62

List of Tables

Table	Title	Page
Table 6.3	Growth in health expenditure	62
Table 6.4	Financing health care	63
Table 6.5	Private health insurance	63
Table 6.6	Out-of-pocket medical expenses	63
Table 6.7	Foregoing health services because of cost	64
Table 6.8	Health expenditure by type of service	64
Table 6.9	Consultations with doctors	65
Table 6.10	Hospital Beds	65
Table 6.11	Average length of stay in hospital	65
Table 6.12	Doctors	66
Table 6.13	Nurses	66
Table 6.14	Doctors aged 55 and over	67
Table 6.15	Foreign-trained doctors	67
Table 6.16	Male life expectancy	68
Table 6.17	Female life expectancy	68
Table 6.18	Major causes of death among males	68
Table 6.19	Major causes of death among females	68
Table 6.20	Mortality and causes of death	69
Table 6.21	Infant mortality	70
Table 6.22	Deaths from Ischaemic heart disease	70
Table 6.23	Deaths from cerebrovascular diseases	70
Table 6.24	Deaths from cancer	71
Table 6.25	Breast cancer survival rates	71
Table 6.26	Colon cancer survival rate	72
Table 6.27	Smoking	72
Table 6.28	Obesity	73
Table 6.29	Diabetes	73
Table 7.1	Educational Attainment of adult population	76
Table 7.2	Educational attainment of the adult population 2000	76
Table 7.3	Young adults with tertiary qualifications	76
Table 7.4	Relative earnings of workers by educational attainment	76
Table 7.5	Total education spending	77
Table 7.6	Public expenditure on education	77
Table 7.7	Public share of education spending	78
Table 7.8	Public and private shares and educational levels	78
Table 7.9	Reading skills	79
Table 7.10	Maths skills	79
Table 7.11	Science skills	79
Table 7.12	Inequality in science performance	80
Table 7.13	Tertiary education and parents' education	80
Table 7.14	Students with low skills	81
Table 7.15	Science literacy and environmental awareness	81
Table 7.16	Teachers' salaries	82
Table 7.17	Teacher–student ratios and class sizes	82
Table 7.18	Teaching hours	82
Table 7.19	Students' sense of belonging	83
Table 7.20	Primary students' reading	83
Table 7.21	Primary students' maths	84
Table 7.22	Primary students' science	84
Table 7.23	Continuity of skills year 4 to year 8	85
Table 7.24	Enrolments in early childhood education and care	85
Table 7.25	Expenditure on pre-primary education	85

Table 7.26	Public and private pre-school education	86
Table 7.27	Adult literacy and numeracy	87
Table 7.28	Proficiency in literacy, numeracy and problem solving	87
Table 7.29	Low-performing adults	87
Table 7.30	Adult participation in learning	88
Table 8.1	Inequality	90
Table 8.2	Ratio of unequal income	90
Table 8.3	Income inequality in the USA	90
Table 8.4	Inequalities in wealth	90
Table 8.5	Wealth distribution and race in the United States	91
Table 8.6	Poverty	92
Table 8.7	Working poor	92
Table 8.8	Race and poverty in the USA	92
Table 8.9	Prevalence of disability	93
Table 8.10	Public spending on disability benefits	93
Table 8.11	Disability and educational achievement	94
Table 8.12	Disability and poverty	94
Table 8.13	Expected years of life in retirement	95
Table 8.14	Public expenditure on aged pensions	95
Table 8.15	Poverty among the elderly	96
Table 8.16	Social expenditure	96
Table 8.17	Net social spending	97
Table 8.18	Government action and inequality	97
Table 8.19	Areas of public social spending	98
Table 8.20	Children in poverty	98
Table 8.21	Child poverty and family structure	99
Table 8.22	Persistence of poverty	99
Table 8.23	Intergenerational mobility	100
Table 9.1	Scale of immigration	102
Table 9.2	Immigration and population growth	102
Table 9.3	Countries with most immigrants	102
Table 9.4	Countries with highest emigration	102
Table 9.5	Unemployment	103
Table 9.6	Poverty	103
Table 9.7	Adult literacy	104
Table 9.8	Citizenship	104
Table 9.9	World totals of refugees	105
Table 9.10	Internally displaced persons	105
Table 9.11	National origins of refugees	106
Table 9.12	Refugees' country of asylum	106
Table 9.13	Asylum applications	106
Table 9.14	Types of migrant intake	107
Table 10.1	Male labour force participation	110
Table 10.2	Female labour force participation	110
Table 10.3	Males paid and unpaid work	110
Table 10.4	Females paid and unpaid work	110
Table 10.5	Gender and tertiary degrees	111
Table 10.6	Female doctors	111
Table 10.7	Women with science and technology degrees	112
Table 10.8	Gender and IT specialists	112
Table 10.9	Median pay of males and females	112
Table 10.10	Female public servants	113

Table 10.11	Females in managerial employment	113
Table 10.12	Females on company boards	113
Table 10.13	Female members of legislatures	114
Table 10.14	Female cabinet ministers	114
Table 10.15	Female heads of government	115
Table 10.16	Global gender gap	116
Table 11.1	Military expenditure	118
Table 11.2	Arms trade	118
Table 11.3	Foreign aid	118
Table 11.4	International attitudes to America	119
Table 11.5	Deaths from terrorism	120
Table 11.6	Countries most impacted by terrorism	120
Table 11.7	Terrorist fatalities in the selected democracies	121
Table 11.8	Globalisation	122
Table 11.9	Components of globalisation	123
Table 12.1	Mammals and threatened species	126
Table 12.2	Birds and threatened species	126
Table 12.3	Land cover	126
Table 12.4	Protected areas	127
Table 12.5	Global temperature anomalies	127
Table 12.6	Atmospheric carbon dioxide	128
Table 12.7	Global greenhouse gas emissions	128
Table 12.8	Global carbon dioxide emissions	128
Table 12.9	Major greenhouse gas emitters	129
Table 12.10	National greenhouse gas emissions per person	130
Table 12.11	National greenhouse gas emissions and the economy	130
Table 12.12	World energy totals and sources	131
Table 12.13	Energy intensity	131
Table 12.14	Structure of primary energy supply	131
Table 12.15	Carbon pricing	132
Table 12.16	Environmentally related taxes	133
Table 12.17	Municipal waste	133
Table 12.18	Disposal and treatment of waste	133
Table 12.19	Environmental performance index	134
Table 12.20	Air pollution	135
Table 12.21	Worst air pollution	135
Table 13.1	Research and development	138
Table 13.2	Researchers	138
Table 13.3	Business research and development	138
Table 13.4	Global innovation index	139
Table 13.5	Intellectual property receipts	139
Table 13.6	High-tech exports	139
Table 13.7	Patents	140
Table 13.8	Mobile telephones	141
Table 13.9	Internet users	141
Table 13.10	Mobile internet penetration	141
Table 13.11	Households with broadband Internet access	142
Table 13.12	Internet usage by age groups	142
Table 13.13	Internet usage and education	142
Table 13.14	Urban and rural broadband	143
Table 13.15	E-government	143
Table 13.16	Online purchases	144

Table 13.17	Generic top-level domains	144
Table 13.18	Robots	145
Table 14.1	Newspaper circulation	148
Table 14.2	Use of internet and social media for news	148
Table 14.3	Facebook as a news source	148
Table 14.4	Paying for online news	148
Table 14.5	Television and public broadcasting	149
Table 14.6	Average television viewing time	150
Table 14.7	Journalists' opinions on letting people express their views	151
Table 14.8	Journalists' views on changes in journalism's ethical standards	151
Table 14.9	Journalists' views on the changing credibility of journalism	151
Table 14.10	Journalists' views on journalism's relevance	152
Table 14.11	How news organisations cover political issues	152
Table 14.12	Trust in media	153
Table 14.13	Fake news	153
Table 14.14	World press freedom index (RSF)	154
Table 14.15	Freedom of the press	154
Table 14.16	Cinema attendance	155
Table 14.17	National origin of films	155
Table 14.18	Cultural exports	156
Table 15.1	Females' age at first marriage	158
Table 15.2	Males' age at first marriage	158
Table 15.3	Females' marital status	158
Table 15.4	Males' marital status	159
Table 15.5	Mothers' age at birth of first child	159
Table 15.6	Births to adolescent mothers	160
Table 15.7	Living arrangements of children	160
Table 15.8	Household size	161
Table 15.9	Types of household	161
Table 15.10	Partnership and cohabitation	161
Table 15.11	Women, motherhood and employment	162
Table 15.12	Parents and employment	162
Table 15.13	Income levels of different family types	163
Table 15.14	Parental leave	163
Table 15.15	Public expenditure on families	163
Table 15.16	Public spending on early childhood education and care	164
Table 15.17	Public spending on family benefits	164
Table 15.18	Costs of childcare	165
Table 15.19	Participation of young children in childcare	165
Table 15.20	Out of school care	166
Table 15.21	Abortion	166
Table 15.22	Global abortion trends	166
Table 15.23	Safety of abortions	167
Table 16.1	Home ownership	170
Table 16.2	Housing and dwelling stock	170
Table 16.3	House price to income ratio	170
Table 16.4	Rooms per person	170
Table 16.5	Total food consumption	171
Table 16.6	Consumption of fat	171
Table 16.7	Consumption of sugar	172
Table 16.8	Eating fruit and vegetables daily	172
Table 16.9	Alcohol consumption	172

Table 16.10	Types of alcohol consumed	173
Table 16.11	Heavy drinking	173
Table 16.12	Alcohol consumption and traffic fatalities	174
Table 16.13	Drinking coffee	174
Table 16.14	Drinking tea	174
Table 16.15	Eating meat	175
Table 16.16	Eating fish and seafood	175
Table 16.17	Urban sprawl	176
Table 16.18	Commuting time	176
Table 16.19	Cars	176
Table 16.20	Cities and public transport	177
Table 16.21	Most liveable city	178
Table 16.22	Global cities index	179
Table 16.23	Happiness	179
Table 16.24	Trust in other people	179
Table 16.25	Volunteering	180
Table 17.1	Change in the crime rate	182
Table 17.2	Changing incidence of crime	182
Table 17.3	Public fear of Burglary	182
Table 17.4	Homicides	183
Table 17.5	Gun-related deaths	183
Table 17.6	The rule of law (1)	184
Table 17.7	Rule of law (2)	185
Table 17.8	Safe living conditions	185
Table 17.9	Citizens' confidence in the legal system	185
Table 17.10	Imprisonment	186
Table 17.11	Capital punishment	186
Table 17.12	Suicide	187
Table 17.13	Teenage suicides	188
Table 17.14	Motor vehicle deaths	188
Table 18.1	Religious affiliation	192
Table 18.2	Attending religious services	192
Table 18.3	Belief in God	192

People and Life Expectancy

1.1 Global Population

The population of the world on 1 January 2018 was 7,444,443,881, according to the US Census Bureau.[1] This was an increase of 78.5 million, or 1.07%, over the previous year. In other words, the world is now producing extra population each year that approximately equals the size of Germany.

It took thousands of years for humankind to reach its first billion, which was achieved in 1803. It is estimated that the world's population was 300 million at the time of Christ and 100 million at 500 BC.

However, in recent times, the earth's population has seen much more rapid increases. From 1959 until 2012, when the population topped seven billion, the earth added another billion people every 12–15 years. According to the Nobel Prize-winning economist Robert Fogel, the increase in the world's population between 1900 and 1990 was four times as great as the increase during the whole previous history of humankind. Although such calculations are difficult, the best guess seems to be that roughly five per cent of the people who have ever lived are alive at the moment.

The rate of growth is now slowing. From 1950 to around 1990, it was above 1.5% per annum. From 2020 onwards, the US Census Bureau estimates, it will be below one per cent and from 2050 around half a per cent or less.

The further forward our projections, the more tentative they must be. Some predict that the earth's population may stabilize at somewhere near 10 billion. The United Nations demographers, however, predict that the global population will be 11.2 billion by the year 2100, or about half as big again as it is now.

Thomas Malthus famously predicted in 1798 that population growth would produce a catastrophe. Instead, the earth's population is almost eight times what it was then, and life expectancy has increased enormously. Malthus's crucial flaw was not to see the transforming capacity of technology, and he was writing on the eve of what was the most technologically dynamic period of history.

This population explosion is a testimony to humankind's success. It was the mastery of agriculture, the ability to live in cities, and reduce disease that made the increase in longevity and improvement in material living conditions possible.

However, success threatens to bring its own problems. Human activity itself now shapes the planet's environment, so that some people have labelled the current and coming geological era the Anthropocene, as the cumulative impact of people is the central driving force. There is more pressure on arable land, on shrinking wilderness areas and on the oceans. Humans have had to construct much bigger cities than anything previously contemplated. Carbon dioxide gases are generated on an unprecedented scale.

---

[1] US Census Bureau 'Census Bureau projects US and World Populations on New Year's Day' Tip Sheet CB17-TPS.88;United Nations *World Population Prospects, the 2017 Revision* (NY, United Nations, 2017);Robert William Fogel *The Escape from Hunger and Premature Death 1700–2100. Europe, America and the Third World* (CUP 2004). See also Alberto Alesina and Enrico Spolace *The Size of Nations* (Cambridge, Mass., the MIT Press, 2005).

Table 1.1 Global population milestones
Year earth's population reached each billion
(Years for 8 and 9 billion are estimates)

Billions	Year
1	1803
2	1927
3	1959
4	1974
5	1987
6	1999
7	2012
8	2026
9	2043

US Census Bureau International Database. https://www.census.gov/programs-surveys/international-programs/about/idb.html

Table 1.2 National population sizes
40 most populous countries (plus smaller selected democracies)
2017 populations in millions

Rank	Country	Population
1	China	1379.3
2	India	1281.9
3	United States	326.6
4	Indonesia	260.6
5	Brazil	207.4
6	Pakistan	204.9
7	Nigeria	190.6
8	Bangladesh	157.8
9	Russia	142.3
10	Japan	126.5
11	Mexico	124.6
12	Ethiopia	105.4
13	Philippines	104.3
14	Egypt	97.0
15	Vietnam	96.2
16	Congo	83.3
17	Iran	82.0
18	Turkey	80.8
19	Germany	80.6
20	Thailand	68.4
21	France	67.1
22	United Kingdom	64.8
23	Italy	62.1
24	Burma	55.1
25	South Africa	54.8
26	Tanzania	54.0
27	South Korea	51.2
28	Spain	49.0
29	Colombia	47.7
30	Kenya	47.6
31	Argentina	44.3
32	Ukraine	44.0
33	Algeria	41.0
34	Uganda	40.0
35	Iraq	39.2
36	Poland	38.5
37	Sudan	37.3
38	Canada	35.6
39	Afghanistan	34.1
40	Morocco	34.0
56	Australia	23.2
66	Netherlands	17.1
77	Belgium	11.5
91	Sweden	10.0
95	Austria	8.8
98	Switzerland	8.3
116	Denmark	5.6
117	Finland	5.5
120	Norway	5.3
121	Ireland	5.0
126	New Zealand	4.5

US Census Bureau International Database. https://www.census.gov/programs-surveys/international-programs/about/idb.html

Moving from a global to a national perspective, the US Census Bureau lists 228 countries and entities. (Entities include some colonies and contested territories.) This division of the world reflects history rather than any rational design. Nation states are not eternal or natural entities. They typically embody a sense of common destiny, imagined communities in the phrase of the scholar Benedict Anderson. Or as Karl Deutsch expressed it more sardonically—'a group of people united by a common error about their ancestry and a common dislike of their neighbours'. They can be enlarged or divided. Most spectacularly, in recent history, the Soviet Union, then the third most populous country in the world, broke into 15 different countries, while what was Yugoslavia more violently dissolved into seven different countries.

Countries come in all sizes. Sixty-seven have a population of less than one million. At the other extreme, by far the two most populous, with populations over one billion are China and India. China is currently and has throughout history been the largest country. However, its growth rate has slowed radically. The United Nations predicts that at some time in coming decades the two countries will become equal, after which India will substantially pull ahead. The United States is the third most populous country in the world (Table 1.1).

There is no 'right size' for a country. Population size, by itself, has little to do with national destiny. Table 1.2 shows no correlation with national prosperity, except perhaps that many of the smallest countries are more economically vulnerable. Size of the population does correlate somewhat more with military strength and international power, but this is also very limited.

1.2 Population Growth

A country's population growth rate has two principal sources—fertility plus migration. As we shall see in Table 1.11, the fertility rate has substantially declined in all the selected countries. Immigration as a source of population growth varies considerably (see Chap. 9), but has been an important recent driver of the faster-growing populations in some countries.

Table 1.3 shows that the population growth rate in these economically advanced democracies has slowed considerably, although there was much more variation in the 1950s than recently. In that decade, the English-speaking New World democracies all had growth rates of 1.7% or more, down to Ireland's population which was then decreasing.

While the differences in these figures for annual growth rates seem small, sustained over time they produce large variations as Table 1.4 demonstrates. During the twentieth century, especially the second half, and continuing into the twenty-first century, the four English-speaking New World democracies had substantially higher growth rates than the West European countries. In 2000, nine of the European countries had populations that were less than double what they had been a century earlier. In contrast, Canada's increased by 5.8 times, Australia's by five times, New Zealand's just below that and the USA's almost four times. In 1950, Australia's population was just less than Belgium's. Fifty years later, Australia had nine million people more. In 1950, America's population was less than double Japan's; by 2000, it was about two and a half times Japan's size.

Table 1.3 Population growth rates
Average Annual Growth Rate (%)

Country	1950–1960	1990–2000	2012–14
Australia	2.3	1.2	1.7
Switzerland	1.3	0.7	1.3
Norway	0.9	0.6	1.2
Canada	2.7	1.0	1.0
New Zealand	2.2	1.3	0.9
Sweden	0.7	0.4	0.8
United States	**1.7**	**1.2**	**0.8**
United Kingdom	0.4	0.3	0.6
Belgium	0.6	0.3	0.5
Finland	1.0	0.4	0.5
Austria	0.2	0.4	0.4
Denmark	0.7	0.4	0.4
France	0.9	0.4	0.4
Italy	0.6	0.0	0.4
Netherlands	1.3	0.6	0.4
Germany	0.6	0.3	0.3
Ireland	−0.5	0.8	0.3
Japan	1.2	0.3	−0.2
Mean	1.0	0.6	0.7

First two columns calculated form US Census Bureau International Database; last column from *OECD Factbook 2015–2016*

Table 1.4 Changing populations
Millions

Country	1900	1950	2000	2050 (est)
United States	76.0	152.3	282.6	398.3
Japan	43.8	83.8	126.6	107.2
Germany	56.1	68.4	82.8	71.5
United Kingdom	36.7	50.1	59.5	71.2
France	38.9	41.8	59.3	69.5
Italy	32.4	47.1	57.6	61.4
Canada	5.4	14.0	31.3	41.1
Australia	3.8	8.3	19.2	29.0
Netherlands	5.2	10.1	15.9	17.9
Belgium	6.7	8.6	10.2	12.8
Sweden	5.1	7.0	8.9	12.0
Switzerland	3.3	4.7	7.3	9.5
Austria	5.8	6.9	8.1	9.1
Norway	2.2	3.3	4.5	6.4
Ireland	3.1	3.0	3.8	6.3
Denmark	2.4	4.3	5.3	5.6
Finland	2.7	4.0	5.2	5.5
New Zealand	0.8	1.9	3.8	5.2

Figures for 1900 are from B.R. Mitchell *International Historical Statistics. Africa, Asia and Oceania 1750–1993* (3rd ed, NY, Stockton Press, 1998) and the *United Nations Statistical Yearbook 1955* (UN, NY, 1957). Figures for 1950, 2000 and 2050 from US Census Bureau International Data Base
Note: In 1900, Austria was still part of the Austro-Hungarian Empire and Ireland was united as a British colony. The table above gives estimates for the 1900 population of the territories comprising the contemporary nation states. Similarly in 1950, Germany was divided into East and West, but the table figure is for a united Germany

Projecting forward to 2050 by the US Census Bureau—an exercise which necessitates assumptions about birth rates and immigration levels—the differences become even more dramatic. Two countries—Japan and Germany—are projected to become less populous, while some others—Italy, the Netherlands, Belgium, Austria, Denmark and Finland—will grow only slightly. The United States, however, will grow substantially.

Taking a more global view, the world population is currently growing at just under 1.1% per year. This average though does not reveal the growing variation between countries. Table 1.5 lists the 21 fastest growing countries in the world. They are concentrated in the Middle East and Africa. Some of them have witnessed the substantial conflict in recent times. None of them is a high-income country.

When the rate of population growth is combined with current population size, it is estimated that between 2017 and 2050 half the world's population growth will be concentrated in just nine countries: (in order of their expected contribution) India, Nigeria, the Congo, Pakistan, Ethiopia, Tanzania, the USA, Uganda and Indonesia.

In contrast, there are 51 countries whose population is expected to decrease in the same period. Table 1.6 lists the 21 countries whose population is currently declining at the

Table 1.5 Fastest growing countries globally
Annual % change 2017

Country	Rate
Syria	4.8
South Sudan	3.9
Angola	3.5
Malawi	3.3
Burundi	3.3
Uganda	3.2
Niger	3.2
Mali	3.0
Burkina Faso	3.0
Zambia	2.9
Ethiopia	2.9
Tanzania	2.8
Benin	2.7
Western Sahara	2.7
Iraq	2.7
Togo	2.7
Guinea	2.6
Cameroon	2.6
Madagascar	2.5
Rwanda	2.5
Egypt	2.5

US Census Bureau International Database

Table 1.6 Most sharply declining populations globally
Annual % change 2017

Country	Rate
Cook Islands	−2.8
Puerto Rico	−1.8
American Samoa	−1.3
Saint Pierre and Miquelon	−1.1
Latvia	−1.1
Lithuania	−1.1
Moldova	−1.0
Bulgaria	−0.6
Estonia	−0.6
Croatia	−0.5
Micronesia	−0.5
Northern Mariana Islands	−0.5
Serbia	−0.5
Ukraine	−0.4
Saint Barthelemy	−0.4
Montenegro	−0.3
Romania	−0.3
Slovenia	−0.3
Cuba	−0.3
Saint Vincent and the Grenadines	−0.3
Hungary	−0.2

US Census Bureau International Database

greatest rate. They fall into two categories. Nine come from islands, and apart from Cuba, all are relatively small. Some of these islands may seem idyllic, but presumably for economic reasons they also have a high rate of emigration.

The other twelve countries are in Eastern Europe, including countries that were part of former Yugoslavia and Soviet Union, or were under Soviet domination.

1.3 Urbanisation

All these economically advanced stable democracies are overwhelmingly urban societies and have been for generations. Urbanisation tends to accompany economic development. According to the United Nations demographers, in 1950 more than two-thirds of the world lived in rural areas; by 2050 around two-thirds of the world's population will live in urban areas. The year 2007 was the first time that the world's urban population exceeded its rural population.

These 18 countries have long manifested much higher urbanisation than the global average. Already in 1950, as Table 1.8 shows, only three countries had less than half their population living in towns and cities. In the decades since, that trend has increased and in 12 countries now more than eight in ten people are urban dwellers.

However, there is still a substantial difference between the countries at the top of the table and the more rural and provincial distributions of population among those at the bottom. It is notable that a few European countries—especially Ireland, Austria and Italy—have barely shifted in their urbanisation rates.

One would think that it is a simple matter to determine how many people live in urban areas and to give the size of

Table 1.7 Area and population density

Country	Population per square kilometre (2015)	Area (thousand square kilometres)
Australia	3	7687
Canada	4	9976
Norway	13	324
New Zealand	17	269
Finland	16	338
Sweden	22	450
United States	**34**	**9372**
Ireland	67	70
Austria	102	84
France	118	549
Denmark	131	43
Switzerland	200	41
Italy	202	301
Germany	231	357
United Kingdom	263	245
Japan	336	378
Belgium	366	31
Netherlands	406	41

Area is from *OECD in Figs. 2000 edition*; population density is from United Nations Department of Economic and Social Affairs *World Population Prospects. The 2017 Revision* (NY, UN, 2017)

1.3 Urbanisation

Table 1.8 Urbanisation
Percentage of population living in urban areas

Country	1950	1980	2015
Belgium	92	95	98
Japan	53	76	93
Netherlands	56	65	90
Australia	77	86	89
Denmark	68	84	88
New Zealand	73	83	86
Sweden	66	83	86
Finland	43	72	84
Canada	61	76	82
United Kingdom	79	79	82
United States	**64**	**74**	**81**
Norway	51	71	80
France	55	73	79
Germany	68	73	75
Switzerland	44	57	74
Italy	54	67	69
Austria	64	65	66
Ireland	40	55	63
Mean	62	74	81

United Nations Department of Economic and Social Affairs *World Urbanisation Prospects. The 2014 Revision* (NY, UN, 2015)

Table 1.9 Biggest city
Largest city's population 2014; its share of national population that year; and number of cities over one million in population

Country	Largest city	Population (millions)	City's share national population %	Number of big cities (> one million)
Japan	Tokyo	38.0	30	8
USA	**New York**	**18.6**	**6**	**45**
France	Paris	10.8	17	4
UK	London	10.3	16	5
Canada	Toronto	6.0	17	6
Australia	Sydney	4.5	19	5
Italy	Rome	3.7	6	4
Germany	Berlin	3.6	4	4
Belgium	Brussels	2.0	18	1
Austria	Vienna	1.8	21	1
Sweden	Stockholm	1.5	16	1
Denmark	Copenhagen	1.3	23	1
NZ	Auckland	1.3	26	1
Switzerland	Zurich	1.2	15	1
Finland	Helsinki	1.2	22	1
Ireland	Dublin	1.2	26	1
Netherlands	Amsterdam	1.1	7	1
Norway	Oslo	1.0	23	1

United Nations Department of Economic and Social Affairs *World Urbanisation Prospects. The 2014 Revision* (NY, UN, 2015)

cities, but in fact, the published figures jump around alarmingly. There is no agreed operational definition of what constitutes an urban area, and apparent changes in urbanisation sometimes simply reflect differences in methodology.

There is even more difference in estimating the size of individual cities. The first source of difference concerns how to draw their boundaries, and there are two main variants. One is to follow the administrative borders, the city proper. This has the virtue of clarity, but is not valid in any sense to do with the workings of the social unit, and is normally much smaller than the 'real' city. The other measure is called urban agglomeration. The United Nations defines an urban agglomeration as the city or town proper and also the suburban fringe or thickly settled territory lying outside, but adjacent to, its boundaries. This is more realistic, but more subject to variable estimates, as the functional limits of a city are more ambiguous than its legal boundaries.

The UN World Urban Prospects data, from which Table 1.9 is also drawn, gives larger figures for some cities because they consider a common urban agglomeration as one when some others cite them as two distinct cities. Thus, while Tokyo is certainly the largest city among the selected countries, this figure is its population combined with Yokohama's, and other estimates put its population at less than half the 35 million given here. Similarly, they treat New York and Newark as if they are a single urban unit.

In more than half the countries, mainly European with relatively smaller populations, there is one dominant city, the only one with a population greater than one million. It is usually, but not always, the political capital (Amsterdam and Zurich are exceptions) and the most important business and cultural centre.

The United States is at the other end of any scale of demographic concentration. The biggest city, New York, comprises only six per cent of the American population, and there are fully 45 cities with a population in excess of one million, almost one per state. On a much smaller scale, Canada and Australia are similar in having several large and influential cities.

The data on population density (Table 1.7) suggests that to some extent at least geography is destiny. The seven countries—including the United States—with the lowest population density all have substantial areas inhospitable to human settlement, with mountains, desert or arctic wastes. But just as the population has grown far more than the Malthusian generation could have envisaged, so population density, thanks to the growth of big cities, is much greater than earlier generations could have predicted.

1.4 The Ageing Society

Policy-makers and social commentators are increasingly talking about the problems caused by the ageing of society.[2] Although there are substantial policy issues posed by this demographic trend, it should be remembered that its most basic cause is good news—people are living longer. The ageing society was a problem the caveman never had to contend with.

The figures in Table 1.10 tell a great success story. During the course of the twentieth century, average life expectancy in these affluent democracies rose by more than half—from around 50 years to nearly 80. Indeed according to Nobel Prize-winning economist Robert Fogel, the increase in life expectancies during the twentieth century was more than double what it had been during the previous 200,000 years.

The most notable aspect of the data is the commonality between the countries. Life expectancy in all of them increased substantially and is still fairly closely grouped. In 2015, Japan had the highest life expectancy, at 83.9 years, but 16 of the other 17 countries were 80 years or over. The exception is the United States, which in 1950 was above average but which has not improved as much as the others in the decades since.

The trend towards greater longevity is continuing. Even in the first 15 years of this century, the mean improved by 3.4 years, although the USA improved only by 1.7 years.

The OECD notes that these gains have been made possible by rising standards of living, improved working conditions, public health interventions and progress in medical care. Improvements in life expectancy at birth actually reflect a decline in mortality rates at all ages, ranging from a sharp reduction in infant mortality to higher survival rates at older ages. The Australian Bureau of Statistics—in a pattern that is also likely to be found elsewhere—observed that in Australia longer life expectancy in the first half of the century was because of a decline in deaths from infectious diseases, due to cleaner water and better sewerage systems, as well as initiatives like mass immunisation. Rises in life expectancy slowed in the decades after World War II largely because of increases in cardiovascular disease. While the earlier improvements were due to the increasing number surviving into old age, more recently the major source of increase is that older people are living longer.

Apart from increased life expectancy, the other cause of the ageing society is that people are having fewer children. Such demographic revolutions move at a glacial pace, but their long-term impact is dramatic. In all these countries, the fertility rate is now below the natural replacement level of 2.1 children per woman. In other words, if this rate continues, and without immigration, all these countries will eventually experience a declining population.

Table 1.11 shows the reduction in the number of children each woman is having—from a mean across the selected countries of 4.1 in 1900 to 1.7 in 2015. By 2000 the figure was less than half what it had been in 1900. In the twenty-first century, it has actually increased very slightly. If the mean is expressed to two decimal places, it crept up from 1.66 to 1.74.

The reasons behind the decline are probably some mixture of the availability of improved contraception, the changed aspirations of women, the financial pressures of contemporary society and the cost of raising children.

The inevitable result of increased longevity and reduced fertility is a change in society's generational balance. The most common figure to indicate social ageing is the old-age dependency ratio which expresses the number of people aged 65 and over as a percentage of those aged 15–64 (considered as the working-age population). In these countries overall, the figure essentially doubled (from 15.7 to 30.9) between 1950 and 2015. However, it is projecting the figure into the future that drives the consternation. By 2050

Table 1.10 Trends in life expectancy
Life Expectancy at Birth, Years

Country	1900	1950	2000	2015
Japan	44.5	63.9	80.7	83.9
Switzerland	50.7	69.2	79.6	83.0
Italy	44.5	66.0	79.0	82.6
Australia	56.5	69.6	79.8	82.5
France	47.0	66.5	78.8	82.4
Norway	56.3	72.7	78.7	82.4
Sweden	55.8	71.8	79.6	82.3
Canada	–	69.1	79.4	81.7
New Zealand	59.4	69.6	77.8	81.7
Finland	46.7	66.3	77.4	81.6
Netherlands	56.1	72.1	78.3	81.6
Ireland	49.5	66.9	76.8	81.5
Austria	40.1	65.7	77.7	81.3
Belgium	47.1	67.5	77.8	81.1
United Kingdom	50.5	69.2	77.7	81.0
Denmark	54.6	71.0	76.5	80.8
Germany	46.6	67.5	77.4	80.7
United States	**49.3**	**69.0**	**77.1**	**78.8**
Mean	*50.3*	*68.5*	*78.3*	*81.7*

Figures for 1900 are from the *United Nations Statistical Yearbook 1955* (UN, NY, 1957). (For the Netherlands, the figure is for 1910.) Figures for 1950 are from the United Nations *World Population Prospects. The 1996 Revision* (UN, NY, 1996) Table A26, p. 318ff. Figures for 2000 from US Census Bureau International Data Base. 2015 data is from OECD *Pensions at a Glance. OECD and G20 data* (Paris, 2017)

---

[2]US Census Bureau 'Older people projected to outnumber children for first time in US history' News release 13 March 2018.

1.4 The Ageing Society

Table 1.11 Fertility rates
Average number of children borne by a woman during her lifetime at each year

Country	1900	1960	2000	2015
France	2.8	2.8	1.9	2.0
Ireland	–	4.1	2.0	2.0
New Zealand	–	3.9	2.0	2.0
Sweden	3.9	2.3	1.7	1.9
United Kingdom	3.4	2.8	1.7	1.9
United States	**3.8**	**3.2**	**2.0**	**1.9**
Australia	3.4	3.3	1.8	1.8
Belgium	4.0	2.7	1.7	1.8
Denmark	4.0	2.6	1.8	1.8
Finland	4.8	2.7	1.8	1.8
Netherlands	4.5	3.2	1.7	1.8
Norway	4.1	2.9	1.8	1.8
Canada	4.8	3.7	1.5	1.6
Switzerland	3.3	2.6	1.4	1.6
Austria	4.9	2.8	1.4	1.5
Germany	4.8	2.5	1.4	1.5
Italy	4.4	2.5	1.3	1.5
Japan	5.2	2.0	1.3	1.5
Mean	*4.1*	*2.9*	*1.7*	*1.7*

1900 data is from Jean-Claude Chesnais *The Demographic Transition. Stages, Patterns and Economic Implications. A Longitudinal Study of Sixty-Seven Countries Covering the Period 1720–1984* (Oxford University Press, 1992). More recent data is from OECD *Pensions at a Glance. OECD and G20 data* (Paris, 2017)

Table 1.12 Old-age dependency ratio
Number of people aged 65+ as a percentage of those aged 15–64

Country	1950	2000	2015	2050
United States	**14.2**	**20.9**	**24.6**	**40.3**
Australia	14.0	20.6	25.0	41.2
Norway	16.0	25.9	27.4	43.1
New Zealand	16.3	20.3	25.1	43.6
Denmark	15.6	24.2	33.0	45.3
Sweden	16.8	29.5	33.8	45.5
United Kingdom	17.9	27.0	31.0	48.0
Canada	14.0	20.5	26.1	48.1
Finland	11.9	24.8	35.0	48.8
Ireland	20.9	18.0	22.3	49.9
Belgium	18.1	28.3	30.6	51.0
France	19.5	27.3	33.3	52.3
Netherlands	13.9	21.9	30.2	53.0
Switzerland	15.8	24.9	29.0	54.6
Germany	16.2	26.5	34.8	59.2
Austria	17.3	24.9	30.5	59.4
Italy	14.3	29.2	37.8	72.4
Japan	9.9	27.3	46.2	77.8
Mean	*15.7*	*24.6*	*30.9*	*51.9*

OECD *Pensions at a Glance. OECD and G20 data* (Paris, 2017)

in these countries, there will be one older person for every two of working age. In Japan, there will be almost eight older people for every ten of working age. The US Census Bureau projects that in 2035, for the first time, older people (65+) will outnumber younger ones (aged 18 or less).

The ageing society brings changes and challenges, but there is considerable fuzziness in the framing of the issues—costs of welfare, health and the increased ratio of dependents to those in the labour force, which will be considered in later chapters.

Government and Politics

2.1 Constitutional History

The 18 countries compared in this book have fulfilled the minimum requirements for liberal democracy for 70 years or more.[1] To be regarded as a liberal democracy for this period, each country has met the basic criteria of inclusiveness, competitiveness and constitutionality, which means that governments have always changed according to constitutional processes and have had to face regularly scheduled, fairly conducted and competitive elections in which (close to) all the adult population could vote. However, the United States is the oldest continuing democracy among them (Table 2.1).

Table 2.1 shows that democracies rarely emerge fully formed, nor do they form at the same time in different places. For many countries, the struggle for national independence was tied up with the establishment of democracy, whether by peaceful transition or after violent conflict, as the United States War of Independence brought liberal democracy to the Confederation, and the establishment of the Irish Republic resulted from armed conflict with Britain, followed by Civil War.

For around half a dozen countries, including the United States, Canada and the United Kingdom, liberal democracy has existed continuously throughout the twentieth century and into the twenty-first. The United Kingdom is an interesting case as the institutions of democracy began to form from as early as the Magna Carta (1215), but the country does not have a written Constitution that articulates the rules for government in a single document. Another half a dozen or so West European countries were always democratic except for periods of foreign occupation during war, including Austria, in which parliamentary democracy was suspended from 1933 to 1945. Finally, a third group achieved varying degrees of representative democracy but later relapsed into authoritarian rule, before becoming fully fledged liberal democracies after the end of World War II. This group includes the vanquished Axis powers (Germany and Italy), but also France (which had the most constitutionally problematic change during the contemporary period, namely the 1958 change from the Fourth to Fifth Republic, and the accession of Charles de Gaulle to a self-created presidency).

As the experience of each one of these countries illustrates, achieving a fully inclusive democracy tends to be a gradual process whereby countries move through varying degrees of competition and pluralism. The extension of suffrage to the whole adult population is one example of this democratic evolution. The dates shown in Tables 2.2 and 2.3 follow consensual scholarly judgements as to when the nature of the country's politics was substantially transformed in a democratic direction rather than when democratic principles were fully embraced.

However, the neat listing of dates hides the messiness of the process. Sometimes suffrage was achieved incrementally as increasing concessions were won. Some countries moved through a series of half-way houses, such as imposing property or literacy requirements. In some federations, including the United States, different states had different regulations for permitting voter registration. Kentucky, for example, abolished property qualifications for voting for white men in 1792, whereas these remained until 1856 in North Carolina.

As women gained the right to vote in some countries, they were still subjected to more restrictions than men, for example, having a higher minimum voting age. Some countries maintained a prohibition on women standing for parliament even after they achieved the vote. The United States lagged behind other liberal democracies in granting voting rights to women. New Zealand was the first democracy to allow women to vote, and Finland was the first to allow them to vote and stand for parliament simultaneously.

---

[1]Arend Lijhart (1984) *Democracies: Patterns of Majoritarian and Consensus Government in Twenty-One Countries*. New Haven: Yale University Press. Pippa Norris and Ronald Inglehart (2018) *Cultural Backlash: The Rise of Authoritarian Populism*. New York: Cambridge University Press.

Table 2.1 Constitutional history

Country	Continuous national elections since	Date of independence	Date of current constitution
United States	**1788**	**1776**	**1789**
Norway	1814	1905	1814
Belgium	1831	1830	1931
United Kingdom	1832	–	–
Netherlands	1848	1814	1814
Switzerland	1848	–	1874
New Zealand	1852	1907	1852
Denmark	1855	–	1953
Sweden	1866	–	1975
Canada	1867	1867	1982
Australia	1901	1901	1900
Finland	1906	1917	1919
Ireland	1921	1921	1937
Austria	1945	1918	1920
France	1946	–	1958
Italy	1946	1861	1948
Japan	1946	–	1947
Germany	1949	–	1949

– Denotes not applicable

The dates from the beginning of continuous elections come from Robert Dahl (1971) *Polyarchy: Participation and Opposition*, Yale University Press, pp. 42, 249. The table does not include interruptions due to external occupation, e.g. some European countries during the Nazi occupation in World War II. The dates for independence and current constitution come from Jan-Erik Lane, David McKay and Kenneth Newton (1991) *Political Data Handbook. OECD Countries*. Oxford University Press, p. 112

Table 2.2 Male suffrage
Year when male suffrage was substantially achieved

Country	Year
France	1848
Germany	1869
United States	**1870**
New Zealand	1879
Belgium	1893
Norway	1897
Australia	1901
Denmark	1901
Finland	1906
Austria	1907
Sweden	1909
Italy	1912
Netherlands	1917
Canada	1917
United Kingdom	1918
Ireland	1918
Switzerland	1919
Japan	1925

Jan-Erik Lane, David McKay and Kenneth Newton (1991) *Political Data Handbook. OECD Countries*. Oxford University Press, p. 111; and Inter-Parliamentary Union at: www.ipu.org

Table 2.3 Women's suffrage
Year when suffrage for women was substantially achieved

Country	Year
New Zealand	1893
Australia	1902
Finland	1906
Norway	1913
Denmark	1915
Germany	1918
Austria	1918
Canada	1918
United Kingdom	1918
Ireland	1918
Sweden	1919
Netherlands	1919
United States	**1920**
France	1944
Italy	1946
Japan	1947
Belgium	1948
Switzerland	1971

Jan-Erik Lane, David McKay and Kenneth Newton (1991) *Political Data Handbook. OECD Countries*. Oxford University Press, p. 111; and Inter-Parliamentary Union at: www.ipu.org

Because they establish the rules of the political game and foster political stability, constitutions are regarded as the backbones of liberal democracies. The United States is a leader in this sense, with its constitution having served as the model for the constitutions of many newly independent nations. So much so, that some form of separation of powers has become the norm in democratic states. But they are also fluid documents, which can be changed to reflect evolving ideals of democratic practice. The United States Constitution has been amended 27 times since 1787, ten of which constitute the Bill of Rights. Therefore, constitutions evolve to expand democracy and maintain their longevity as working documents. But as history has shown, there is always the possibility that they can be suspended, rewritten or thrown out when threatened by autocratic leaders, wars and political instability.

2.2 Heads of State and Heads of Government

The United States is unique among these stable democracies because it is the only country that does not formally distinguish between the head of the state and the executive head of government. In the United States, both roles are embodied in the office of the presidency, whereas in most other liberal democracies, the president or the monarch is the head of state and the prime minister, chancellor or premier (different countries use different titles) is the head of the executive government.

Three other countries (grouped just above the United States in Table 2.4) mix or share these roles. The Swiss system reflects that country's peculiar traditions, with a rotating presidency (and prime ministership) investing less power in any individual leader and more in the collective, multi-party cabinet than any other country and making it extremely stable. France and Finland have what is sometimes called a semi-presidential system or dual executive. They have a popularly elected president holding the highest office in the land, elected for a longer period than parliament and with the power to dissolve it, but also needing to rule with parliament, which is the institution where governments must be formed. Both systems arose out of problems with parliamentary instability, which have now largely disappeared. In the other 14 cases, the head of state lacks substantial executive power.

Only five countries elect their heads of state: Austria, Ireland, Finland, France and the United States. Compared to the United States, partisan competition is less fierce in Austria and Ireland: there have been instances in Ireland where there has only been one candidate, and in Austria nearly all the presidents have been former diplomats. In Italy, parliament elects the president, and both the role and selection of the president have been a matter of some dissatisfaction. In Germany, a specially convened assembly, nominated by both national and provincial parliaments, elects the president without debate.

While in practice, the President of the United States is elected by the people, this is mediated through the Electoral College—one of the quirks of American democracy. The Electoral College was designed as a check on public power, placing a layer of elites between the people and their selected leaders. Voters elect members of the Electoral College who pledge their support for a particular candidate, who in turn elect the President.

In the countries where heads of state are elected, they cannot remain in that position indefinitely and there is some variation in the length of their terms. The President of the United States is limited to serving two four-year terms, which allows for more frequent turnover and hence accountability than say, for example, Italy—where the president may serve for an unlimited number of seven-year terms.

Table 2.4 Heads of state

Country	Title	Executive power	Selected by	Maximum duration of office
Belgium	Monarch	Weak		
Denmark	Monarch	Weak		
Japan	Monarch	Weak		
Netherlands	Monarch	Weak		
Norway	Monarch	Weak		
Sweden	Monarch	Weak		
United Kingdom	Monarch	Weak		
Australia[a]	Monarch	Weak	Government	One 5-year term
Canada[a]	Monarch	Weak	Government	(by convention)
New Zealand[a]	Monarch	Weak	Government	
Germany	President	Weak	Legislature—special	Two 5-year terms
Italy	President	Weak	Legislature	Unlimited 7-year terms
Austria	President	Weak	Public	Two 6-year terms
Ireland	President	Weak	Public	Two 7-year terms
Switzerland	President	Strong	Legislature	Unlimited non-consecutive 1-year terms
Finland	President	Strong	Public	Two consecutive 7-year terms
France	President	Strong	Public	Two consecutive 5-year terms
United States	**President**	**Strong**	**Public**	**Two 4-year terms**

[a]Australia, Canada and New Zealand have as head of state the British Monarch, represented nationally by a Governor-General, selected by the national government

Arend Lijhart (1984) *Democracies: Patterns of Majoritarian and Consensus Government in Twenty-One Countries*. New Haven: Yale University Press

So why is it the norm among liberal democracies to maintain two separate roles—head of state and head of government? Typically, there are three components of the head of state's role. The first is symbolic—to preside at ceremonial events and embody national unity above the fray of political conflict. The second common role is to certify that proper procedures are being followed in legislation and elections. The third is to have a 'reserve power' role in times of crisis. These latter two roles are infrequently exercised. They arise most often when the rules of the game—the national constitution—do not unambiguously cover an eventuality that has arisen. In particular, they occur when the workability of the national parliament is in doubt.

When heads of state do intervene in political conflicts, it is likely to involve considerable tension—potentially threatening their capacity to fulfil the consensual parts of the role. In 1990, the King of Belgium refused to provide royal assent for a new and liberal abortion law. This created a significant political crisis, which was resolved only when parliament used its constitutional prerogatives creatively to 'suspend' the King from ruling for a day so that the law could be passed.

Perhaps the most surprising aspect of Table 2.4 is the persistence of monarchies. If the three former British colonies (whose head of state is the Governor-General representing the British monarchy) are included, then a majority of countries remain monarchies. These Monarchs enjoy varying degrees of prestige and popularity in their respective countries, sometimes spurred on by the modernisation of many royal families. However, their current roles and the routes to them are essentially similar. They retain their privileges and ceremonial roles, often religious as well as national, in return for renouncing all attempts to influence politics.

2.3 Federalism

All states of any size and complexity devolve some power to more local units of administration.[2] What differentiates a federal system from a unitary one is that the powers of regional governments are constitutionally entrenched and therefore cannot be reduced on the whim of a national government. The 'division of power' between the national government and regional governments is guaranteed by the constitution where each is independent within defined spheres.

Whether or not a country is a federation is most often explained by historical factors. In almost all the federations in Table 2.5, the current nation state was formed by the coming together of existing local units of government, and in the formation of the new country, some federal guarantees were enshrined. Federations also tend to occur more frequently in countries that are larger in geographic area (the United States, Canada, Australia) or where there are distinctive social interests (e.g. linguistic or ethnic) in different areas of the country (Belgium). The Belgian federation, for example, evolved through demands for greater regional autonomy rather than a 'coming together' of pre-existing entities. In most cases, there has been no change in the regional boundaries since the original constitutions were framed. The United States is an exception here: it consisted of only 13 states when the original constitution was adopted, since growing to 50 (Alaska and Hawaii were the last two states, incorporated in 1959).

The arguments for federation include that it encourages greater responsiveness to local needs and variations and brings government closer to the people, that it allows

Table 2.5 Federal and unitary state structures

Country	System	Constitutional amendment	Regional governments
Australia	Federal	Referendum/Veto	6 States
Austria	Federal	Referendum/Veto	9 *Länder*
Belgium	Federal	Referendum/Veto	10 Provinces
Canada	Federal	Referendum/Veto	12 Provinces
Germany	Federal	Referendum/Veto	16 *Länder*
Switzerland	Federal	Referendum/Veto	26 *Kanton*
United States	**Federal**	**Referendum/Veto**	**50 States**
Denmark	Unitary	Referendum majority	
Finland	Unitary	Referendum/Veto	
France	Unitary	Referendum majority	
Ireland	Unitary	Referendum majority	
Italy	Unitary	Referendum majority	
Japan	Unitary	Referendum/Veto	
Netherlands	Unitary	Referendum/Veto	
New Zealand	Unitary	Parliamentary majority	
Norway	Unitary	Referendum/Veto	
Sweden	Unitary	Parliamentary majority	
United Kingdom	Unitary	Parliamentary majority	

Arend Lijhart (1984) *Democracies: Patterns of Majoritarian and Consensus Government in Twenty-One Countries*. New Haven: Yale University Press

---

[2]John Loughlin, John Kincaid and Wilfried Sweden (2013) *Routledge Handbook of Regionalism and Federalism*. London: Routledge.

diversity and experimentation in government, and that it provides a break on the growth of centralised power. Federal structures are also important mechanisms for mitigating or circumventing political conflict, and accommodating demands for some degree of autonomy. From time to time, however, renewed calls for regional independence may arise, as sporadic debates over the status and sovereignty of Quebec in Canada illustrate.

The arguments against federalism involve issues of duplication and inefficiency, and a lack of accountability through buck-passing the responsibility for problems between different levels of government.

Some institutional characteristics follow almost automatically from federalism. One is judicial review of government decisions to ensure that one level of government is not abrogating the prerogatives of the other (see Sect. 2.9 'The Judiciary'). Switzerland with its unique mix of institutions is the only federation not to have such judicial review.

In addition, federal constitutions typically place restrictions on constitutional change in order to encourage stability. Although three countries (Sweden, the United Kingdom and New Zealand) allow the possibility of change through a simple parliamentary majority, most others require a referendum. In addition, a change in federal countries typically requires not only a popular majority, but to meet 'federal' criteria as well. In the United States, a constitutional amendment must be approved by three quarters of the states. In Germany, it must be approved by two-thirds of the *Bundesrat*, the legislative body representing the *Länder*, and in Switzerland and Australia, changes require both an electoral majority and a majority of regions (known as the 'double majority' requirement).

Finally, federalism should not be confused with decentralisation. As Table 2.6 shows, central governments tend to raise a greater share of tax in unitary systems than in federal ones, but there is considerable overlap. The United States, as a federal democracy, raises around two-thirds of its total taxation revenue through the central government. But Sweden, for example, which is a unitary state, is also highly decentralised—regions and municipalities have autonomous taxation powers, supported by the Local Government Act.

Austria lies at the other extreme. Despite being a federal state, 95% of its taxation revenue is collected by the central government. This arrangement originated in the constitutional and economic rebuilding of Austria after two world wars and the necessity of having a strong role for the state in this process. This is one of federalism's dilemmas. Either there is an administratively messy system with each state imposing its own taxes or there is 'vertical fiscal imbalance', where one layer of government is responsible for raising money that is spent on services provided by another, and so a potential recipe for mutual irresponsibility.

Table 2.6 Taxation by level of government
Proportion of all taxes raised by central government

Country	Type	1975	1995	2015
Australia	Federal	80.1	77.5	79.3
Austria	Federal	77.0	94.1	95.0
Germany	Federal	67.5	70.4	68.2
Belgium	Federal	94.1	92.3	86.5
United States	**Federal**	**65.9**	**66.6**	**67.0**
Switzerland	Federal	52.7	58.6	60.4
Canada	Federal	57.6	53.1	50.1
Ireland	Unitary	90.5	95.8	97.0
Netherlands	Unitary	97.3	95.5	95.2
New Zealand	Unitary	92.3	94.7	93.2
United Kingdom	Unitary	88.0	95.3	94.6
France	Unitary	91.8	88.6	86.6
Norway	Unitary	77.6	80.4	84.7
Italy	Unitary	99.1	94.2	83.2
Finland	Unitary	76.4	77.4	76.0
Japan	Unitary	74.5	74.8	76.1
Sweden	Unitary	70.8	68.7	63.7
Denmark	Unitary	69.0	68.2	72.9
	Mean Federal	70.7	73.2	72.4
	Mean Unitary	84.3	84.9	83.9

OECD (2017) *Revenue Statistics 1965–2016*, OECD Publishing: Paris, p. 28

2.4 Legislative Structures

How legislatures are designed has a significant impact on the character of the law-making process.[3] Almost three quarters of the democracies in Table 2.7 have a legislature that is bicameral (comprised of two chambers). However, while bicameralism may be the norm, having a strongly bicameral system—as the United States does—is the exception.

In order to be considered a strong bicameral system, a country must have two houses whose composition is distinctly different (incongruent) but have substantially similar powers (symmetrical). The United States Congress fits the bill: the Senate comprises of two members chosen from each state, whereas House of Representatives members are apportioned between the states on the basis of population. With the exception of taxation bills, the legislative powers of the two chambers are equal. If legislation is to pass, it must obtain a majority in both houses.

Among the four countries with strong bicameralism, the situation derived from their federal origins. In each, the lower house directly reflects population size, while the upper house is based on ensuring all the regions are equally represented. Although there is no genuine sense today in which these second chambers act as states' houses, their distinctive

---
[3] George Tsebelis and Jeanette Money (1997) *Bi-Cameralism*, Cambridge: Cambridge University Press.

Table 2.7 Legislative structures

Country	Number of chambers	Strength of bicameralism	Method of election	Powers of second house
Australia	Bicameral	Strong	Incongruent	Symmetrical
Germany	Bicameral	Strong	Incongruent	Symmetrical
Switzerland	Bicameral	Strong	Incongruent	Symmetrical
United States	**Bicameral**	**Strong**	**Incongruent**	**Symmetrical**
Belgium	Bicameral	Weak	Congruent	Symmetrical
Italy	Bicameral	Weak	Congruent	Symmetrical
Netherlands	Bicameral	Weak	Congruent	Symmetrical
Austria	Bicameral	Weak	Congruent	Asymmetrical
Canada	Bicameral	Weak	Incongruent	Asymmetrical
France	Bicameral	Weak	Incongruent	Asymmetrical
Ireland	Bicameral	Weak	Congruent	Asymmetrical
Japan	Bicameral	Weak	Congruent	Asymmetrical
United Kingdom	Bicameral	Weak	Incongruent	Asymmetrical
Denmark	Unicameral			
Finland	Unicameral			
New Zealand	Unicameral			
Norway	Unicameral			
Sweden	Unicameral			

Arend Lijhart (1984) *Democracies: Patterns of Majoritarian and Consensus Government in Twenty-One Countries*. New Haven: Yale University Press

composition can provide a check upon the lower house majority.

Weak bicameral systems fall into two types. In the first, the method of election tends to produce a mirror of the lower house, and so the second house tends to be a rubber stamp for the government of the day. In the second are those where the upper house lacks the power of the lower house. They may have the power to criticise or delay legislation but not to block it. This varies widely between countries: the British House of Lords can delay legislation for one year but the Japanese House of Councillors can only delay it for 60 days. The influence of these second chambers rests in moral suasion, their power to propose, disclose or embarrass. In the face of a patient and determined majority government, however, they are powerless.

In contrast, strong bicameral legislatures have real potential to frustrate the government's legislative agenda. For example, the United States Senate has routinely used its powers to block judicial appointments, controversial legislation and even funding bills. The Senate's power to block the latter has seen the United States federal government shut down 19 times since 1975. Because the House of Representatives and the Senate are elected at different times and geographic area is weighted differently (large urban areas are more heavily represented in the House, and rural and less populous states in the Senate), it is possible for different parties to have majorities in the different houses. This has happened in six of last 42 Congresses, between 1947 and 2019.

So why do so many countries have a weak bicameral system? The answer probably lies in the origins and evolution of legislative rule. In the transition to popular rule, upper houses were established because of the anxieties of established elites about what a popularly elected lower house might do. Most evolved beyond these anti-democratic origins, either by changing their method of selection or by increasingly limiting their powers.

Only five countries are unicameral. They include five of the six smallest countries in population and area. All are unitary rather than federal systems and the Scandinavian countries have relatively homogenous populations. New Zealand, Denmark and Sweden all became unicameral legislatures in the second half of the twentieth century. In each of these cases, the upper houses that were abolished were either appointed, indirectly elected by politicians, or membership was restricted on the basis of wealth.

In 2013, the Irish people voted on a referendum proposal to abolish the *Seanad Éireann*, the upper house of the Irish *Oireachtas*. Proponents of the reform argued that the upper house was unrepresentative, merely a rubber stamp for government legislation and expensive to run. Advocates against its abolition suggested that it was a valuable check on the power of government and acted to disperse power within the Irish system. The referendum was narrowly defeated, 51.7% against and 48.3% in favour, and Ireland remains a weak bicameral system.

2.5 Governments, Executives and Legislatures

The legislature is the central institution of representative democracy.[4] It is the forum where the elected representatives are meant to express the will of the people on a continuing basis, and through which executive government is responsible to the people. However, the institutional means by which different countries seek to achieve responsible, representative government differ enormously.

Perhaps the most fundamental issue is whether the survival of the government depends on having the continuing confidence of the legislature. Different liberal democracies have devised two diametrically opposed institutional solutions to achieving responsible executive government. In the British-derived system, cabinet members must be members of the legislature, and answer to it on a continuing basis. As Table 2.8 shows, the most common pattern among the selected countries is the British one, where governments must retain the support of the legislature to stay in office.

In other systems, which emphasise the separation of powers, cabinet members must not be members of the legislature. The United States falls into this category, and it perhaps better thought of as the 'President's cabinet' rather than a collective body responsible to the legislature. In the middle sits a range of countries, where nearly all members of the executive are also members of the legislature, but which occasionally go outside for some appointments. In Canada, ministers are drawn from time to time from the appointed Senate, in order to secure representation from a particular region, or where the Senator has special competencies.

The problem with members of the executive not being members of the legislature is that it runs the risk of the legislature lagging behind in knowing what executive government is doing. The problem with cabinet members being part of the legislature is that if the government has a secure and disciplined majority, the legislature simply 'rubber stamps' what executive government wants.

As Table 2.8 shows, the United States sits among a small group of countries (Japan, Italy and Switzerland) where scholars of comparative democracy judged that the cohesion of the governing parties was low. In Japan and Italy, party cohesion was low because the major parties were so factionalised. In the United States, parties often reflected regional differences internally, and there was more emphasis on 'hands across the aisle' in negotiating policy.

In institutional terms, cohesion is seen as desirable as it enables collective action—for legislators to come together in order to sustain a government: to pass bills and make policy. The counter-argument is that party cohesion weakens the role of the legislator as a representative of the people, and compromises the freedom to vote according to conscience.

Yet summary judgments about the relative power of different legislatures can be misleading. In the United States, for example, despite the President's power to hire and fire his departmental Secretaries, Cabinet departments are created and their responsibilities defined by Congress, which also decides their budgets. Congress has the power to pass, or not, legislation advocated by the departments, and exercises oversight through the committee system, where departmental personnel can be called to testify. This both limits the President's power and even creates divided loyalties for departmental heads. On the other hand, the American Congress is a much less predictable institution—as party cohesion is low and the coalitions supporting particular pieces of legislation often cut across party lines, the party that is not in office has more scope to influence deliberations.

In addition, however, degrees of party cohesion are not eternal. As American politics has become more polarised, so the party divisions have become more rigid, and party voting patterns in Congress more predictable.

To a considerable extent, the differences in the flavour of national parliaments and relations between executive governments and their legislatures are determined by the logic of institutional structures and partisan competition. However, beyond this, countries have built their own traditions about how legislatures should function. Institutionally, the relationship between executive government and the legislature in Sweden is not so different from a British-style Westminster system, but their traditions are very different. The Swedish parliamentary system works much more through negotiation and deliberation in committees. Most legislation emerges in this way and then has a very high probability that parliament will approve it. Therefore, while we see that nations such as Sweden are categorised as having 'low' government control over the legislature, culture and working modes develop over time to ensure that there is usually a workaround.

---

[4]Richard S. Katz (2007) *Political Institutions in the United States*. Oxford: Oxford University Press.

Table 2.8 Governments, executives and legislatures

Country	Does government depend on the confidence of the legislature?	Are members of cabinet members of the legislature?	Cohesion of governing parties	Government control over the legislature
Australia	Y	Y	H	H
Ireland	Y	Y	H	H
Japan	Y	Y	L	H
New Zealand	Y	Y	H	H
United Kingdom	Y	Y	H	H
Austria	Y	Y+	H	M
Belgium	Y	Y+	H	M
Canada	Y	Y+	H	H
Denmark	Y	Y+	H	L
Germany	Y	Y+	H	M
Italy	Y	Y+	L	L
Netherlands	Y	N	H	L
Norway	Y	N	H	M
Sweden	Y	N	H	L
Finland	N	Y+	H	L
France	N	N	H	H
Switzerland	N	N	L	H
United States	N	N	L	L

Y = Yes; Y+ = Yes, plus some others; N = No; H = High; M = Medium; L = Low

Jaap Woldendorp, Hans Keman and Ian Budge (2000) *Party Government in 48 Democracies (1945–1998). Composition—Duration—Personnel*. Dordrecht: Kluwer Academic Publishers; G. Bingham Powell, Jr. (2000) *Elections as Instruments of Democracy. Majoritarian and Proportional Visions*. New Haven: Yale University Press

2.6 Electoral Systems

The countries covered in this book are all representative democracies, so how they turn the wishes of the people into elected representatives is crucial. Electoral systems long fascinated scholars, who recognised that the formula by which people are elected has a large impact on who is elected. In recent years, their importance has come into popular view as legislatures often fail to reflect the diversity of a country's citizens (e.g. see Sect. 10.4 below on gender).

The United States is distinctive in that although some aspects of national elections are regulated by federal law, they should more properly be seen as simultaneous state events—with each state able to choose important aspects of its electoral system.

Among the different electoral systems countries (or states) use, the first key variable is whether each constituency chooses one member or several. If there is only one winner, it means that those who voted for another candidate will not be represented. Multi-member systems, which commonly used in European countries (Table 2.9), tend to produce more proportional outcomes, that is, the representatives elected more closely match the votes that are cast. Since 1842, federal law in the United States has required that candidates for the House of Representatives be chosen from single member districts.

Another, less commented on aspect of electoral methods is whether voters must choose only one option (categorical) or whether they can express their preferences among candidates (ordinal). In single member systems where there are more than two candidates, under a categorical system (as in the United States and the United Kingdom), the voter must make a strategic as well as a preferential decision. Which candidate do I prefer? Do they have a chance of winning? Many voters who might otherwise prefer a minority candidate decide not to 'waste' their vote on someone who has no chance of winning.

The ordinal, or preferential, system is used in Australia, the Oscars, and from 2018, the US State of Maine. In 2011, a referendum was held in the United Kingdom to ask voters if they wanted to move from a first past the post (categorical) to an alternative vote (ordinal) system. Opinion among parties and politicians was divided and, in the end, UK voters elected to stay with the first-past-the-post system, with 68% support).

Apart from preferential voting, another solution to this problem is the one used in France and, within the United States, in Louisiana. If no candidate obtains a majority in the first round, there is a run-off between the leading candidates with the most votes.

2.6 Electoral Systems

Table 2.9 Electoral systems

Country	Single or multi-member constituencies	Type of vote	Index of Disproportionality** (2010–2017)
Plurality systems			
Canada	Single	Categorical	12.22
United Kingdom	Single	Categorical	12.21
United States	**Single**	**Categorical**	**4.38**
Majority Systems			
Australia	Single	Ordinal	10.77
France	Single	Categorical/Double ballot	19.39
Mixed Systems			
Italy	25:75 Single: Multi	Categorical	17.34
Japan	63:37 Single: Multi	Categorical	17.52
Germany	50:50 Single: Multi MMP*	Categorical	4.89
New Zealand	42:58 Single: Multi MMP*	Categorical	2.94
Proportional Systems			
Austria	Multi	Categorical	3.52
Netherlands	Multi	Categorical	0.92
Denmark	Multi	Categorical	0.76
Sweden	Multi	Categorical	1.95
Belgium	Multi	Categorical	4.19
Finland	Multi	Categorical	2.99
Norway	Multi	Categorical	2.79
Switzerland	Multi	Ordinal	3.73
Ireland	Multi	Ordinal	7.16

For bi-cameral systems, the table gives the electoral system of the lower house only
*MMP means mixed-member proportional
**Index of Disproportionality: the higher the score, the larger the distortion between parties' vote shares and their seat shares. The figure reported is the average of all national elections between 2010 and 2017 Michael Gallagher (2018) *Election indices dataset*. Available at: https://www.tcd.ie/Political_Science/people/michael_gallagher/ElSystems/index.php

Multi-member, proportional representation (PR) systems generate different problems. People can be elected with a low percentage of the vote. In the Netherlands, where the whole country is one single electorate, which elects 150 members, a candidate or party is assured a seat if he or she wins 0.67% of the vote. This often results in numerous parties being represented in the legislature, and often protracted processes of coalition and government formation. After the 2017 election, it took 208 days for a coalition government to be formed. In some variants of proportional representation (now largely discarded) when voters could only choose one party list or another, they had no influence over which individuals were elected. This gave the party machines, which decided the list rankings, great power. Most list systems now give voters some choice among individual candidates. Some, such as the Irish and Australian Senate systems, also allow voters to express preferences across parties.

The most common criticism of proportional representation systems is that they rarely produce clear legislative majorities, and that the result can therefore be weak and unstable government. Small groups holding the 'balance of power' can also exercise disproportionate power.

The United States occupies a median position among the countries covered here requiring Presidential elections to be held every four years (Table 2.10). Fixed-term elections, also practiced Switzerland and Norway, avoid the situation that is often observed in Australia and Japan where governments call early elections for political advantage—to avoid damaging debates in the legislature or to exploit a lead in the opinion polls. Too long a term means that governments are held accountable less frequently. Too short a term can be criticised on the ground that it encourages an almost constant process of electioneering and campaigning and that it does not leave enough time for voters to properly judge the competence of the government and the policies it has implemented.

Table 2.10 Number of national elections

Country	Number of national elections 1945–2018	Maximum interval between elections (years)	Average interval between elections (years)
United States	18	4	4.0
Switzerland	18	4	4.0
Germany	19	4	3.8
Norway	19	4	3.8
Italy	19	4	3.8
Finland	20	4	3.7
France	20	5	3.7
Ireland	20	5	3.7
United Kingdom	20	5	3.7
Sweden	21	4	3.5
Austria	22	4	3.3
Belgium	22	4	3.3
Netherlands	22	4	3.3
Canada	23	5	3.2
New Zealand	25	3	2.9
Denmark	27	4	2.7
Japan	27	4	2.7
Australia	28	3	2.6

Michael Gallagher (2018) *Election indices dataset*. Available at: https://www.tcd.ie/Political_Science/people/michael_gallagher/ElSystems/index.php

2.7 Party Systems and Electoral Choice

The most obvious difference when looking at political contests in these democracies is that some involve an essentially two-sided competition, while in others there are a large number of competing parties. It would seem a simple matter to count the number of parties, but in fact it is a complicated exercise. To be relevant, some account has to be taken of the relative size of political parties and their role in forming government.

Political scientists have used the concept of the 'effective' number of parties to count not just their existence but their importance and support. The numbers in Table 2.11 represent the effective number of parties in the legislature and provide a good indication of the level of party competition, or fragmentation, in democracies. As can be seen from the descriptions in the right-hand column, they fall into four broad groups, from essentially two-party to strongly multi-party.

Of all the democracies included in this volume, the United States ranks as that with the 'purest' two-party system. Although there are many minor parties in US politics, they rarely win more than a few per cent of the vote or elect a candidate to office. Since 1899, the Republican Party and the Democrats have held more than 95% of the seats in both Houses of Congress.

Table 2.11 Party systems

Country	Effective number of parties (1977–2017)	Capsule description of system
United States	**1.7**	**Essentially two-party**
Australia	2.2	Essentially two-party
United Kingdom	2.3	Essentially two-party
Canada	2.6	Essentially two-party
New Zealand	2.7	Essentially two-party
Japan	2.8	Essentially two-party
France	3.1	Principally two-party with a significant third
Ireland	3.1	Principally two-party with a significant third
Austria	3.3	Principally two-party with a significant third
Germany	3.7	Moderately multi-party
Sweden	4.0	Moderately multi-party
Norway	4.2	Moderately multi-party
Italy	4.8	Strongly multi-party
Denmark	5.1	Strongly multi-party
Netherlands	5.1	Strongly multi-party
Finland	5.2	Strongly multi-party
Switzerland	5.4	Strongly multi-party
Belgium	7.5	Strongly multi-party

Michael Gallagher (2018) *Election indices dataset*. Available at: https://www.tcd.ie/Political_Science/people/michael_gallagher/ElSystems/index.php

The association between electoral system and party system is strong. However, parties with a strong regional basis can lead to more than two parties even in single member electoral systems, and this has become more pronounced in Canada and the United Kingdom with the success of regionalist parties such as the Scottish National Party (SNP) and Plaid Cymru. The New Zealand party system changed with its change of electoral system. With mixed-member proportional representation, parties such as the Greens and NZ First routinely win parliamentary representation.

Next is a grouping of three countries, where there is a third party whose support can influence the formation of governments. In each, there has been principally a choice between two main parties for government, but some variability or uncertainty about who might join with whom in coalition. In recent years, right wing populist parties such as the National Front in France and the Austrian People's Party have assumed important roles in coalition formation across Europe.

As we move into multi-party systems, the patterns become ever more varied. Some revolve around one dominant party. For most of the contemporary era, Italy for example, had a dominant two-party system. The Christian Democrats in Italy and the Liberal Democratic Party in Japan were far bigger than their competitors and invariably until the early 1990s, formed the basis of government. After Italy's anti-corruption and electoral reforms, the Christian Democrats disappeared, and party competition is increasingly based around two broad party groupings. In Sweden, most governments have either been based upon the Social Democrats (often able to form government in their own right) or a coalition of smaller conservative parties.

As the number of parties increases, the nature of the electoral choice changes. G. Bingham Powell has analysed (Table 2.12) how in half these countries the nature of the government (either single party or coalition) the public is electing is usually clear to them before the election. But in four strongly multi-party systems, there is not such a clearly identifiable choice between competing aspirants for government.

Similarly, although no one can predict all the permutations of party balances an election might throw up, in the two-party systems it is normally clear after the election who will form the government. In other countries, with many different groups represented, there can still be considerable uncertainty about what coalition will form government. A party's own vote might go down, but because of the balance of competing parties its chance of being in government may increase. The lottery aspects of who forms government should not be exaggerated, but in some countries post-election negotiations can be protracted. Belgium, for example, the country with the strongest multi-party

Table 2.12 Electoral choice and government formation

Country	Likelihood of prospective governments being identified in pre-election choice	Formation of government post-election
Australia	High	Usually clear result
Canada	High	Usually clear result
France	High	Usually clear result
Germany	High	Usually clear result
Japan	High	Usually clear result
New Zealand	High	Usually clear result
United Kingdom	High	Usually clear result
United States	**High**	**Usually clear result**
Sweden	High	Variable
Norway	Variable	Usually clear result
Austria	Variable	Variable
Ireland	Variable	Variable
Denmark	Variable	Negotiation after
Netherlands	Variable	Negotiation after
Belgium	Low	Negotiation after
Finland	Low	Negotiation after
Italy	Low	Negotiation after
Switzerland	Low	Negotiation after

G. Bingham Powell, Jr. (2000) *Elections as Instruments of Democracy. Majoritarian and Proportional Visions*. New Haven: Yale University Press

Table 2.13 Electoral participation
Voting turnout as a proportion of registered voters in each period

Country	1945–1970	1971–1990	1991–2007	2008–2018
Australia	94	95	95	92
Belgium	92	93	92	89
Denmark	84	87	86	87
Sweden	83	90	84	86
New Zealand	91	88	83	78
Austria	95	91	81	78
Netherlands	95	84	78	77
Norway	81	82	77	77
Italy	92	91	84	76
Germany	86	87	80	73
Ireland	74	74	66	68
United States	**93**	**76**	**69**	**67**
Finland	79	76	67	67
United Kingdom	77	75	67	67
Canada	76	74	65	63
Japan	73	70	57	60
Switzerland	68	51	45	50
France	79	74	64	49
Mean	84	81	74	72

IDEA Voter Turnout Database https://www.idea.int/data-tools/data/voter-turnout

system, also holds the record for the longest time to form a government. Following the 2010 general election, in which 11 parties were elected to the parliament, none with a vote share greater than 20%, it took 541 days to form a government.

2.8 Political Participation

Increasing alienation and detachment from politics is a concern in nearly every advanced liberal democracy. The figures in Tables 2.13 and 2.14 offer some limited support for this concern. Table 2.13, which depicts voter turnout in our 18 democracies and how this has changed over time, broadly supports the claim that voters are becoming increasingly alienated from representative institutions, but it needs to be treated with some caution. The trend in the most recent decades is for turnout to be on average 12 percentage points lower than in the post-World War II decades. This decline has been most significant in France and the United States, but at the same time, Denmark and Sweden have experienced modest increases in turnout.

How to interpret these trends is a contentious subject among political scientists. Some would argue that declining voter turnout is related to cynicism with governments and

Table 2.14 Political participation beyond elections
Percentage of respondents/electorate who have undertaken various forms of political action

Country	Petitions	Attending peaceful demonstrations	Boycotts	Party membership
New Zealand	84.1	18.2	15.4	2.1
Australia	78.6	19.8	15.1	1.6
Sweden	77.6	30.9	27.5	3.6
Switzerland	77.2	27.8	18.8	3.9
Canada	70.7	25.4	22.4	–
Norway	69.2	29.1	24.0	4.4
United States	**68.9**	**14.7**	**19.2**	**–**
France	66.4	37.2	13.9	1.2
United Kingdom	65.9	15.9	16.2	1.2
Japan	54.9	8.0	5.6	4.2
Italy	52.1	34.3	18.6	4.5
Finland	49.0	9.9	15.3	9.7
Germany	48.4	29.5	8.9	2.1
Netherlands	42.1	18.5	11.9	2.4
Austria	–	–	–	13.5
Belgium	–	–	–	4.8
Denmark	–	–	–	3.7
Ireland	–	–	–	2.2
Mean	64.4	23.2	16.5	4.2

Project MAPP (Members and Activists of Political Parties), Political Party Database Project (PPDB). World Values Survey, 2005–2009 Wave

politicians, as well as the decline of traditional political parties in many established democracies—an observation also supported by the extremely low rates of party membership shown in Table 2.14.

Others might suggest that it is a problem of too many riches. Switzerland, which historically has the lowest turnout at elections, also has a multitude of opportunities to participate with quarterly referenda. High election frequency has also been cited as a culprit in France's downward turnout trend. French voters can typically participate in legislative, municipal, departmental, regional, European parliament and presidential elections—all of which take place in multiple rounds.

Not surprisingly, the figures show that the best way to achieve high turnout for voting is to make it compulsory. Australia and Belgium both have compulsory voting, though this has not stopped election turnout declining in these two democracies over the last decade.

Countries have different traditions about whether elections are held on a holiday or work day, whether there are two voting days or only one, and if the voter cannot vote in person in their own constituency how easy it is to cast an absentee or postal ballot. While modifying some procedures would probably increase participation in the more restrictive countries, logistical arrangements do not correlate strongly with overall levels of turnout.

There can be marked variations in the same country at different elections. Apart from the lack of enthusiasm for all politics, one variable affecting turnout is whether the outcome is predictable or uncertain. It can also vary with political strategies. In the 2008 presidential election, the Obama campaign was able to mobilise significant support from black voters and overall turnout rose from 55.7 to 58.2% of the voting age population. In 2012, with Obama once again on the ballot, the turnout rate among black voters (67%) surpassed white voters (64%) for the first time in history.

There are two ways of measuring voter turnout, and neither is universally satisfactory. The better option, which is used here, is as a proportion of registered voters, and the other is as a proportion of the voting age population. In many countries, registration is compulsory and so all-but-identical with citizenship. In countries, most especially the United States, registering to vote is voluntary, and sometimes—especially for minority groups—has proved difficult to achieve. For example, US State laws have been passed in recent years that require strict photo identification when voting. Research has shown that black and Latino voters are particularly likely to lack this identification and are disproportionately likely to be asked for it at polling stations.

Voting, however, is only one part of the political participation story. Party membership (Table 2.14) has traditionally been an important indicator of engagement. In recent decades, however, the number of people joining political

Table 2.15 Bills of rights and judicial review of government decisions

Country	Bill of rights	Judicial review of government decisions	Highest national court that can review government decisions, give advice or enforce rights
United States	**Y**	**Y (strong)**	**Supreme Court**
Canada	Y	Y (strong)	Supreme Court
Germany	Y	Y (strong)	Federal Constitutional Court
Australia	N	Y (medium)	High Court
Austria	Y*	Y (medium)	Constitutional Court
Italy	Y	Y (medium)	Constitutional Court
Belgium	Y*	Y (weak)	Constitutional Court
Denmark	Y	Y (weak)	Supreme Court
Ireland	Y	Y (weak)	Supreme Court
Japan	Y	Y (weak)	Supreme Court
Norway	Y	Y (weak)	Supreme Court
Sweden	Y	Y (weak)	Supreme Court
France	Y	N (weak)	Constitutional Council
Finland	Y	N (none)	Supreme Court
Netherlands	Y*	N (none)	Supreme Court
New Zealand	Y	N (none)	Supreme Court
Switzerland	Y	N (none)	Supreme Court
United Kingdom	Y*	N (none)	Supreme Court

*Protections provided by the European Convention for the Protection of Human Rights and Fundamental Freedoms
Arend Lijhart (1984) *Democracies: Patterns of Majoritarian and Consensus Government in Twenty-One Countries.* New Haven: Yale University Press

parties has declined dramatically. Comparable figures are not available for North America, where membership does not have the same meaning as in European democracies. In the USA, the concept of membership as an ongoing voluntary commitment is unheard of, with citizens expressing partisan support by registering as party voters. Membership in Canada fluctuates with the electoral cycle, as citizens typically join to vote in leadership primaries.

Although comprehensive global data is not available, the World Values Survey gives us some indication of how many people participate in protests, boycotts and petitions in most of our countries. The data presented in Table 2.14 reveals some interesting differences. In contrast to party membership, participating in protests and boycotts is a means of political expression for many people, particularly in European countries. In the United States and Canada, more than two-thirds of survey respondents claimed to have signed a

Table 2.16 Method and length of judicial appointments

Country	Method of appointment	Tenure/retirement
Australia	Government appointment	Compulsory retirement at 70
Austria	Government appointment	Compulsory retirement at 70
Belgium	Government appointment	Compulsory retirement at 70
Canada	Government appointment	Compulsory retirement at 75
Denmark	Independent Judicial Appointments Council	Compulsory retirement at 70
Finland	Government appointment	Compulsory retirement at 65
France	Presidential and parliamentary appointments	9 year non-renewable terms
Germany	Elected by the House of Representatives and the Senate	12 year terms with compulsory retirement at 68
Ireland	Government appointment	Compulsory retirement at 70
Italy	Presidential appointment, parliamentary election, judicial election	9 year terms
Japan	Government appointment subject to popular referendum every ten years	Face popular referendum every ten years
Netherlands	Government appointment	Compulsory retirement at 70
New Zealand	Government appointment	Life
Norway	Appointed by the Monarch on the recommendation of the Judicial Appointments Board	Compulsory retirement at 70
Sweden	Government appointment	Following probation, permanent tenure
Switzerland	Parliamentary election	6 year terms
United Kingdom	Appointed by judicial selection committee	Compulsory retirement at 70
United States	**Presidential appointment approved by the Senate**	**Life**

petition, which is consistently the most practiced type of political activity after voting in all our countries.

2.9 The Judiciary

As the third arm of government, the judicial system performs a series of vital functions in democratic states. Apart from having the power to impose punishments, courts in some democracies are granted the power to review government legislation and decisions against constitutional principles or bills of rights. The principles enshrined in these documents can include freedoms of religion, expression and association and are instrumental in achieving political equality and social and economic wellbeing.

Table 2.15 shows that almost three quarters of our countries allow their courts to invalidate government legislation if it is incompatible with the constitution. The United States, Germany and Canada have particularly strong systems of judicial review. As early as 1803 in the landmark judgment *Marbury v. Madison*, the United States Supreme Court established its own authority to review the decisions of the elected government against the constitution.

Courts are not afraid to show their independence from politicians. The Italian Constitutional Court, for example, invalidated a controversial law passed by parliament in 2004 that would have given senior politicians immunity from prosecution. Between 1951 and 1990, the German Constitutional Court invalidated almost 5% of all federal laws. In 2015, the US Supreme Court legalised same sex marriage nationwide, overriding numerous state laws (*Obergefell v. Hodges*).

The constitutions of several democracies explicitly deny the power of judicial review to their courts. The logic of this resides in the view that important decisions as to whether or not laws conform with the constitution should be made by elected representatives rather than by an appointed and frequently unrepresentative judicial body. Article 120 of the Constitution of the Netherlands, for example, explicitly denies the courts the power to review the constitutionality of laws and treaties.

Other countries have reached compromise positions. Although Sweden provides for judicial review, there is a wariness about courts overruling elected representatives. The Swedish solution has been to establish a judicial body that gives advice on the constitutionality of proposed legislation. France is an interesting case in this respect. Judicial review is prohibited, but the Constitutional Council acts to review bills immediately after they have passed through parliament. In Belgium, judicial review can only be exercised where the legislation concerns the balance of power between different levels of government.

Bills of rights provide another mechanism by which governments can be held accountable. These documents typically codify a range of civil and political rights and invest the courts with the power to enforce them. The United States Constitution was amended to include a Bill or Rights in 1789, and now most Americans identify their Constitution entirely with its statement of rights.

Bills of rights are extremely common among established democracies. From our 18 countries, Australia is the only democracy without one. The reason for this stems from the belief that as an elected and accountable body, the legislature is well equipped to provide for rights and address social problems when they occur. The need has also been mitigated in some countries such as Australia, Ireland and the United Kingdom, where international instruments are seen as a source of protection, and judicial precedent has evolved over centuries to create a body of implied, rather than express, rights that citizens can look to. Many of the countries in Table 2.15 are party to the Convention for the Protection of Human Rights and Fundamental Freedoms, which has the status of constitutional law and is enforced through the European Court of Human Rights.

How judges are appointed varies between democracies. In the United States, the process of appointing new judges is an open contest between conflicting ideological positions and party affiliations. In Germany, care is taken not only to balance the nominations between the parties but also the *Länder*. In the Netherlands, the government picks one of the parliament's nominations. This gives wide scope for political appointments, but this is tempered by party competition, where each side knows that a blatantly political appoint would invite retaliation.

Once a judge is appointed, it is most common for them to continually serve on the bench until he/she retires. Several European democracies, France, Italy, Germany and Switzerland, require their judges to serve terms of between six and 12 years. The choice democracies make here is finding a balance between protections of the court's independence and providing some measure of accountability. Japanese Supreme Court judges are subject to popular referendum every ten years, but this is largely a formality. The United States is the only democracy to appoint judges for life, without compulsory retirement.

2.10 Political Finance

Alongside the different ways in which they structure their electoral systems, these 18 democracies also adopt quite different approaches to regulating money in politics and campaigning.[5] With the increasing cost and scale of election campaigns, political finance has become one of the most pressing issues for established democracies and strict regulatory regimes have become increasingly common.

Political finance regulation has three core aims: to resource political actors such as candidates and political parties, to reduce reliance on private money and to increase political equality. To achieve these aims, countries adopt a variety of different measures, shown in Tables 2.17 and 2.18.

Most countries place some restrictions on the money that candidates and political parties can receive. This can either be in the form of a limit on the amount of political donations or by regulating the source from which they are received. In Belgium, for example, individuals can only donate a maximum of 500 Euro to a political party. In Canada, the limit is $1500. In the United States, it is $2700. The aim here is to find a balance between preserving the democratic freedoms of citizens to use donations to parties and candidates as a form of support or political expression, with the need to circumvent the potential corrupting influence of money in politics.

The United States, like Canada and France, bans political donations from foreign sources, unions and corporations. The rationale behind banning donations from unions and corporations is twofold: to reduce the influence of 'big money' in politics in light of these actors' ability to accumulate funds and give precedence to the individual as the appropriate participant in election campaigns. Banning donations from foreign sources reflects the view that domestic politics should be only be influenced by participants from within that particular country.

Either in tandem with putting restrictions on the source of money, or as an alternative to regulating its supply, countries might also restrict the amount of money that political parties and candidates can spend on electioneering. Once again, this varies widely. In Canada, for example, the maximum amount a party can spend it tied to the number of candidates it fields in a general election. In Belgium, the maximum spend is one million Euro per party; in Austria, it is 7 million. One criticism of caps on political expenditure is that

---

[5]Pippa Norris, Thomas Wynter and Sarah Cameron (2018) *Corruption and Coercion: The Year in Elections 2017*. Electoral Integrity Project. Pippa Norris, Holly Ann Garnett and Max Groemping (2016) Electoral Integrity in all 50 US states, ranked by experts. *Vox*. Available at: https://www.vox.com/the-big-idea/2016/12/24/14074762/electoral-integrity-states-gerrymandering-voter-id [Accessed 7 January 2019].

2.10 Political Finance

Table 2.17 Political donations and expenditure
As of 2018

Country	Donation limit	Ban on foreign donations	Ban on corporate donations	Ban on union donations	Expenditure limit
United States	Y	Y	Y	Y	Y
Canada	Y	Y	Y	Y	Y
France	Y	Y	Y	Y	N
Finland	Y	Y	N	N	N
Ireland	Y	Y	N	N	N
Japan	Y	Y	N	N	N
United Kingdom	Y	Y	N	N	Y
Belgium	Y	N	Y	Y	Y
Italy	Y	N	N	N	Y
Norway	N	Y	N	N	N
Germany	N	N	Y	Y	N
Australia	N	N	N	N	N
Austria	N	N	N	N	Y
Denmark	N	N	N	N	N
Netherlands	N	N	N	N	N
New Zealand	N	N	N	N	Y
Sweden	N	N	N	N	N
Switzerland	N	N	N	N	N

Compiled by author from the International IDEA Political Finance Database https://www.idea.int/data-tools/data/political-finance-database

Table 2.18 Public funding to political parties
As of 2018

Country	Public funding to parties	Criteria
Australia	Y	4% of first preference vote
Austria	Y	1% of the vote
Belgium	Y	Representation
Canada	Y	2% of the vote
Denmark	Y	More than 1000 votes
Finland	Y	Representation
France	Y	1% of the vote in at least 50 constituencies
Germany	Y	Share of vote in previous election
Ireland	Y	2% of votes
Japan	Y	Representation and 2% of votes
Netherlands	Y	Representation and members
New Zealand	Y	Registration
Norway	Y	Share of votes and representation
Sweden	Y	2.5% of votes
United Kingdom	Y	Representation
United States	Y	**Limit spending and donations**
Italy	N	–
Switzerland	N	–

Compiled by author from the International IDEA Political Finance Database https://www.idea.int/data-tools/data/political-finance-database

they are often placed so high that they are meaningless in practice.

Although political finance regulation in the United States might appear restrictive when compared to countries such as Australia, Austria, Switzerland and Denmark, which do not impose limitations on donations and expenditure, achieving effective political finance regulation in America has been impossible due to successive decisions of the Supreme Court that prioritise the freedom of political speech over regulating donations and spending.

The second arm of political finance regulation is the provision of public funding to political parties and candidates in order to contest elections. Proponents of public funding argue that it is necessary to preserve the role of political parties as institutions that are central to representative democracy, to offset the increasing costs of campaigning for both parties and candidates and to mitigate the potentially corrupting role of private money in politics. Critics of public funding question the value of using taxpayers' money in this way and suggest that parties and candidates become too reliant on money from the state where they should be out fundraising and connecting with voters.

As Table 2.18 shows, all but two countries—Italy and Switzerland—provide direct public funding to political parties and candidates. In both these countries, however, parties are still indirectly supported through funding to legislators and tax deductions for party donations. Those countries that provide public funding to parties do so according to a number of different rationales. The United Kingdom, for example, provides funding to parties who have gained parliamentary representation, with the aim of supporting policy development. Other countries, such as Australia and Canada, provide payments for election expenses that are tied to the number of votes that a party or candidate receives.

The United States is unique in providing an 'opt in' system of public financing. In the mid-1970s, legislation was enacted in response to the Watergate scandal to provide public funding for presidential primaries and elections. However, in receiving state funding, a candidate has had to adhere to expenditure limits and as such the scheme has reduced in popularity with major party candidates. It was not used by either Barack Obama or Donald Trump in their successful presidential campaigns.

2.11 Electoral Integrity

While the 18 countries compared in this book are all liberal democracies—that is, they meet basic criteria of inclusiveness, competitiveness and constitutionality with regularly scheduled, fairly conducted and competitive elections—there is still a significant degree of variation between them in how robust their electoral processes actually are. In recent years, many political scientists have expressed widespread concern surrounding falling turnout, public disaffection and party polarisation.

In some countries, electoral malpractices fuel violence with severe consequences for national stability and personal safety. In stable, established democracies such threats are rarely relevant. However, elections continue to suffer from disinformation campaigns, barriers to electoral and party competition and the underrepresentation of women and minority candidates. Elections in the stable democracies are not overturned, but they are often flawed.

The perceptions of electoral integrity index is a tool to assess the quality of elections based on a rolling survey of experts in over 160 countries, covering more than 280 elections from 2012 to 2017. Experts are asked to provide a score for each country on several sub-dimensions that reflect different points in the electoral cycle: electoral laws, electoral procedures, district boundaries, voter registration, media coverage, campaign finance, voting processes, vote count, results and the electoral authorities that oversee the process.

Table 2.19 compares the scores of the selected countries. Denmark, Finland and Norway top the list, with scores in the mid- to high-80s. These countries are considered to have elections that have very high degrees of electoral integrity across nearly all stages of the electoral process. Nonetheless, the elections are not perfect, with their lowest scores in media coverage and campaign finance regulation.

Table 2.19 Electoral integrity 2012–2017

Country	Perceptions of electoral integrity score
Denmark	87
Finland	86
Norway	83
Germany	81
Sweden	80
Netherlands	80
Switzerland	79
Austria	77
New Zealand	76
Canada	75
France	75
Belgium	71
Ireland	71
Australia	70
Japan	68
Italy	67
United Kingdom	66
United States	**61**

The categories are constructed from the average score for each country in national presidential and parliamentary elections held from 2012 to 2017 in the 100 point perceptions of electoral integrity index
70+ is judged very high; 60–69 high
Corruption and Coercion: The Year in Elections 2017—Pippa Norris, Thomas Wynter and Sarah Cameron

All 18 democracies score in 'high' levels of electoral integrity when compared to countries such as Venezuela (with a score of 45) and Cambodia (32). However, the United States comes out at the bottom of the 18 with a score of 61. This is due to a series of important vulnerabilities that characterise the US electoral system. Foremost are concerns over gerrymandering, where district boundaries are purposefully drawn to produce partisan advantages, as well as disparities between the popular and Electoral College votes. The electoral college system delivered victory in 2016 to a presidential candidate who lost the popular vote by 2.8 million votes—more than 2% of the national total.

Allegations of electoral malpractice also reflect partisan divides. Republicans are typically concerned about the threat of electoral fraud through double voting, impersonation and non-qualified voting. A recent example is President Trump's allegation that three million fraudulent votes were cast in the 2016 presidential election. Democrats, on the other hand, argue that stricter requirements for registration and balloting pose a greater threat to elections in the United States by suppressing turnout among sections of the population such as the poor, the disabled and minority groups.

The United States is not alone within this group of countries to have significant problems with its electoral system. The 2017 UK general election rated poorly among country experts on electoral laws and voter registration processes. This has, in part, been due to a new process that shifted from household to individual voter registrations linked to a National Insurance number. This resulted in many individuals dropping off the electoral roll, especially the mobile, the young and those in rented accommodation.

Table 2.20 compares the perceptions of electoral integrity scores for all US States. These range from a high of 75 in Vermont (assessed as very high) to 53 in Arizona (assessed as moderate). The Southern states, with a history of racial discrimination, generally perform poorly, while the Pacific West and New England are evaluated most positively by the experts. Election stages that perform best are the vote count, voting processes and the role played by election authorities. Areas where electoral integrity needs to be improved are how district boundaries are determined (gerrymandering), media reporting (including incidences of fake news), campaign finance and electoral laws.

Interestingly, there is a correlation between assessments of electoral integrity in the United States, and which party controls the state legislature. According to these evaluations, Democrat-controlled states usually have significant greater electoral integrity than Republican-controlled states throughout all stages of the electoral processes, except one: the declaration of the results. The gap was largest when it came to district boundaries, voter registration, electoral laws and the performance of electoral officials. Similarly, in the 2016 presidential election, there was a clear tendency for Republican presidential candidate for Donald Trump to win more of the states with low electoral integrity scores.

Table 2.20 Electoral integrity—United States (2016)

State	PEI index of electoral integrity	State	PEI index of electoral integrity
Vermont	75	New Jersey	63
Idaho	73	Arkansas	63
New Hampshire	73	Indiana	63
Iowa	73	North Dakota	63
New Mexico	73	Kentucky	62
Maine	72	South Dakota	62
Washington	72	Kansas	62
Hawaii	72	Nevada	62
Louisiana	71	New York	61
Colorado	71	Virginia	60
Maryland	70	Texas	59
Oregon	69	Florida	58
Minnesota	69	North Carolina	58
Delaware	68	Alabama	58
Connecticut	68	Michigan	57
Montana	67	Ohio	57
Massachusetts	67	Georgia	57
Wyoming	67	Rhode Island	57
DC	67	Pennsylvania	56
West Virginia	66	South Carolina	56
Alaska	66	Mississippi	56
Nebraska	66	Oklahoma	55
California	65	Tennessee	55
Utah	65	Wisconsin	54
Illinois	64	Arizona	53
Missouri	64		
		Mean	64

The Electoral Integrity Project PEI-US 2016 (1.0)

Table 2.21 Corruption perception index
Ranges from 0 (highly corrupt) to 100 (very clean)

Country	2002	2007	2017
New Zealand	95	94	89
Denmark	95	94	88
Finland	97	94	85
Norway	85	87	85
Switzerland	85	90	85
Sweden	93	93	84
Canada	90	87	82
Netherlands	90	90	82
United Kingdom	87	84	82
Germany	73	78	81
Australia	86	86	77
Austria	78	81	75
Belgium	71	71	75
United States	**77**	**72**	**75**
Ireland	69	75	74
Japan	71	75	73
France	63	73	70
Italy	52	52	50

Transparency International *Corruption Perceptions Index 2017*

Table 2.22 Bribe payers' index
Ranges from 10 (least corrupt) to 0 (most corrupt)

Country	2002	2006	2008	2011
Netherlands	7.8	7.3	8.7	8.8
Switzerland	8.4	7.8	8.7	8.8
Belgium	7.8	7.2	8.8	8.7
Germany	6.3	7.3	8.6	8.6
Japan	5.3	7.1	8.6	8.6
Australia	8.5	7.6	8.5	8.5
Canada	8.1	7.5	8.8	8.5
United Kingdom	6.9	7.4	8.6	8.3
United States	**5.3**	**7.2**	**8.1**	**8.1**
France	5.5	6.5	8.1	8.0
Italy	4.1	5.9	7.4	7.6

Data is not available across all four years of the survey for: Austria, Denmark, Finland, Ireland, New Zealand, Norway and Sweden
Deborah Hardoon and Finn Heinrich. 2011. Bribe Payers Index 2011. Berlin: Transparency International

Table 2.23 Index of public integrity
Ranges from 10 (most integrity) to 0

Country	2015	2017
Norway	9.8	9.8
Denmark	9.7	9.6
Finland	9.5	9.5
Netherlands	9.4	9.4
New Zealand	9.4	9.3
Sweden	9.1	9.2
Switzerland	9.0	9.1
United Kingdom	9.1	9.1
Belgium	8.9	8.9
Germany	8.8	8.8
United States	**8.8**	**8.8**
Canada	8.8	8.7
France	8.8	8.7
Ireland	8.7	8.7
Australia	8.6	8.6
Austria	8.2	8.3
Italy	7.8	7.9

No data on Japan
Index of Public Integrity. https://integrity-index.org

2.12 Corruption

Corruption is corrosive of good governance and democratic accountability.[6] The total economic cost of corruption worldwide is estimated by the World Economic Forum to be equivalent to 5% of global GDP. However, because successful corruption often means that no offence or transgression is officially recorded or even publicly known, it is impossible to measure its extent authoritatively.

Since 1995, Transparency International (TI), an international non-government organisation dedicated to combatting corruption, has been conducting and assembling annual polls of business people and country analysts on their perceptions of corruption in the countries they work in. Their methodology assigns a score to each country ranging from zero (highly corrupt) to 100 (most clean). Around 70% of all countries globally scored less than 50 in 2017.

Table 2.21 shows that the 18 countries are ranked among the less corrupt governments worldwide. The countries fall into some broad clusters. First is the cleanest group, ranking 85 and above, and led by New Zealand, Denmark and Finland. Next is a mid-range grouping of countries scoring 80 and above, including Canada and the United Kingdom. The United States ranks on par with Austria and Belgium, in a third group of countries scoring in the 70s. Italy is the most corrupt of all our countries, scoring well behind the others on only 50.

Since 2002, corruption has worsened in the majority of the countries, including top-ranked nations such as Finland. Previously, six countries had scores of 90 and above, but as at 2017, no country ranks higher than 89. Finland, once regarded as the bastion of good governance, has dropped from a ranking of 97 (2002) to 85 (2017). This has largely been attributed to conflicts of interest that have emerged when public office holders, who are not subject to financial disclosures, have not recused themselves from decisions that may affect them.

While its ranking has not declined as severely, the United States has historically performed relatively poorly among stable democracies due to the culture of 'pay to play' politics in Washington, facilitating the undue influence of lobbying interests and wealthy individuals over government.

Perception of corruption is not the same as the incidence of corruption, and perceptions can be shaped by factors beyond direct experience. Sometimes scores can be shaped by the prevalence of scandals in the news. Sometimes in surveys of expatriates about the countries they are living in (TI predominantly uses surveys of business people around the globe), cultural distance, the opaqueness of local procedures and other frustrations can too easily become labelled as corruption. Moreover, although a convenient indicator, a single number obscures the complexity of corruption and the significant variations in how it manifests in different country settings. Such qualifications have led to debates within TI itself about the usefulness of the exercise.

More recently, TI has also constructed a Bribe Payer's Index (BPI), which it has measured four times, in 2002, 2006, 2008 and 2011. The BPI is a ranking of leading export countries, according to the propensity of their firms to bribe abroad. It is based on interviews with business executives in many countries throughout the world. Different exporting countries were included in different surveys.

This measure of corruption has shown significant improvement, stemming from extensive efforts to combat bribery in international business. While the United States once again ranks towards the bottom of the list, from 2002 to 2011 its score improved from 5.3 to 8.1. With the Foreign Corrupt Practices Act (1977), the United States has had the legislative means to punish firms from paying and accepting bribes overseas, but only more recently has the global community followed suit with initiatives such as the OECD Anti-Bribery Convention (1997) and the UN Convention Against Corruption (2003).

A further way in which we can look at corruption is not through its incidence or perceptions, but by measuring a country's capacity to safeguard against it. The Index of Public Integrity provides such an assessment, comparing countries' judicial independence, the extent of administrative discretion, trade openness, budget transparency, electronic

---

[6]Transparency International Corruption Perceptions Index 2017; Alina Mungiu-Pippidi and Ramin Dadsov (2016) Measuring Control of Corruption by a New Index of Public Integrity. *European Journal of Criminal Policy Research* 22: 415–438.

empowerment of citizens and the freedom of the press. The United States ranks in the middle of our countries on this measure, scoring highly on trade openness and budget transparency, but lower than other established democracies on judicial independence and the freedom of the press. As with the TI Index of Corruption, the Scandinavian countries and New Zealand top the list—highlighting the relationship between these two measures and the importance of institutional safeguards against corruption.

2.13 Assessing Democracy

This chapter has illustrated the complex and varied institutional arrangements that underpin government and politics in these 18 democracies, including their constitutional histories, electoral and party systems, legislatures, executives and judiciaries.[7] While each country no doubt is built on robust democratic foundations that have evolved over time, challenges continue to emerge, including corruption, gaps in political participation and electoral malpractice.

The chapter concludes by looking at how citizens and experts view democracy in the 18 countries using two different measures: scores that reflect the level of freedom in a particular country and trust in political institutions. We do so because institutional arrangements have much greater resilience when viewed positively by a country's citizens.

Table 2.24 shows the Freedom House score for each country, which is an aggregate rating of countries based on an assessment of political rights and civil liberties. In 2018, 88 (or 45% of the world's 195 countries) were designated as 'free'. Freedom House has published these indictors since 1972—relying on assessments by on-the-ground analysts who perform research, consult local professionals, and collect and analyse information from news articles, NGOs, governments and other sources.

Three democracies, Finland, Norway and Sweden, top the list with a perfect score of 100, followed closely by Canada and the Netherlands on 99. The United States sits at the bottom of the table on a score of 86. This should be some cause for alarm. As the world's oldest existing democracy, US citizens have benefited from a strong democratic system with robust freedoms of expression and civil liberties. In recent years, however, democratic institutions in the United States have experienced erosion due to partisan manipulation of the electoral process (through, e.g., gerrymandering), growing disparities in wealth and political influence. The United States' political rights rating declined from 1 to 2 (one of only

Table 2.24 Freedom scores 2018

Notes Political rights and civil liberties scores range from 1 (most free) to 7 (least free). The aggregate score ranges from 0 (least free) to 100 (most free)

Country	Political rights (1–7)	Civil liberties (1–7)	Aggregate score (0–100)
Finland	1	1	100
Norway	1	1	100
Sweden	1	1	100
Canada	1	1	99
Netherlands	1	1	99
Australia	1	1	98
New Zealand	1	1	98
Denmark	1	1	97
Ireland	1	1	96
Japan	1	1	96
Switzerland	1	1	96
Belgium	1	1	95
Austria	1	1	94
Germany	1	1	94
United Kingdom	1	1	94
France	1	2	90
Italy	1	1	89
United States	**2**	**1**	**86**

Freedom House (2018) *Democracy in Crisis: Freedom in the World 2018*. Freedom House

two of these countries to receive that lower score) due to growing evidence of Russian interference in the 2016 elections, violations of basic ethical standards by the new administration and a reduction in government transparency.

The evidence provided in the Freedom House scores is corroborated by other indices, for example, the *Economist* Democracy Index and the perceptions of electoral integrity index (see Sect. 2.11 'Electoral Integrity' above). The United States' northern neighbour, Canada, does better on several indicators, including the political power of interest groups and the proportion of women in parliament. The Canadian government has actively championed freedom of expression and cultural tolerance in recent years.

Table 2.25 compares levels of trust in political institutions using the Edelman Trust Barometer. The Barometer produces an average index of trust in government, business, the media and non-government organisations (NGOs). It collects data from two groups: the general population and a sample of the 'informed public'. The latter must be college educated, significant media consumers and sit within the top 25% of household incomes. Levels of trust are higher among members of the informed public when compared to members of the general public across all democracies, perhaps reflecting their better appreciation of democratic checks and balance, perhaps their lesser alienation.

While the Netherlands and Canada lead the table on scores of 67 and 62, what is notable is that with an index of

---

[7]Carroll Doherty, Jocelyn Kiley and Bridget Johnson (2018) The Public, the Political System and American Democracy. Pew Research Centre.

Table 2.25 Trust in institutions

Country	2012 Index general population	2018 Index	2017 Index informed public	2018 Index
Netherlands	48	54	62	67
Canada	51	49	62	62
Italy	47	43	61	57
Sweden	36	41	47	56
France	36	40	56	56
Australia	40	40	54	55
Germany	34	41	54	54
United Kingdom	35	39	56	52
Japan	32	37	49	46
United States	**40**	**43**	**68**	**45**
Ireland	34	38	–	–

Note Countries not included are Austria, Belgium, Denmark, Finland, Ireland, New Zealand, Norway and Switzerland. Trust = 60–100; neutral = 50–59; distrust = 1–49
Edelman 2018 Global Trust Barometer

1–100, none of the countries score particularly highly. Again, when compared with the other liberal democracies, the United States does not perform well.

Levels of trust in the United States' institutions peaked in 2017 on a score of 52, before crashing to 43 in 2018. America's decline in trust is the steepest one-year change ever measured by the Barometer. It is backed up by a recent survey of Americans from the Pew Research Centre, which reported that although 84% of the public say it is important that the rights and freedoms of all people are respected, only a minority (47%) felt that reflects the current situation of the country. Democracies such as Japan and the United Kingdom have also experienced declining levels of trust, particularly among the informed public, while the Netherlands and Sweden have both improved their scores.

Nonetheless, the overall picture is one of democratic recession among longstanding democracies: declining popular participation in elections and politics, weakness in the functioning of government, declining trust in institutions, the dwindling appeal of mainstream representative parties and decline in media freedoms.

Economics

3.1 Contemporary Economic Income and Growth

If you compare the size of economies the way we always used to, the news for Americans is reassuring: the United States' economy is still the biggest. That way was simply to convert other countries' gross domestic product to the same currency, usually US dollars, to make them comparable. The modern and more accurate way to compare economies, however, takes account of the reality that one US dollar can buy more in some countries than others, including than in the USA itself. The OECD, a club of mainly rich nations, does a lot of careful (but not necessarily perfect) price calculations to allow comparisons between economies to be made in US dollars after allowing for differences the US dollar's purchasing power in each country, thus approximating PPP—purchasing power parity.

When you do this, however, there is news for Americans. As Table 3.3 shows, with annual GDP of $21.4 trillion, China has already overtaken the USA, on $19 trillion, as the world's largest economy, measured (as GDP does) by the value of annual production of goods and services. And allowing for purchasing power means that if you count the 28 countries making up the European Union as one economy —which you probably should, since they have a common market—it is about $1 trillion bigger than the USA. Exclude the United Kingdom from the EU, however, and its size falls below America's. As Table 3.3 shows, the United Kingdom is the world's 10th biggest economy in its own right. Notice that allowing for purchasing power causes India to move up to third biggest, ahead of Japan. Indonesia's position as eighth biggest would also surprise many.

To put it crudely, there are two ways to rank high on economic size: have a huge number of poor people adding to GDP, or have a smaller number of relatively rich people. As can be seen from Table 1.2 in Chap. 1, China (population of 1.4 billion), India (1.3 billion), Indonesia (260 million) and Brazil (210 million) are big economies because of their big populations. America, on the other hand, does well on both counts, with its third largest population of more than 325 million and its high standard of living. Surely, then, if you divide a country's GDP by its population to get annual income per capita, America returns to its accustomed place at the top of the charts as the country whose people are richest. Sorry, not these days, and not after you allow for purchasing power.

As Table 3.1, which focuses on our group of 18 developed democracies shows, the USA is outranked by three small special cases: Ireland, the Celtic Tiger so vibrant it bounded back from the financial crisis of 2008, Switzerland, and Norway, which had the good fortune to find offshore oil and the good sense to invest rather than spend most of the proceeds. Special cases aside, America remains by far the richest of the rich countries. The notable feature of the remaining countries is how similar their incomes are, with half of the 18 clustered $5000 above or below the median annual income of $47,400 per person.

Income per person is the simplest and commonest way of measuring the average material standard of living of a country's population, but it tells us nothing about how evenly income is actually distributed between individuals or households. As Table 8.1 below attests, the US rates particularly highly on income inequality.

Table 3.2 shows how fast GDP (income) per capita has been growing in the selected economies since the turn of the century. It divides the 18 years into three periods: before, during and after the peak years of the Great Recession. Some countries' economies—Australia, for example—grow more strongly than others because of high growth in their populations. Examining growth *per capita* gives a clearer idea of the advance in *average* material living standards. Clearly, America's growth performance is far from outstanding, neither before nor after the global financial crisis of October 2008. Paradoxically, however, America's modest growth performance is a mark of its international leadership, even its exceptionalism. Because it is responsible for so much of the world's invention and innovation, economists regard the USA as being at the frontier of technological advance.

Table 3.1 GDP per capita
US $ per head of population, current prices and current PPP, 000, 2015

Country	$US PPP
Ireland	68.4
Switzerland	62.5
Norway	62.0
United States	**56.1**
Netherlands	49.6
Austria	49.4
Denmark	49.0
Germany	48.0
Sweden	47.8
Australia	47.0
Belgium	45.9
Canada	44.2
Finland	42.3
United Kingdom	41.8
France	41.0
Japan	40.7
New Zealand	37.7
Italy	37.2
Mean	*48.4*

OECD *Compendium of Productivity Indicators 2017*

Table 3.2 Contemporary economic growth
GDP growth (%) per capita per year for each period

Country	2000–07	2008–09	2010–17
Ireland	3.9	−5.8	5.9
Germany	1.7	−2.0	1.8
Sweden	2.8	−3.7	1.8
Japan	1.3	−3.3	1.6
New Zealand	2.3	−0.8	1.4
United States	**1.8**	**−2.3**	**1.4**
Canada	1.8	−2.1	1.2
United Kingdom	2.3	−3.1	1.2
Australia	2.0	−0.1	1.1
Denmark	1.6	−3.3	0.9
Netherlands	1.8	−1.5	0.9
Austria	2.0	−1.5	0.8
France	1.4	−1.9	0.8
Belgium	1.9	−1.5	0.7
Switzerland	1.8	−1.3	0.7
Finland	3.2	−4.2	0.6
Norway	1.8	−1.9	0.4
Italy	1.1	−3.9	0.0
Mean	*2.0*	*−2.4*	*1.3*

OECD *Compendium of Productivity Indicators 2017*

The bigger you get, the harder it is to grow at a high percentage rate. But, when you are the technological leader, growth depends on the hard graft of continuous innovation. Those following you can grow simply by adopting up your recent advances.

Table 3.3 World's 20 biggest economies
Total Size of GDP US$ billions PPP 2016 (EU figure is for 2017)

Global rank	Country	GDP $US billions (PPP) 2016
1	China	21,365
	(European Union)	(19,970)
2	**United States**	**18,969**
3	India	8609
4	Japan	5434
5	Germany	4110
6	Russian Federation	3306
7	Brazil	3081
8	Indonesia	2934
9	France	2818
10	United Kingdom	2763
11	Italy	2329
12	Mexico	2265
13	Turkey	1921
14	Korea, Republic	1834
15	Saudi Arabia	1803
16	Spain	1693
17	Iran, Islamic Republic	1610
18	Canada	1575
19	Australia	1109
20	Thailand	1109

World Bank *World Development Indicators* http://wdi.worldbank.org/tables

3.2 Long-Term Economic Development

All 18 of the democratic developed economies on which this book focuses experienced a huge increase in living standards over the previous century. Table 3.4 shows how, overall, real living standards in these economies rose by a factor of more than nine over almost 130 years. It is based upon the heroic efforts of the veteran scholar Angus Maddison, who devoted his career to estimating the world's economic growth over past centuries. No doubt many of his estimates and assumptions could be argued with, but they are the best available over such a long period. Maddison achieved comparable purchasing power by using 'international dollars'. And because those dollars are all of the 1990 vintage, there is no need to allow for inflation when comparing amounts between years. Their increase over the periods reflects real growth in income.

The table well demonstrates the joint phenomena of 'catch-up and convergence' between the economies of the developed world. Over the period, the gap between the richest and poorest of the selected countries was narrowed from a factor of more than five to one of less than two. At one extreme, Japan's standard of living is estimated to have risen by a factor of 29; at the other, New Zealand's rose 5.5 times. America's early rise to its historical position as the biggest and richest economy can be seen in the table, as can the United Kingdom's steady decline from near the top of

Table 3.4 Income per capita 1870–1998
Per capita income in thousands of 1990 International dollars

Country	1870	1913	1950	1973	1998
United States	**2.4**	**5.3**	**9.6**	**16.7**	**27.3**
Norway	1.4	2.5	5.4	11.2	23.7
Denmark	2.0	3.9	6.9	14.0	22.1
Switzerland	2.2	4.3	9.1	18.2	21.4
Canada	1.7	4.4	7.4	13.8	20.6
Japan	0.7	1.4	1.9	11.4	20.4
Australia	3.6	5.7	7.5	12.8	20.4
Netherlands	2.8	4.0	6.0	13.1	20.2
France	1.9	3.5	5.3	13.1	19.6
Belgium	2.7	4.2	5.6	12.2	19.4
Austria	1.9	3.5	3.7	11.2	18.9
United Kingdom	3.2	4.9	6.9	12.0	18.7
Sweden	1.7	3.1	6.7	13.5	18.7
Finland	1.1	2.1	4.3	11.1	18.3
Ireland	–	–	3.4	6.9	18.2
Germany	1.8	3.6	3.9	12.0	17.8
Italy	1.5	2.6	3.5	10.6	17.8
New Zealand	2.7	5.2	8.5	12.5	14.8
Mean	*2.1*	*3.8*	*5.9*	*12.6*	*19.9*

Angus Maddison *The World Economy. A Millennial Perspective* (Development Studies Centre, OECD, Paris, 2001) p. 185, 215

Table 3.5 Economic growth 1820–1998
Average per capita annual growth rates, 1820–1998, %

Country	1820–1870	1870–1913	1913–1950	1950–1973	1973–1998
Ireland	–	–	–	3.0	4.0
Norway	0.5	1.3	2.1	3.2	3.0
Japan	0.2	1.5	0.9	8.1	2.3
Austria	0.9	1.5	0.2	4.9	2.1
Italy	0.6	1.3	0.9	5.0	2.1
Finland	0.8	1.4	1.9	4.3	2.0
United States	**1.3**	**1.8**	**1.6**	**2.5**	**2.0**
Belgium	1.4	1.1	0.7	3.6	1.9
Australia	4.0	1.1	0.7	2.3	1.9
Denmark	0.9	1.6	1.6	3.1	1.9
United Kingdom	1.3	1.0	0.9	2.4	1.8
Netherlands	0.8	0.9	1.1	3.5	1.8
France	0.9	1.5	1.1	4.1	1.6
Germany	1.1	1.6	0.2	5.0	1.6
Canada	1.3	2.3	1.4	2.7	1.6
Sweden	0.7	1.5	2.1	3.1	1.3
New Zealand	3.9	1.5	1.4	1.7	0.7
Switzerland	1.1	1.6	2.1	3.1	0.6
Mean	*1.3*	*1.4*	*1.2*	*3.6*	*1.9*

Angus Maddison *The World Economy. A Millennial Perspective* (Development Studies Centre, OECD, Paris, 2001) p. 185, 215

the league to the bottom half. Japan's post-war ascent is evident, as is the more recent rise of oil-rich Norway.

Australia's decline from being the world's richest country on a per capita basis in the latter part of the nineteenth century to today being in the middle of this league of high-income nations is explained by its inevitable fall from an initial position of being a country with a small population efficiently producing a significant share of the world's rural and mineral commodities at a time when prices were particularly high.

Table 3.5 reveals that it is only since World War II that economic growth has been consistently achieved over time and across countries. Whereas there were two periods—World War I and the depression of 1929–32—when economic disaster was almost universal, there were few periods before World War II when economic growth was universal. The post-war improvement is commonly attributed to the advent of Keynesian demand management and the greater share of the economy accounted for by the relatively more stable government spending and the services sector generally. For all these countries, the period of nearly 30 years following World War II was the 'golden age' of rapid economic growth, unlike any period in world history before or since.

The 18-nation average annual growth rate of 3.6% more than doubled any preceding period. The golden age finished with the oil price shock of 1973 and the advent of 'stagflation'—simultaneous high unemployment and inflation. The economic times since then have been more turbulent and the rate of growth lowers. Even so, the last period shown was one of shared and continuing growths in income.

The table shows the USA growing significantly faster than the rich-country average over the 80 years from 1870 to 1950 as it overtakes the United Kingdom as economic leader of the developed world. In the golden age, however, its growth fell well short of the average. America's relatively modest rate of growth was shared by its World War II allies —the United Kingdom, Canada, Australia and New Zealand. By contrast, Germany and Japan, and also France, grew strongly as they rebuilt their economies after the devastation of war.

Another significant boost to growth during the golden age was the significant reduction in trade barriers between the developed economies under the US-promoted General Agreement on Tariffs and Trade. Thus, the golden age was the period in which America's post-war developed country allies made great strides towards catching up with, and converging on, its high standard of living. The 25 years following the end of the golden age saw most countries growing at very similar rates per capita.

3.3 Inflation and Interest Rates

Table 3.6 shows snapshots of the chequered history of the developed countries' experience with inflation over the past 45 years. In the post-war period to 1973—not shown in the table—inflation in most countries was manageable, though not negligible. The remainder of the 1970s (first column),

Table 3.6 Inflation
Consumer price index, annual rate

Country	1973–79	2008	2012	2017
Ireland	14.9	3.1	1.9	0.3
Japan	9.9	1.4	0.0	0.4
Switzerland	4.0	2.4	−0.7	0.6
Finland	12.6	3.9	3.2	1.0
France	10.7	3.2	2.2	1.1
Denmark	10.8	3.4	2.4	1.2
Netherlands	7.2	2.2	2.8	1.3
Italy	20.9	3.5	3.3	1.4
Canada	9.2	2.4	1.5	1.5
Germany	4.6	2.8	2.1	1.7
Australia	12.2	4.3	1.7	1.9
New Zealand	13.8	4.0	1.1	1.9
Norway	8.7	3.8	0.7	1.9
Sweden	9.8	3.4	0.9	1.9
United States	**8.5**	**3.8**	**2.1**	**2.0**
Austria	6.2	3.2	2.6	2.2
Belgium	8.4	4.5	2.6	2.2
United Kingdom	15.6	3.6	2.8	2.7
Mean	*10.4*	*3.3*	*1.8*	*1.5*

OECD *Economic Outlook November 2017*

however, saw a dramatic acceleration in the rate of price increase, with annual inflation rates reaching an exceptionally high 8.5% in the United States and double figures in almost half of our selected 18 economies. Though the world prices of many rural and mineral commodities rose strongly in the early 1970s, the 1973 watershed is widely attributed to the first OPEC oil price shock. As well as a sharp jump in gasoline prices, this brought about a sudden and massive transfer of wealth from the mainly oil-importing developed economies to the oil-exporting countries.

For the developed economies, the shock was both inflationary for prices and contractionary for economic activity—a rare and difficult combination for the economic managers to respond to. It was the end of the post-war 'golden age' of trouble-free economic growth, and the start of the turbulent era of 'stagflation'—the previously unknown combination of a stagnant economy with rapidly rising prices.

Whereas the post-war period to 1973 saw countries' inflation rates contained within a fairly narrow band, the 1973–79 period saw not only a much higher level of inflation overall, but a far wider range as some economies proved more susceptible to inflationary pressure than others, and as different countries responded in different ways. In the USA, Federal Reserve Chairman Paul Volcker responded firmly, raising the 'fed funds' interest rate to a peak of 20% in mid-1981 to halt the inflationary boom. Inflation reached 14.8% in early 1980, but had fallen below 3% by 1983. The cost, however, was the severe recession of the early 1980s, in which the rate of unemployment rose above 10%, and which spread to most other developed economies, helping them bludgeon inflation out of their systems.

As the 1980s turned to the 1990s, most countries had inflation back under control. Japan's economy dipped in and out of recession throughout the 1990s, which caused its average inflation rate to be particularly low, and its general level of prices actually to fall during the 2000s. Such 'deflation' is not to be welcomed because it brings problems by discouraging spending, production and investment.

In the 2000s, other countries had cause to worry that deflation might be looming. However, the second column of Table 3.6 shows that by the end of the prosperous years leading up to the global financial crisis in September 2008, inflation had started to creep up, including in the USA. The Great Recession soon put an end to that and, during the weak and protracted recovery, central bankers have been more inclined to worry that inflation was too low rather than too high—as shown by the snapshots taken in 2012 and 2017. In hindsight, inflation can be seen as the problem of an earlier age. It's not compatible with contemporary worries that economic growth is too weak.

Interest rates are linked to the inflation rate because lenders require to be compensated for the expected loss in purchasing power of their money while it is in the hands of the borrower, as well as receive a 'real' interest rate as a reward for giving up the use of their money for the duration of the loan. According to one version of economic theory, in a world of highly integrated national financial markets, a country's long-term interest rate should reflect its inflation rate and a uniform global real (after-inflation) interest rate, plus or minus a premium or discount reflecting the country's peculiar circumstances, if any. For instance, countries with large current account deficits or high levels of foreign debt may have to pay a premium to encourage continued lending from abroad.

Table 3.7 offers rough and ready support for this theory. If we make the imperfect comparison of the 2007 column of this table with the 2008 column in Table 3.6, then we find 12 of the 18 countries' real long-term interest rates falling in a narrow band from 0.5 to 1.7%. A stronger conclusion is that, even before the onset of the financial crisis, real long-term interest rates now seem a lot lower, even immediately before the financial crisis, than they were in the 1980s and 1990s, and they've fallen further in the following 10 years. Note, however, that half of the 18 countries are members of the euro currency zone, which would do much to keep their long-term interest rates low.

Table 3.7 Long-term interest rates
Percent, per annum

Country	2007	2017
Switzerland	2.9	−0.1
Japan	1.7	0.1
Germany	4.2	0.3
Denmark	4.3	0.5
Netherlands	4.3	0.5
Austria	4.3	0.6
Finland	4.3	0.6
Sweden	4.2	0.6
Belgium	4.3	0.8
France	4.3	0.8
Ireland	4.3	0.9
United Kingdom	5.0	1.3
Norway	4.8	1.6
Canada	4.3	1.9
Italy	4.5	2.2
United States	**4.6**	**2.4**
Australia	6.0	2.6
New Zealand	6.3	3.0
Mean	4.4	1.1

OECD *Economic Outlook November 2017*

Table 3.9 Employment in industry
% of labour force

Country	1975	1995	2016
Germany	45	36	27
Italy	39	34	26
Austria	41	32	26
Japan	36	34	25
Finland	36	27	22
Belgium	40	26	21
New Zealand	36	25	20
Australia	34	23	20
Switzerland	42	29	20
France	39	26	20
Ireland	32	28	20
Norway	35	23	19
Canada	29	22	19
Denmark	32	27	19
United Kingdom	40	27	18
Sweden	37	26	18
United States	**31**	**24**	**18**
Netherlands	35	23	15
Mean	37	27	21

Earlier columns are from OECD Historical Statistics 1960–1995 (1997)
Last columns are from OECD *Labour Force Statistics 2007–2016* (2017)

3.4 Changing Economic Structures

A casual glance at Table 3.8 suggests that, in the United States and, indeed, in all the other 17 developed democracies, employment in agriculture has fallen over the past

Table 3.8 Employment in agriculture
% of labour force

Country	1975	1995	2016
New Zealand	10.7	9.7	6.5
Ireland	22.4	11.7	5.6
Austria	12.5	7.5	4.3
Finland	14.9	8.1	3.9
Italy	16.7	6.7	3.9
Japan	12.7	5.7	3.4
Switzerland	7.6	4.4	3.3
France	10.3	4.6	2.8
Australia	6.8	5.0	2.6
Denmark	9.8	4.4	2.5
Netherlands	5.7	3.7	2.1
Norway	9.4	5.2	2.1
Canada	6.1	4.1	1.9
Sweden	6.4	3.1	1.9
United States	**4.1**	**2.9**	**1.6**
Belgium	3.8	2.4	1.3
Germany	6.8	3.1	1.3
United Kingdom	2.8	2.1	1.1
Mean	9.4	5.2	2.9

Earlier columns are from OECD Historical Statistics 1960–1995 (1997)
Last columns are from OECD *Labour Force Statistics 2007–2016* (2017)

40 years or so. An equally casual glance at Table 3.9 suggests that employment in "industry"—mainly manufacturing, but also mining, utilities (electricity, gas and water) and construction—in the US and everywhere else has fallen even more dramatically over the same period. But casual glances can be misleading. Both tables show the two sectors' *share* of the total workforce declining, and a decline in a sector's absolute level of employment is just one possible explanation for a decline in its share. It is likely that employment *has* fallen in both sectors in the US and all the selected economies, but this would be a less important reason for the decline in the sectors' shares of the total. Rather, their shares have declined mainly because of the rapid growth in the absolute size of employment in the services sector which, as Table 3.10 shows, has greatly increased its share of total employment.

In a similar vein, nor should it be assumed that a decline in the two sectors' share of total employment—or even a decline in their absolute levels of employment—implies an absolute decline in their output of goods. In fact, their output has continued to grow in absolute terms in the US and most of the other economies. In other words, we are producing more rather than fewer agricultural, manufactured and other goods than we used to, but are using fewer workers to do so.

How? By exploiting advances in technology, which are increasing the productivity of the machines—including, these days, computers and computerised machines—used to produce goods. Producing more goods using fewer workers is the epitome of greater productivity and technical

Table 3.10 Employment in services
% of labour force

Country	1975	1995	2016
Netherlands	59	74	83
United Kingdom	57	71	81
United States	**65**	**73**	**81**
Sweden	57	71	80
Canada	65	74	79
Denmark	59	68	79
Norway	56	71	79
Belgium	57	71	78
Australia	60	72	77
France	51	69	77
Switzerland	50	67	77
Ireland	46	60	75
Finland	49	65	74
New Zealand	54	65	73
Germany	48	61	71
Japan	52	61	71
Austria	47	60	70
Italy	44	59	70
Mean	*54*	*67*	*76*

Earlier columns are from OECD Historical Statistics 1960–1995 (1997)
Last columns are from OECD *Labour Force Statistics 2007–2016* (2017)

Table 3.11 GDP by sector
% 2016

Country	Agriculture	Industry	Service
United States	**1**	**20**	**79**
France	2	20	79
United Kingdom	1	20	79
Netherlands	2	20	78
Belgium	1	22	77
Denmark	1	23	76
Italy	2	24	74
Sweden	1	25	74
Switzerland	1	26	74
Australia	3	24	73
Austria	1	28	71
Canada	2	28	71
New Zealand	6	22	71
Finland	3	27	70
Japan	1	29	70
Germany	1	30	69
Norway	2	32	66
Ireland	1	39	60
Mean	*2*	*26*	*73*

World Bank *World Development Indicators*

efficiency. It involves businesses pursuing ever greater economies of scale. And it is this unending push for higher productivity and more economising that is by far the greatest reason our material living standard is today many times higher than it was at the start of the Industrial Revolution.

But if we have used decades of advances in labour-saving technology in the production of goods to become ever more prosperous, why isn't the rate of unemployed workers many times higher than it is? Because as employment opportunities in agriculture and industry have diminished, job opportunities have grown just as strongly in the sector of the economy performing many and varied services for us. The shift in economies' industrial composition from goods to services is driving primarily by technological advance, but also by our growing affluence. There are limits to how many more goods we want to consume as we get richer: limits to how much we can eat, how many clothes we need, even how many automobiles, TV sets and digital devices we can cope with. But we have yet to reach a limit in how many services we would like to pay others to perform for us—including many things which, in less affluent days, we used to do for ourselves.

Many people lack the imagination to envision the wide and ever-growing range of services encompassed by the services sector. They think services imply servility and think of unskilled jobs: cleaners, hotel chambermaids, waiters, dishwashers and people serving behind counters. They don't think that, going from the top down, service workers start with the president or prime minister, all politicians, scientific advisers, doctors, dentists, veterinarians, business executives, fund managers, professors and school teachers, lawyers, accountants, bankers, realtors, nurses, paramedics, celebrities and chefs, plus the ever-growing ranks of carers: childcare, aged care, invalid care, even pet care workers. Come back in 10 years' time and the list will be much longer.

Table 3.9 charts the course of 'deindustrialisation' in the US and other developed economies over the past 40 years. Remember, however, that the industrial structure of the developed economies—the relative shares of the agricultural, industrial and services sectors—changed continuously over the previous century and will continue changing in this century, driven primarily by technological advance and growing affluence.

Table 3.11 shows more clearly that the long-term progression from the farm to city-based manufacturing to services is universal among the developed economies (and reaching the more advanced developing countries), led by the country that has always led the way in technological innovation and changing tastes in response to growing affluence: America.

3.5 International Trade

Tables 3.12 and 3.13 are a powerful demonstration of globalisation. Their outstanding feature is the way both exports and imports have grown steadily over the past 40 years for the United States and virtually all the selected countries. This has been brought about by falling transport and telecommunication costs, but mainly by the successive

Table 3.12 Exports
Exports of goods and services as % GDP

Country	1974–79	1990	2005	2014
Ireland	44	57	83	114
Belgium	56	69	87	84
Netherlands	52	56	71	83
Switzerland	32	36	46	64
Denmark	29	37	49	54
Austria	32	38	53	53
Germany	24	25	40	46
Sweden	29	30	49	45
Finland	27	22	39	38
Norway	38	40	45	38
Canada	24	26	39	32
Italy	22	19	26	30
New Zealand	27	27	29	30
France	19	21	26	29
United Kingdom	28	24	26	28
Australia	15	16	18	21
Japan	13	10	13	18
United States	**8**	**10**	**10**	**14**
Mean	*29*	*31*	*42*	*45*

First two columns are from OECD *Historical Statistics* CD-Rom
Second last columns are from UNDP *Human Development Report 2007–08*
Last columns are from OECD *Factbook* 2016

Table 3.13 Imports
Imports of goods and services as % GDP

Country	1974–79	1990	2005	2014
Ireland	55	52	68	95
Belgium	57	68	85	83
Netherlands	51	52	63	72
Switzerland	31	34	39	53
Austria	33	37	48	50
Denmark	32	33	44	48
Sweden	29	30	41	41
Finland	28	24	35	39
Germany	22	25	35	39
Canada	25	26	34	33
France	20	23	27	31
Norway	41	34	28	30
United Kingdom	29	27	30	30
Italy	22	19	26	27
New Zealand	31	27	30	27
Australia	16	16	21	21
Japan	12	10	11	21
United States	**9**	**11**	**15**	**17**
Mean	*30*	*31*	*42*	*42*

First two columns are from OECD *Historical Statistics* CD-Rom
Second last columns are from UNDP *Human Development Report 2007–08*
Last columns are from OECD *Factbook* 2016

Table 3.14 Current account balance
Current account balance as % GDP

Country	2000	2007	2017
Switzerland	11.9	10.1	10.2
Netherlands	1.9	7.0	9.4
Denmark	1.6	1.4	8.5
Germany	−1.8	6.8	7.9
Sweden	4.0	8.2	4.7
Norway	14.7	12.4	4.5
Japan	2.7	4.7	3.9
Ireland	−0.4	−6.5	3.0
Italy	0.1	−1.4	2.8
Austria	−0.9	3.8	2.0
Belgium	3.5	2.0	−0.4
Finland	7.5	3.8	−0.4
Australia	−3.8	−6.7	−1.1
France	1.2	−0.3	−1.5
United States	**−3.9**	**−4.9**	**−2.4**
New Zealand	−3.2	−6.8	−3.0
Canada	2.5	0.8	−3.1
United Kingdom	−2.4	−3.8	−4.7
Mean	*2.0*	*1.7*	*2.2*

OECD *Economic Outlook November 2017*

reductions in tariff barriers to trade achieved by many rounds of multilateral negotiations under the GATT (predecessor to the WTO), culminating in the huge Uruguay Round of 1994.

In these tables, each country's exports and imports are expressed as a proportion of that country's national income (GDP) to facilitate comparisons between countries and also over time for a particular country (because this takes account of inflation and the real growth in the country's income). It can be seen that the economies with the highest ratios of exports and imports to national income are the smaller European countries, many of them with contiguous borders and most of them members of the EU. The EU's expansion and efforts to increase the economic integration of its members are another factor explaining the growth in trade over the period. The USA's low ratios of exports and imports occur not because of high barriers to trade but because the sheer size of its economy causes it to be more self-sufficient.

The high percentages shown in Table 3.15, which shows a country's exports of services as a proportion of its total exports of goods and services, and the same for imports of services, are explained by advances in technology, which have increasingly made services tradeable across national borders. By greatly reducing the cost of travel, the advent of the jumbo jet not only precipitated an explosion in international travel, but also made it possible for foreign students and patients to travel abroad for education or health care, as well as for engineers, architects and many other professions to go overseas to sell their services as consultants. Advances in telecommunications and the advent of the Internet have

Table 3.15 Trade in services
Exports/imports of services as percentage of total exports/imports

Country	Exports 2016	Imports 2016
United Kingdom	45.0	18.7
Ireland	41.6	45.9
Denmark	36.9	33.7
United States	**34.1**	**14.0**
Sweden	32.2	24.3
France	31.8	24.5
New Zealand	30.7	19.7
Finland	30.4	27.1
Austria	29.6	20.9
Norway	29.6	30.4
Belgium	28.6	24.2
Switzerland	27.4	18.5
Netherlands	22.7	18.6
Australia	21.6	16.9
Japan	21.6	20.7
Italy	18.2	18.0
Germany	17.5	19.2
Canada	17.1	16.1
Mean	*28.7*	*22.9*

OECD *Quarterly International Trade Statistics*, Vol 2017/2

also opened the way for trade in services, including call centres and processing of administrative data. The table shows that, by now, services account for a significant proportion of exports, but also of imports. High levels of both exports and imports are a sign of globalisation: the ever-increasing integration of national economies. Many Americans would be surprised to learn that exports of services now account for more than a third of all exports. This is a sign that, with the rise of digitisation and ecommerce, the USA has become the world's dominant exporter of IP—intellectual property—in the form of software programs, films, videos and TV shows, video games, recorded music and books. This would do much to explain why, unlike most of the other countries, America's exports of services greatly exceed its imports.

The term 'current account' has many meanings in the financial world, but in Table 3.14 it refers to the current account on a country's balance of payments—a summary record of all that country's many transactions with other countries during a period. The current account includes the balance of a country's trade in exports and imports of goods and services (the trade balance), but also the balance of its receipts and payments of interest, dividends and other forms of income arising from its financial investments in other economies and their investments is its economy (the 'net income' balance). In the post-war era when countries fixed their exchange rate to the US dollar, governments desiring to maintain that rate needed to limit the size of their current account deficits or surpluses. In the era of floating exchange rates that followed the US government's breaking of the link between the dollar and gold in 1971, there is more scope for countries to run sustained current account deficits or surpluses. The wide range of deficits (minus signs) and surpluses (no minus sign) seen in the table are a product of this change. Whereas many people see all deficits as a bad thing —and a sign a country is 'living beyond its means'— economists see that some countries (such as China, Japan and Germany) run a perpetual surplus because their people save more each year than they are able to use to finance profitable domestic investment projects, whereas other countries (such as the USA) have more potentially profitable investment projects than they are able to finance from their own saving. This is the economic justification for America's perpetual modest current account deficit, which few economists are greatly concerned about.

3.6 Globalising Economies

While the effects of globalisation can be seen in growing proportions of exports and imports (Tables 3.12 and 3.13 on the previous page), they can also be seen in many other areas. Tables 3.16 and 3.17 chart another important dimension: the rise and rise of the transnational corporation—companies whose activities extend beyond their home country's borders to a number of other countries. The term 'foreign direct investment' (FDI) refers to foreigners' investment in a country's business corporations where investment in the stock of particular companies is great

Table 3.16 Outward foreign direct investment
% GDP

Country	2005	2016
Ireland	–	276
Netherlands	94	180
Switzerland	–	163
Belgium	–	122
Canada	59	82
Sweden	–	70
Denmark	33	57
United Kingdom	49	56
Austria	24	53
France	28	52
Norway	–	48
Finland	–	47
Germany	29	39
United States	**28**	**34**
Australia	27	31
Japan	8	27
Italy	–	26
New Zealand	10	9
Mean	*35*	*76*

OECD *FDI in Figures* April 2018

3.6 Globalising Economies

Table 3.17 Inward foreign direct investment
% GDP

Country	2005	2016
Ireland	–	277
Switzerland	–	128
Netherlands	71	107
Belgium	–	102
Canada	55	63
United Kingdom	31	56
Sweden	–	55
Australia	33	44
Austria	27	40
Norway	–	40
New Zealand	38	38
United States	**22**	**35**
Finland	–	34
Denmark	28	32
France	17	29
Germany	23	23
Italy	–	19
Japan	2	4
Mean	*31*	*64*

OECD *FDI in Figures* April 2018

Table 3.18 Import penetration
Goods and services import volume as % of total final expenditure, at constant prices

Country	2000	2017
Ireland	44	50
Belgium	39	47
Netherlands	34	43
Switzerland	32	37
Austria	29	35
Denmark	25	34
Germany	22	30
Finland	23	29
Sweden	25	29
France	19	25
New Zealand	19	25
Canada	23	24
Norway	19	24
Italy	19	23
United Kingdom	19	23
Australia	12	17
Japan	11	15
United States	**12**	**14**
Mean	*24*	*29*

OECD *Economic Outlook 2017*

enough to give the foreigners a significant influence over the company's management. FDI may involve the foreigners establishing a new business, their purchase of an existing local business or the merger of their corporation with a local one. So FDI is to be distinguished from other, more volatile forms of foreign capital inflow to a country such as for the purchase of small parcels of stocks or lending by foreign banks.

Table 3.16 shows the size of total amounts of FDI flowing from the United States and other selected economies during the years 2005 and 2016, expressed as a proportion of each economy's GDP to aid comparison between countries and over time. The missing data for 2005 tells us more about formerly inadequate record keeping than anything else. Even so, it's clear from those countries for which there is complete data that both outward and inward FDI (Table 3.17) grew significantly over the 11-year period.

Unfortunately, the almost unbelievably high rates of both inflow and outflow of the four small countries topping both tables in 2016 tell us about a less attractive feature of globalisation: the ease with which transnational corporations are able to avoid tax by moving money into and out of low-tax countries. Ignoring those four countries, what the two tables show is that, for all the developed economies, the growth of transnational firms is a two-way trade. My country's firms spread to your country, while your country's firms spread to my country. The national economies of the world—both developed and developing—become evermore intertwined. This is true of the country rightly seen as the biggest player in the spread of transnational corporations, the USA. Many big US companies aspire to do business in most of the other countries of the world but, equally, most non-American transnationals aspire to a slice of the action in the biggest and most technologically advanced developed economy, the USA.

Table 3.18 shows yet another instance of the way globalisation involves national economies becoming more intertwined: a steadily growing proportion of a country's total spending on goods and services (including both public and private sector spending on consumption and new investment projects—'total final expenditure') imported from other countries. Many people can see this phenomenon just by looking at the labels on supermarket shelves. What this table's list of high and rising rates of importation in 18 countries shows is something locals can't see: my country may be buying more of your exports, but your country is buying more of our exports. America's much lower rates of importation than the European countries are explained by the simple fact that its much greater size makes it more able to supply its own needs internally without any artificial assistance from protection measures.

Table 3.19 demonstrates one further way in which globalisation and the spread of transnational corporations are intertwining economies and businesses. 'Global value chains' refer to the growing practice of firms—often from developed countries—bringing parts from many countries to be assembled in another country, usually a developing country where labour is cheap. This is done for automobiles,

Table 3.19 Global value chains
% of country's exports that involve imported parts

Country	1995	2011
Ireland	38.5	43.6
Finland	24.2	34.7
Belgium	31.0	34.5
Denmark	23.2	32.6
Sweden	26.3	29.2
Austria	21.4	27.8
Italy	17.2	26.5
Germany	14.9	25.5
France	17.3	25.1
Canada	24.4	23.5
United Kingdom	18.3	23.1
Switzerland	17.6	21.8
Netherlands	23.2	20.1
Norway	19.9	17.2
New Zealand	16.9	16.7
United States	**11.5**	**15.0**
Japan	5.6	14.7
Australia	12.1	14.1
Mean	20.2	24.8

OECD *Factbook 2016*

Table 3.20 Exchange rates
Value of US$1 expressed in units of other currencies, average of daily rates
US$ = 1.00

Country	2007	2012	2017
Australian $	1.20	0.97	1.30
Canadian $	1.07	1.00	1.30
Danish Krone	5.44	5.79	6.62
Japanese Yen	117.80	79.80	112.30
New Zealand $	1.36	1.24	1.41
Norwegian Krone	5.86	5.82	8.26
Swedish Krona	6.76	6.77	8.55
Swiss Franc	1.20	0.94	0.99
British Pound	0.50	0.63	0.78
Euro	0.73	0.78	0.89

OECD *Economic Outlook 2017*

cell phones and many other electronic goods. The table shows the proportion of a country's exports accounted for by the value of previously imported parts.

America's proportions are lower than other countries' because, although US-based transnationals initiate many value chains, having initially designed the final products in the USA, the parts generally come from other countries to be assembled offshore. Most of the finished products may be *imported* to the USA, while other are exported from the country of assembly to third countries. Little assembling and subsequent export are done in America.

3.7 Exchange Rates

Exchange rates are a *relative* price—the value of one country's currency relative to another country's. Table 3.20 shows the value of 17 other selected countries' currencies relative to the world's reserve currency, the US dollar. Thus, from an American perspective, the table tells how much of a particular foreign currency one US dollar would buy in 2007 (immediately before the global financial crisis reach its height) and then in 2012 and 2017. From a non-American's perspective, the table shows how a country's own currency's value has changed relative to the greenback over the 11-year period. So, for example, whereas one US dollar was worth 118 yen in 2007, by 2012 this had fallen to 80 yen, meaning the yen's value had appreciated (risen) against the greenback. From an American perspective, the greenback's value against the yen had depreciated (fallen). The Euro is the common currency of eight of the selected countries: Germany, France, Italy, Austria, Netherlands, Belgium, Finland and Ireland.

It can be seen that, over the 10 years, the US dollar appreciated in value against all the other currencies bar two—the yen and the Swiss franc. By contrast, the US dollar generally depreciated between 2007 and 2012. This depreciation is explained by the US Federal Reserve's resort during the Great Recession to the unconventional practice of 'quantitative easing' (creating money) when, in its efforts to stimulate demand, it was unable to lower its policy interest rate below zero. Increasing the supply of US dollars relative to the demand for them lowered the US dollar exchange rate, imparting a modest degree of stimulus to the US economy by making its export- and import-competing industries more internationally price competitive. As the quantitative easing was unwound between 2012 and 2017, however, the US dollar generally appreciated.

Table 3.20 shows considerable potential to mislead (but it is not easy to report exchange rate movements in a way that does not). As we have seen, it should not be thought that the value of the US dollar stayed constant over the 11 years while all other currencies changed around it. Nor is the table meant to imply that a country's exchange rate with the US dollar is the only one that matters to anyone bar an American. A country has separate exchange rates with the currencies of all the countries with which it trades, and the importance of those other exchange rates is determined by each trading partner's share of that country's trade. Finally, it should not be assumed that it is good to have an appreciating currency and bad to have one that is depreciating. Depreciation and appreciation each have (opposing) sets of both advantages and disadvantages. Which direction happens to be desirable, on balance, is determined by a country's economic circumstances at the time and, even then, will be a matter of debate.

3.7 Exchange Rates

Table 3.21 Big Mac index
Costs of a Big Mac in each country when local currency is converted to US$ at current exchange rate, mid-2017
If costing more than US price, then US$ is undervalued; if less, then US$ is overvalued

Country	Cost Big Mac ($US)
Switzerland	6.74
Norway	5.91
Sweden	5.82
United States	**5.30**
Canada	4.66
Australia	4.53
Euro Area	4.47
United Kingdom	4.11
Japan	3.36

www.economist.com/news/finance-and-economics
Published July 13, 2017

The *Economist* magazine's famous Big Mac Index, Table 3.21, is a light-hearted but enlightening exercise. We live in an era of floating exchange rates in which relativities are changing continuously. Speculative trading plays a large part in international currency markets to the point where, at any particular time, it is not uncommon for markets to have 'overshot' and caused currencies to be significantly over- or undervalued. But overvalued relative to what—and to what precise extent? Economists use varying models to attempt to answer these questions—but never with any certainty.

The theory of purchasing power parity states that, over time, exchange rates should adjust to ensure that the prices of internationally traded commodities remain the same throughout the world. The *Economist* has applied this theory to just one commodity, the Big Mac hamburger which, though not traded between countries, is produced by the McDonald's company in many countries to the same recipe. If the PPP theory held perfectly, the national-currency retail price of each country's Big Mac should, after conversion to US dollars, be identical to the hamburger's price in the United States ($US5.30 in mid-2017). Hence, the extent to which the hamburger's actual price in other countries exceeds or falls short of the home US price is a quick but, of course, imperfect measure of the extent to which the US dollar is undervalued or overvalued, relative to the other country's currency.

3.8 Productivity

If you want to summarise in two words, the reason America and the other developed countries have got richer over the past 20 years—notwithstanding the setback of the Great Recession—and, indeed over the past two centuries, they are productivity improvement. Here, we take a country's wealth to be its annual production of goods and services. It can increase its output of goods and services by applying more labour and more physical capital (machines and buildings etc.). But what if it were to increase its output by more than the increase in its inputs of labour and capital? This seemingly magical result is called an increase in productivity (productiveness), measured as output divided by input to give output *per unit* of input.

Dividing a country's output by its inputs gives its *level* of productivity at a point in time. The United States is the richest large economy mainly because it has the highest productivity *levels* in most industries. This puts it at the 'technological frontier' and means it can achieve an increase in its productivity only by coming up with inventions and innovations that push out the frontier. In consequence, it has relatively low *rates of annual improvement* in productivity. All other countries, by contrast, are back from the frontier and so can improve their productivity at a faster rate than the USA simply by appropriating American technology. The further back from the frontier a country is, the faster the rate at which it can catch up. This goes a fair way towards explaining Ireland's remarkably rapid productivity growth. Another part of the explanation is its greatly expanded production of IT equipment. When the computer you produce this year has twice the capacity of the one you produced last year, but has the same amount of inputs, this is equivalent to a doubling in output.

The most commonly quoted productivity measure is the productivity of labour—output per worker or, better, output (GDP) per hour worked. As can be deduced from Table 3.22, almost all countries achieve an improvement in

Table 3.22 Growth in labour productivity
GDP per hour worked, total economy, percentage change at annual rate

Country	1996–2000	2009–2015
Ireland	3.8	6.2
Denmark	1.8	1.5
Australia	2.5	1.4
Sweden	2.5	1.4
Japan	1.0	1.3
Germany	1.2	1.2
Austria	1.9	1.0
Canada	2.0	1.0
France	1.4	1.0
Netherlands	1.5	0.9
Belgium	1.6	0.7
Finland	2.5	0.7
United States	**2.0**	**0.7**
Italy	0.9	0.6
Switzerland	1.4	0.6
United Kingdom	1.9	0.6
New Zealand	1.5	0.5
Norway	1.9	0.5
Mean	*1.9*	*1.2*

First column from *OECD Economic Outlook* No 82 December 2007 Statistical Annex
Final column from *OECD Compendium of Productivity Indicators 2017*

the productivity of their labour almost every year. The five years to 2000 were the last period of strong productivity growth in the USA and the developed countries. The seven years to 2015 saw much slower improvement in all the countries bar Ireland, the rebounding Celtic Tiger. You might expect this weaker performance to be explained by the Great Recession during the period, but many economists believe the slowdown began earlier and has deeper causes—even though they continue to debate what those causes are.

Table 3.23 shows an exercise in 'growth accounting'—measuring the three main contributions to a country's economic growth (first column): increased input of labour, increased input of capital equipment (here divided between ICT capital and other capital), with 'multi-factor productivity' as the remainder.

Multi-factor productivity measures all those factors that add to output that cannot be explained by the application of more labour or more capital equipment: technological advances in the quality rather than the quantity of the machines, advances in know-how that aren't embodied in machinery (such as improvements in the way firms are managed), improvements in the quality of labour (the increased skill of the workforce through greater education and training—that is, greater 'human capital'), greater economies of scale, the removal of government-imposed policy constraints on efficiency and changes (for better or worse) in the composition of a country's industries (since some industries have higher

Table 3.23 Contributions to GDP growth
GDP growth 1995–2015 and its components

Country	GDP growth	Labour input	ICT capital	Non-ICT capital	Multi-factor productivity
Ireland	4.32	0.99	0.33	1.28	1.74
Australia	3.15	1.08	0.49	0.88	0.69
New Zealand	2.74	1.22	0.62	0.53	0.35
Canada	2.43	0.94	0.39	0.52	0.58
Sweden	2.40	0.46	0.54	0.45	0.95
United States	**2.37**	**0.51**	**0.44**	**0.42**	**1.00**
United Kingdom	2.05	0.59	0.28	0.35	0.83
Finland	2.03	0.43	0.23	0.30	1.08
Netherlands	1.87	0.56	0.41	0.44	0.47
Switzerland	1.85	0.57	0.44	0.38	0.46
Belgium	1.75	0.57	0.44	0.57	0.17
Austria	1.74	0.27	0.36	0.46	0.65
France	1.54	0.22	0.30	0.39	0.63
Denmark	1.39	0.27	0.45	0.43	0.25
Germany	1.30	0.06	0.28	0.22	0.75
Japan	0.82	−0.38	0.37	0.21	0.62
Italy	0.47	0.14	0.24	0.32	−0.22
Mean	*2.01*	*0.50*	*0.39*	*0.48*	*0.65*

No data on Norway
OECD *Compendium of Productivity Indicators 2017*

Table 3.24 Investment in intellectual property products
Share of investment, as a percentage of gross fixed capital formation

Country	1995	2015
Ireland	9.5	43.3
Sweden	24.5	27.6
Switzerland	14.6	26.6
Denmark	13.8	25.4
United States	**20.1**	**25.3**
Netherlands	14.8	24.2
France	19.8	24.0
Japan	12.2	23.7
United Kingdom	25.8	21.5
Finland	16.8	20.8
Austria	9.6	20.5
Belgium	11.5	19.3
Germany	11.4	17.9
Italy	11.5	16.3
New Zealand	9.9	14.8
Norway	10.1	14.3
Australia	11.1	11.7
Canada	12.9	11.2
Mean	*14.4*	*21.6*

OECD *Compendium of Productivity Indicators 2017*

levels of productivity than others). It can be seen that the average annual rates of improvement in the productivity of labour shown in Table 3.22 are higher than the average annual rates of multi-factor productivity improvement over the 20 years to 2015. This is because measures of labour productivity *include* multi-factor productivity. Economists consider 'MFP' to be the refined essence of productivity growth, the true source of our ever-increasing prosperity over the centuries. It is driven by advances in technology and a more highly skilled workforce. Note, however, that while, like many concepts in economics, the idea of MFP is conceptually sound, it cannot be measured directly. Its measurement as a residual means this measurement is susceptible to any mismeasurement of the other items in the sum.

Table 3.24 shows the increase over 20 years in each country's proportion of total annual capital investment devoted to investment in intellectual property (IP) products—those protected by patents, copyright and trade names. Since the USA is at the technological frontier, it is no surprise to see it leading the list of larger economies.

3.9 Global Competitiveness and Economic Freedom

The Global Competitiveness Index, Table 3.25, is prepared annually by the World Economic Forum, a forum for discussions between top business and political leaders, based in Davos, Switzerland. Competitiveness is a woolly concept

3.9 Global Competitiveness and Economic Freedom

Table 3.25 Global competitiveness index
Score (0 = least competitive)

Country	2008 global rank	2017–18 global rank	2008 score	2017–18 score
Switzerland	2	1	5.61	5.86
United States	**1**	**2**	**5.74**	**5.85**
Netherlands	8	4	5.41	5.66
Germany	7	5	5.46	5.65
Sweden	4	7	5.53	5.52
United Kingdom	12	8	5.30	5.51
Japan	9	9	5.38	5.49
Finland	6	10	5.50	5.49
Norway	15	11	5.22	5.40
Denmark	3	12	5.58	5.39
New Zealand	24	13	4.93	5.37
Canada	10	14	5.37	5.35
Austria	14	18	5.23	5.25
Belgium	19	20	5.14	5.23
Australia	18	21	5.20	5.19
France	16	22	5.22	5.18
Ireland	22	24	4.99	5.16
Italy	49	43	4.35	4.54

World Economic forum: https://www.weforum.org/reports/the-global-competitiveness-report-2017-2018

much revered by business people, but out of step with orthodox economic analysis. It takes the objectives of a business—to capture market share from its competitors, or to be the most profitable firm—and assumes these are relevant to the objectives of countries in their economic interactions with other countries. It implies a view of international trade as a zero-sum game in which the object is to be a winner—the biggest winner—not a loser. But economists see trade as win-win—both sides are left better off.

A global competitiveness report has been issued for many years, but in recent years some leading American economists have been engaged to give the exercise greater academic rigour. In the process, competitiveness has been redefined to mean 'the set of institutions, policies and factors that determine the level of productivity of a country'. The level of productivity—output per unit of input—sets the sustainable level of the material prosperity that can be attained by a country.

For each of the 137 countries assessed, the index examines many indicators, grouped into 12 categories.

Some variables are measured using publicly available statistics, but most rely on the results of an annual survey of executive opinion. A sample of the business executives in each country is asked to assess their country's performance on a particular variable on a seven-point scale. This process introduces a large element of subjectivity to the exercise, subjecting it to the preferences and prejudices of senior business people and making it susceptible to changing intellectual fashions. This may help explain why countries' rankings change more than would be expected.

The variables are weighted differently according to a country's level of economic development but, even so, the weights remain essentially arbitrary. Many variables are given equal weight. All of them seem to be of some relevance in determining a country's productivity but, in reality, some will be more influential than others. This may explain why the index's rankings aren't highly correlated with measures of economic success such as income per capita, Table 3.1, or contemporary rates of economic growth, Table 3.2. But if a country's level of productivity is the prime objective, the United States' high ranking makes sense.

The Index of Economic Freedom, Table 3.26, is prepared annually by the Heritage Foundation, a conservative American think tank. The index scores 180 countries on 12 components of four key aspects of economic freedom: rule of law, government size, regulatory efficiency and market openness. It uses publicly available statistics and the published subjective assessments of other organisations. The 12 components are weighted equally so that, for example, market openness is given the same importance as size of government (with small government rated more favourably than big government). Depending on their scores, countries are divided into five categories ranging from 'free' to 'repressed'. The top four countries shown in the table are classed as 'free' and the next 11—including the USA—are

Table 3.26 Economic freedom
100 = highest score

Country	Global rank 2009	Global rank 2018	Score 2009	Score 2018
New Zealand	5	3	82.0	84.2
Switzerland	9	4	79.4	81.7
Australia	3	5	82.6	80.9
Ireland	4	6	82.2	80.4
United Kingdom	10	8	79.0	78.0
Canada	7	9	80.5	77.7
Denmark	8	12	79.6	76.6
Sweden	26	15	70.5	76.3
Netherlands	12	17	77.0	76.2
United States	**6**	**18**	**80.7**	**75.7**
Norway	28	23	70.2	74.3
Germany	25	25	70.5	74.2
Finland	17	26	74.5	74.1
Japan	19	30	72.8	72.3
Austria	23	32	71.2	71.8
Belgium	20	52	72.1	67.5
France	64	71	63.3	63.9
Italy	76	79	61.4	62.5

Economic Freedom Index: https://www.heritage.org/index/about

Table 3.27 Human development index
Scores can range from 0.000 (lowest) to 1.000 (highest)

Country	2015 HDI global rank	2015 HDI score	1990 HDI score	Average annual change 1990–2015
Top 30				
Norway	1	0.949	0.849	0.45
Australia	2	0.939	0.866	0.32
Switzerland	2	0.939	0.831	0.49
Germany	4	0.926	0.801	0.58
Denmark	5	0.925	0.799	0.59
Singapore	5	0.925	0.718	1.02
Netherlands	7	0.924	0.830	0.43
Ireland	8	0.923	0.762	0.77
Iceland	9	0.921	0.797	0.58
Canada	10	0.920	0.849	0.32
United States	**10**	**0.920**	**0.860**	**0.27**
Hong Kong, China	12	0.917	0.781	0.64
New Zealand	13	0.915	0.818	0.45
Sweden	14	0.913	0.815	0.45
Liechtenstein	15	0.912		
United Kingdom	16	0.909	0.775	0.64
Japan	17	0.903	0.814	0.42
Korea (Republic of)	18	0.901	0.731	0.84
Israel	19	0.899	0.785	0.54
Luxembourg	20	0.898	0.782	0.56
France	21	0.897	0.779	0.57
Belgium	22	0.896	0.805	0.42
Finland	23	0.895	0.783	0.53
Austria	24	0.893	0.794	0.47
Slovenia	25	0.890	0.767	0.60
Italy	26	0.887	0.768	0.58
Spain	27	0.884	0.755	0.64
Czech Republic	28	0.878	0.761	0.57
Greece	29	0.866	0.760	0.52
Estonia	30	0.865	0.728	0.69
Selected others				
Poland	36	0.855	0.712	0.74
Chile	38	0.847	0.700	0.76
Saudi Arabia	38	0.847	0.698	0.77
Portugal	41	0.843	0.711	0.68
Argentina	45	0.827	0.705	0.64
Russian Federation	49	0.804	0.733	0.37
Cuba	68	0.775	0.676	0.55
Iran	69	0.774	0.572	1.22
Turkey	71	0.767	0.576	1.15
Mexico	77	0.762	0.648	0.65
Brazil	79	0.754	0.611	0.85
China	90	0.738	0.499	1.57
Colombia	95	0.727	0.592	0.83
India	131	0.624	0.428	1.52
Lowest				
Guinea	183	0.414	0.271	1.71
Burundi	184	0.404	0.270	1.62
Niger	187	0.353	0.212	2.06
Central African Republic	188	0.352	0.320	0.39

UNDP *Human Development Report* 2017

rated 'mostly free', leaving Belgium, France and Italy rated as 'moderately free', in company with Rwanda, Bahrain and Uganda.

The index is unashamedly ideological, being 'grounded in the classical liberal economic theories of Adam Smith and Fredrich Hayek', which leaves it measuring a 'time-tested formula for sustained economic growth'. However, the rankings in Table 3.26 show little correlation with the rankings for either income per capita, Table 3.1, or contemporary rates of economic growth, Table 3.2. Nor does economic freedom seem to equate with political freedom. The index's highest rankings go to Hong Kong and Singapore, neither of which is a genuine democracy.

3.10 Human Development Index

The United Nations Development Programme developed an index designed to create a broader view of a country's development than using average income alone which, on the face of it, takes no account of the diffusion of economic benefits through a society or other aspects of human wellbeing. The Human Development Index (HDI) is a simple summary measure of three dimensions of the human development concept: living a long and healthy life, being educated and having a decent standard of living. The UNDP's rationale is that:

> Human development is a process of enlarging people's choices ... The three essential ones are for people to lead a long and healthy life, to acquire knowledge and to have access to resources needed for a decent standard of living. If these choices are not available, many other opportunities remain inaccessible.

The HDI combines the three dimensions into one index, and scores each country for each year, with a summary measure between zero and one, a higher score meaning greater human development. While national income correlates with strongly with the HDI, the measure also gives weight to the distribution of income and the development of social infrastructure. Two components of the HDI—longevity and educational attainment—by their nature reflect upon the wellbeing of the population as a whole.

The idea of a composite scale is to go beyond the limits of individual measures to capture more of the complexity of the social experience. However, an intrinsic problem of constructing composite indicators is that even if all the elements can be scored satisfactorily, there is always an arbitrariness about their weightings—how the components are combined into one scale. Such constructs are inevitably surrounded by methodological disputes. They should not be viewed as more than a convenient means of encapsulating and simplifying complex realities in order to facilitate comparisons between countries and over time.

The HDI is a relatively blunt instrument for distinguishing the finer aspects of social development within the United States and the 17 selected rich countries, all of which score very highly. While Norway tops the list, only 0.024 points separate the first five selected countries. All 18 are in the top 24 places, at the top of the 'very high human development' category. The USA would have been at the top based solely on income per person, but scored less well on life expectancy at birth and expected years of schooling.

The final column of the table, giving a country's average annual percentage change since 1990, shows that life is still improving for people in these 18 high-income democracies, and that their relatively greater wealth is also translating into greater life chances to a substantial proportion of their citizens. Finally, the table reminds us how much better our citizens are doing than most of the people in the world, especially in Africa.

Work and Labour

4.1 Labour Force Participation and the Ageing Society

The alarm often expressed about the ageing society—that it will lead to higher taxes, slower economic growth, and divert more resources to caring for the elderly—stems from a simple but far-reaching change in the aged dependency ratio. That ratio is those of working age (usually defined as 15–64) compared with those retired from the labour force. As we saw in Table 1.12 above, the long-term projections are dramatic. By 2050, across these 18 democracies, the average will be one aged person for every two of working age. The United States is the best placed with two for every five, but the change will be unprecedented in all these countries.

The labour force participation rate in Table 4.1 is the proportion of the population of working age (15–64 years) that participates in the labour force either by working or actively seeking work. It makes no distinction between full-time and part-time employment. There are many reasons why the rate is likely to be well below 100%: young people still in full-time education, older people in early retirement, people who don't have paid employment because they are looking after children or other dependents, people who are disabled, and people who would like to work, but have become discouraged from actively seeking it (and who thus no longer meet the tight definition of 'unemployed').

Before approaching the changes in the aged dependency ratio, we should begin by noting that the latest labour force participation rates are at or near the historical peak for most countries, principally because of the rising participation rate of women (see Table 10.2). The great majority of these 18 countries had stable or increasing labour force participation in the first 16 years of this century, with for whatever reason, the United States being the major exception, with a four-point decline. This anomaly may be due to the impact of the Great Recession, the slow recovery in employment after it, and discouraged workers leaving the labour force.

For some decades in many countries, the trend was towards earlier retirement. Table 4.2 shows that that has gone into reverse, with the participation rate of the 55-to-64-year-old cohort lifting substantially in 16 years. Remember that this figure includes part-time as well as full-time work, which may help explain some of the dramatic rises at the bottom of the table. Probably, the most important reasons for the rise are that people at this age are now healthier than in the past and that they are more aware of making sure they have sufficient savings for their retirement. It also reflects the higher participation rate of women coming into that cohort and remaining in the labour force.

Table 4.3 gives a more differentiated view of employment around retirement age. It shows that around three quarters of 55–59-year-olds are still working across these 18 affluent democracies. That drops to half in the next age bracket, while among those aged 65–69 only one in five are still working. Again the differences between countries are substantial, with the USA clearly above the mean in the older cohort. Japanese and New Zealanders in this cohort are eight times more likely to be working than Belgians, who are clearly the leaders in early retirement.

People now live a lot longer in retirement than they used to. With slight variations, and occasionally differences between men and women, the normal pensionable age in these 18 countries is around 65. Table 4.4 shows the average life expectancy for people aged 65. For women, it is just on 22 years and men 19, which means that most people will be living the best part of two decades in retirement. This worsens the aged dependency ratio, but despite the doomsayers, more people living longer is a good problem to have.

Table 4.1 Labour force participation
% in the labour force of all people aged 15–64

Country	2000	2016
Switzerland	81	84
Sweden	79	82
Denmark	80	80
New Zealand	75	80
Netherlands	74	80
Norway	81	78
United Kingdom	76	78
Canada	76	78
Germany	71	78
Australia	74	77
Japan	73	77
Austria	71	76
Finland	75	76
United States	**77**	**73**
France	68	72
Ireland	68	71
Belgium	65	68
Italy	60	65
Mean	74	76

OECD *Employment Outlook 2017*

Table 4.3 Employment rates of older people
% employed within each age group 2015

Country	55–59	60–64	65–69
Japan	80	64	43
New Zealand	80	72	43
United States	**69**	**54**	**31**
Norway	80	65	28
Australia	70	54	26
Canada	71	51	25
Switzerland	82	60	23
Sweden	83	68	22
United Kingdom	73	52	21
Ireland	66	47	19
Denmark	81	55	19
Germany	79	56	16
Finland	76	47	14
Netherlands	73	53	13
Italy	62	37	9
Austria	67	27	9
France	71	28	6
Belgium	63	26	5
Mean	74	51	21

OECD *Pensions at a Glance 2017*

Table 4.2 Labour force participation among older people
People aged 55–64 in the labour force as % of that cohort

Country	2000	2016
Sweden	69	80
New Zealand	60	79
Switzerland	65	74
Norway	68	74
Japan	67	74
Germany	43	71
Denmark	58	71
Netherlands	39	68
Finland	47	66
United Kingdom	53	66
Canada	51	66
Australia	48	65
United States	**59**	**64**
Ireland	47	61
France	37	54
Italy	29	53
Austria	30	52
Belgium	27	48
Mean	50	66

OECD *Employment Outlook 2017*

Table 4.4 Life expectancy at 65
Average expected remaining years of life, 2015

Country	Females	Males
Japan	24.5	19.5
France	23.5	19.8
Switzerland	22.7	19.9
Australia	22.4	19.9
Italy	22.4	19.5
Canada	22.3	19.7
New Zealand	21.7	19.5
Sweden	21.6	19.4
Finland	21.6	18.6
Belgium	21.6	18.4
Norway	21.5	19.2
Austria	21.5	18.7
United Kingdom	21.4	19.1
Netherlands	21.2	18.8
Germany	21.1	18.3
United States	**21.0**	**18.5**
Ireland	21.0	18.2
Denmark	20.7	18.1
Mean	*21.9*	*19.1*

OECD *Pensions at a Glance 2017*

4.2 Unemployment

A central aim of economic management is to provide full employment or as close to full employment as possible. As the first data column in Table 4.5 shows, in the golden age of economic growth from World War II until 1973, there was very low unemployment in these countries. But then with the oil shock and with stagflation—high inflation and high unemployment occurring simultaneously—economic management became much more difficult. For a long time, it looked as if unemployment was on an ever-upward trajectory, which fortunately stabilised by the turn of the century in most of these countries, although at a much higher level than the pre-1973 norm.

Unemployment is heavily influenced by the economy's progress through the business cycle, with the rate likely to rise sharply when the economy drops into recession. The table reflects the impact and slow recovery from the 2008–09 Great Recession. Unemployment peaked in 2010 both in the United States and the OECD as a whole. In a few countries—the United States, Ireland and the United Kingdom—it rose dramatically. In the years since, in most of these countries, unemployment has improved, although only in six of 18 countries has it returned to pre-crisis levels or lower. In a few, notably France and Italy, the rate has worsened rather than improved, suggesting that the unemployment is more structural than cyclical, that their economies are not generating enough jobs.

Table 4.5 Unemployment
Harmonised rate as % civilian labour force

Country	1970–73	1980–89	2000–06	2010	2016
Japan	1.3	2.5	4.8	5.1	3.1
Germany	0.8	6.1	9.6	7.0	4.1
Switzerland	0.4	0.6	4.1	4.5	4.6
Norway	1.2	2.8	4.2	3.6	4.7
United Kingdom	2.6	9.7	5.0	7.8	4.8
United States	**5.2**	**7.2**	**5.4**	**9.6**	**4.9**
New Zealand	0.2	4.5	4.2	6.2	5.1
Australia	2.0	7.2	5.5	5.2	5.7
Austria	1.2	3.3	4.6	4.8	6.0
Netherlands	1.7	9.8	3.9	5.0	6.0
Denmark	0.9	8.1	4.8	7.5	6.2
Canada	5.8	9.3	7.1	8.1	7.0
Sweden	2.3	2.5	6.2	8.6	7.0
Belgium	2.1	11.1	8.1	8.3	7.9
Ireland	6.1	14.0	4.5	13.9	7.9
Finland	2.2	4.8	8.6	8.4	8.8
France	2.7	9.1	9.4	9.3	10.1
Italy	5.8	9.9	7.9	8.4	11.7
Mean	2.5	6.8	6.0	7.3	6.4

OECD *Employment Outlook 2017*

Table 4.6 Youth unemployment
Labour force participation of young people, aged 15–29, 2014
Percentage in education, employment, both or neither

Country	Employed and in education	In education, not employed	Employed, not in education	Not in education or employment
Netherlands	32	25	34	8
Norway	22	31	38	9
Germany	20	33	37	9
Switzerland	28	21	42	9
Japan	7	36	47	10
Denmark	31	30	29	10
Sweden	14	35	41	10
Austria	19	27	43	11
Australia	23	23	41	12
Finland	19	35	33	12
United Kingdom	11	27	47	14
United States	**15**	**30**	**40**	**15**
Canada	15	22	48	15
Belgium	3	44	38	15
France	7	39	37	17
New Zealand	7	41	33	19
Ireland	8	39	35	19
Italy	2	44	26	27
Mean	16	32	38	13

OECD *Society at a Glance 2016*

Countries varied over time in the severity of their unemployment, and in where they are placed in these league tables. The United States began the period with higher unemployment than the mean, but more recently has been below the mean. Japan and Germany have been through several cycles, but now have returned to relatively low unemployment, while Switzerland has usually had close to the lowest unemployment during the whole period.

Unemployment is sad at whatever stage of the life cycle it occurs. For older people, it is a bitter blow to become unemployed after a lifetime of work. For young married people with a family and mortgage, it hits with immediate force. But none is sadder than youth unemployment, which may have long-term impacts on a person's self-confidence and ability to function in the wider society.

According to the OECD, the global recession severely impacted on young people entering the labour force. Table 4.6 shows the situation some years later. Firstly, it should be noted that youth here covers a 15-year age range, from 15 to 29. One would expect to find substantial differences between those in adolescence and those approaching 30. The first three data columns include those who are both employed and in education, in education only, and employed but no longer in education. Over the 18 countries as a whole, these three categories cover 86% of the age cohort. The last column covers those sometimes referred to as NEETs—not in education, employment or training. In seven of these countries, this group forms up to 10% of young people—worrying enough if it signals long-term disengagement from work and society. In Italy, however, the group comprises more than one in four young people and almost one in five young people in Ireland and New Zealand, and with several other countries lower, but still worryingly high, including the United States.

While a temporary experience of unemployment is distressing, a long-term absence from work becomes much more serious. Table 4.7 shows that in 2016 people unemployed for 12 months or more were less than 2% of the labour force in 12 of the countries. Apart from how the market is generating opportunities or not, there are contrasting stick or carrot public policies to encourage people moving back into employment. Speculating, the United States and Norway are both succeeding but for different reasons. Long-term unemployment is much more of a problem in the bottom four countries, and especially in Italy, where it is approaching 7%. Another way the OECD approaches the issue is what percentage of the unemployed have been out of work 12 months or longer, and in 2016 in three countries—Italy, Ireland and Belgium—it was more than half.

4.3 Part-Time Work and Working Hours

Part-time work has become an increasingly important aspect of employment in many countries.[1] Indeed, Table 4.8 shows it now comprises one in five of all jobs across these 18 countries, and Table 4.9 shows it is one in three of all women's jobs. The term 'total employment' simply adds full-time and part-time jobs together.

As Table 4.8 shows, in the first 16 years of this century, the proportion of part-time jobs continued to rise, and especially quickly in some European countries. By 2016, one in five of the jobs in these countries overall was part-time, while more than one in three Dutch jobs was part-time. For whatever reason, this growth has been least marked in the United States.

It is sometimes assumed that part-time employment is, almost by definition, inferior to full-time employment. Such a conclusion is too sweeping. The growth in part-time employment is partly a function of increased demand from employers. It is likely that many formerly full-time jobs in retailing, hospitality and elsewhere were divided into several part-time jobs, with the advantage to employers of more closely matching their staffing levels with their busiest times of the week, thus increasing the productivity of labour.

Table 4.7 Long-term unemployment
% of labour force unemployed for one year or more

Country	2005	2016
United States	**0.6**	**0.6**
Norway	0.4	0.6
New Zealand	0.4	0.7
Canada	0.6	0.8
Japan	1.5	1.2
Sweden	0.8	1.2
Denmark	1.1	1.3
United Kingdom	1.0	1.3
Australia	0.9	1.4
Germany	5.9	1.7
Austria	1.4	1.9
Switzerland	1.7	1.9
Finland	2.1	2.3
Netherlands	2.1	2.6
Belgium	4.4	4.0
France	3.5	4.3
Ireland	1.6	4.7
Italy	3.8	6.8
Mean	*1.9*	*2.2*

OECD *How's Life 2017*
The sharp reduction in Germany is mainly due to a change in measurement methods

Table 4.8 Part-time employment
As % of total employment
Defined as people normally working fewer than 30 h per week in main job

Country	2016
Netherlands	38
Switzerland	27
Australia	26
United Kingdom	24
Ireland	23
Japan	23
Germany	22
Denmark	22
New Zealand	21
Austria	21
Canada	19
Norway	19
Italy	19
Belgium	18
France	14
Finland	14
Sweden	14
United States	**13**
Mean	*21*

OECD *Employment Outlook 2017*

[1] Also draws on: https://eh.net/encyclopedia/hours-of-work-in-u-s-history/.

4.3 Part-Time Work and Working Hours

Table 4.9 Female part-time employment
As % of total female employment
Normally working fewer than 30 h per week in main job

Country	2016
Netherlands	60
Switzerland	45
Australia	38
United Kingdom	38
Japan	37
Germany	37
Ireland	35
Austria	35
Italy	33
New Zealand	32
Belgium	30
Norway	27
Denmark	27
Canada	26
France	22
Sweden	18
Finland	18
United States	**18**
Mean	*32*

OECD *Employment Outlook 2017*

Table 4.10 Annual hours worked
Average annual hours actually worked per person in employment
Includes part-time and part-year workers as well as full-time workers

Country	1995	2016
Ireland	–	1879
United States	**1841**	**1783**
New Zealand	1841	1752
Italy	1856	1730
Japan	1884	1713
Canada	1775	1703
United Kingdom	1731	1676
Australia	1794	1669
Finland	1776	1653
Sweden	1640	1621
Austria	1783	1601
Switzerland	1700	1589
Belgium	1585	1551
France	1605	1472
Netherlands	1479	1435
Norway	1488	1424
Denmark	1419	1410
Germany	1528	1363
Mean	*1690*	*1612*

OECD *Employment Outlook 2017*

But the growth is also a product of increased willingness to supply such labour on the part of some workers. Many mothers with young families would prefer to work less than the full 35–40 h a week, as would most full-time students, and some people around retirement age.

At its best, the growth of part-time work reflects the growing flexibility of the labour market. On the other hand, many people working part-time would prefer to be working full-time if such work was available. It is also a form of employment dominated by women, and sometimes this reflects their limited opportunities for more full-time involvement in the workforce.

The availability of part-time work as a major part of the economy is a relatively recent innovation. Historically, onerous hours of work were a great problem for working people. The Economic History Association estimates that in the late nineteenth century, the average American work week was around 60 h, while earlier in the century working weeks of 70+ h were common. Reducing the hours worked has been a central part of the labour struggles over the last century—the eight hour day and the 40 h week were significant legal landmarks in several countries. While harsh working conditions continue, especially in poorer countries, in these affluent democracies, concerns about working hours are usually at a more refined level, to do with work–life balance, combining family and career, and with productivity.

The measurement of working hours is complicated. The crude totals in Table 4.10 demand many qualifications.

The table mixes full-time and part-time work, all year with part-year (e.g. seasonal) employment, and employees and the self-employed. Data are drawn from surveys and from administrative data. There are many differences in how countries collect the data—hours actually worked, usually worked, or hours paid for or contracted. There are also issues of both unpaid overtime at work and paid absences from work (e.g. paid sick leave). Countries differ both in the structure of a normal working week and the number of such weeks per year. Different numbers of national holidays, and of annual leave, some of which may be legally required and others which are based on negotiations between employer and employee, further complicate the measurement. Another easily forgotten factor is where a particular national economy happens to be in the business cycle. One would expect average hours to be higher when the economy was booming and lower when it was in the doldrums.

Remembering these many qualifications, Table 4.10 suggests that total working hours are gradually trending down. If the Irish figure (present and highest in 2016, but absent in 1995) is excluded, the mean has trended down from 1690 to 1596, almost 100 fewer hours a year, and that workers in European countries (apart from Italy) tend to work fewer hours a year than the English-speaking democracies and Japan.

A more modest measure is those who say they usually work 50 h or more a week. Table 4.11 shows four English-speaking countries, including the United States, rank highest here.

Table 4.11 Employees working very long hours
% of employees usually working 50 h or more per week 2015

Country	50+ h
New Zealand	15.0
Australia	13.2
United Kingdom	12.7
United States	**11.4**
France	7.8
Austria	6.8
Ireland	4.7
Germany	4.6
Belgium	4.3
Italy	3.9
Finland	3.9
Canada	3.7
Norway	3.2
Denmark	2.2
Sweden	1.1
Netherlands	0.5
Mean	6.2

No data on Japan or Switzerland
OECD *How's Life 2017*

Table 4.12 Low-income work
Share of working-age persons (18–65 years) living with less than 50% of median household disposable income, 2013

Country	2006	2013
Switzerland	6.8	6.3
Denmark	5.3	6.7
Finland	7.1	7.9
France	6.9	7.9
Austria	7.0	8.5
Netherlands	6.8	9.0
Norway	7.5	9.0
Germany	8.7	9.1
New Zealand	10.9	9.1
Ireland	9.4	9.2
Belgium	8.5	9.4
Sweden	5.6	9.4
United Kingdom	10.4	9.8
Australia	11.1	10.2
Canada	12.4	12.8
Italy	10.7	13.4
Japan	13.4	14.5
United States	**14.7**	**15.7**
Mean	9.1	9.9

OECD *Employment Outlook 2017*

Much more sophisticated measures, however, are needed before more penetrating comparisons of working hours, productivity or quality of life can be made.

4.4 Underemployment, Unsatisfactory and Vulnerable Work

The unemployment rate is the proportion of the total labour force that is out of work, but available for, and seeking, work. A person is defined as employed if working for pay, profit or family gain for at least one hour per week. Note that someone who is seeking a full-time job, but nonetheless accepts a few hours of casual employment to earn a little cash, is not classed as unemployed. Similarly, someone who would like to have a job, but is not actively seeking one, will not be classed as unemployed. Thus, the tight definition of unemployment means that the official estimates often understate the full extent of joblessness and underemployment.

The tables on this page explore aspects of those who work but whose situation is still, by various considerations, unsatisfactory. While unemployment is the most basic measure of deprivation, its narrow parameters mean that among the employed there are the working poor and those who for various reasons are vulnerable or dissatisfied.

Table 4.12 uses the common definition of relative poverty —less than 50% of median household disposable income— and its incidence among people of working age. It is notable how much larger these percentages are than those who are unemployed in Table 4.5. The difference is what we might call the working poor. While the United States has lower than average unemployment, it has the greatest proportion of working-age people in relative poverty. The relative lack of change in either numbers or rankings between 2006 and 2013 suggests that this is a fairly stable aspect of these societies. Italy, Japan, Canada and Australia are closest to the USA in their proportion of low-income persons of working age.

Table 4.13 shows the proportion of those working part-time who would prefer to be working full-time, another measure of 'under-employment'. It is low in Norway and the United States but constitutes five out of eight part-time workers in Italy, four in ten in France, and more than one in four in several other countries. It is likely that a substantial number of those in involuntary part-time employment are young people who have not yet secured full-time employment.

The OECD has constructed a measure of job strain, which is defined as a situation in which job demands reported by employees (e.g. time pressure and exposure to physical health risks) exceed their job resources (e.g. work autonomy and good workplace relationships). This subjective measure showed considerable variation in several countries when measured in 2005 and 2015 and should perhaps be viewed with caution at this stage. In Table 4.14, Switzerland leapt from being near average in 2005 to the top of the list in 2015, while Norway and Germany moved in the other direction. Japan was near the top in both years. The United States was close to the mean in both years.

4.4 Underemployment, Unsatisfactory and Vulnerable Work

Table 4.13 Involuntary part-time employment
2016

Country	As % PT employment
Norway	6.6
United States	**7.3**
Switzerland	8.0
Netherlands	8.7
Belgium	8.8
Germany	11.2
Austria	12.4
Denmark	13.1
United Kingdom	14.3
Japan	19.5
New Zealand	24.5
Canada	25.0
Finland	26.3
Sweden	26.3
Australia	28.0
Ireland	29.5
France	41.6
Italy	62.5
Mean	20.8

OECD *Employment Outlook 2017*

Table 4.14 Job strain
Proportion of employees who experience a number of job demands exceeding their job resources

Country	2005	2015
Norway	20	15
Denmark	20	21
Finland	22	23
Sweden	24	26
Ireland	25	27
Belgium	26	28
Canada	28	28
Netherlands	25	28
United States	**27**	**29**
France	30	30
New Zealand	23	30
United Kingdom	27	30
Austria	29	31
Australia	30	33
Germany	49	34
Italy	40	40
Japan	48	43
Switzerland	27	43
Mean	29	30

Canada LAY = 2005
OECD: *How's Life 2017*

Table 4.15 Risks from automation
% of jobs at high (estimated 70%+ chance) of being automated or significantly changed (50–70% chance) in the next 10–20 years 2015

Country	Automated	Significantly changed
Finland	7	21
Belgium	7	22
Japan	7	22
Sweden	7	23
Australia	7	26
Ireland	8	23
France	9	21
Canada	9	24
Denmark	9	24
United States	**9**	**25**
New Zealand	9	26
Norway	10	23
United Kingdom	10	25
Netherlands	10	27
Italy	10	34
Austria	12	29
Germany	12	31
Mean	9	25

No data on Switzerland
OECD *Employment Outlook 2017*

most at risk of being substituted by technology are those involving basic exchange of information and simple manual dexterity. On the other hand, occupations that entail creative tasks, those that involve inter-personal relationships and greater socio-economic skills are at a lower risk. The risk of automation has been said to be particularly severe for workers from the most disadvantaged socio-demographic groups, in low-skill and semi-skilled occupations.

The two columns of Table 4.15, however, suggest far more jobs will be transformed rather than lost through increases in automation. There are not huge differences between countries, but it is likely to impact work in several European countries most.

4.5 Trade Unions

Table 4.16 documents dramatic changes over time and between countries. The trend over 35 years was for trade union membership to substantially decline as a percentage of all employees, so that in 2015 it was just two-thirds what it had been 35 years earlier. However, the contrasts between countries are also large. In 2015, five countries still had union memberships that were more than half of all employees, while in nine others it was less than one in five.

Unions in the United States never had the extensive membership coverage that they achieved in several other countries, but even from that small base, they halved during this period (22 → 11). The sharpest declines elsewhere

The final table in this section (4.15) examines the risks to current jobs from automation. In a technologically dynamic economy, new jobs are continuously being created and old ones made redundant. According to the OECD, the tasks

Table 4.16 Trade union membership
Union members as % of all employees

Country	1980	1995	2015
Denmark	76	77	67
Sweden	80	83	67
Finland	69	80	65
Belgium	53	56	55
Norway	57	57	52
Italy	49	38	37
Ireland	64	46	30
Austria	49	41	27
Canada	35	33	27
United Kingdom	52	33	25
New Zealand	60	28	19
Germany	35	29	18
Netherlands	31	26	18
Australia	50	32	17
Japan	31	24	17
Switzerland	27	23	16
France	19	9	11
United States	**22**	**14**	**11**
Mean	*48*	*40*	*32*

First columns: Jelle Visser 'Union membership statistics in 24 countries' *Monthly Labor Review* January 2006 p. 38–49. Final column from OECD Employment Outlook 2017

Table 4.17 Trade union membership in public and private sectors 2015

Country	Private sector %	Public sector %
Denmark	63	74
Sweden	61	79
Finland	60	75
Belgium	56	53
Norway	37	80
Italy	24	73
Austria	23	46
Ireland	20	57
Japan	16	28
Germany	16	25
Netherlands	15	24
Switzerland	15	21
United Kingdom	14	55
Canada	14	72
Australia	12	42
New Zealand	10	52
France	8	19
United States	**6**	**35**
Mean	*26*	*50*

OECD *Employment Outlook 2017*

occurred in Australia (50 → 17), Ireland (64 → 30), the United Kingdom (52 → 25) and Austria (49 → 27). In contrast, the countries with the highest memberships only had slight declines.

The figures on trade union membership are based on both surveys and administrative data, the latter sometimes giving a higher estimate by a couple of percentage points, due to the reporting organisation inflating figures, or members (or their spouses) forgetting their memberships when polled in surveys. On the whole, these discrepancies are relatively small. Occasionally, there are larger discrepancies. Normally, this is because one source is using gross figures and the other net. Net membership only includes those employed, while gross union density also counts members when they are retired or unemployed. The discrepancy tends to be greatest in those countries (Denmark, Finland, Belgium and Sweden) where unions play a publicly subsidised role in welfare schemes. Whatever the measurement issues, the substantial trends and differences are not in doubt.

Trade union membership has always varied with the characteristics of the workforce. It has always been lower among part-time and temporary workers, often lower in the service sector than when there are large concentrations of workers in manufacturing or mining. Table 4.17 provides another contrast in membership rates—between the public and private sectors, essentially across the 18 countries, there is just half the membership rate in the private as in the public sector. These differences may stem from greater worker rights in the public sector, different employer attitudes, but also simply, as noted, because larger concentrations of workers make it easier to organise.

In the countries at the bottom of the table, the contrasts are even starker because of just how low union membership in the private sector is. Just one American private sector worker in 16 is a union member.

The wage-setting mechanisms differ greatly among the 18 democracies (Table 4.18), and there are many idiosyncrasies which make blanket comparisons misleading. For example, French trade unions seem to still wield considerable influence even though their official memberships are low.

The differences are becoming sharper. In the countries at the bottom of the table, the trend is towards an ever more decentralised model, with more enterprise bargaining at the company level, and with agreements made covering a smaller proportion of the workforce. At the top, key agreements are still industry-wide and cover the great majority of workers. It is in the countries at the bottom of the table that union membership has declined most sharply. In the West European countries at the top where official forums establish society- and industry-wide agreements, trade union membership has held up more.

Within the United States, Western and Rosenfeld note that between 1973 and 2007, union membership in the private sector declined from 34 to 8% among men and 16 to 6% among women. During this time, wage inequality rose by 40%. Changes in market factors are part of the explanation for the changing wage distribution. But the authors, after

4.5 Trade Unions

Table 4.18 Collective bargaining systems 2015

Country	Predominant level	Degree centralisation
Belgium	Sectoral/National	Centralised
Finland	Sectoral/National	Centralised
Austria	Sectoral	Organised decentralised
Denmark	Sectoral	Organised decentralised
France	Sectoral	Centralised
Germany	Sectoral	Organised decentralised
Italy	Sectoral	Centralised
Netherlands	Sectoral	Organised decentralised
Norway	Sectoral	Organised decentralised
Sweden	Sectoral	Organised decentralised
Switzerland	Sectoral	Organised decentralised
Australia	Company/Sectoral	Decentralised
Canada	Company	Decentralised
Ireland	Company	Decentralised
Japan	Company	Decentralised
New Zealand	Company	Decentralised
United Kingdom	Company	Decentralised
United States	**Company**	**Decentralised**

OECD *Employment Outlook 2017*

Table 4.19 Industrial disputes
Annual averages of work days lost per 1000 salaried employees

Country	1970s	1980s	1990s	2000–07	2008–15
Japan	74	6	2	0	0
Austria	7	2	4	50	1
Switzerland	2	0	2	4	1
United States	**322**	**90**	**40**	**35**	**5**
Germany	41	24	12	5	6
Sweden	140	78	49	22	7
Netherlands	32	15	22	8	10
New Zealand	245	344	63	15	10
Australia	512	245	122	36	16
United Kingdom	511	249	30	29	23
Finland	488	302	167	81	27
Ireland	528	264	118	29	34
Italy	980	246	158	94	43
Norway	37	87	82	57	59
Canada	728	411	233	174	98
Belgium	205	37	31	74	106
France	155	50	463	265	122
Denmark	192	147	169	37	142
Mean	288	144	98	56	39

First two columns derived from the *ILO Yearbook of Labour Statistics 2002* (ILO, Geneva, 60th ed) plus several earlier editions for total days lost. There were several gaps in the data for industrial disputes, which have been averaged out (a less than perfect procedure given the volatility of annual rates of industrial disputation.)
Final three columns OECD *Employment Outlook 2017*

doing stringent statistical analysis, conclude that the decline in unions accounts for between one-fifth and one-third of the rising inequality.

4.6 Industrial Disputes

The decline in industrial disputes in Table 4.19 is even more dramatic than the decline in trade union membership in Table 4.16.[2] When looking at the average work days lost per 1000 employees, the 18-country mean in 2008–2015 was just one-seventh what it had been in the 1970s. The 1970s were the peak of days lost through industrial disputes, partly because it was a period of inflation and economic instability.

The periods since have seen a steady drop, with each decade being less than the preceding one. Individual countries however show great variations, sometimes reflecting a period of upheaval before returning to long-term patterns. The countries at the bottom of the table—Denmark, France, Belgium and Canada—have all had major variations but often have been among the countries with the most time lost in industrial disputes. Canada has always presented a sharp contrast to its southern neighbour in industrial relations.

There are eight countries where in the latest period ten days a year or less per 1000 employees were lost. This includes the United States, plus the almost perennially industrially peaceful countries of Japan, Austria, Switzerland, Germany and the Netherlands.

In calculating the rates for time lost, there are divergences in how both the numerator and denominator are counted. Countries have different minima for the number of days of labour lost before strikes are counted in their statistics. Some types of strike ('political' and unofficial and 'wildcat') or stoppages among some groups (public sector and armed forces) are excluded in some countries. Proportions are sometimes given of all employed (as here); sometimes of civilian employees, and sometimes of some ill-defined group called workers.

So these figures cannot be used to explore nice distinctions and small differences. However, the overwhelming trends over time and the extreme differences between countries still stand, even allowing for the substantial measurement problems.

Interestingly, the rankings in Tables 4.20 and 4.21 show little relationship to that in 4.19. Table 4.19 is based on surveys of senior executives about how cooperative trade unions are in their country. It is not surprising that Switzerland tops the list, but Denmark at number two has a record of industrial volatility. With many exceptions, and perhaps counter-intuitively, there is more of a relationship to the relative size of unions in Table 4.16. The general tendency is for managers to judge unions as more cooperative

---

[2]Also draws on Bruce Western and Jake Rosenfeld 'Union, norms, and the rise in US wage inequality' *American Sociological Review* 76(4), 513–537, 2011.

Table 4.20 Quality of labour relations
Cooperation in labour-employer relations as judged by senior executives
Scale of 1 (generally confrontational) to 7 (generally cooperative)

Country	2014
Switzerland	6.2
Denmark	6.0
Norway	5.8
Japan	5.6
New Zealand	5.5
Netherlands	5.5
Ireland	5.4
Austria	5.4
Sweden	5.4
Germany	5.2
United Kingdom	5.1
Canada	5.0
Finland	5.0
United States	**4.7**
Belgium	4.2
Australia	3.9
France	3.6
Italy	3.4
Mean	*5.0*

OECD *Employment Outlook 2017*

Table 4.21 Public trust in trade unions
% in surveys saying they trust—or have quite a lot of confidence in—trade unions

Country	2000	2010
Finland	58	67
Denmark	59	66
Norway	66	66
Netherlands	61	59
Belgium	50	55
Sweden	47	55
Austria	45	52
Germany	41	45
France	40	43
Japan	43	40
Switzerland	37	40
United Kingdom	44	35
Canada	36	32
Ireland	53	32
Italy	34	31
New Zealand	23	30
Australia	26	27
United States	**34**	**25**
Mean	*44*	*44*

OECD *Employment Outlook 2017*

in those countries where union membership is more encompassing. Managers in the United States and Australia view unions as more confrontational even though both countries have relatively few days lost through strikes.

Similarly, public trust in trade unions bears only a very limited relationship to the frequency of industrial disputes. The Canadian public is more positive towards unions than the Americans, even though the latter has far fewer days lost. Nor is it clear why the American public opinion declined by 11 points over that decade, when there seem to have been few manifestations of union abuse of power. The countries of Scandinavia and northwest Europe have the most positive attitudes, something that is perhaps related to their greater confidence in their social institutions overall.

Together with Tables 4.16 and 4.19 represent a significant shift in social power, most especially in the English-speaking democracies, with trade unions having much less influence now than some decades ago.

Government Taxes and Spending

5.1 Government Taxes and Spending

The decades of strong economic growth following World War II were a period of growing expectations of what governments should do for their citizens. It was a time when the welfare state expanded greatly, as did government spending on education and health. Table 5.1 shows how government spending as a percentage of GDP—the most common method of measuring the size of government—expanded between the 1960s and 1990s.

Equally, it shows that since the 1990s, government spending (and this includes all levels of government—national, regional and local) has remained broadly in line with GDP growth. For government spending to rise as a percentage of GDP, it must grow at a faster real rate than the economy overall. When its percentage remains constant, it is growing at a similar rate to the economy. By this measure, government spending has been broadly stable in these decades, and the 18-country mean is slightly lower in 2015 than it was in the 1990s.

The table also shows how much the size of government in these economically advanced, stable democracies varies. Indeed, the biggest governments, France and Finland, take almost double the percentage of GDP as the bottom country, Ireland. (Ireland is a relatively small economy, which in recent decades has had periods of both spectacular growth and sharp recession (see Table 3.2), which is part of the reason that its percentage jumps around much more than any of the other countries.)

Most countries tend to be placed at a similar ranking over the decades. The top nine countries were always in the top half, and in 2015, seven of these governments had spending that was more than half of GDP. Apart from Ireland, the other bottom four countries, including the United States, were always among the smallest. The relative amounts spent on social welfare seem to be one reason for countries' rankings in size of government.

Governments' share of GDP may have stopped growing since the 1990s because of increasing voter resistance to high taxes. As would be expected, Table 5.2 shows a similar pattern for taxes as for spending. The 18-country mean grew by one-third—from 27 to 36%—between 1965 and 1990, but it has been almost constant since.

The proportions for taxes are consistently lower than for spending. Sometimes, this is because the governments are running a deficit, but it is also because government revenue is not only composed of taxes. On average, for these 18 countries, taxes comprise 85% of government revenue with the remainder coming from sales, grants and small other sources.

The fact that government spending and taxes have been a fairly stable proportion of GDP since the 1990s may indicate that there is unlikely to be radical change in the near future. For all the talk about smaller government and all the demands for greater government services, it may be that there are strong political obstacles to the size of government either expanding or shrinking too much.

Table 5.1 Government spending
Total government outlays as % of GDP

Country	1960s	1990s	2007	2009	2015
Finland	30.3	57.8	46.8	54.8	57.0
France	38.0	52.9	52.2	56.8	57.0
Denmark	33.8	57.9	49.6	56.5	54.8
Belgium	39.1	52.2	48.2	54.1	53.9
Austria	38.7	54.0	49.5	54.5	51.7
Italy	33.7	52.5	46.8	51.2	50.5
Sweden	38.9	65.3	49.7	53.1	50.2
Norway	36.7	51.5	41.4	46.1	48.8
Netherlands	40.8	51.6	42.5	48.2	45.3
Germany	37.5	47.5	42.8	47.6	44.0
United Kingdom	36.7	43.0	41.3	47.9	42.9
Canada	31.6	48.3	39.4	44.4	41.1
New Zealand	–	44.9	38.4	41.9	39.5
Japan	19.5	35.1	35.0	40.7	39.4
United States	**29.1**	**36.6**	**36.9**	**43.0**	**37.7**
Australia	24.4	36.6	34.4	38.1	37.2
Switzerland	20.3	33.8	31.0	33.1	33.9
Ireland	34.4	40.7	35.8	47.1	29.5
Mean	*33.1*	*47.9*	*42.3*	*47.7*	*45.2*

1960s = average of 1960–1973; 1990s is average of 1990–1999
Last three columns from OECD *Government at a Glance 2017*; earlier years from OECD Historical Statistics CD Rom

5.2 Government Debt and Budget Balances

Unlike the pursuit of growth and lower unemployment, the budget balance is not an end in itself, but a means to those ends.[1] Nor can it be assumed that a balanced budget is better than a budget deficit or that a budget surplus is better still. Because budgets are an instrument of economic management rather than an objective of that management, the desirable size and sign on the budget balance will be a function of where the economy happens to be in the business cycle at the time.

The judgment will be influenced also by the degree of investment (as opposed to recurrent) spending included in the budget. Most economists have no objection to borrowing to help cover the cost of public works that will deliver benefits over many years.

Operating (or recurrent) deficits are appropriate—and, indeed, helpful—when economies are entering or leaving recessions, whereas operating surpluses are desirable when economies are growing strongly. As the eminent economist John Maynard Keynes wrote, 'the boom, not the slump, is the time for austerity at the Treasury'. Following such a rule will limit the build-up of government debt over the medium term, thus 'reloading the fiscal cannon' ready for use during the next downturn.

Table 5.3 shows that in 2007 when economic conditions were fairly buoyant in most of these countries, 14 out of 18

Table 5.2 Total tax
Total taxation as % GDP

Country	1965	1990	2007	2010	2015
Denmark	29.1	44.4	46.4	44.8	45.9
France	33.6	41.0	42.4	42.0	45.2
Belgium	30.6	41.2	42.7	42.6	44.8
Finland	30.0	42.9	41.5	40.8	43.9
Austria	33.6	39.4	40.8	41.1	43.7
Italy	24.7	36.4	41.7	41.9	43.3
Sweden	31.4	49.5	45.0	43.2	43.3
Norway	29.4	40.2	42.1	42.0	38.3
Netherlands	30.9	40.2	36.0	36.1	37.4
Germany	31.6	34.8	34.9	35.0	37.1
New Zealand	23.2	36.2	33.9	30.3	33.0
United Kingdom	30.1	32.9	33.2	32.6	32.5
Canada	25.2	35.2	32.1	30.6	32.0
Japan	17.6	28.2	27.5	26.5	30.7
Australia	20.6	28.0	29.5	25.4	28.2
Switzerland	16.6	23.6	26.1	26.5	27.7
United States	**23.5**	**26.0**	**26.7**	**23.5**	**26.2**
Ireland	24.5	32.4	30.4	27.0	23.1
Mean	*27.0*	*36.3*	*36.3*	*35.1*	*36.5*

OECD *Revenue Statistics 1965–2016*

Table 5.3 Government deficits and surpluses
General government budget balance as % of GDP

Country	2007	2009	2015
Norway	18.3	12.1	7.7
Switzerland	1.9	1.9	1.9
Netherlands	5.8	−0.8	1.8
Sweden	4.3	0.3	1.3
Germany	0.9	−2.1	1.1
Austria	0.3	−3.0	0.4
Denmark	5.0	−2.5	0.2
Canada	3.0	−2.1	−0.6
Ireland	2.6	−9.1	−0.6
Australia	2.2	−2.5	−1.6
Italy	0.3	−3.7	−1.6
New Zealand	0.8	−3.6	−1.8
Belgium	0.5	−4.4	−2.0
Finland	5.5	−1.8	−2.3
France	−1.0	−5.2	−2.8
United Kingdom	−1.1	−6.9	−2.8
Japan	−2.1	−8.0	−3.6
United States	**−2.3**	**−10.6**	**−4.0**
Mean	*2.5*	*−2.9*	*−0.5*

OECD *Government at a Glance 2017*

---

[1]Paul Krugman 'Fraudulence of the Fiscal Hawks' *NYT* February 8, 2018. Ruth Marcus 'Billing the Grandkids' WP 11-6-2008.

countries had a budget surplus. In the four that had deficits, arguably, this reflected a long-term failure to balance taxes and spending. The United States, under the Bush Administration, had a deficit, in contrast to the late Clinton period of surpluses. This deficit was due to a combination of large tax cuts coupled with the very large cost of its military operations in Iraq and Afghanistan. Some economic historians said that this was the first time in American history that there was no attempt to raise taxes to pay for a military involvement.

After the dramatic recession of 2008–2009, all but three countries had budget deficits in 2009. This was partly due to taxes raising less money in a time of subdued economic activity and also due to governments seeking to stimulate economic growth.

Six years later, overall the deficits are much more modest than in 2009. However, more than half the countries still had them. The four countries which were in deficit in 2007—France, Britain, Japan and the United States—also had the biggest deficits in 2015.

The long-term consequence of always running budget deficits is a build-up of government debt. Table 5.4 shows gross government debt as a percentage of GDP. Overall, these countries had considerably greater debt in 2015 than they had had 20 years earlier. Eight countries now had debt that was greater than 100% of GDP.

When Table 5.4 is compared with Table 5.1, it is clear that there is no relationship between the size of government and the size of government debt. In particular, the Scandinavian countries and some others in northern Europe, while having relatively large governments, have also had strong financial discipline. Norway is a special case. Almost uniquely, it has shown prudence in salting away for the future part of the proceeds from its exploitation of North Sea oil deposits.

Some other European countries—notably Italy, Belgium and France—have large governments but not the tax base to support them. Japan and the United States have smaller governments, but large debts, and in Japan's case, this has become dramatically worse.

Measuring national debt brings several issues. It is most common, as here, to use the figure for gross debt. Gross debt is the key in what immediate interest repayments governments have to make. Even here there are differences about whether or not to include unfunded public pensions liabilities (They are included in Table 5.4 making the figure for the United States, Australia, Canada and Sweden greater).

Governments always have financial assets (including their own bonds) that bring income as well as debt. Table 5.5 is a figure for net debt. Norway with its far-sighted use of its North Sea bonanza heads this table, although three other governments are also in positive territory.

Each different measure is useful for particular purposes. The key point, however, is that a large government debt will impact substantially on future budget management. There is little indication that the countries with the largest debts have made serious efforts to address this.

Table 5.4 Government debt
General government gross debt as % of GDP

Country	1995	2015
Norway	37	39
Switzerland	53	45
Denmark	82	54
Sweden	77	62
Australia	59	68
Finland	63	75
Netherlands	86	78
Germany	54	79
Ireland	61	89
Austria	69	100
United Kingdom	51	112
Canada	124	116
France	67	121
United States	**83**	**125**
Belgium	140	127
Italy	121	157
Japan	92	234
Mean	78	99

No data on New Zealand
OECD *Government at a Glance* database

Table 5.5 Financial net worth of government
General government financial net worth as % GDP

Country	2005	2015
Norway	122	285
Finland	56	54
Sweden	7	28
Australia	27	14
Denmark	−9	−5
Switzerland	−13	−5
Canada	−31	−30
Netherlands	−30	−42
Germany	−48	−43
Austria	−45	−57
Ireland	−6	−58
France	−41	−76
United Kingdom	−26	−79
United States	**−46**	**−79**
Belgium	−89	−98
Japan	−65	−126
Italy	−96	−132
Mean	−20	−26

No data on New Zealand
OECD *How's Life 2017*

Table 5.6 Structure of government spending
Spending on each function as % total general government spending 2015

Country	General public service	Defence	Public order and safety	Economic affairs	Environmental protection
Australia	12.5	4.4	4.9	10.0	2.4
Austria	13.3	1.1	2.7	11.9	0.9
Belgium	15.1	1.6	3.3	12.0	1.6
Denmark	13.5	2.0	1.8	6.7	0.8
Finland	14.9	2.4	2.2	8.3	0.4
France	11.0	3.1	2.9	10.0	1.8
Germany	13.5	2.3	3.6	7.1	1.4
Ireland	13.9	1.2	3.7	11.5	1.4
Italy	16.6	2.4	3.7	8.1	1.9
Japan	10.4	2.3	3.2	9.5	2.9
Netherlands	11.1	2.5	4.0	8.8	3.2
Norway	9.6	3.1	2.2	10.5	1.8
Sweden	14.1	2.3	2.6	8.4	0.6
Switzerland	12.6	2.8	5.0	11.0	2.1
United Kingdom	10.6	5.0	4.7	7.1	1.8
United States	**13.8**	**8.8**	**5.4**	**8.7**	**0.0**
Mean	*12.9*	*3.0*	*3.5*	*9.4*	*1.6*

Country	Housing and community services	Heath	Recreation, culture and religion	Education	Social protection
Australia	1.6	19.4	2.0	14.6	28.2
Austria	0.7	15.5	2.4	9.6	42.0
Belgium	0.6	14.2	2.2	11.9	37.5
Denmark	0.4	15.6	3.2	12.8	43.0
Finland	0.7	12.6	2.6	11.0	44.9
France	1.9	14.3	2.3	9.6	43.1
Germany	0.9	16.3	2.3	9.6	43.1
Ireland	2.0	19.3	2.0	12.4	32.7
Italy	1.2	14.1	1.5	7.9	42.6
Japan	1.7	19.4	0.9	8.7	40.7
Netherlands	0.7	17.7	3.1	12.0	36.8
Norway	1.5	17.2	3.0	11.2	39.8
Sweden	1.5	13.8	2.2	13.0	41.6
Switzerland	0.6	6.5	2.4	17.2	39.9
United Kingdom	1.1	17.8	1.5	12.0	38.4
United States	**1.4**	**24.2**	**0.7**	**16.2**	**20.8**
Mean	*1.2*	*16.1*	*2.1*	*11.9*	*38.4*

No data on Canada and New Zealand
OECD *Government at a Glance 2017*

5.3 Structure of Government Spending

Tables 5.1 and 5.2 were concerned with the size of governments in relation to the total economy. This table examines the priorities in government spending irrespective of its size. It is not a guide to the absolute totals spent in particular areas, but rather their relationship to the sum of government spending. Nor of course is it a guide to how well or wisely that money is spent.

The OECD has divided areas of spending into ten functions. The largest area of spending in nearly all governments is social protection, with almost two dollars in every five that these 16 governments spend devoted to it. It includes a range of activities, supporting people in old age or suffering from disabilities, help for the unemployed, housing and community services. Eight countries devote more than 40% of government spending to social protection, with Finland the highest. By far the lowest, with just 20%, is the United States.

5.3 Structure of Government Spending

The second largest area of government spending is health. While most countries are clustered in the range between 13 and 19% of government spending, there are two extreme outliers. At the low end is Switzerland with less than half the average of the others, and at the top is the United States, the only country which devotes more government money to health than to social protection.

Other OECD data shows that between 2007 and 2015, these two, social protection and health, are the only two that have grown, while all others have decreased. This does not mean that spending in those areas has become less. It is more likely to mean that they have not grown as quickly, and so, their *share* of government spending has decreased. So the two biggest areas of government spending are the ones where the pressure for further growth is the greatest.

Some of the labels for the functions are self-explanatory, but others are not. The most obscure is the first column—the third biggest area for government spending—labelled 'general public services'. This includes legislative organs, and central government departments, foreign aid, basic research and public debt transactions. Most of the countries are clustered close to the mean, but the lowest percentage is Norway (9.6) and the highest is Italy (16.6). It is likely that public debt interest payments play a role in determining relative positions here.

The fourth priority for these governments is education, which includes all institutions from preschool to tertiary. There is a surprising spread here. Switzerland and the United States give it the highest relative priority; both double the lowest which is Italy.

The relatively non-descript area of economic affairs is the highest of the rest. It includes public money spent on transport and communications, fuel and energy and direct support to different industries from agriculture to mining to construction. All countries, including the United States, are within a few percentage points of the mean.

In terms of total spending, the remaining five areas are much less significant. Among them, defence and public order and safety are the most important and show some marked contrasts among the countries. 'Defence' refers to money spent on the military, on civil defence, foreign military aid and so forth. The United States devotes 8.8% of its government spending here, by far the highest. At the other end is Austria, with just 1.1%.

Public order and safety refer mainly to money spent on police services, fire protection, law courts and prisons. Again the United States is the leader, with 5.4% of its government expenditure. The overall mean for spending here is slightly greater than for the military, with most countries closely clustered around the mean of 3.5%.

One suspects that environmental protection, referring to such activities as waste management, pollution abatement and protection of biodiversity and landscape, might be growing, but it still remains low compared with other functions. The figure for the USA of zero does not literally mean that it spends nothing, but rather that its spending here is less than 0.5% of total government spending.

So countries vary greatly not only in the size of their governments, but in the relative priorities that government spending is directed towards. America has a distinctive pattern, quite different from some West European countries, with health, defence and public order and safety demanding more and with much less given to social protection.

Health

6.1 Health Expenditure

Health spending has been rising inexorably. In 2016, across the 18 selected countries, it consumed two and a half times the share of GDP it did in 1960. In every country, its share had at least doubled. It should be remembered that when spending on any item rises over time as a proportion of GDP, this means it is growing at a faster real rate than the overall economy. When one remembers how much these economies grew over this 56-year period, the greater growth of health spending is even more remarkable.

There is no shortage of speculation about what is driving the rise in health spending. One is the good news on greater life expectancy, reported in Tables 1.10, 6.16 and 6.17. Dieleman and his colleagues in their rigorous study of health expenditures in the United States confirmed that, excluding infants, health spending per person generally increases with age. So, future increases in demand are likely as the proportion in older age groups increases.

Health care is a very technologically dynamic area, subject to continuous research and improvements in treatment. The introduction of new goods and services—new drugs and surgical procedures, for example—allows medicine to expand into areas where effective treatments were not previously possible. These typically produce better outcomes, but often also increase costs.

Apart from the growing spending in all countries, Table 6.1 also shows dramatic differences between the countries in the amounts they spend. Until 1980, the countries were fairly closely grouped. In that year, the United States ranked equal third by this measure of health spending, and was only 1.3 points above the 18 nation mean. But then the United States grew far more quickly than any other countries. By 2000, America is 4.4 points above the mean, and by 2016, it is 6.6 points above the mean. It is almost five points above the next ranked country, Switzerland, and its 2016 share of GDP is almost double what it was in 2000, an increase not remotely matched by any other of the countries.

In few other areas is one of these countries such an outlier. It raises two questions: What produced this huge rise? And does the increased American spending produce superior services and outcomes?

Because the United States has the largest economy in the world, a greater share of its GDP translates into an even greater contrast in spending per person (Table 6.2). The average American's spending is all but three times the amount in the bottom ranking Italy, and almost $2000 more than in second-ranked Switzerland.

Table 6.3 shows a strong contrast between the rise in spending in the two periods, with the rate of increase in the later period only about 40% of the earlier one. In the earlier one, most economies were growing strongly, but then came the Great Recession of 2008–2009, and health spending was strongly affected. The contrasts between countries in each period are strong. In the second period, health spending actually contracted on a per-person basis in Italy, and growth was very small—in contrast to the earlier period—in Ireland, Denmark, New Zealand and the United Kingdom. In contrast in the countries at the top of the table—Switzerland and Australia—spending increased unabated, and in the United States, it was almost as strong as in the previous period.

By itself, an increase in health spending is neither a good nor a bad thing. Rather that spending must be related to needs and outcomes. Balancing the many demands for increased health funding against optimal health outcomes will continue to be a vexed policy issue in all the selected countries.

The data for all the tables in this chapter comes either from OECD Health at a Glance 2017, or the OECD Health Database.

Table 6.1 Health expenditure and GDP
Total spending on health as proportion of gross domestic product

Country	1960	1980	2000	2016
United States	**5.1**	**8.7**	**13.1**	**17.2**
Switzerland	4.9	7.6	10.7	12.4
Germany	4.8	8.8	10.6	11.3
France	4.2	7.4	9.3	11.0
Sweden	4.7	9.1	8.4	11.0
Japan	3.0	6.5	7.6	10.9
Canada	5.4	7.2	9.2	10.6
Netherlands	3.9	7.5	8.6	10.5
Norway	2.9	7.0	7.7	10.5
Austria	4.3	7.5	9.9	10.4
Belgium	3.4	6.4	8.7	10.4
Denmark	3.6	6.8	8.3	10.4
United Kingdom	3.9	5.7	7.3	9.7
Australia	3.8	6.3	8.3	9.6
Finland	3.9	6.4	6.7	9.3
New Zealand	4.3	6.0	8.0	9.2
Italy	3.6	7.0	8.2	8.9
Ireland	3.8	8.7	6.4	7.8
Mean	4.1	7.4	8.7	10.6

Table 6.2 Health expenditure per person
$US PPP 2016

Country	$
United States	**9892**
Switzerland	7919
Norway	6647
Germany	5551
Ireland	5528
Sweden	5488
Netherlands	5385
Austria	5227
Denmark	5205
Belgium	4840
Canada	4753
Australia	4708
France	4600
Japan	4519
United Kingdom	4192
Finland	4033
New Zealand	3590
Italy	3391
Mean	5304

Table 6.3 Growth in health expenditure
Percentage annual average growth in per capita health expenditure

Country	2003–2009	2009–2016
Switzerland	1.4	2.8
Australia	2.7	2.7
United States	**2.5**	**2.1**
Germany	2.2	1.8
Japan	2.9	1.8
Norway	2.1	1.8
Canada	3.1	1.1
Austria	2.1	1.0
Belgium	2.7	1.0
Finland	3.4	1.0
Netherlands	3.2	1.0
France	1.6	0.9
Sweden	1.8	0.9
United Kingdom	3.9	0.9
New Zealand	4.5	0.6
Denmark	3.4	0.3
Ireland	6.9	0.1
Italy	1.6	−0.3
Mean	2.9	1.2

6.2 Financing Health Care

Health care can be catastrophically expensive for an individual, and much of the need for it is unpredictable.[1] Both public funding and private insurance schemes are designed to protect people from having to choose between financial ruin and loss of health. Public funding can allow for treatment to be matched to need rather than the ability to pay. Some critics argue that government provision of health care leads to over-servicing and abuse, while others argue that for budgetary reasons governments too often are unable or unwilling to fund health at the needed levels.

There are often institutional peculiarities about how things are done in different countries, but the first two columns in Table 6.4 are essentially public schemes. It can be seen that in most countries, the bulk of funding is from the public purse. In all but three, they comprise 70% or more of total funding. However, they only sum to 50% in the United States, the only country lacking universal health insurance coverage.

All countries, however, have some mix of public and private funding. Out-of-pocket payments annoy the public

---

[1]Joseph L. Dieleman et al 'US spending on Personal Health Care and Public Health, 1996–2013' *JAMA* 2016; 316(24):2627–2646.Eric C. Schneider et al Mirror, Mirror 2017: International Comparison Reflects Flaws and Opportunities for Better US Health Care (The Commonwealth Fund 2017) (www.commonwealthfund.org). Gerard F. Anderson et al 'It's the Prices, Stupid: Why the United States is so different from other countries' *Health Affairs* V22, N3, 2003.Rodney Tiffen and Ross Gittins *How Australia Compares* (2nd ed., Melbourne, Cambridge University Press, 2009) (on maternal mortality rates).

6.2 Financing Health Care

Table 6.4 Financing health care
% total expenditure by each source, 2015

Country	Government schemes	Compulsory insurance	Out of pocket	Voluntary insurance	Other
United States	**27**	**23**	**11**	**35**	**4**
France	4	75	7	14	1
Canada	69	1	15	13	2
Ireland	70	0	15	12	3
Australia	67	0	20	10	4
Switzerland	22	42	28	7	1
Netherlands	9	71	12	6	1
Austria	31	45	18	5	2
Belgium	18	59	18	5	0
New Zealand	71	9	13	5	3
Finland	61	13	20	3	3
United Kingdom	80	0	15	3	2
Denmark	84	0	14	2	0
Italy	75	0	23	2	1
Japan	9	75	13	2	1
Germany	7	78	13	1	2
Sweden	84	0	15	1	1
Norway	74	11	14	0	0
Mean	48	28	16	7	2

Table 6.6 Out-of-pocket medical expenses
Out-of-pocket medical expenses as % household expenditure, 2015

Country	%
France	1.4
United Kingdom	1.5
Germany	1.8
New Zealand	2.1
Canada	2.2
Netherlands	2.4
Ireland	2.5
United States	**2.5**
Denmark	2.6
Japan	2.6
Norway	2.9
Austria	3.0
Finland	3.0
Australia	3.1
Italy	3.1
Belgium	3.2
Sweden	3.3
Switzerland	5.3
Mean	2.7

Table 6.5 Private health insurance
% total population 2015 and % for primary care

Country	Total	Primary
Sweden	0.1	0
United Kingdom	10.6	0
Finland	15.4	0
Switzerland	27.9	0
New Zealand	28.8	0
Germany	33.9	10.8
Austria	36.2	0
Denmark	36.5	0
Ireland	45.4	0
Australia	55.8	0
United States	**63.0**	**55.3**
Canada	67.0	0
Belgium	81.6	0
Netherlands	84.1	0
France	95.5	0
Mean	45.5	–

No data on Italy, Japan or Norway

but are beloved by economists, who believe they discourage overuse of services that otherwise appear to be 'free'. The third column of Table 6.4 shows that they comprise around one in six of healthcare dollars spent in the 18 countries. They are highest in Switzerland, and Table 6.6 shows that it is also in that country that they comprise by far the largest share of household expenditure. Indeed, one dollar of every 20 a Swiss household spends goes on medical expenses.

Voluntary insurance schemes are most important in the United States. Most OECD countries have achieved universal or near universal coverage of healthcare costs for a defined basket of services. There are many variations about what the basket comprises of, but they usually include consultations with doctors and specialists, tests and examinations, and surgical and therapeutic procedures. Dental care and pharmaceutical drugs may be partially covered, although these are the two areas most frequently financed by out-of-pocket payments.

Table 6.5 shows great variations in the percentage of people with private health insurance, but apart from Sweden in every other country, it is a substantial part of the health funding mix. The OECD distinguishes four purposes of private health insurance. They may involve cost-sharing left after basic coverage (complementary insurance), additional services (supplementary insurance) or provide faster access or larger choice to providers (duplicate insurance). In nearly all the countries, all of the private health insurance is for one or more of these three purposes.

It is only in the United States, and to a lesser extent Germany, where private health insurance serves a fourth purpose, where it plays such a large role in financing primary health care. In every other countries, primary health care such as seeing a general practitioner is solely or principally paid for through universal public insurance schemes.

Private insurance as a major means of funding has its own dynamics and incentives. Out-of-pocket payments provide constraints based on market disciplines. The universalism of

Table 6.7 Foregoing health services because of cost
% population, 2016, who forwent a medical consultation or prescribed drugs because of cost

Country	Consultation	Prescribed drugs
Germany	2.6	3.2
Sweden	3.9	6.8
United Kingdom	4.2	2.3
Italy	4.8	–
Norway	5.9	3.6
Canada	6.6	10.5
France	8.5	4.0
Netherlands	10.3	6.7
New Zealand	14.5	5.7
Australia	16.2	7.8
Switzerland	20.9	11.6
United States	**22.3**	**18.0**
Mean	*10.1*	*7.3*

No data on Austria, Belgium, Denmark, Finland, Ireland or Japan

Table 6.8 Health expenditure by type of service
2015, % each type

Country	In-patient care	Out-patient care	Long-term care	Medical goods	Collective services
United States	**17**	**47**	**5**	**14**	**16**
Canada	22	34	14	20	10
Switzerland	22	34	19	16	9
United Kingdom	29	30	18	14	9
Netherlands	26	28	25	13	9
France	33	28	11	20	8
Germany	28	28	16	20	8
Italy	32	31	10	21	6
Austria	34	28	15	17	6
Ireland	31	26	23	14	6
Belgium	30	24	24	16	5
Finland	26	38	17	15	5
Sweden	22	33	26	12	5
Denmark	26	34	24	10	5
Japan	28	29	19	20	4
Norway	29	29	28	11	3
Mean	*27*	*31*	*18*	*16*	*7*

No data on Australia or New Zealand

public funding is watched by the guardians of the public purse. It has been argued that in the American system, there is less scope for containing costs than in either of these.

The Commonwealth Fund is a pioneering American organisation, which has over many years looked at that country's health services in international perspective, and it is their research on which Table 6.7 is based. In 11 of the selected countries, it surveyed the public and also surveyed primary care physicians.

Its public survey, in Table 6.7, found that more than one in five Americans said they had skipped a medical consultation because of its cost, not only the highest among the 11 countries but double their average. Switzerland with its high out-of-pocket costs is the next highest, while the figure is less than five per cent in the four European countries with strong public systems.

The second column gives the data on the percentage of the public who say they skipped buying drugs that were prescribed for them because of the cost. The figures and rank orderings are a little different, but again the United States (and Switzerland) top the list, and again the American figure is more than double the mean for the other countries.

Just as America has uniquely high spending on health, so it has a unique mix of financing it, but one that is failing to be fully inclusive.

6.3 Healthcare Services

The previous section examined how health is financed, while this one looks at where the money goes. Table 6.8 showing the share of spending in five broad areas for just one year, 2015, is a useful starting point but with important limits.

Out-patient care includes consultations with doctors. One reason why this figure has been rising, and in-patient care declining, is that an increasing number of procedures, including surgical procedures, are conducted on a same day, out-patient basis.

In-patient care refers to money spent on hospitals, which some decades ago was rising fastest, but as we shall see, much effort has gone into containing these costs. The category of medical goods consists mainly of pharmaceuticals, which like in-patient care, was once the fastest growing area of spending. This has been less so recently, especially as patented medicines in several key areas have been replaced by generics.

It is hard to believe that in the table, long-term care is consistently demarcated because the range is so large. It is likely though that at least at the top and bottom (US) they do reflect, even if very imperfectly, real differences in practice. The high figures for the Scandinavian countries and the Netherlands do reflect their greater commitment to formal, publicly subsidised care for the aged.

The final category of collective services is not further disaggregated. It includes prevention and public health services but also, and probably more importantly, overall governance and administration of the health system. Here, the United States spends a much higher proportion, more than double the mean of the other countries.

The Commonwealth Fund study ranked the United States 10th out of 11 on administrative efficiency. Its surveys found that more US doctors reported problems related to coverage restrictions, and that both doctors and patients in America complained of what they saw as time wasting on billing and insurance claims.

6.3 Healthcare Services

Table 6.9 Consultations with doctors
Number of times on average a person consults a doctor each year

Country	2000	2015
Japan	14.4	12.7
Germany	7.7	10.0
United Kingdom	2.8	8.4
Netherlands	5.9	8.2
Canada	7.4	7.7
Australia	6.4	7.4
Belgium	7.6	6.8
Italy	6.1	6.8
Austria	6.7	6.6
France	6.9	6.3
Ireland	–	5.7
Denmark	4.2	4.4
Finland	4.3	4.3
Norway	–	4.3
United States	**3.7**	**4.0**
Switzerland	3.4	3.9
New Zealand	4.0	3.7
Sweden	2.9	2.9
Mean	*5.9*	*6.4*

Table 6.10 Hospital Beds
Number per 1000 population

Country	2000	2015
Japan	14.7	13.2
Germany	9.1	8.1
Austria	8.0	7.6
Belgium	–	6.2
France	8.0	6.1
Switzerland	6.3	4.6
Finland	7.5	4.4
Netherlands	4.8	4.2
Australia	4.0	3.8
Norway	5.0	3.8
Italy	4.7	3.2
Ireland	–	3.0
United States	**3.5**	**2.8**
New Zealand	–	2.7
Canada	3.8	2.6
United Kingdom	4.1	2.6
Denmark	–	2.5
Sweden	3.3	2.4
Mean	*6.2*	*4.7*

Table 6.11 Average length of stay in hospital
Days

Country	2000	2015
Australia	6.3	5.5
Denmark	8.1	5.5
Sweden	7.1	5.9
United States	**6.8**	**6.1**
Netherlands	9.0	6.2
Ireland	7.4	6.4
Norway	8.9	6.7
New Zealand	9.5	6.8
United Kingdom	10.7	7.0
Canada	7.2	7.4
Belgium	8.4	7.6
Italy	7.5	7.8
Switzerland	12.8	8.4
Austria	9.8	8.5
Germany	10.7	9.0
Finland	12.6	9.4
France	11.7	10.1
Japan	24.8	16.5
Mean	*10.0*	*7.8*

One factor which is not driving health costs up is people going to the doctor more often. Table 6.9 shows that this edged up between 2000 and 2015, but not by a great amount. The table shows a surprising range of variations among the countries. Sweden and the other Scandinavian countries have a low number of consultations with doctors, and this may be due to nurses and other health professionals playing a more important role in primary care there.

The outlier is Japan. The average Japanese has twice as many consultations with a doctor each year as the average person from the other countries even though Japan has a lower density of doctors than the others (Table 6.12), meaning that either Japanese doctors work long hours or their consultations are very brief.

Interestingly, as health spending continues its inexorable rise, the number of hospital beds in relation to population has been falling rather than growing. Indeed, Table 6.10 shows that the number fell by around a quarter in the first 15 years of the twenty-first century. The greatest number of hospital beds is for curative care (77%), but they also include long-term care (12%) and rehabilitation (9%). The high number of Japanese beds probably reflects that country devoting more of them to long-term care of its aging population.

The average length of stay in hospital is often regarded as an indicator of efficiency (Table 6.11). Like all such indicators, however, it is far from foolproof. If hospital stays are too short, the comfort or recovery of patients may be compromised, and shorter stays may transfer costs to other parts of the health system or onto the patients and their families. On the other hand, the reasons for shorter stays in hospital also include technological advances in anaesthetics, the development of less invasive surgical techniques, and improved pre- and post-operative treatment regimes.

In sum, the tables on hospital resources and hospital care suggest reductions rather than increases. The reasons include the vigorous efforts by governments and health authorities to limit ever-spiralling health costs. The rather limited OECD data on the percentage of health expenditure devoted to in-patient care suggest that up until 1980 hospital spending was rising more rapidly than general health spending but since then has been growing less rapidly.

In both these tables, although there are substantial national contrasts, the more fundamental fact is the shared downward trend. The reductions derive from improved procedures but there are also many complaints of inadequate resources. For all the selected countries, balancing financial pressures against the accessibility and quality of hospital care will continue to be a critical issue.

6.4 Healthcare Personnel

Just as spending on health has risen dramatically, so have the number of people employed to deliver health services.[2] Table 6.12 shows that in relation to population, there were three times as many doctors in the selected countries in 2015 as in 1960. The countries were very closely grouped in 1960, when 15 out of 18 had between 1.0 and 1.4 doctors per 1000 population. They were still fairly closely grouped in 2015. Japan, the United States and some other English-speaking countries are now at the bottom of the table, largely because their number of doctors has grown at a slower rate.

The largest group in the health labour force is nurses. Table 6.13 shows that in 2015, the countries on average had three times as many nurses as doctors. Nurses have always had a central role in hospitals, but increasingly they also play a part in primary care and home care settings. This is due to both the expansion of needed medical roles and also financial constraints, where it is cheaper (but just as effective) to have a nurse rather than a doctor perform a task.

While it is almost certain that the number of doctors will keep on increasing, both in total and in relation to their share of the population, there are some prospective issues regarding supply. Table 6.14 shows the rapidly changing age profile of doctors. Although one can only guess at what age these doctors will move into partial or total retirement, in the four European countries at the bottom of the table, it could be a problem. In the most dramatic cases, Italy and France, the proportion of doctors aged 55 and over increased two and a half fold in just 15 years.

---

[2]Joseph L. Dieleman et al 'US spending on Personal Health Care and Public Health, 1996–2013' *JAMA* 2016; 316(24):2627–2646.Eric C. Schneider et al Mirror, Mirror 2017: International Comparison Reflects Flaws and Opportunities for Better US Health Care (The Commonwealth Fund 2017) (www.commonwealthfund.org).Gerard F. Anderson et al 'It's the Prices, Stupid: Why the United States is so different from other countries' *Health Affairs* V22, N3, 2003.Rodney Tiffen and Ross Gittins *How Australia Compares* (2nd ed., Melbourne, Cambridge University Press, 2009) (on maternal mortality rates).

Table 6.12 Doctors
Practising doctors per 1000 population

Country	1960	2000	2015
Austria	1.4	3.9	5.1
Norway	1.2	3.4	4.4
Sweden	1.0	3.1	4.2
Switzerland	1.4	3.5	4.2
Germany	1.4	3.3	4.1
Italy	0.7	–	3.8
Denmark	1.2	2.9	3.7
Australia	1.1	2.5	3.5
Netherlands	1.1	3.2	3.5
France	1.0	3.3	3.3
Finland	0.6	2.5	3.2
Belgium	1.3	2.8	3.0
New Zealand	1.1	2.2	3.0
Ireland	1.0	2.2	2.9
United Kingdom	0.8	2.0	2.8
Canada	1.2	2.1	2.7
United States	**1.4**	**2.3**	**2.6**
Japan	1.0	1.9	2.4
Mean	*1.1*	*2.7*	*3.5*

Table 6.13 Nurses
Practising nurses per 1000 population

Country	2000	2015
Switzerland	12.9	18.0
Norway	–	17.3
Denmark	12.4	16.7
Finland	10.7	14.7
Germany	10.5	13.3
Ireland	12.3	11.9
Australia	–	11.5
United States	**10.2**	**11.3**
Sweden	9.9	11.1
Japan	8.4	11.0
Belgium	8.8	10.8
Netherlands	–	10.5
New Zealand	9.0	10.3
Canada	8.5	9.9
France	6.7	9.9
Austria	7.2	8.1
United Kingdom	–	7.9
Italy	–	5.4
Mean	*9.8*	*11.6*

An emerging trend in healthcare personnel is evident in Table 6.15. In 2015, one in five doctors in the selected countries trained in another country. A medical degree is an internationally portable qualification, with many degrees now being internationally recognised, or fairly easily upgraded. Not surprisingly Table 6.15 shows that the proportion of foreign-trained doctors is much higher in English-speaking countries, where graduates would have

6.4 Healthcare Personnel

Table 6.14 Doctors aged 55 and over
% of practising doctors

Country	2000	2015
United Kingdom	11	13
Ireland	–	22
Norway	23	25
Australia	23	26
Netherlands	14	26
Finland	15	27
New Zealand	16	27
Austria	16	32
Canada	24	32
Sweden	21	33
Switzerland	19	34
Japan	28	35
United States	**26**	**35**
Denmark	22	37
Belgium	24	44
Germany	32	44
France	16	47
Italy	19	53
Mean	*20*	*33*

Table 6.15 Foreign-trained doctors
Share of foreign-trained doctors 2015

Country	%
New Zealand	42
Ireland	39
Norway	38
Australia	32
Sweden	27
Switzerland	27
United Kingdom	27
United States	25
Canada	24
Finland	20
Belgium	12
France	10
Germany	10
Austria	5
Denmark	5
Netherlands	2
Italy	1
Mean	*20*

No data on Japan

also often learnt English as part of their studies. The proportion is lowest in Italy, the Netherlands and Denmark, countries whose languages are less studied elsewhere.

The Commonwealth Fund's latest report concluded that 'based on a broadly inclusive set of performance metrics, we find that US healthcare system performance ranks last among 11 high-income countries'.

In the tables in this chapter so far, the United States is often an outlier, and in seemingly paradoxical ways. Despite the fact that it has the highest health spending by a considerable margin, it has a below average number of doctors in relation to population, an average number of nurses, a below average number of public consultations with doctors and a below average number of hospital beds. It has the highest proportion of people saying they have forgone treatments because of their cost. Finally, although not by a large margin, it has the lowest life expectancy among these countries.

This all suggests more attention needs to be paid to American cost structures and the effectiveness of that country's health expenditure.

6.5 Gender and Mortality

In almost every human society, women tend to live longer than men. Many have pondered whether there is a biological basis for this, for example, whether the female body's needs to accommodate pregnancy and breastfeeding have other advantages leading to greater longevity.[3] Biological reasons almost certainly have some relevance, but it is hard, and increasingly difficult, to disentangle them from social factors.

The importance of social factors is suggested by how much the gap in life expectancy between the sexes jumps around at different times and between different societies. In every one of the 18 countries, female life expectancy at birth is greater than male life expectancy (Tables 6.16 and 6.17). The mean difference is four and a half years, with the smallest being in the Netherlands (3.3 years), New Zealand (3.5) and the United Kingdom (3.6). The gap is largest in France and Japan (both 6.3 years), which are also the two countries where female life expectancy is highest.

Tables 6.18 and 6.19 give the 12 major causes of death among males and females. The commonalities probably outweigh the differences, but males are more likely to die from ischaemic heart disease, lung cancer, accidents and intentional self-harm.

Each of these would seem to relate primarily to social factors: Males are more likely to smoke tobacco, which is related to deaths from lung cancer and ischaemic heart disease. They tend to drink more alcohol, related to deaths from heart disease and to be associated with deaths in car

---

[3]Anne Case and Angus Deaton 'Rising morbidity and mortality in midlife among white non-Hispanic Americans in the twenty first century' *PNAS* December 8, 2015 Vol 12 No 49, 15078–15083. Thomas R. Frieden 'US life expectancy is dropping. Here's how to fix it' *WP* January 11, 2018. Jessica Y Ho and Arun S Hendi 'Recent trends in life expectancy across high income countries: retrospective observational study' *British Medical Journal*, 2018; 362: k2562.

Table 6.16 Male life expectancy
Expected lifespan at birth, years

Country	1970	2015
Japan	69.3	80.8
Switzerland	70.0	80.8
Norway	71.2	80.5
Australia	67.4	80.4
Sweden	72.3	80.4
Italy	69.0	80.3
Netherlands	70.8	79.9
New Zealand	68.5	79.9
Canada	69.3	79.6
Ireland	68.8	79.6
France	68.4	79.2
United Kingdom	68.7	79.2
Austria	66.5	78.8
Denmark	70.7	78.8
Belgium	67.9	78.7
Finland	66.5	78.7
Germany	67.5	78.3
United States	**67.1**	**76.3**
Mean	*68.9*	*79.5*

Table 6.17 Female life expectancy
Expected lifespan at birth, years

Country	1970	2015
Japan	74.7	87.1
France	75.9	85.5
Switzerland	76.2	85.1
Italy	74.9	84.9
Australia	74.2	84.5
Finland	75.0	84.4
Norway	77.5	84.2
Sweden	77.3	84.1
Canada	76.4	83.8
Austria	73.5	83.7
Belgium	74.2	83.4
Ireland	73.5	83.4
New Zealand	74.5	83.4
Netherlands	76.5	83.2
Germany	73.6	83.1
United Kingdom	75.0	82.8
Denmark	75.9	82.7
United States	**74.7**	**81.2**
Mean	*75.2*	*83.9*

Table 6.18 Major causes of death among males
Causes of death among males, all OECD countries, 2015

Causes of death	% deaths
Ischaemic heart diseases	13.0
Lung cancer	7.0
Stroke	6.0
Accidents	4.8
Chronic obstructive pulmonary diseases	4.1
Diabetes	3.1
Colorectal cancer	2.9
Prostate cancer	2.5
Intentional self-harm	2.2
Dementia	2.1
Alzheimer's disease	1.3
Parkinson's disease	0.9
All other	50.0

Table 6.19 Major causes of death among females
Causes of death among females, all OECD countries, 2015

Cause of death	% deaths
Ischaemic heart diseases	11.0
Stroke	8.2
Dementia	4.5
Lung cancer	3.9
Chronic obstructive pulmonary diseases	3.4
Diabetes	3.4
Breast cancer	3.2
Accidents	3.1
Alzheimer's disease	3.0
Colorectal cancer	2.5
Intentional self-harm	0.8
Parkinson's disease	0.7
All other	53.0

accidents and assaults. Males' higher suicide rate almost certainly also owes more to social than biological factors.

A more subtle difference is that women tend to be more attentive to their bodies, and are more likely to consult doctors. Dieleman and his colleagues found that in America, females spent 24.6% more than males on health care in 2013.

On the whole, however, especially in contemporary societies, the most important factors are equally relevant to both sexes. Obesity rates and deaths from drug overdoses tend to be equal destroyers of life opportunities, for example.

As we saw in Table 1.10, life expectancy for both sexes greatly increased over the twentieth century, so that the 18-nation mean in 2015 was 31 years longer than in 1900. Both sexes increased life expectancy between 1970 and 2015, by 10.6 years on average for men (Table 6.16) and 8.7 years for women (Table 6.17). The commonality in the movements far outweighs the differences.

One historical source of premature mortality among females has become much less frequent. Giving birth has become much safer. As late as 1960, the average across these countries was 64 maternal deaths for every 100,000 live births, which by 2000 was down to less than one-tenth that number, at 5.6 deaths per 100,000 live births.

While consistently rising life expectancy has become the expectation, in recent years, the trend has sometimes faltered. Ho and Hendi found that in 11 of the 18 countries in

2014–15, it slightly decreased. In the great bulk of the countries, there was a robust recovery in 2015–16, but less so in the United Kingdom and especially the United States. Perhaps curiously, Case and Deaton pointed to how the worsening mortality and morbidity rates in America were mainly affecting non-Hispanic whites.

In late 2018, the United States Center for Disease Control published figures showing that American life expectancy had had a dip of 0.1 years in each of the last three years. The leading cause was what they call deaths from unintentional injuries, with drug overdoses account for just under half of these deaths. The opioid crisis is centrally implicated. The rate of drug overdose deaths involving synthetic opioids, other than methadone, has more than tripled since 1999. In the United States, suicide is the tenth leading cause of death, and the CDC reports the number of suicides has also been increasing. Both these trends towards premature deaths are —at least so far—much more pronounced in the United States than the other selected democracies.

It remains to be seen whether this is a temporary setback in the trend towards longer life expectancy or a turning point with long-term implications.

6.6 Mortality and Causes of Death

Table 6.20 gives a good insight into contemporary causes of mortality. The first column is the mortality rate for an age-standardised population. Because Japan has the highest life expectancy it has the lowest mortality rate in the table. The other columns all give the percentages that each cause of death contributes to that country's mortality. (It should be remembered that because the countries have different mortality rates, the same percentage involves a different number of people dying from that cause. For example, five countries all have 11% of deaths associated with dementia, but this means 90 people in an age-standardised population of 100,000 people in America, and 72 in Australia.)

The two largest causes, by far, are circulatory system diseases and cancer. These are the highest overall, and they are also the two highest in every single country. The other causes show far more variation between countries, and the reasons for the differences are far from obvious.

Deaths from external causes include suicide, assault and accidents, which can include drownings, poisonings, falls and traffic accidents. It is the smallest of all the listed causes. However, whereas most deaths from illness are more prevalent among older people, death from external causes is no respecter of age. External causes of death are more important than the percentage in the table because they are strongly associated with premature and untimely death. The range is not great, but the United States has the highest rate.

While Table 6.20 is a snapshot, the other three tables on the page show trends, and all are strongly positive. We have a particularly long run of data on infant mortality, and Table 6.21 records the remarkable fall in infant mortality over the course of the twentieth century. The infant mortality rate is the number of babies who die aged less than one year per 1000 live births during the same year.

Table 6.20 Mortality and causes of death
Mortality rate for 100,000 age-standardised population 2015
% for major causes

Country	All causes	Dementia	Circulatory system	Respiratory system	External causes	Cancer	All other
Japan	583	3	26	15	7	31	18
Australia	654	11	29	9	7	29	15
Switzerland	674	11	33	6	6	27	16
Canada	683	10	27	9	7	31	16
France	686	9	24	6	7	30	23
Italy	709	6	36	7	4	30	16
Norway	718	10	28	9	7	28	18
New Zealand	727	9	35	9	6	30	12
Sweden	728	11	34	7	6	27	15
Austria	736	4	41	5	6	28	16
Belgium	746	8	28	9	7	28	20
Netherlands	760	12	27	9	5	31	17
Finland	761	18	37	3	7	23	11
Germany	773	6	38	7	4	27	18
United Kingdom	778	11	28	14	4	30	14
Denmark	794	9	24	11	4	30	23
Ireland	801	8	33	12	5	29	12
United States	**822**	**11**	**31**	**10**	**8**	**23**	**17**
Mean	*730*	*9*	*31*	*9*	*6*	*28*	*16*

Table 6.21 Infant mortality
Deaths per 1000 live births

Country	1900	1950	2000	2015
Finland	153	44	3.8	1.6
Japan	155	60	3.2	1.9
Norway	91	28	3.8	2.3
Sweden	99	21	3.4	2.3
Austria	231	66	4.8	2.6
Germany	229	60	4.4	2.8
Denmark	128	31	5.3	2.9
Italy	174	64	4.5	2.9
Switzerland	150	31	4.9	3.1
Australia	83	25	5.2	3.2
United Kingdom	148	31	5.6	3.2
Belgium	172	53	4.8	3.4
Ireland	109	45	6.2	3.4
France	162	52	4.6	3.7
Netherlands	155	25	5.1	3.9
New Zealand	62	28	5.8	4.0
United States	**142**	**29**	**6.9**	**4.4**
Canada	–	41	5.3	4.7
Mean	*144*	*41*	*4.8*	*3.1*

Table 6.22 Deaths from Ischaemic heart disease
Deaths per 100,000 age-standardised population

Country	1990	2015
Japan	57	34
France	89	39
Netherlands	182	46
Belgium	120	54
Denmark	311	60
Norway	264	72
Switzerland	161	78
Italy	135	84
Australia	271	85
Canada	234	93
Sweden	272	95
United Kingdom	297	98
Germany	222	106
United States	**255**	**113**
Ireland	335	127
New Zealand	291	129
Austria	225	131
Finland	340	147
Mean	*226*	*88*

Its reduction is one important reason life expectancy has increased so much over the last century and a bit. In round figures, in 1900 one in seven babies from the selected countries died before their first birthday. By 2000, the figure was one in 200. A notable feature is the process of convergence over the century. Whereas in 1900 mortality rates ranged from New Zealand's 62 to Austria's 231, and by 2000, the range from best to worst was a tiny 3.2 to 6.9.

Between 2000 and 2015, improvement continued, so that the 2015 average was two-thirds the 2000 figure. Although the countries are closely grouped, the United States and Canada now come at the bottom of the table.

A major reason for increasing life expectancy in the first part of the twentieth century was the reduction of premature deaths due to infectious diseases. In recent decades, the more important contributor has been older people living to greater ages. The single biggest contributor to this success is the reduction of people dying from circulatory diseases, and/or dying from them at older ages. Table 6.22 shows that deaths from ischaemic heart disease (IHD) in 2015 were less than 40% of what they had been in 1990 in the 18 selected countries, while Table 6.23 shows that deaths from cerebrovascular diseases declined by slightly less.

Circulatory or cardiovascular disease covers all diseases and conditions involving the heart and blood vessels. IHD is caused by the accumulation of fatty deposits lining the inner wall of a coronary artery, restricting blood flow to the heart. IHD alone was responsible for nearly 12% of all deaths in OECD countries in 2015.

The first main feature of Table 6.22 is the strength and commonality of the trend. Every country shows a marked decline in the mortality rate from IHD. The second is that there is still substantial variation between them. IHD is striking at four times the rate in Finland as it is in Japan. The United States has shared in the improvement, but is still worse than average on this measure.

Cerebrovascular disease refers to a group of diseases that relate to problems with the blood vessels that supply the brain. One major manifestation is stroke, which can introduce disability burdens short of death. Like the previous table, the first notable feature of Table 6.23 is the strong

Table 6.23 Deaths from cerebrovascular diseases
Deaths per 100,000 age-standardised population

Country	1990	2015
Canada	79	36
France	87	36
Switzerland	93	37
United States	**76**	**42**
Austria	159	45
Australia	113	46
Belgium	112	47
Norway	135	47
Germany	139	48
Sweden	110	48
Netherlands	106	50
Denmark	111	51
Japan	139	51
United Kingdom	137	53
Ireland	132	55
Finland	152	63
New Zealand	119	64
Italy	146	67
Mean	*119*	*49*

universal trend to improvement. Mortality rates from cerebrovascular diseases are much more closely grouped than from IHD, and with somewhat different rankings. Here, the United States does better than average.

These three tables are all testimony to dramatic improvements. Hopefully, each will continue improving, although future movements are likely to be on a more modest scale.

6.7 Cancer

While the previous section detailed the dramatic successes in reducing the mortality rates from circulatory diseases, the tale of deaths from cancer is one of substantial but much more modest success. Table 6.24 shows that the standardised death rate from cancer in 2015 was just under 80% what it had been in 1990, less than half the improvement shown in relation to ischaemic heart disease in Table 6.22.

All the countries improved but at rather different rates and the rankings in 2015 were different from in 1990. Finland, the worst performer in IHD, is the best on cancer. Denmark, the worst on cancer, was a high performer on IHD. The United States is above average and showed one of the best improvements over the period. The rankings in Table 6.24 show some similarity to the rankings for the year 2000 (rather than 2015) for smoking rates in Table 6.27.

Cancers are a diverse group of diseases that all involve the growth and spread of abnormal cells which invade and destroy surrounding tissue. Analysts now distinguish more than 100 types. A small number, perhaps five to ten per cent are genetic, but the rest stem from environmental and behavioural causes.

Different cancers have very different profiles. Prevention has been more successful with some than others, while early detection and better treatment regimes now mean there is a much higher survival rate in most forms. The worst prognoses are for lung cancer and pancreatic cancer. Lung cancer accounts for 22% of cancer-related deaths among men and 16% for women. The male rate has declined while the female rate hasn't, probably reflecting the sharper decline in smoking among men.

The other two tables on this page show the survival rates for two major cancers. Breast cancer is the second most common cause of cancer mortality in women, although survival rates have increased due to earlier diagnosis and better treatment. One in nine women will have breast cancer at some point in their life. Risk factors include age, a family history of breast cancer, genetic predisposition, oestrogen replacement therapy and lifestyle factors including obesity, physical activity, diet and alcohol consumption.

Table 6.25 shows that survival rates for breast cancer were already high early in the twenty-first century and improved somewhat further in the next decade. The countries are closely grouped, all with five-year survival rates between 82 and 90%, and 16 between 86 and 90%, with the United States and Australia at the top.

Table 6.24 Deaths from cancer
Rate for 100,000 age-standardised population

Country	1990	2015
Finland	224	172
Switzerland	254	176
Japan	208	177
Sweden	215	185
Australia	241	187
United States	**250**	**188**
France	254	196
Austria	261	197
Norway	231	198
Belgium	278	199
Germany	257	201
Italy	259	205
Canada	258	207
New Zealand	271	210
United Kingdom	281	222
Netherlands	280	224
Ireland	280	227
Denmark	293	233
Mean	*255*	*200*

Table 6.25 Breast cancer survival rates
Five-year survival %

Country	2000–2004	2010–2014
United States	**89**	**90**
Australia	87	90
Finland	87	89
Japan	86	89
Sweden	86	89
Canada	86	88
New Zealand	83	88
Norway	85	88
France	87	87
Netherlands	84	87
Belgium	85	86
Denmark	80	86
Germany	84	86
Italy	84	86
Switzerland	84	86
United Kingdom	80	86
Austria	82	85
Ireland	77	82
Mean	*84*	*87*

Table 6.26 Colon cancer survival rate
Five-year survival rate

Country	2000–2004	2010–2014
Australia	64	71
Belgium	64	68
Japan	63	68
Canada	62	67
Norway	60	67
Switzerland	63	67
Finland	61	65
Germany	62	65
Sweden	60	65
United States	**65**	**65**
Austria	61	64
France	61	64
Italy	59	64
New Zealand	61	64
Netherlands	58	63
Denmark	52	62
Ireland	53	61
United Kingdom	52	60
Mean	*60*	*65*

Colorectal cancer is the third most commonly diagnosed form of cancer for men after prostate and lung cancers and the second most common after breast cancer for women. Its incidence is higher for men than women. Risk factors include age, family history of colorectal cancer or polyps and lifestyle factors such as a diet high in fat and low in fibre, lack of physical activity, obesity, and tobacco and alcohol consumption.

Table 6.26 gives the five-year survival rates for colon cancer. Generally, rectal cancer is more difficult to cure than colon cancer due to a higher probability of spreading to other tissue, recurrence and post-operative complications. The survival rate for colon cancer is not as high as for breast cancer, although it did rise in the ten-year period, so that now on average around two in three people diagnosed with colon cancer survive for at least five years. Australia leads the way here, with the United States right on the mean, and Britain and Ireland trailing the field.

The fight to reduce the death toll from cancer is not a single struggle. Prevention, earlier detection and improved treatments are all part, and these take different forms with different cancers.

6.8 Non-medical Determinants of Health

The first scientific articles drawing a link between smoking and health problems appeared around 1950.[4] In the following decades, an overwhelming array of evidence linked smoking to cancer, heart disease, and many lesser medical problems, and these gradually penetrated into the public consciousness. Public health bodies in many countries said that smoking was the largest single preventable cause of premature death.

Given the strength of the evidence and the magnitude of the problems, perhaps the amazing thing is how tobacco consumption has persisted. However, its downward trend is now clear. In Table 6.27, the proportion of the adult population smoking daily halved in 35 years in the 18 democracies overall. In the countries at the top of the table, including the United States, the figure in 2015 was one-third what it was in 1980. (The table does not look at how many cigarettes people smoke nor at the numbers who may be more occasional smokers.)

There are important variations between countries. OECD historical data suggests that smoking grew most in the English-speaking countries in the decades after World War II, but it was also in those countries that the reduction in smoking began soonest, most starting to trend down from some time in the 1960s. Except for Ireland, the other five are all in the top seven places in the table.

Some Scandinavian countries responded more slowly, with the 2000 rates being particularly high in Norway and Denmark, but all have now declined substantially, as has Japan. At the bottom of the table are several European countries where one in five or more adults still smoke daily. Indeed in Austria, there was no reduction between 2000 and 2015. It is an interesting issue about why there has been so little behavioural change in those countries despite the strong public health warnings.

Table 6.27 Smoking
% adult population smoking daily

Country	1980	2000	2015
Sweden	32	19	11
United States	**34**	**19**	**11**
Australia	36	20	12
Norway	36	32	12
Canada	33	22	14
New Zealand	35	25	14
United Kingdom	40	27	16
Denmark	51	31	17
Finland	26	23	17
Japan	42	27	18
Belgium	35	24	19
Ireland	37	27	19
Netherlands	43	32	19
Italy	36	24	20
Switzerland	37	26	20
Germany	35	25	21
France	31	27	22
Austria	29	24	24
Mean	*36*	*25*	*17*

---

[4] John Bacon "'We are losing too many Americans': Suicides, drug overdoses rise as US life expectancy drops" *USA Today*, November 29, 2018.

6.8 Non-medical Determinants of Health

Table 6.28 Obesity
% adults (some countries measured, some self-reported) with BMI 30+

Country	2000	2015
Japan	3	4
Italy	9	10
Switzerland	7	10
Norway	7	12
Sweden	9	12
Netherlands	10	13
Austria	9	15
Denmark	10	15
France	9	17
Belgium	12	19
Ireland	11	23
Germany	12	24
Finland	11	25
Canada	15	26
United Kingdom	21	27
Australia	21	28
New Zealand	17	32
United States	**31**	**38**
Mean	12	19

Table 6.29 Diabetes
% adult population with Type 1 or Type 2 diabetes 2015

Country	2015
Ireland	4.4
Sweden	4.7
United Kingdom	4.7
Australia	5.1
Belgium	5.1
Italy	5.1
France	5.3
Netherlands	5.5
Japan	5.7
Finland	6.0
Norway	6.0
Switzerland	6.1
Austria	6.9
Denmark	7.2
New Zealand	7.3
Canada	7.4
Germany	7.4
United States	**10.8**
Mean	6.2

Even in 2017, the OECD estimated that across its member countries, if smoking rates and alcohol consumption were halved, life expectancies would rise by 13 months.

The figures on obesity provide a stark contrast to those on tobacco. There is no trend to improvement, rather the reverse. In Table 6.28, the five English-speaking countries are at the bottom, with the United States having the highest rate. The American figure is double the mean for the 18 selected countries, 38:19.

Obesity is defined as a body mass index (BMI) of 30 or more. The BMI is the ratio of a person's weight (in kilograms) to the square of their height (in metres). A person six feet tall (1.83 m) becomes defined as obese when they weigh 100 kg or more. The term overweight is defined as having a BMI from 25 to less than 30.

The table shows that in every single country, the percentage of obese adults increased in those 15 years, several spectacularly so, so that the 18 nation mean rose by over 50%. Japan is still by far the country with the lowest proportion of obese people.

There has been much speculation about the causes of this rapid change. While individual differences are due to a mix of genetic and environmental factors, the trend towards greater proportions of the population becoming obese must be found in behavioural changes, and by looking both at patterns of activity and diet.

While there is doubt about all the causes of increasing obesity, there is none about the negative health consequences it brings. Excess body weight is a major risk factor for many health problems including coronary heart disease, Type 2 diabetes, respiratory disease and some cancers.

Table 6.29 shows the proportion of the population suffering from diabetes. Diabetes is a chronic disease characterised by high levels of glucose in the blood, and itself associated with a range of other serious health problems.

The United States is clearly the worst affected among the selected countries. This may be due partly to better detection than just higher incidence: The International Diabetes Federation estimates that a further 33 million adults have undiagnosed diabetes in the OECD countries.

In an innovative and exhaustive study, Joseph L. Dieleman and his colleagues examined all categories of health spending in the United States between 1996 and 2013. They discovered that the costliest illness in 2013 was diabetes (ahead even of heart disease). More than half the cost was in prescription drugs, and spending on diabetes increased by 6.1% per year over the period.

Obesity, clearly, is one of the most important public health challenges in the United States and many other countries for the foreseeable future.

Education

7.1 Educational Attainment

In a complex sophisticated economy, education is a key both to individual prospects and to national economic performance.[1] Before World War II, most people finished their schooling at the junior secondary level or below. In the United States in 1940, of the population aged 25 and above, just 24% had finished four or more years of high school. In 2017, for the first time, 90% of the adult population had completed senior high school or a higher qualification.

Although each educational system grew up with its own assumptions and methods, international bodies have devoted considerable attention to standardising the types of institutions and qualifications in different countries. While they are broadly comparable, one should not assume that someone graduating from secondary school in one country has exactly the same skills as a graduate from another country or equally that a high school graduate from 1959 has the same skills as one in 2019.

The tables in this section show just how quickly educational expectations have been changing. Tables 7.1 and 7.2 —based as they are on the great majority of the adult population, whose composition only changes very marginally from year to year–are by their nature slow to reflect the change. However, the contrast in the educational attainments of the adult population between 2000 and 2017 shows how rapidly change has been occurring. The 18-nation mean for the percentage of tertiary educated in the adult population rose from 28 to 41, while those whose highest qualification is lower secondary or less dropped from 28 to 17%.

Canada topped the number of tertiary-educated adults in both years, with the United States dropping behind Japan to come in third in 2017. The bottom five places in both years were held by the same countries, although their order changes. Italy is bottom both times, and in 2017, by a considerable margin—now with less than half the number of tertiary-educated adults as the mean of the other countries.

Germany, Austria and the Netherlands, for whatever reason, seem to be less encouraging of their young people going on to tertiary education.

Table 7.3 shows the same trend towards increasing educational attainments more sharply. Looking only at young adults, aged between 25 and 34, over the 26 years from 1991 to 2017, the mean for the 18 nations as a whole more than doubled, up from 22 to 47%. Italy, Germany and Austria again are near the bottom of the table, with Canada and Japan again at the top.

The change has been faster in some countries than others. The average rise was by 25 percentage points, but Canada, Ireland and Britain all rose by 30 or more, while Australia and Switzerland rose by 29. Finland had the smallest rise, by just eight points, and Germany only rose by 11.

In 1991, the United States was one of the top three countries, but its more modest growth in the proportion of tertiary graduates means that it has dropped back to the middle of the field, just one point above the 18-nation mean.

So within the context of a universal trend towards increasing educational attainments, there have been somewhat contrasting trajectories.

Table 7.4 shows a central reason why the trend will continue: the strong association between educational attainment and future income. Taking upper secondary education, as the norm (100) against which to measure others in each country, the table shows that across the 18 countries, those with only a lesser qualification earn four-fifths as much, while those with a bachelor's degree earn one-third more. Moreover, the general pattern holds true in every country (except strangely Austria among graduates). Moreover, a higher degree, a masters or doctorate, is associated with still higher incomes.

To a large extent, the differences between countries in this table mirror their degree of income inequality more generally (see Table 8.1). Looking only at the first two columns, Finland has the smallest spread, and over all three columns, Sweden does. The United States is at the other end of the spectrum: those with less education have the lowest relative incomes; and those with bachelor and higher degrees have the highest relative incomes among the 18 democracies.

---

[1]Also draws on Erik Schmidt 'For the First Time, 90 percent completed High School or More' America Counts, July 31, 2018, US Census Bureau.

Table 7.1 Educational Attainment of adult population
% of those aged 25–64 in each category 2017

Country	Primary/ lower secondary	Upper secondary	Tertiary
Canada	9	35	57
Japan	0	49	51
United States	**10**	**44**	**47**
Australia	19	35	46
Ireland	18	36	46
United Kingdom	19	34	46
Finland	11	44	45
Norway	17	39	43
Sweden	15	41	43
Switzerland	12	45	43
Belgium	23	37	40
Denmark	19	42	40
New Zealand	21	41	38
Netherlands	22	41	37
France	22	43	35
Austria	15	53	32
Germany	14	58	29
Italy	38	42	18
Mean	*17*	*42*	*41*

Upper secondary includes post-secondary, non-tertiary qualifications
The Japanese figures do not disaggregate to lower levels
OECD Educational Database

Table 7.2 Educational attainment of the adult population 2000
% of those aged 25–64 in each category 2000

Country	Primary/ lower secondary	Upper secondary	Tertiary
Canada	18	40	42
United States	**12**	**50**	**37**
Ireland	42	22	36
Japan	17	49	34
Sweden	19	49	32
Finland	26	42	32
New Zealand	24	46	29
Australia	41	30	29
Norway	15	57	28
Denmark	20	54	27
Belgium	42	31	27
United Kingdom	37	37	26
Switzerland	13	62	25
Germany	17	59	23
France	36	41	23
Netherlands	45	32	22
Austria	24	62	14
Italy	57	33	10
Mean	*28*	*44*	*28*

OECD Education at a Glance 2003

Table 7.3 Young adults with tertiary qualifications
% of 25–34-year-olds in each year with tertiary qualifications

Country	1991	2000	2007	2017
Canada	33	48	56	61
Japan	–	47	54	60
Ireland	20	30	44	53
Australia	23	31	41	52
United Kingdom	19	27	43	52
Switzerland	21	26	35	50
Norway	27	35	43	48
United States	**30**	**38**	**40**	**48**
Denmark	19	29	36	47
Netherlands	22	27	37	47
Sweden	27	34	40	47
Belgium	27	36	41	46
France	20	32	41	44
New Zealand	23	27		44
Finland	33	38	39	41
Austria	8	15	31	40
Germany	20	22	23	31
Italy	7	10	19	27
Mean	*22*	*31*	*39*	*47*

OECD Education at a Glance 2018

Table 7.4 Relative earnings of workers by educational attainment
Earnings of (full-time and part-time) workers, where upper secondary education earnings = 100, 2016

Country	Lower secondary or below	Tertiary bachelors	Tertiary higher degree
United States	**74**	**169**	**233**
France	80	142	210
Ireland	80	167	208
Canada	83	152	186
Netherlands	82	132	184
Germany	76	165	183
Austria	69	93	174
United Kingdom	76	148	172
Finland	98	125	169
Switzerland	78	141	167
Denmark	80	111	166
Belgium	82	126	165
Norway	76	114	156
New Zealand	87	130	154
Australia	87	135	152
Japan	78	152	–
Italy	78	138	138
Sweden	82	105	135
Mean	*80*	*136*	*174*

Japanese figure is for all tertiary qualified employees
OECD Education at a Glance 2018

7.2 Education Spending

Health and education present strongly contrasting trends in expenditure.[2] Total health spending in 2015 was exactly double the share of GDP as education spending (Tables 6.1 and 7.5). Health's share of GDP has been steadily increasing, up from 8.7 to 10.6% over 16 years, while education's has fallen very slightly from 5.7 to 5.3%.

It should be remembered that GDP was itself growing in these countries most of the time, so a declining figure does not normally mean decreased expenditure but usually that education spending has not kept pace with increased national income. This is especially pertinent to Ireland, whose sharp reduction in education's share was more a result of its recent rapid economic growth than of cutbacks in education spending.

Several European countries are near the bottom of the table, most notably Italy, Germany, Austria and France, and this aligns with their low position in Table 7.1. The English-speaking countries are all in the top half of the table, including the United States, which is among the top third in its education spending.

Education expenditure's relative lack of growth may surprise many. In the last section, we saw how much educational attainments have risen. In addition, the constant change in knowledge-based economies means that expectations surrounding education keep growing. One reason why educational expenditure as a share of GDP has not been increasing more is that the school-aged cohort as a proportion of the total population is decreasing with the ageing of society. But perhaps the health-spending lobbies also tend to be stronger than the educational lobbies.

In all the selected democracies, education is primarily a public responsibility, and in most of them, it is overwhelmingly so. Overall, public expenditure on education as a share of GDP dropped substantially between 2005 and 2015 (Table 7.6). Top-ranking Norway was the only country where it increased. Several others, including Japan, had sharp declines, which at least partly reflect more general budgetary constraints. The United States declined more than most, and it is now in the bottom third of these countries in its public education spending.

Table 7.7 shows that in the countries overall more than four in every five dollars spent on education come from the public purse. This proportion declined somewhat over the 20 years from 2005 to 2015. Interestingly, in most of the countries where the public share was greatest, it dropped the least. In the top five countries in the table, the public share is still 94% plus. Between 2005 and 2015, the public share dropped most sharply in Britain. Australia and the United States have the smallest public share.

The contrast between public share of total educational expenditure at primary and secondary levels compared with tertiary is sharp (Table 7.8). More than 90% of spending at the school level is done by governments, including in the

Table 7.5 Total education spending
Total education expenditure as a % of GDP

Country	1995	2005	2015
Denmark	6.2	7.4	–
Norway	6.3	5.7	6.4
New Zealand	4.8	6.7	6.3
United Kingdom	5.5	6.2	6.2
Switzerland	6.0	6.1	–
United States	**6.6**	**7.1**	**6.1**
Canada	7.0	6.2	6.0
Australia	5.5	5.8	5.9
Belgium	5.8	6.0	5.7
Finland	6.3	6.0	5.7
Netherlands	4.8	5.0	5.4
Sweden	6.2	6.4	5.3
France	6.2	6.0	5.2
Austria	6.1	5.5	4.9
Germany	5.4	5.1	4.2
Japan	4.7	4.9	4.1
Italy	4.7	4.7	3.9
Ireland	5.2	4.6	3.5
Mean	5.7	5.9	5.3

No 2015 data on Denmark or Switzerland, ordered as if their 2005 figure was still current
OECD Education at a Glance 2018

Table 7.6 Public expenditure on education
Public expenditure on education as a % of GDP

Country	2005	2015
Norway	5.7	6.3
Finland	5.9	5.6
Belgium	5.8	5.4
Sweden	6.2	5.0
New Zealand	5.2	4.7
Austria	5.2	4.6
France	5.6	4.5
Switzerland	5.6	4.5
Canada	4.7	4.4
Netherlands	4.6	4.3
United Kingdom	5.0	4.2
United States	**4.8**	**4.1**
Australia	4.3	4.0
Germany	4.2	3.6
Italy	4.3	3.3
Ireland	4.3	3.1
Japan	3.4	2.9
Mean	5.0	4.4

No 2015 data on Denmark
OECD Education at a Glance 2018

---

[2] Also draws on data reported in Rodney Tiffen and Ross Gittins *How Australia Compares* (2nd ed, Cambridge University Press, 2009).

Table 7.7 Public share of education spending
Public expenditure as % of total education expenditure

Country	1995	2005	2015
Finland	98	98	98
Norway	94	98	98
Sweden	98	97	96
Belgium	92	94	95
Austria	93	91	94
Ireland	90	94	89
France	92	91	88
Italy	91	91	87
Germany	82	82	86
Netherlands	90	91	81
New Zealand	–	78	75
Canada	81	76	73
Japan	76	69	73
United Kingdom	87	80	69
Australia	79	73	67
United States	**71**	**67**	**67**
Mean	*88*	*86*	*83*

No data on Switzerland or Denmark
OECD Education at a Glance 2018

Table 7.8 Public and private shares and educational levels
Public expenditure as % of total expenditure at each level, 2015

Country	Primary and secondary	Tertiary
Finland	99	97
Norway	99	96
Austria	95	94
Sweden	100	89
Belgium	97	86
Germany	87	85
France	91	80
Ireland	95	74
Netherlands	88	71
Italy	95	65
New Zealand	83	52
Canada	90	49
Australia	81	38
United States	**91**	**35**
Japan	92	32
United Kingdom	87	29
Mean	*92*	*67*

No data on Denmark or Switzerland
OECD Education at a Glance 2018

United States. In seven countries, it is 95% or more. In contrast, just two in every three dollars on tertiary education comes from the public sector and the spread among the countries is much greater. In three countries, it is over 90%, while in five it is less than half. The English-speaking countries and Japan are clustered at the bottom of the table. In 1995, the United States was the lowest ranking of these countries, its shares then being 37%, while the 18-country mean was 78%. The country where cost shifting has changed most radically is Britain. In 1995, 80% of tertiary education costs were borne by the government, but by 2015, this had dropped to 29%, placing it at the bottom of the table.

7.3 Maths, Science and Reading Skills

For a long time, comparative studies in education had a vacuum at their heart. Over the years, scholars had carefully built-up data on comparative educational expenditures, levels of attainment, and participation in educational institutions. But there was no solid comparative data on the end product of the educational process—the skills that students took into their adult working and social life. In recent years, some major projects have addressed this gap.

The Programme for International Student Assessment (PISA), an initiative of the OECD, is the most important and ambitious attempt so far to comparatively chart students' literacy skills. PISA surveys 15-year-old students, an age at which students in most of the participating countries are nearing the end of their compulsory schooling, but have not yet specialised too much in particular disciplines.

The tests gauge how well students are able to use their knowledge and skills to meet real-life opportunities and challenges, rather than assessing their mastery of a specific curriculum. PISA says it uses 'the term "literacy" to encompass [a] broad range of competencies relevant to coping with adult life in today's rapidly changing societies'. This emphasis on acquisition and application of skills underlines the approach to the three main domains they test —reading, mathematical and scientific literacy.

Reading literacy involves students' ability to understand, use, reflect on and engage with written texts. Mathematical literacy involves students' capacity to reason mathematically and use mathematical concepts and procedures. Scientific literacy is the ability to engage in reasoned discourse about science and technology, explain phenomena scientifically and interpret data. These foundational competencies carry into many other aspects of learning.

Since 2000, PISA has been conducted every three years. In each cycle, the three-core assessment domains are rotated, so one domain is the major focus each time. PISA 2015 was the sixth cycle, and science was the selected domain. It was conducted in 72 countries, with an average sample of around 6000 students in each, and 540,000 in total. In each domain, the answers are scaled so that the mean for the OECD countries is 500.

In reading literacy (Table 7.9), eight countries, including the United States, are clustered within plus or minus three points of the OECD mean. Austria and Italy substantially trail the other selected countries, while Canada and Finland are clearly in the lead, and Ireland, Japan and Norway also perform well.

7.3 Maths, Science and Reading Skills

Table 7.9 Reading skills
Mean scores 2015, scaled so that OECD mean = 500

Country	Mean	Change since 2000 or EAY
Canada	527	−7
Finland	526	−20
Ireland	521	−6
Japan	516	−6
Norway	513	8
Germany	509	25
New Zealand	509	−20
Australia	503	−25
Netherlands	503	−10
Denmark	500	3
Sweden	500	−16
Belgium	499	−8
France	499	−6
United Kingdom	498	−3
United States	**497**	**−7**
Switzerland	492	−2
Austria	485	−7
Italy	485	−2
Mean	505	−6

PISA 2015 Results (Volume 1): Excellence and Equity in Education, PISA, OECD Publishing, 2016

Table 7.10 Maths skills
Mean scores 2015, scaled so that OECD mean = 500

Country	Mean	Change since 2003 or EAY
Japan	532	−2
Switzerland	521	−6
Canada	516	−16
Netherlands	512	−26
Denmark	511	−3
Finland	511	−33
Belgium	507	−22
Germany	506	3
Ireland	504	1
Norway	502	7
Austria	497	−9
New Zealand	495	−28
Australia	494	−30
Sweden	494	−15
France	493	−18
United Kingdom	492	−3
Italy	490	24
United States	**470**	**−13**
Mean	502	−11

PISA 2015 Results (Volume 1): Excellence and Equity in Education, PISA, OECD Publishing, 2016

Table 7.11 Science skills
Mean scores 2015, scaled so that OECD mean = 500

Country	Mean	Change since 2006
Japan	538	7
Finland	531	−32
Canada	528	−6
New Zealand	513	−17
Australia	510	−17
Germany	509	−7
Netherlands	509	−16
United Kingdom	509	−6
Switzerland	506	−6
Ireland	503	−5
Belgium	502	−8
Denmark	502	6
Norway	498	11
United States	**496**	**7**
Austria	495	−16
France	495	0
Sweden	493	−10
Italy	481	6
Mean	507	−6

PISA 2015 Results (Volume 1): Excellence and Equity in Education, PISA, OECD Publishing, 2016

The countries show a wider spread on mathematical literacy (Table 7.10). Japan is clearly in the lead, followed by Switzerland and Canada. Eight countries have a mean lower than the OECD mean of 500. By far the lowest is the United States, 20 points lower than the next lowest Italy, and 62 points lower than Japan.

Japan, Finland and Canada are also in the lead on science literacy (Table 7.11). Italy is the bottom-performing country, quite a bit lower than the others. Sweden is the second bottom.

In all three domains, the United States scores at or beneath the OECD mean of 500, as do Italy, France, Sweden and Austria. This is a strange mix of countries with very different characteristics, but their consistently mediocre performance must raise questions about how their education system is performing. Other countries score very differently on different domains—Switzerland a low 492 on reading but a very high 521 on maths—for unknown reasons.

The second column in each table shows the change between that country's 2015 mean and the earliest available year for it on that measure. Reading literacy results go back to 2000, maths to 2003 and science to 2006, in each case, the earliest year to which PISA thinks subsequent results can be compared. (Occasionally individual countries missed in the early years, and so this column gives the change for the earliest year available.)

The worrying trend is that in all three domains the mean has a minus sign in front of it. Individual countries vary (e.g. Germany improved greatly on reading, Italy did on science and Norway on science), but as a group, these countries' performances are declining rather than improving. Perhaps the most surprising was Finland, which had had outstanding results in earlier rounds of PISA, but in 2015 dropped steeply in every domain, 20, 33 and 32 points, respectively. Australia (−25, −30 and −17) and New Zealand (−20, −28 and −17) were also large sliders. The USA declined substantially in maths and slightly in reading but improved in science. The 2015 results give education policy-makers more concern than comfort.

7.4 Education and Equity

'No child left behind,' declared President George W. Bush as his aspiration for America's educational system, passed into law in 2001. Education is inevitably intertwined with equity issues. The first concern is that in an information age, literacy skills are crucial to many social opportunities both in work and leisure, and those lacking those skills will be substantially disadvantaged. The second concern relates to how education reinforces or qualifies existing inequalities, whether it offers avenues of mobility for disadvantaged people or cements their inferior position.

In all countries, the socio-economic situation of their families has some relationship with students' literacy skills. In Table 7.12, PISA divides students into different socio-economic status backgrounds based on their reporting of various home and family characteristics. It shows that the mean science literacy score for each quartile steadily rises with improved socio-economic circumstances.

The relationship between the socio-economic spread and high scoring is slight, but there is some suggestion that those with the smaller spread are the better performing countries. The top two countries, Japan and Finland, perform substantially above the 18-country mean at every level, which results in their having close to the average spread (90 points). France (117) and Belgium (110) have the largest spread because their bottom quartile scores are well below the mean, and their highest quartile scores slightly above. America is close to the average spread (89), consistently just below the mean at each level.

A different view on education's role in the transmission of inequality is seen in Table 7.13. As we have seen in earlier tables, the percentage of tertiary educated is steadily increasing with each generation. This table looks at those currently aged 30–44, neither of whose parents had a tertiary education, which in all the countries is a majority of this age cohort. It then looks at how many of this group gained a tertiary education. Although not directly comparable with earlier tables, this suggests that those with parents who lacked a tertiary education are themselves less likely themselves to gain one.

Nevertheless one in three did. Only in Canada did half do so. The three bottom countries in the table are ones which tend to have a low proportion of tertiary education anyway, but it is much lower among this group. The United States has

Table 7.12 Inequality in science performance
Socio-economic status quartiles, with mean science score in each 2015

Country	Bottom quartile	Second quartile	Third quartile	Top quartile
Japan	498	533	549	578
Finland	494	517	542	572
Canada	492	518	542	563
United Kingdom	473	490	525	557
Australia	468	497	525	559
Denmark	467	489	512	543
Germany	466	503	527	569
Ireland	465	489	513	545
Netherlands	465	494	519	559
New Zealand	463	504	533	565
Norway	463	489	512	535
United States	**457**	**478**	**508**	**546**
Switzerland	455	496	513	561
Belgium	450	482	522	560
Sweden	450	478	513	543
Austria	448	478	512	545
Italy	442	476	490	518
France	441	477	515	558
Mean	464	494	521	554

PISA 2015 Results (Volume 1): Excellence and Equity in Education, PISA, OECD Publishing, 2016

Table 7.13 Tertiary education and parents' education
30–44-year-olds, neither of whose parents had tertiary education, 2012 or 2015

Country	% of age cohort in this group	% of these who completed tertiary education
Canada	58	50
Finland	78	48
New Zealand	58	46
Japan	64	41
United Kingdom	71	38
Norway	63	37
Ireland	78	35
Belgium	69	35
Denmark	63	35
Australia	68	33
Netherlands	73	32
France	80	31
Sweden	60	28
United States	**60**	**27**
Germany	65	25
Austria	81	16
Italy	95	14
Mean	70	34

Includes tertiary education A and B
No data on Switzerland
PISA 2015 Results (Volume 1): Excellence and Equity in Education, PISA, OECD Publishing, 2016

a much higher rate of tertiary graduates than these three, but this slightly below average figure of 27% suggests somewhat less upward educational mobility.

Apart from education as a means of transmitting privilege, the other big equity concern is students being left behind. Table 7.14 addresses this. In addition to the scaled scores, the PISA study divides each sample into performance bands or levels of proficiency, where the cut-off points are designated as having skills to perform designated tasks and problems. On all the tests, Level Two is designated as the minimum acceptable level. For students in the two lowest levels, Level One and an unbounded region below that, their lack of literacy skills inhibits their capacity to learn and understand other subjects.

In contrast, in the top proficiency level, 6, 'students can consistently identify, explain and apply scientific knowledge and knowledge about science in a variety of complex life situations. They can link different information sources and explanations and use evidence from those sources to justify decisions'. They use scientific reasoning and their scientific understanding to seek solutions to unfamiliar scientific and technological situations.

Table 7.14 thus highlights how many students are in danger of being excluded from future opportunities, by showing the percentages not able to perform at what is considered the minimum level. Across the 18 countries, one in every ten students is failing to perform at this acceptable level in any of the three domains. The figure is highest in France, with the United States coming next.

While the greatest focus is on how those with inadequate levels of literacy are less able to cope with their work and in their personal lives, another dimension is their capacity to participate in civic life. Many contemporary issues require scientific capacity. Table 7.15 looks at levels of scientific proficiency and the students' awareness of greenhouse gases in the atmosphere. The last column reveals overall substantial differences between the countries with Swedish students having the highest awareness and Americans the lowest. Equally, there are clear differences between the different levels of scientific proficiency and their levels of awareness. In the top group, overall, 19 in 20 students have awareness; in the bottom group just one in three.

Table 7.14 Students with low skills
The first column is the percentage of students who performed below level 2 in all three tests. Last three columns = % below level 2 in each domain; but also includes those who have dropped out of school and those unable to satisfactorily complete the PISA test

Country	Low in all three	Reading	Maths	Science
Japan	6	18	15	14
Canada	6	25	29	26
Finland	6	14	16	14
Ireland	7	13	18	18
Denmark	8	24	23	25
Norway	9	22	24	26
Germany	10	20	21	21
Switzerland	10	23	19	22
United Kingdom	10	31	34	31
New Zealand	11	25	29	26
Netherlands	11	22	21	23
Australia	11	26	29	25
Sweden	11	24	26	27
Italy	12	37	38	38
Belgium	13	25	26	25
Austria	14	35	35	34
United States	**14**	**32**	**41**	**34**
France	15	29	30	29
Mean	10	25	26	25

OECD Education at a Glance 2017

Table 7.15 Science literacy and environmental awareness
% of among 15-year-olds at each level of science proficiency who are aware or very aware of the increase of greenhouse gases in the atmosphere, PISA 2015

Country	Below level 2	Levels 2–3–4	Level 5 and above	All levels
Sweden	53	86	99	81
United Kingdom	51	84	98	80
Ireland	44	83	98	79
Canada	47	78	97	78
Finland	35	75	97	74
Italy	50	79	97	73
Norway	42	77	98	73
Denmark	41	76	98	73
Australia	40	70	95	69
Netherlands	27	73	98	69
France	31	70	96	66
Germany	32	66	93	65
Belgium	26	65	95	62
New Zealand	29	61	90	60
Switzerland	27	63	92	60
Japan	19	57	90	59
Austria	26	61	94	57
United States	**33**	**56**	**88**	**55**
Mean	36	71	95	69

OECD Education at a Glance 2018

7.5 Schools' Resources and Learning Environments

PISA has provided unprecedented international benchmarking, but also provides a basis for considering educational policies and practices. No magic bullet seems to emerge when considering the patterns of results, as national idiosyncrasies defeat most attempts at simple generalisations. Nevertheless, it reveals many suggestive contrasts.

Table 7.16 Teachers' salaries

Lower secondary teachers' salaries, in public institutions, relative to earnings for tertiary-educated workers, which = 100

Country	Scale
Finland	99
Germany	99
Australia	93
Netherlands	92
Austria	90
United Kingdom	90
Sweden	89
France	88
New Zealand	87
Belgium	86
Denmark	83
Norway	75
Italy	69
United States	**65**
Mean	86

No data on Canada, Ireland, Japan or Switzerland
OECD Education at a Glance 2018

Table 7.17 Teacher–student ratios and class sizes

Number of students per teacher, plus average size of classes in year nine

Country	Ratios	Class size
Belgium	9.1	19.7
Norway	10.2	23.9
Finland	10.3	19.1
Italy	10.5	23.3
Japan	11.5	36.1
Sweden	11.5	23.3
Austria	11.7	24.2
Switzerland	12.2	20.1
France	12.3	29.3
Denmark	12.7	21.6
Australia	13.1	25.1
Ireland	14.4	24.6
New Zealand	14.6	25.3
Germany	14.7	25.0
United Kingdom	14.7	24.4
Canada	15.9	26.4
United States	**16.0**	**25.8**
Netherlands	20.4	25.7
Mean	13	25

PISA 2015 Results (Volume 1): Excellence and Equity in Education, PISA, OECD Publishing, 2016

Table 7.18 Teaching hours

Net statutory contact time in public institutions per year 2017

Country	Hours
Belgium	533
Finland	589
Austria	607
Japan	610
Italy	626
Norway	663
France	684
Ireland	722
Canada	745
Germany	747
Netherlands	750
Switzerland	760
Australia	797
New Zealand	840
United Kingdom	855
United States	**966**
Mean	718

No data on Denmark or Sweden
OECD Education at a Glance 2018

Most teachers in lower secondary classes in most countries have tertiary qualifications. Table 7.16 compares their salaries to the rest of the tertiary-educated labour force, where an index of 100 represents that group's salaries. In none of the countries do lower secondary teachers exceed 100, but in most, it is not very different. The exceptions are the United States and Italy. In America, junior secondary teachers receive only about two-thirds as much as their tertiary-educated peers. Does this considerably lesser salary mean that many suitably qualified people are not attracted to teaching?

It is a favourite argument of those wanting more resources for education that smaller class sizes will lead to better outcomes. It is important to distinguish class sizes from the related issue of teacher–student ratios, and probably the latter is the more basic. It may be that more staffs are desirable not to cut class sizes, but to better prepare for fewer contact hours or provide other support for students' learning.

This might seem to be the case for high-performing Japan, which has the largest class sizes but a relatively small staff–student ratio. The national differences in Table 7.17 provide mixed evidence. High-performing Finland has a low staff–student ratio, but so does underperforming Italy. Canada and the United States have almost identical teacher–student ratios, but Canada performs much better on PISA.

Apart from reducing average class size, another intuitive argument for improving student performance would be to spend more time in class—the longer they're there, the more they learn. Table 7.18 gives no support to this view. Top-performing countries Finland and Japan have fewer statutory contact hours than the mean. Curiously, the four countries with the highest hours are all English-speaking, and the one with by far the highest hours is the United States. American students spend 221 h more than Canadian students and 356 h more than Japanese students in class each year, but seem to have little to show for it.

PISA has also ventured into the non-cognitive aspects of learning. Table 7.19 reports on students' sense of belonging. A sense of belonging has to do with feelings of being

7.5 Schools' Resources and Learning Environments

Table 7.19 Students' sense of belonging
Index constructed on students' responses to six questions, higher = greater sense of belonging

Country	Index score
Austria	0.44
Switzerland	0.36
Germany	0.29
Norway	0.21
Netherlands	0.17
Denmark	0.14
Finland	0.09
Italy	0.05
Sweden	0.04
Belgium	0.01
Ireland	−0.02
Japan	−0.03
France	−0.06
United States	**−0.09**
United Kingdom	−0.09
Canada	−0.11
Australia	−0.12
New Zealand	−0.17
Mean	*0.06*

Lisa de Bortoli *Sense of Belonging at School*, PISA Australia in Focus Number 1, Melbourne, ACER, 2018

accepted and valued by their peers and by others at their school. It is an important part of students' self-esteem and motivation. It may sometimes at least be associated with educational success and long-term well-being.

PISA explored students' sense of belonging by asking them to respond (from strongly agree to strongly disagree) to six statements (such as 'I feel like an outsider at school', or 'I make friends easily at school'). The responses were combined to construct a sense of belonging index, standardised to have a mean of zero, with higher scores indicating a greater sense of belonging at the school.

Table 7.19 indicates a range of national differences, with the three most German-influenced countries—Austria, Switzerland and Germany—having by far the greatest sense of belonging, with the Scandinavian and low countries broadly coming next. They all come out, on balance, on the positive side of the ledger. The bottom five places are taken by English-speaking countries, including the United States, with Australia and New Zealand doing particularly badly.

Such international comparisons help to move beyond the taken-for-granted discussions within which debates about education take place within countries. In particular, it would seem that the English-speaking democracies share some assumptions about educational practices, but looking at some of the other selected democracies would expand their sense of opportunities.

7.6 Primary Students' Learning Skills

PISA has contributed greatly to our knowledge of the educational skills of 15-year-old students around the world. The International Association for the Evaluation of Educational Achievement (IEA) has performed a similar task for primary school students.

The 2016 Progress in International Reading Literacy Study (PIRLS) study of reading literacy among Year 4 students, directed by the IEA, was its fourth cycle. It involved 580,000 Year 4 students in 50 countries. Reading is one of the most important abilities students acquire as they progress through their early school years. Year 4 was chosen because it is a pivotal point at which students are no longer just learning to read but using their reading skills to advance their other learning.

The rankings in Table 7.20 provide interesting similarities and contrasts to Table 7.9 which looks at 15-year-olds' reading skills. Ireland, Finland and Norway are high on both tables, while France and Belgium rank low on both. The American, Swedish and Italian figures for primary school reading are much higher than their PISA rankings.

Another major international project on primary school children's skills is the Trends in International Mathematics and Science Study (TIMSS), also conducted by the IEA. TIMSS conducts tests on Year 4 and Year 8 students in maths and science; the focus here will be mainly on the Year 4 results.

Table 7.20 Primary students' reading
PIRLS Mean scores 2016

Country	Mean	% Low and below low
Ireland	567	11
Finland	566	9
Norway	559	10
United Kingdom	559	14
Sweden	555	12
United States	**549**	**17**
Italy	548	13
Denmark	547	14
Netherlands	545	12
Australia	544	19
Canada	543	17
Austria	541	16
Germany	537	19
New Zealand	523	27
Belgium	516	27
France	511	28
Mean	*544*	*17*

No data on Japan or Switzerland
United Kingdom figure = England only
Sue Thomson et al. *Highlights from PIRLS 2016, Australia's Perspective*, Melbourne, ACER, 2017. TIMSS and PIRLS, International Study Centre, IEA

The TIMSS scores make 500 the score for the mean of all their countries. This makes the scores appear higher than they do on PISA. It is true that taking all 49 countries in TIMSS 2016 into account the highest scoring countries were from East Asia: Singapore, Hong Kong, Korea, Taiwan and Japan. But there were also many poorer countries whose scores were substantially below our 18 selected democracies.

TIMSS has been conducted on a four-year cycle since 1995, and TIMSS 2015 is the sixth assessment. Forty-nine countries took part, with samples of 5000+ students in each. Year 4 students are mostly 10-years-old. France, New Zealand and Italy rank low on maths performance (Table 7.21), prefiguring their later performance in PISA maths. Canada's performance here is much weaker than it later becomes in PISA, while America is above average here, but ranked bottom in PISA maths.

The top countries in primary school science (Table 7.22) are Japan and Finland as they were in PISA's science results. This is by far the US's best relative performance, coming third in the rankings. Again Italy, Belgium, New Zealand and France's mean score is at the bottom.

The mean is not the only important measure. Both TIMSS and PIRLS divide students into four proficiencies: Advanced International Benchmark (625+); High International Benchmark (550–624); Intermediate International Benchmark (475–549); Low International Benchmark (400–474).

Table 7.21 Primary students' maths
Mean for each country, scored so that overall TIMSS mean = 500, 2016

Country	Mean	% Low and below low
Japan	593	4
Norway	549	14
Ireland	547	16
Belgium	546	12
United Kingdom	546	20
Denmark	539	20
United States	**539**	**21**
Finland	535	18
Netherlands	530	17
Germany	522	23
Sweden	519	25
Australia	517	30
Canada	511	31
Italy	507	31
New Zealand	491	41
France	488	42
Mean	*530*	*23*

United Kingdom figure = England only; Belgian figure = Flemish only
No data on Switzerland or Austria
Sue Thomson *TIMSS 2015. Reporting Australia's Results*, Melbourne, ACER, 2017; Ina V. S. Mullis et al. *TIMSS 2015 International Results in Mathematics* (International Study Center, Boston University); Michael O. Martin et al. *TIMSS 2015 International Results in Science* (International Study Center, Boston University)

Table 7.22 Primary students' science
Mean for each country, scored so that overall TIMSS mean = 500, 2016

Country	Mean	% Low and below low
Japan	569	6
Finland	554	11
United States	**546**	**19**
Sweden	540	18
Norway	538	15
United Kingdom	536	19
Ireland	529	21
Germany	528	22
Denmark	527	22
Canada	525	23
Australia	524	25
Netherlands	517	24
Italy	516	25
Belgium	512	27
New Zealand	506	33
France	487	42
Mean	*528*	*22*

United Kingdom figure = England only; Belgian = Flemish only
No data on Switzerland or Austria
Sue Thomson *TIMSS 2015. Reporting Australia's Results*, Melbourne, ACER, 2017; Ina V. S. Mullis et al. *TIMSS 2015 International Results in Mathematics* (International Study Center, Boston University); Michael O. Martin et al. *TIMSS 2015 International Results in Science* (International Study Center, Boston University)

The second column in each of the tables gives the percentage banded as low and below low. These can be considered the students at risk of falling behind in their subsequent studies. There are some differences between the three areas but broadly Japan and Finland have very few such at-risk students. France has by far the most, and in maths and science, four in ten of their students fall into this category.

PIRLS and TIMMS also allow us to examine changes over the cycles. This trend data is not presented in the tables, but in contrast to the downward trend in many countries on PISA, the findings on primary school students suggest either stability or improvement for most countries including the United States (+21 on maths and +4 on science, compared to the earliest year of testing). The contrast presents a puzzle. Taken at face value, they suggest that early student learning is improving, but learning later is not.

The final table on the page (7.23), for which unfortunately we only have data for eight countries, compares the maths score for Year 4 and in the next TIMSS cycle Year 8 students. The rank orderings stay roughly the same, but the movement overall is downward, with the positive scoring countries, except Japan, moving closer to the mean. America's Year 8 figure here is still above the TIMSS mean and thus far superior to its PISA maths score.

7.6 Primary Students' Learning Skills

Table 7.23 Continuity of skills year 4 to year 8
Mean for each country in relation to overall TIMSS score of 500 Maths for Year 4 in 2011 and then Year 8 in 2015

Country	2011 year 4	2015 year 8
Japan	85	86
United Kingdom	42	18
United States	**41**	**18**
Australia	16	5
Italy	8	−6
Sweden	4	1
Norway	−5	−13
New Zealand	−14	−7
Mean	22	13

No data for other countries
Sue Thomson *TIMSS 2015. Reporting Australia's Results*, Melbourne, ACER, 2017; Ina V. S. Mullis et al. *TIMSS 2015 International Results in Mathematics* (International Study Center, Boston University); Michael O. Martin et al. *TIMSS 2015 International Results in Science* (International Study Center, Boston University)

These movements and the contrasts between the relative performance of different countries in primary school and secondary school assessments pose more questions than they give answers, but they provide an evidential base for more substantial policy discussions.

7.7 Pre-primary Education

Educational institutions are expanding in both directions: students are staying more years in school and university, while at the same time there are increasing moves for them to start at earlier ages. Partly, the financial pressures and career aspirations of parents in contemporary societies mean there is more demand for high quality and affordable childcare from an early age (see Sect. 15.6 below). Beyond this, however, that demand has been heightened because of the increasing recognition of the importance of early education in children's cognitive and emotional development.

Early enrolment in pre-school education is also seen as a means of reducing unequal educational opportunities. Many inequalities are already present when children begin school and often persist through subsequent years. So, pre-primary education is seen as one solution.

Pre-primary education consists less of formal lessons in a curriculum and more of programmes designed to develop the cognitive, physical and socio-emotional skills on which primary education will build.

Table 7.24 charts the percentage of each age group enrolled in early childhood education and care (ECEC). Note that this mixes—as is often done—two distinct activities. Most day care centres are not centrally committed to pre-primary education. As would be expected, enrolments steadily increase with age. Until the age of two, less than one

Table 7.24 Enrolments in early childhood education and care
ECEC enrolments % age cohort 2016

Country	Aged 3	Aged 4	Aged 5
United Kingdom	100	100	97
Belgium	99	99	99
France	99	100	100
Denmark	97	98	98
Norway	96	97	97
Sweden	95	94	95
Germany	92	96	97
Italy	92	96	96
New Zealand	89	93	98
Netherlands	88	96	99
Japan	84	95	96
Austria	76	92	97
Finland	73	79	84
Australia	64	91	100
Ireland	49	90	92
United States	**38**	**67**	**91**
Switzerland	2	48	99
Mean	78	90	96

No data on Canada
OECD Education at a Glance 2018

Table 7.25 Expenditure on pre-primary education
% of GDP, public and private institutions, 2015

Country	2015
Sweden	1.35
Norway	0.93
Finland	0.86
France	0.74
Belgium	0.71
Germany	0.56
Italy	0.54
New Zealand	0.54
Austria	0.52
United States	**0.42**
United Kingdom	0.41
Switzerland	0.40
Netherlands	0.39
Australia	0.25
Japan	0.20
Ireland	0.07
Mean	0.56

No data on Canada or Denmark
OECD Education at a Glance 2018

in two children across the 18 countries are enrolled in formal day care (see Table 15.19 below). At age three, three quarters are enrolled, and by age five, it is almost 100%. Switzerland is a radical outlier with young children there having little involvement in ECEC. Among other countries, the United States is the next lowest.

Table 7.25 gives the total (public and private) expenditure on pre-primary education. There is a very large range. The

Table 7.26 Public and private pre-school education

% of those enrolled attending public or private institutions 2015

Country	Public	Private
Switzerland	95	5
Canada	93	7
Finland	92	8
France	87	13
Denmark	83	17
Sweden	83	17
Italy	72	28
Austria	71	29
Netherlands	71	29
United States	**60**	**40**
Norway	53	47
United Kingdom	51	49
Belgium	47	53
Germany	35	65
Japan	27	73
Australia	21	79
Ireland	2	98
New Zealand	1	99
Mean	*58*	*42*

OECD Education at a Glance 2017

Scandinavian and several other European countries lead the way. The United States is just below the mean, but clearly in the middle range. Ireland (most markedly), Japan and Australia have been much slower to invest in this emerging area.

Table 7.26 shows there are very strong contrasts between the countries on whether pre-primary education occurs principally at public or at private institutions. While more than 90% of enrolments in Switzerland, Canada and Finland are in public institutions, in Ireland and New Zealand more than 90% of enrolments are in private institutions. The United States is in the middle.

Apart from Canada, the other English-speaking democracies have been slow to invest in pre-primary education. Does this contribute to Canada's superior performance compared to the other English-speaking democracies at higher levels of education? Perhaps the slowness to invest is because of budgetary pressures or because the developmental importance of early education has not yet been fully recognised. However, it is a safe prediction that there will be increasing pressure to expand the public commitment in this area.

7.8 Adult Competencies

Economists may express the most important long-term goal of education as developing a society's human capital—the knowledge, skills and competencies embodied in individuals that are relevant to economic activity. Others may emphasise that education enables adults to lead fulfilling lives, to participate in society and in their social milieu, to find satisfying work.

But it is very difficult to know with certainty about how well equipped the adult population, post-education, is to achieve these goals. While students form a captive sample, it is much more difficult and expensive to study the intellectual skills and capacities of adults. The OECD Programme for the International Assessment of Adult Competencies (PIAAC) coordinated a Survey of Adult Skills. Over two rounds, one in 2011–2 and the other in 2014–5, 33 countries participated. The national samples ranged from 4000 up to 27,300 persons. The survey was administered by trained interviewers and took 30–45 min to complete.

The Survey of Adults Skills assessed the proficiency of 16–65-year-olds in literacy, numeracy and problem solving in technology-rich environments. These are key information-processing skills that are relevant to adults in many social contexts and work situations, broadly generic, information-processing competencies which provide a foundation for developing other competencies rests.

The results are reported on a 500-point scale; a higher score indicates greater proficiency. As with the student surveys (PISA, TIMSS and PIRLS), the scale is divided into proficiency levels; six levels for literacy and numeracy (from below Level 1 up to Level 5) and four in problem solving in technology-rich environments (from below Level 1 to Level 3).

Individuals were assigned to levels based on their ability to complete certain tasks. A person at Level 1, reading literacy can successfully read short texts where there is little competing information, to locate a single piece of information. A person at Level 5 can search for and integrate information across multiple, dense texts, evaluating evidence and arguments.

Table 7.27 shows the mean scores for literacy and numeracy. As in the student tests, Japan and Finland top the rankings, and Italy brings up the rear. The Netherlands, Belgium and Sweden are high in the adult table, but their performance in the student tests is more problematic, which raises questions about whether their current educational standards are as good as they used to be. The United States is close to the mean on reading literacy, but as in PISA its performance in numeracy is near the bottom.

In literacy and numeracy, levels three to five are considered capable of coping with most situations, and in both cases, the 18-nation mean shows about half the adult population at these levels (Table 7.28). In both cases, the rankings are close to those for the means.

The ability to solve problems in technology-rich environments is increasingly important in contemporary societies. The Survey of Adult Skills included the ability to use digital technology, communications tools and networks to acquire and evaluate information and perform practical tasks.

7.8 Adult Competencies

Table 7.27 Adult literacy and numeracy
Mean scores for literacy and numeracy, 2012 or 2015

Country	Literacy	Numeracy
Japan	296	288
Finland	288	282
Netherlands	284	280
Belgium	275	280
Sweden	279	279
Norway	278	278
Denmark	271	278
Austria	269	275
Germany	270	272
New Zealand	281	271
Australia	280	268
Canada	273	265
United Kingdom	273	262
Ireland	267	256
France	262	254
United States	**270**	**253**
Italy	250	247
Mean	274	270

No data on Switzerland
OECD (2016) *Skills Matter: Further Results from the Survey of Adult Skills* (OECD Skills Studies, Paris)

Table 7.28 Proficiency in literacy, numeracy and problem solving
% of levels 3–5 in literacy and numeracy, and levels 2–3 in problem solving, 2012 or 2015

Country	Literacy	Numeracy	Problem-solving
Japan	71	63	35
Finland	63	58	42
Netherlands	60	56	42
Sweden	58	57	44
Australia	56	46	38
New Zealand	56	48	44
Norway	55	55	41
Belgium	51	54	35
Canada	51	45	37
Denmark	50	55	39
United Kingdom	49	41	35
Germany	47	49	36
Austria	46	51	32
United States	**46**	**34**	**31**
Ireland	45	36	25
France	42	37	–
Italy	30	29	–
Mean	51	48	37

No data on Switzerland; problem-solving tests not administered in France and Italy
OECD (2016) *Skills Matter: Further Results from the Survey of Adult Skills* (OECD Skills Studies, Paris)

The final column of Table 7.28 shows a considerably lower proportion of people performing at satisfactory levels than in literacy and numeracy (and the two lowest countries on reading literacy, Italy and France, did not participate). Perhaps the outstanding feature of the findings is how closely clustered the countries are, plus or minus seven points around the mean of 37. The United States is the lowest among the cluster, but substantially ahead of Ireland.

This lack of competence is limiting the possibilities for many people in the selected countries. Around one in four adults has no or only limited experience with computers or lacks confidence in their ability to use computers.

Table 7.29 examines how many are in danger of exclusion because of their lack of skills in literacy and numeracy. The rankings differ somewhat from those of the mean scores, but Italy is clearly the outlier, with five times as many low-performing adults as Japan. The United States again ranks low, and especially so because of numeracy.

Increasingly, it is important that adults can go on learning after school is completed. Table 7.30 reports on those who do and those who don't participate in formal adult learning programs. The percentage of participating in informal programs can be calculated by subtracting the sum of these two from 100.

France and Italy have substantial majorities not participating, and Japan has a very low number in formal programs. To an extent, the English-speaking countries and those of northwest Europe offer the most chances to participate in adult learning.

Table 7.29 Low-performing adults
Level 1 and below in literacy and/or numeracy, % adults, 2012 or 2015

Country	Both	Literacy only	Numeracy only
Japan	4	1	4
Finland	8	3	5
Netherlands	9	2	4
Austria	10	5	4
Belgium	10	4	3
New Zealand	10	2	9
Norway	10	2	5
Sweden	10	3	4
Australia	11	1	9
Denmark	11	5	3
Germany	13	4	5
Canada	14	3	9
United Kingdom	14	2	10
Ireland	15	3	10
United States	**16**	**1**	**13**
France	18	3	10
Italy	21	6	10
Mean	12	3	7

No data on Switzerland
OECD (2016) *Skills Matter: Further Results from the Survey of Adult Skills* (OECD Skills Studies, Paris)

Table 7.30 Adult participation in learning
% of 2012 or 2015

Country	Some formal	None
New Zealand	18	32
Denmark	14	34
Finland	16	34
Sweden	14	34
Netherlands	14	36
Norway	16	36
United States	**14**	**41**
Canada	14	42
Australia	17	44
United Kingdom	16	44
Germany	7	47
Ireland	15	49
Belgium	8	51
Austria	6	52
Japan	3	58
France	5	64
Italy	6	75
Mean	*12*	*45*

No data on Switzerland
OECD Education at a Glance 2017

Inequality and Social Welfare

8.1 Income Inequality

National summary measures of economic growth or income take no account of the income distribution. They measure the size of the cake, but not how it is divided up. But distribution is central to peoples' sense of their well-being and their capacity to use the national wealth for their own goals.

Table 8.1 uses the most common measure, the Gini coefficient, a measure of dispersion invented by the Italian statistician, Corrado Gini. This index takes a value of 0 if every household has identical income and a value of 1 if one household has all the income. Thus, an increase in the coefficient represents an increase in inequality.

The Gini coefficient is a ratio measure, which includes all members of a population, and is the best summary measure to make comparisons over time and between countries. Generally, richer countries such as the selected countries have a lower Gini coefficient than poorer countries. Most Third World countries have coefficients of between 0.40 and 0.65, compared with a mean of just over 0.30 for these 18 affluent democracies.

Table 8.1 shows that the Scandinavian countries are the most equal, and the predominantly English-speaking nations are the most unequal. Sweden has the highest level of income equality based on the Gini coefficient measurement and the United States the highest level of income inequality. From 1980 to 2013, income inequality increased in most nations in the table with noteworthy exceptions of France and Ireland. In France, progressive taxation policies are credited with making a difference; in Ireland, dramatic swings in its economic growth rates (Table 3.2) interact with its income distribution.

Table 8.1 illustrates that in 2013 income inequality in the USA was much higher than in the other 17 countries. This was not the case in 1980 when income inequality in the USA was high, but similar to France, Ireland, Italy and Switzerland. Table 8.2, based on the income of the tenth richest group to the tenth poorest, shows that once again, in 2013, no country comes close to the level of income inequality in the USA, whereas there were similar levels of inequality, based on this measure, in the USA, Ireland, Italy, Canada, Australia and France in 1980. A significant gap has opened up from 1980 to 2013, with the USA now alone as clearly the most unequal.

The high rate of income inequality in the USA is felt particularly by black and Hispanic Americans. US census data from 2016 has the median household income for whites at $65,000, Hispanics at $48,000 and blacks at $39,000. The top 5% of household income earners were being paid at least $225,000 per year in 2016, which is nearly four times the median for all American households. The story of American income inequality today is that those at the top of the income ladder have been paid a lot more in relative terms since the 1970s, and those in the middle and bottom experienced long periods of relative wage stagnation.

In 1965, the average American CEO was earning 27 times more than the average worker per year, while in 2010 they were earning 243 times more. Since the 1980s, the booming financial services sector in the USA has also had a significant impact on incomes with employees in that industry paid substantially more than other sectors of the economy. Moreover, the financialisation of incomes has been broadly felt with stock options increasingly given to senior managers across a range of businesses to avoid income taxation. At the same time as incomes at the top have gone up substantially, the highest marginal tax rate has gone down for top income earners putting more money in their bank accounts.

Table 8.3 is in many ways a very good historical overview of the impact of progressive taxation, and unionisation, on income inequality in America. In 1929, the top marginal tax rate was 25%, and by 1946 it was 95%. By the mid-1970s, it was down to 70%. By the end of the Reagan presidency, it was back down to 29% and the top 1% of income earners were nearly earning as much as the bottom 50%. By 1995, they were earning as much as the bottom 50% of income earners. In 2014, the top 1% were earning considerably more income than the bottom 50%. This has

© Springer Nature Singapore Pte Ltd. 2020
R. Tiffen et al., *How America Compares*, How the World Compares,
https://doi.org/10.1007/978-981-13-9582-6_8

Table 8.1 Inequality
Gini index of disposable income, earliest available year and latest available year

Country	Near 1980	Near 2013
Sweden	0.197	0.237
Norway	0.224	0.248
Denmark	0.255	0.249
Finland	0.207	0.259
Netherlands	0.252	0.264
Austria	0.227	0.279
Belgium	0.227	0.279
France	0.312	0.289
Germany	0.244	0.293
Ireland	0.328	0.294
Switzerland	0.309	0.295
Japan	–	0.302
Italy	0.306	0.319
Canada	0.284	0.321
Australia	0.281	0.330
United Kingdom	0.267	0.330
United States	**0.310**	**0.381**
Mean	*0.264*	*0.292*

No data on New Zealand
Luxembourg Income Study database

Table 8.2 Ratio of unequal income
Ratio of disposable income of those at the 90th percentile with those at the 10th percentile
Earliest and latest available years

Country	Near 1980	Near 2013
Sweden	2.4	2.8
Denmark	3.2	2.9
Norway	2.8	3.0
Finland	2.6	3.1
Netherlands	2.9	3.1
Belgium	2.7	3.3
Austria	2.9	3.4
France	3.9	3.6
Switzerland	3.4	3.6
Germany	2.9	3.7
Ireland	4.2	3.8
Japan	–	3.9
United Kingdom	3.5	4.1
Italy	4.0	4.3
Australia	3.9	4.5
Canada	4.1	4.5
United States	**4.6**	**5.9**
Mean	*3.4*	*3.7*

No data on New Zealand
Luxembourg Income Study database

Table 8.3 Income inequality in the USA
Share of all annual income for highest income earners and those below average in selected years

	% going to top 1% of income earners	% going to bottom 50%
1928	24	–
1932	16	–
1936	19	–
1946	13	–
1962	13	20
1970	11	21
1980	11	20
1988	15	17
1995	15	15
2000	18	15
2006	20	14
2009	19	14
2014	20	13

http://wid.world/country/usa/

8.2 Wealth Inequality

Thomas Piketty in *Capital in the Twenty-First Century* popularised a focus on wealth inequality as well as income inequality. Household wealth is much more unequally distributed than household income—compare Table 8.1 with Table 8.4—due to the very high levels of concentrated wealth at the top. In the USA, the top 10% own half of the total wealth, while the bottom 40% own just over 3%. This concentration of wealth tends to be intergenerational and therefore cements economic class relations.

Table 8.4 Inequalities in wealth
Shares of net wealth distribution for each quintile
Final column is ratio of those at the 5th percentile of wealth to the median

Country	Q1	Q2	Q3	Q4	Q5	Ratio P5: median
Belgium	0.2	4.6	12.4	21.7	61.2	10.1
Italy	0.4	4.5	12.6	20.9	61.6	9.3
Australia	0.5	4.6	12.2	21.0	61.8	9.5
United Kingdom	0.5	4.1	11.3	20.6	63.4	11.1
Finland	−1.1	2.2	10.8	23.3	64.9	10.6
France	−0.1	1.8	9.9	20.9	67.5	14.8
Canada	0.3	3.0	9.2	19.5	68.0	15.1
Norway	−5.1	1.5	10.7	23.5	69.5	12.7
Germany	−0.5	1.3	5.7	17.2	76.3	33.8
Austria	−0.6	1.3	6.0	16.2	77.1	34.7
Netherlands	−3.3	0.6	4.7	19.3	78.7	43.9
United States	**−0.9**	**0.6**	**2.9**	**9.3**	**88.2**	**90.7**
Mean	*−0.8*	*2.5*	*9.0*	*19.5*	*69.9*	*24.7*

No data on Denmark, Ireland, Japan, New Zealand, Sweden or Switzerland
OECD *In It Together. Why Less Inequality Benefits All* (2015)

started to find its way into political rhetoric, with Bernie Sanders' campaign of 2016 targeting explicitly the 'top 1%' for having too much of the pie at everyone else's expense.

8.2 Wealth Inequality

Table 8.5 Wealth distribution and race in the United States
Median family wealth ($000) in each racial group 1983–2016

Year	White	Black	Hispanic
1983	105	13	10
1989	135	8	9
1998	142	23	15
2007	199	24	24
2013	146	13	14
2016	171	17	21

Urban Institute calculations from Survey of Financial Characteristics of Consumers 1962 (December 31), Survey of Changes in Family Finances 1963, and Survey of Consumer Finances 1983–2016

This is particularly apparent when looking at the wealth profile of black Americans compared to white Americans. Wealth creates further wealth for affluent white Americans. Data from the respected policy think tank, the Urban Institute, shows that between 1983 and 2016 the median wealth of both white and black Americans grew, by 60 and 30%, respectively. The raw numbers are more revealing. Black median household wealth was a paltry $13,000 in 1983 and a not particularly impressive $17,000 in 2016. For whites, it was $105,000 in 1983 and $171,000 by 2016. The gap between white wealth and black wealth has gotten much bigger during a period in which racism and discrimination had by many measures declined. This points to the persistence of structural racism in the USA, not just between black and white Americans, but also between white and Hispanic Americans as Table 8.5 illustrates.

The table also shows that the 1980s were not a period of positive wealth accumulation for the median black or Hispanic household; however, the 1990s and early 2000s were. The global financial crisis and its associated housing market collapse in many places across America hit the wealth of all races hard, but it was particularly devastating for the wealth of black Americans as the table shows. By 2013, the median wealth of blacks was back to the levels of 1983, whereas whites and Hispanics still held on to a significant amount of the increases in wealth they had accumulated since 1983.

Wealth in most countries relates very significantly to home ownership. As the work of Ta-Nehisi Coates has ably shown, black Americans were cut out of the housing market well into the twentieth century due to racist lending, real estate and employment practices. This has had an enduring impact and led Coates and others to call for reparations to be paid to blacks to compensate.

Wealth inequality, like income inequality, is greater in the USA than in the other nations in Table 8.4. As the table illustrates, the 5th percentile of Americans has accumulated an extraordinary 88% of overall American wealth, a telling indication of the power of the ultra-wealthy in American society. Based on 2017 data from the Survey of Consumer Finances, a very small percentage, often referred to as the '1%', owns as much wealth as the bottom 90%. The average member of the top 1% has $26 million in wealth, whereas the average member of the bottom 40% of the US population is $9,000 in debt.

The ratio of the wealth of those at the 5th percentile in the USA to the median wealth is 91 in the USA. This is substantially higher than any other country. Even the Netherlands, the European nation with the highest ratio (44 times higher), has only half the ratio of the USA. The middle quintile in seven of the countries has 10% or more of the wealth, compared to just three per cent in the United States.

One way of addressing wealth inequality is through an estate tax, a tax on the wealth of deceased persons. Many OECD nations have such a tax. For estates worth over $USD3 million, the UK has a 26% tax. In the USA, the top rate of estate tax is 40%, although the first $USD11 million of an individual's estate is tax exempt. The exemption level was doubled from $USD5.5 million by the Republican Party's *Tax Cuts and Jobs Act of 2017*. A future Democrat-controlled Congress is likely to revisit this issue to increase federal revenue and attempt to create greater equality in America.

8.3 Poverty

Measurements and conceptualisations of poverty are politically and intellectually contentious.[1] In developing countries, to be poor is to have so little money as to be in danger of severe malnutrition or exposure. This is sometimes called subsistence poverty—insufficient income to afford the most basic standards of food, clothing and shelter so that one's very survival is at stake. The fact that very few people in developed countries face poverty of this severity has given rise to two approaches to measuring poverty. The first is an absolute material conception, using some notion of basic needs, and the second is based on relative deprivation, where poverty is determined by reference to the general standard of living and social expectations. The most common relative poverty line used in international comparisons is 50% of a country's median (or dead-middle) income. This is an arbitrary figure, and sometimes either 40 or 60% is used (Table 8.6).

Using a measure of relative poverty, it is apparent from Table 8.6 how persistent poverty has been from 1980 to 2013 in these advanced industrial democracies. Apart from Denmark, no nation substantially reduced poverty in this period. In most countries, the percentage of people living in

---

[1] Also draws on Abbakyn Kurts and Tal Yellin, 'Minimum Wage Since 1938', *CNNMoney*, https://money.cnn.com/interactive/economy/minimum-wage-since-1938/.

Table 8.6 Poverty

% of population living in relative poverty, defined as less than half median income, earliest and latest available years

Country	Near 1980	Near 2013
Denmark	10.1	5.7
Sweden	5.3	6.0
Netherlands	6.3	6.2
Finland	5.1	6.8
Norway	5.0	7.7
Belgium	4.5	8.1
Switzerland	7.6	8.7
Austria	6.7	8.8
France	10.3	9.1
United Kingdom	9.0	9.1
Ireland	11.1	9.4
Germany	5.3	10.0
Japan	–	10.9
Italy	10.5	12.9
Canada	12.4	13.7
Australia	11.3	13.9
United States	**15.0**	**17.2**
Mean	*8.5*	*9.7*

No data on New Zealand
Luxembourg Income Study database

Table 8.7 Working poor

% of households with at least one person working, falling below the relative poverty line, 2013

Country	%
Germany	3.0
Denmark	3.9
Finland	4.1
Australia	4.6
Ireland	5.0
United Kingdom	5.3
Switzerland	5.7
New Zealand	5.8
Sweden	5.8
Belgium	6.1
Netherlands	6.6
Norway	6.7
France	7.3
Austria	7.8
Canada	8.7
United States	**11.9**
Italy	12.0
Japan	12.9
Mean	*6.8*

OECD *In It Together. Why Less Inequality Benefits All* (2015)

Table 8.8 Race and poverty in the USA

Percentage of people below the relative poverty line in each racial group

Year	White	Black	Hispanic
1959	18.1	55.1	–
1964	14.9	–	–
1969	9.5	32.2	–
1974	8.6	30.3	23.0
1982	12.0	35.6	29.9
1988	10.1	31.3	26.7
1993	12.2	33.1	30.6
2000	9.5	22.5	21.5
2007	10.5	24.5	21.5
2011	12.8	27.6	25.3
2016	11.0	22.0	19.4

US Census Data

poverty increased. The Nordic states and the Netherlands had the lowest rates and the USA the highest in both years by a substantial margin.

Central reasons for these high rates of poverty in America include the very limited nature of welfare support, significant income inequality and the large proportion of people who work full-time but are still poor. We see strong evidence of this last factor in Table 8.7 with roughly 12% of American households having a member who is classified as 'working poor'. There are similar percentages of the working poor in Italy and Japan.

A major contributor to poverty in America since the 1980s has been the stagnation of wages for the working poor. The minimum wage was frozen at $3.35 during the eight years of the Reagan presidency from 1981 to 1989. It rose during the George Bush Snr presidency and the Clinton presidency to reach $5.15 by 1997, but remained frozen during the Bush Jnr presidency. Barack Obama spoke frequently during his presidency about the scourge of inequality in America, and one of his key policy responses was a concerted push to increase the minimum wage. The Democrat-controlled Congress increased the minimum wage to $7.25 in 2009 (still low compared with most OECD nations). The Republicans, who controlled the Congress for the last 6 years of Obama's presidency, ignored calls for further minimum wage increases. To sidestep the Congress, Obama issued an executive order in 2014 to increase the minimum wage for federal contractors to $10.10.

Another distinctive feature of American poverty is the large number of people living in what the US Census Bureau defines as 'deep poverty', which is a household 50% below the poverty line. In 2016, the Bureau estimated that 18.5 million Americans—or 5.8%—lived in 'deep poverty'. The miserly nature of government welfare provided to working-age adults without children and the time-limited nature of welfare even to single parents with children at least partly explain the high incidence of 'deep poverty' in America.

The risk of falling into poverty affects people of different races very differently. Poverty among whites in Table 8.8 follows a very different pattern to the experience of blacks and Hispanics. American poverty rates were significantly reduced from the mid-1960s when President Johnson launched his 'War on Poverty'. As the numbers suggest new government programmes and civil rights laws instituted in the mid-1960s saw a reduction in white poverty from 18.1% in 1959 to 8.6% in 1974 and for blacks from a staggering 55.1% in 1959 to 30.3% in 1974. However, Johnson's promise to 'cure' poverty was not achieved and Reagan infamously quipped 'we waged a war on poverty, and poverty won'. This outlook led to a reduction in government support for the poor in the 1980s and not surprisingly a rise in poverty rates in this decade. This set in place a pattern of poverty rates generally decreasing during Democratic presidencies and increasing during Republican presidencies.

Table 8.8 reveals that the rate of black poverty is still twice that of white poverty in the twenty-first century. Hispanic poverty rates have also remained consistently high since 1974 when the Census Bureau started measuring it.

8.4 Disability

Disability has become a major policy concern in many of the selected countries and is likely to become more so. As Table 8.9 shows, an average of one in 14 working-age people is receiving incapacity-related payments across these 18 affluent democracies. Moreover, as Table 8.10 shows, public spending on disability benefits averages 2.5% of GDP.

Disability spending therefore takes a greater proportion of the government budget in some countries than the military or universities. But there is also considerable unmet demand. The last column in Table 8.9 reports the proportion of working-age adults who say they suffer from a disability, and the mean for this column is two and a half times the mean for the recipients' column. Although we should not leap to the conclusion that all those who think they have a disability also think they deserve a public benefit, the gap does suggest that as well as already constituting a major public commitment, there will be continuing demand for it to be increased.

These tables also show strong differences between countries. Denmark, for example, is spending six times as much of its national income on disability benefits as Canada. Similarly, on a proportional basis, five times as many people are receiving incapacity-related benefits in Norway as in Japan. The variation shows that the definition of disability and the generosity of governments towards people with disabilities differ markedly. Interestingly, the proportion in each country saying they suffer from a disability varies as much as the proportions receiving a benefit, from slightly more than one in five to just less than one in ten.

The United States is above the mean in Table 8.9 on the proportion of the working-age population receiving benefits, but near the bottom in Table 8.10 suggesting that the amount paid to each recipient is much lower than in many other countries.

Table 8.9 Prevalence of disability
Recipients of incapacity-related payments as % of population, aged 20–64
Last column is percentage saying they have a disability, c.2008

Country	2000	2012	Self-assessed disability %
Norway	9.4	10.7	16
New Zealand	9.4	7.9	–
Finland	8.8	7.5	21
Denmark	7.0	7.3	21
Sweden	8.6	6.9	18
United States	**5.2**	**6.8**	**12**
United Kingdom	7.4	6.7	17
Belgium	4.9	6.6	13
Ireland	5.2	6.4	13
Italy	7.1	5.9	9
Australia	5.1	5.5	12
France	4.5	4.8	13
Germany	4.5	4.8	17
Switzerland	4.5	4.7	10
Austria	5.1	4.5	14
Canada	4.2	4.4	12
Netherlands	3.1	3.8	17
Japan	1.9	2.1	–
Mean	5.9	6.0	15

OECD Economic Policy Reforms 2016: Going for Growth Interim Report (2016)
2nd column from OECD Sickness, Disability and Work. Breaking the Barriers (2010)

Table 8.10 Public spending on disability benefits
% of GDP 2013

Country	
Denmark	4.7
Sweden	4.3
Finland	3.8
Norway	3.7
New Zealand	3.1
Belgium	2.9
Australia	2.6
Netherlands	2.5
Austria	2.3
Switzerland	2.3
Germany	2.1
Ireland	2.1
United Kingdom	2.0
France	1.7
Italy	1.7
United States	**1.4**
Japan	1.0
Canada	0.8
Mean	2.5

OECD database Public Spending on Incapacity

Table 8.11 Disability and educational achievement

% of those without disability and with disability at each educational level

Country	Low achievement without disability	Low achievement with disability	High achievement without disability	High achievement with disability
United Kingdom	9.9	19.3	25.2	20.7
Sweden	14.8	24.9	25.3	18.3
Finland	22.1	26.5	18.7	15.0
Netherlands	15.7	29.9	30.7	22.5
United States	**15.5**	**32.6**	**26.8**	**8.8**
Ireland	14.1	33.5	26.4	17.1
France	22.1	33.9	28.2	25.4
Austria	24.9	37.9	9.6	10.3
Denmark	27.6	38.1	16.2	14.1
Italy	30.7	39.2	12.3	8.9
Canada	33.6	42.0	21.5	15.3
Belgium	27.1	45.1	26.6	18.0
Germany	36.6	47.7	9.4	6.9
Norway	39.2	48.5	20.8	7.1
Mean	*23.9*	*35.7*	*21.3*	*14.9*

No data on Australia, Japan, New Zealand or Switzerland
Medium educational level omitted
OECD Family Database

Public spending on incapacity, as reported in Table 8.10, refers to spending due to sickness, disability and occupational injury. By far, its greatest component is cash payments, but it may also include providing support, services and rehabilitation. Some disabilities are congenital; others are the result of occupational injury and disease that affect the person's ability to participate in employment. While most people think of physical disability, the OECD notes that mental health problems are now the biggest single cause of disability claims in most countries. At base, there remains considerable latitude for policy-makers and officials in how disability is defined and responded to.

Remembering that the label disability covers a wide range of issues, its impact on the life chances of those affected can be profound and may be helped or hindered by public policies. If, for example, disability affects educational opportunity, this has knock-on effects through the rest of life. Table 8.11 shows considerable variation in levels of educational achievement between countries and also how much disability affects it. The disabled are somewhat over-represented among those with low educational achievement and under-represented among high achievers.

Among the countries on which we have data, having a disability has the greatest impact on educational achievement in America. Twice as many people with disabilities finish with low educational achievements in America as people without disabilities (32.6:15.5%), while those without disabilities outnumber those with three to one (26.8:8.8%) among those with high educational achievement. In contrast, in terms of reducing those with high achievements, the impact

Table 8.12 Disability and poverty

% living in relative poverty in households with or without a member with a disability

Country	No household member has a disability	A household member has a disability
Norway	7.0	5.2
Sweden	8.0	5.4
Finland	4.8	6.7
Netherlands	6.1	7.2
Belgium	11.7	8.7
Germany	10.2	8.7
Ireland	12.2	8.7
United Kingdom	13.0	9.5
Austria	7.3	9.6
Denmark	6.5	9.7
France	8.0	10.0
Italy	15.5	17.1
United States	**19.4**	**30.6**
Mean	*10.0*	*10.5*

No data on Australia, Canada, Japan, New Zealand or Switzerland
OECD Family Database

of disability is very slight in more than half of the countries selected.

Table 8.12 shows considerable variation both in the range of households living below the poverty line and in what impact disability has on that proportion. The United States, as we saw in Sect. 8.3, has the highest proportion living in relative poverty. This table shows that it is also the country where the presence of a disability is most likely to result in poverty. In several other countries, in contrast, households with a disabled member have a lower proportion or around the same proportion living in poverty than others.

In all countries, disability is likely to be an increasingly fraught policy area, with growing demands for scarce public resources. The best way to fight benefit dependence and exclusion among people with disability is to promote their re-integration into employment. While this is universally agreed, resources are yet to follow the rhetoric. Only around 0.1% of GDP across these countries is devoted to rehabilitation and employment programmes.

8.5 Poverty and the Ageing Society

Today's large welfare states began with the introduction of pension schemes for the elderly. By the late nineteenth century, a number of developed economies adopted the view that growing old should not mean becoming poor or at least not desperately poor. The elderly poor were increasingly viewed as the 'deserving poor', resulting in governments developing welfare programmes to protect them from poverty.

The American welfare system emerged relatively late. However, like welfare systems elsewhere, support for the elderly was the starting point. The Social Security Act of 1935 passed by the Congress with overwhelming bipartisan support and signed into law by Franklin D. Roosevelt has been the centrepiece of the American welfare state ever since, accepted even by extremely anti-welfarist and fiscally conservative Republicans.

All countries have distinctive welfare schemes for the aged. America does not mean test benefits, which are based on the direct tax employees and employers contributed to individual social security accounts. In order to gain access to social security, recipients need to have either worked for 10 years or been married to a worker for 10 years. As a result, around three per cent of Americans never receive any social security (Table 8.13).

Because of its contributory nature, social security is not thought of as 'welfare', despite the fact that it will soon be costing the federal government more than one trillion dollars per year. As a result of the social security programme, cash benefit spending on the elderly in the USA is near the middle of Table 8.14, in contrast to spending on the unemployed and sole parents, for example, where the USA ranks much lower.

Table 8.14 generally shows a small but consistent increase in public spending on the elderly, which is likely to keep increasing as governments are faced with ageing populations. So, spending on the aged which is where the contemporary welfare state began is also the greatest current contributor to its continuing expansion.

Table 8.13 Expected years of life in retirement

Country	Females	Males
France	27.6	23.6
Belgium	26.1	21.3
Italy	25.6	21.8
Austria	25.4	21.0
Canada	23.9	18.9
Australia	23.7	19.6
Finland	23.7	20.0
Netherlands	23.6	19.9
Switzerland	23.3	19.0
United Kingdom	22.9	19.3
Germany	22.6	19.5
Denmark	22.2	19.1
Ireland	22.2	16.7
Norway	22.0	18.1
Sweden	21.9	18.7
Japan	21.1	15.5
United States	**20.6**	**17.2**
New Zealand	20.4	16.7
Mean	23.3	19.2

OECD *Pensions at a Glance 2017*

Table 8.14 Public expenditure on aged pensions
Public expenditure on cash benefits for old-age and survivors' pensions as % of GDP

Country	1990	2000	2013
Italy	11.3	13.5	16.3
France	10.4	11.4	13.8
Austria	11.3	12.0	13.4
Finland	7.2	7.4	11.1
Belgium	8.9	8.7	10.2
Japan	4.8	7.3	10.2
Germany	9.5	10.8	10.1
Denmark	6.1	6.3	8.0
Sweden	7.3	6.9	7.7
United States	**5.8**	**5.6**	**7.0**
Switzerland	5.2	6.0	6.4
United Kingdom	4.5	5.1	6.1
Norway	5.5	4.7	5.8
Netherlands	6.3	4.7	5.4
New Zealand	7.2	4.9	5.1
Ireland	4.8	2.9	4.9
Canada	4.2	4.2	4.6
Australia	3.1	4.7	4.3
Mean	6.9	7.1	8.4

OECD *Pensions at a Glance 2017*

The table shows a wide disparity, with Italy spending almost four times the share of its national income on age pensions as Australia, the country which also has the highest rate of the relative poverty among the aged (Table 8.15). The correlation between government expenditures on the

Table 8.15 Poverty among the elderly
% of those aged 65+ living in relative poverty
Earliest and latest available years

Country	Near 1980	Near 2013
Netherlands	5.5	2.2
Denmark	31.8	4.0
Norway	6.3	4.4
France	23.8	5.2
Sweden	2.9	6.6
Finland	12.1	7.1
Italy	13.3	7.5
Ireland	8.2	8.2
Canada	22.1	9.0
United Kingdom	23.1	9.1
Austria	18.5	9.9
Germany	14.4	9.9
Japan	–	13.6
Belgium	10.9	15.4
Switzerland	19.3	19.0
United States	**26.9**	**20.6**
Australia	24.7	33.7
Mean	*16.5*	*10.9*

No data on New Zealand
Luxembourg Income Study database

elderly and poverty rates is far from perfect: two low spenders, Canada and New Zealand, have very low elderly poverty rates (the cost of living and targeted programmes are important factors here also). Nonetheless, it is worth noting that in New Zealand life expectancy after retiring is one of the shortest in the OECD.

Table 8.15 shows the proportion of elderly people living below the poverty line (defined as 50% of each country's median income). This rate varies considerably: the Netherlands, Denmark, Norway and France have very low rates of poverty among the elderly, whereas America has the second highest rate.

The reason lies in America's very low minimum wage and the large number of people receiving it. This not only affects those people's ability to save, but also how much social security they receive. Additionally, more than a third of Americans work in jobs without employer retirement plans. The net impact of this, according to a recent study, is that 42% of Americans have saved less than $10,000 for their retirement.

One result is that many Americans work beyond the official national retirement age. Table 8.13 shows the expected years of life in retirement. This is a product both of life expectancy and of the official and effective retirement ages. In every country, the figure for women is higher, both because they tend to live longer and also retire younger. The countries at the top of the table, such as France, Belgium and Italy, are there not because (as we saw in Chapter One) they live longer, but because they retire earlier. Many men in these countries are retired from the age of 60. In contrast, the longest-living Japanese are near the bottom because they keep working the longest. America has a slightly shorter life expectancy than the other countries, but also a higher effective retirement age.

Overall, the picture of life expectancy is a positive one for the OECD: as a whole, average years in retirement rose from 15 in 1970 to 22 in 2016 for women, and from 11 to 18 for men.

8.6 Government Social Spending and Redistribution

Social spending has been rising in the 18 selected countries and now amounts to almost one-quarter of national income, up from just under one-fifth in 1980 (Table 8.16). This rise is the more remarkable, because as we saw in Table 5.1 government spending has barely increased relative to GDP as taxpayers have become more resistant to higher taxation and governments have begun worrying about the budgetary implications of an ageing population.

Very considerable variation persists among the countries, with the largest spender France spending double the proportion of the smallest, Ireland. Moreover, the rank ordering of spending in this table roughly aligns with the total size of governments in Table 5.1.

Table 8.16 Social expenditure
Public social expenditure as % of GDP

Country	1980	1995	2007	2016
France	21	28	28	32
Finland	18	27	23	31
Belgium	24	26	25	29
Denmark	25	29	25	29
Italy	18	20	25	29
Austria	23	27	25	28
Sweden	29	33	26	27
Germany	23	27	24	25
Norway	17	24	20	25
Japan	10	14	19	23
Netherlands	24	23	20	22
United Kingdom	17	20	20	21
New Zealand	17	19	18	20
Switzerland	14	18	17	20
Australia	11	17	16	19
United States	**13**	**15**	**16**	**19**
Canada	14	19	16	17
Ireland	17	16	16	16
Mean	*19*	*22*	*21*	*24*

First two columns from OECD *Factbook 2007*; Last two columns from OECD *Society at a Glance 2016*

Public social expenditure is spending by governments to provide support to individuals and households during circumstances that adversely affect their welfare. It covers cash transfer payments, but also directs 'in-kind' provision of goods and services and tax breaks for social purposes. The label 'social expenditure' can cover different groupings of spending. The broadest is to include education, health and welfare spending. Most commonly, just health and welfare are included and sometimes only social welfare.

Increases in social welfare spending can result from any of three factors: an increase in the number of people who meet unchanged eligibility criteria; government decisions to widen eligibility criteria; and government decisions to increase the real value of benefits paid. Spending in some areas, particularly unemployment, varies with the business cycle, while in others—age pensions—it is growing with a demographic inevitability.

Table 8.16 on public social spending is the simplest and most commonly used measure and is the best indicator of the size of the welfare state. A rather different view emerges when net social spending is considered, as in Table 8.17. The second column reflects how the amount given by governments in welfare is clawed back through taxation, either through direct taxing of benefits or through indirect taxes which welfare recipients pay because of their consumption. In contrast, some recipients in some countries enjoy some special tax treatments. Examining the post-tax picture of welfare spending only affects the rank ordering slightly, although some of the Scandinavian countries in particular are affected most.

The third column refers to private social expenditure. This is overwhelmingly pensions and other benefits provided by employers, sometimes because they are legally obliged to, but often reflecting social practices surrounding employment. The United States has far more of these than any other country, being around double the next placed countries, Switzerland and the Netherlands. When all these factors are taken together, in the final column, the rankings are quite different from Table 8.16.

A system that relies on employer contributions is not likely to be one aimed at the neediest in society. Table 8.18 looks at the redistributive and equalising impact of government taxes and transfers. All these countries are capitalist societies, and the workings of their economies generate considerable inequality. The United States is one of six of the selected countries, where the market Gini index is over 0.5. What is distinctive about the USA, though, is the relatively small effect government action has on making the society more equal. After government action, it is the most unequal of these 18 democracies, because it is the one where government action has the least effect on redistributing resources. By contrast, Finland has a market Gini index almost the same as America's, but its final Gini score is radically different.

Table 8.17 Net social spending
% of GDP 2013

Country	Gross public social expenditure	Net public social expenditure	Net current private social expenditure	Net total social expenditure
France	31.5	28.0	3.2	31.2
United States	**18.8**	**19.8**	**10.5**	**28.8**
Belgium	29.3	25.7	1.5	27.2
Netherlands	22.9	20.1	5.6	25.6
Denmark	29.0	22.5	2.9	25.4
Japan	23.1	22.1	3.3	25.4
Sweden	27.4	22.9	2.4	25.3
Italy	28.6	24.1	1.1	25.2
United Kingdom	21.9	20.5	4.7	25.0
Germany	24.8	23.0	2.4	24.6
Finland	29.5	23.3	0.8	24.1
Austria	27.6	22.6	1.5	24.0
Switzerland	19.2	16.8	5.0	21.8
Canada	16.9	16.5	3.8	20.0
Australia	18.1	17.8	2.2	19.8
Ireland	20.2	18.6	1.8	19.8
Norway	21.8	18.0	1.3	19.3
New Zealand	19.3	17.1	0.5	17.4
Mean	*23.9*	*21.1*	*3.0*	*23.9*

OECD *Government at a Glance 2017*

Table 8.18 Government action and inequality
Gini indices before and after public taxes and transfers, 2015

Country	Gini (market-based)	Gini (post-taxes and transfers	Proportional change (%)
Finland	0.495	0.257	48
Belgium	0.494	0.268	46
Ireland	0.575	0.309	46
Austria	0.497	0.280	44
Denmark	0.442	0.254	43
Germany	0.508	0.292	43
France	0.504	0.294	42
Norway	0.412	0.252	39
Sweden	0.443	0.281	37
Italy	0.516	0.325	37
Netherlands	0.440	0.283	36
Japan	0.488	0.330	32
United Kingdom	0.527	0.358	32
Australia	0.483	0.337	30
New Zealand	0.461	0.333	28
Canada	0.440	0.322	27
Switzerland	0.387	0.295	24
United States	**0.508**	**0.394**	**22**
Mean	*0.479*	*0.304*	*36*

OECD *Government at a Glance 2017*

Table 8.19 Areas of public social spending
% of GDP for total and specified areas, 2016

Country	Total	Old-age pensions	Income support to working-age pop	Health
France	31.5	13.8	5.4	8.6
Finland	29.5	11.1	6.5	5.8
Belgium	29.3	10.2	8.0	8.0
Denmark	29.0	8.0	5.9	6.7
Italy	28.6	16.3	4.1	6.8
Austria	27.6	13.4	5.0	6.5
Sweden	27.4	7.7	4.3	6.6
Germany	24.8	10.1	3.5	7.9
Japan	23.1	10.2	2.0	7.8
Netherlands	22.9	5.4	6.4	7.9
United Kingdom	21.9	6.1	4.6	7.1
Norway	21.8	5.8	5.0	5.5
Ireland	20.1	4.9	7.0	5.5
New Zealand	19.4	5.1	4.6	7.4
Switzerland	19.2	6.4	4.0	6.6
United States	**18.8**	**6.9**	**2.3**	**8.0**
Australia	18.7	4.3	4.9	6.4
Canada	16.8	4.6	4.1	7.1
Mean	23.9	8.4	4.9	7.0

OECD *Society at a Glance 2016*

Table 8.20 Children in poverty
Percentage of children growing up in relative poverty
Earliest and latest available years

Country	Near 1980	Near 2013
Denmark	5.2	3.6
Finland	3.2	4.4
Sweden	4.8	4.7
Netherlands	4.2	4.9
Norway	4.9	6.7
Belgium	3.5	7.2
Switzerland	4.3	7.9
United Kingdom	7.7	8.8
Austria	4.8	10.1
Ireland	13.8	10.4
Japan	–	11.3
France	7.8	11.4
Germany	2.8	11.4
Australia	13.6	14.4
Canada	14.8	17.8
Italy	11.1	21.0
United States	**18.9**	**21.3**
Mean	7.8	10.4

No data on New Zealand
Luxembourg Income Study database

The final Table (8.19) includes health as well as welfare to see where social spending is devoted. The last three columns do not sum to the first data 'total' column because other small miscellaneous areas are omitted.

The table quickly leads to the conclusion that any rhetoric about cutting back the welfare state is unlikely to succeed. Much of the political anger against welfare is about it going to undeserving people of working age—through unemployment, but also incapacity, benefits—but this is a relatively small area of expense, especially in the United States.

Two areas—old-age pensions and health—make up two-thirds of social spending across these 18 countries, and these are both likely to grow rather than shrink. In most countries, old-age pensions are the largest area of spending and, with the ageing society, will keep increasing. In the United States and other anglophone countries, health often takes a larger share but neither is there any sign of health spending being reduced.

8.7 Child Poverty and Social Mobility

In 2018, Arizona Democratic Party candidate for the US Senate Dr. Kyrsten Sinema claimed: 'There's really no other country in the world where a little girl who grew up homeless living in a gas station could ever dream of serving in the United States Congress and run for the United States Senate'.[2] This log cabin to White House theme is embraced both by conservative figures and by left-of-centre politicians such as Sinema and Barack Obama.

It has been a long-standing American belief that it provides exceptional opportunities for upward mobility. In fact, nearly all these democracies have examples of people rising from poverty to high political office.

What is representative about Sinema's story is how commonplace it is to grow up poor in America. Table 8.20 shows that America has consistently had the highest rate of relative childhood poverty among these 18 democracies. In both the earliest available and the latest available years, the American figure was more than double the average of the others. In both years, the countries of north-western Europe, especially Scandinavia, had the lowest rates, leading presidential contender Bernie Sanders to suggest that America

---

[2] Also draws on: Keon Vleminckx & Timothy Smeeding, *Child Well-Being, Child Poverty and Child Policy in Modern Nations*, (Bristol: Policy Press, 2001). Brendon O'Connor, *A Political History of the American Welfare System*, (Lanham, MD: Rowman & Littlefield, 2001). Emily Badger, Claire Cain Miller, Adam Pearce & Kevin Quealy, 'Extensive Data Shows Punishing Reach of Racism for Black Boys,' *The New York Times*, March 19, 2018. Timothy Noah, *The Great Divergence: America's Growing Inequality Crisis and What We Can Do about it* (New York: Bloomsbury Publishing USA, 2012) Rasmus Landersø & James J. Heckman, 'The Scandinavian Fantasy: The Sources of Intergenerational Mobility in Denmark and the US,' *Scandinavian Journal of Economics*, 119(1) 178–230 (2017).

should learn from Denmark, which had the lowest child poverty figure of 3.6%.

Conservative American politicians have often blamed child poverty rates on children being born out of wedlock and being raised by single mothers. Table 8.21 severely qualifies that claim. In every country, the rate of child poverty is higher among those living with a single mother than in two-parent families and often by a considerable margin. However, the differences in poverty rates in single-mother families are just as notable: Switzerland, Norway, Australia, the United States and United Kingdom all have similarly high numbers of children living with a single mother, but child poverty is much lower in Norway and Switzerland.

David Brady in *Rich Democracies, Poor People* concludes that: 'generous social policies are much more important to achieving low poverty than economic performance or demographic factors like single parenthood'. The table shows that those countries having the greatest commitment to welfare are clustered at the top. Within America itself, analysts of the impact of President Johnson's 'war on poverty' programmes have long demonstrated this, in contrast to the Reagan mantra that 'government is not the solution to our problem; government is the problem'.

To experience poverty is bad enough, but it assumes added dimensions if it is hard for the individuals affected to escape from it, or if growing up in poverty sentences children to a lifetime of deprivation. Table 8.22 shows that the poverty trap is potent in most of the countries. In the top four countries, slightly more than half moved out of the relative poverty in the three-year period under review. In the bottom four—Canada, Italy, the United States and Ireland—six out of ten were still in poverty after three years.

The poverty trap in the USA has a particularly racial aspect to it as a 2018 *New York Times* study illustrates. The *Times* tracked 10,000 poor boys and found that only 2% of black boys in the study were rich as adults whereas 10% of white boys were; whereas 48% of poor black boys were still poor as adults compared to 31% of white boys remaining poor.

The first challenge in measuring social mobility across generations is to gather good longitudinal data. But equally account needs to be taken of the social changes occurring—the changing shape of the economy and so the changing distribution of occupations; of technological change; of the

Table 8.21 Child poverty and family structure
% of children living in poverty, around 2013

Country	Living in two-parent families	Living with single mother	% of children living with single mother
Denmark	2.3	7.9	16.8
Norway	3.3	10.4	18.1
Switzerland	7.5	12.8	21.1
Finland	2.2	15.1	11.7
Netherlands	3.0	18.7	11.6
Sweden	6.4	21.9	9.9
New Zealand	4.0	22.1	13.8
Ireland	6.4	25.0	20.5
Austria	7.0	26.9	15.4
Belgium	4.9	28.0	10.3
France	8.2	29.4	13.7
Germany	7.5	30.1	15.9
Japan	9.7	32.6	6.2
Australia	9.5	35.9	17.3
United States	**9.5**	**35.9**	**17.3**
Canada	13.7	44.0	12.4
United Kingdom	13.6	48.5	20.6
Italy	17.6	49.4	9.8
Mean 2013	*7.5*	*27.0*	*14.4*
Mean 1980	*5.9*	*23.2*	*9.4*

Luxembourg Income Study database

Table 8.22 Persistence of poverty
% of those still in the relative poverty after three years, 2007 approximately

Country	
Netherlands	41
Denmark	44
Germany	46
Austria	48
France	50
United Kingdom	50
Belgium	52
Finland	54
Australia	56
Canada	61
Italy	62
United States	**63**
Ireland	69
Mean	*53*

No data on Japan, New Zealand, Norway, Sweden, Switzerland
OECD *Growing Unequal? Income Distributions and Poverty in OECD Countries* (2008)

Table 8.23 Intergenerational mobility
Intergenerational earning elasticity, father to son
(Lower = more mobility)

Country	Elasticity
Denmark	0.15
Norway	0.17
Finland	0.18
Canada	0.25
Australia	0.26
Sweden	0.27
New Zealand	0.29
Germany	0.32
Japan	0.34
France	0.44
Switzerland	0.46
United States	**0.47**
Italy	0.50
United Kingdom	0.50

No data on Austria, Belgium, Ireland or the Netherlands
Miles Corak 'Inequality from Generation to Generation: the United States in comparison' in Robert S Rycroft *The Economics of Inequality, Poverty and Discrimination in the 21st Century* (Proquest Ebook Central, 2014)

growing participation of women in the labour force; and of the extent and diffusion of economic growth. Table 8.23 gives a measure of father–son mobility, and—consistently with the other tables on this page—it shows that mobility is greatest in the strong welfare states of Scandinavia. While Canada and Australia often are closer to the United States on inequality measures, here they show greater mobility. The United States is among the three countries with the lowest amount of social mobility. Italy and Ireland also tend to do consistently worse when it comes to pathways from poverty.

The American self-image of a land of opportunity and social mobility was formed in the nineteenth century in contrast to the rigidity of European social structures. It is a self-image that is out of step with contemporary realities. The relative poverty among children is greater in America, and poverty is less of a long-term trap in many European countries than it is in America.

9 Immigration and Refugees

9.1 Immigration Flows

Human migration is a major feature of the contemporary world. In 2017, according to the United Nations, there were 258 million people, or 3.3% of the world's population, who lived outside their country of birth. In 2000, it was 175 million, 2.8%. So the number is increasing both absolutely and proportionally.

Migration, both permanent and temporary, is overwhelmingly from poorer to richer countries, and not only to the affluent West. There is a very big inflow of migrants to provide labour to the oil-rich Middle Eastern countries. There are also important regional flows, such as to South Africa from the poorer African countries to its north.

Not only are many migrants seeking to improve their own lives, but many are supporting families in their homelands. Annual remittance flows total $US 580.6 billion, most of which is sent to low- and middle-income economies, with the greatest amounts going to India, China, the Philippines and Mexico.

Some countries (India, Russia and Pakistan) figure in both Tables 9.3 and 9.4, attracting immigrants from poorer nearby countries, while large numbers of their own citizens seek a more affluent life elsewhere. More countries in the world had net emigration than immigration in 2017, although for many the differences were close to zero. Four countries—India, Mexico, Russia and China—had more than 10 million emigrants in 2017 (Table 9.4).

Beyond the very large legal migration is irregular migration. Because of its clandestine nature, it is impossible to get authoritative data. It is estimated that there were 50 million irregular migrants in 2010, many of whom rely on smuggling services. It is a particular issue in the United States, where Pew Research estimated in 2014 there were 11.1 million undocumented migrants, down from the 2007 peak of 12.2 million. Much darker than this, the International Labour Organisation estimated that 21 million individuals are victims of forced labour globally, nearly always associated with gross exploitation.

Apart from permanent migration, as travel has become cheaper and easier, in recent years there has been a sharp increase in temporary unskilled labour migration, with seasonal workers being the most numerous; there were 685,000 in 2016, an increase of 30%.

In recent times, immigration has become a much more politically charged issue. Former British tabloid editor, Kelvin MacKenzie commented after Britain voted to leave the European Union that Brexit was won on immigration 'by a thousand miles'. Right-wing populist parties in Western Europe, such as France's National Front, make hostility to immigration central to their appeal, while in the US 2016 election, candidate Donald Trump denounced Mexicans as thieves and rapists and pledged to build a wall on the country's southern border.

The confluence of several factors—large illegal immigration, economic insecurity, controversy over asylum seekers, pressures to take more refugees, plus anxiety over terrorist attacks and some cultural confrontations—have all contributed to this growth. Nor is there any neat relationship between number of immigrants and anti-immigrant sentiment.

But at the same time as political controversy has increased, some economists have stressed the desirability of increasing immigration as one strategy to address the ageing society. As the natural rate of population growth has declined, migration has become a more important source of population increase. Table 9.2 shows that in particular in European countries, net migration was a more important factor in population growth than natural increase, although this is not so in the United States. In some countries—Italy, Germany, Austria and Finland—natural population growth was either close to zero or negative. Table 9.2 expresses in growth per thousand population. When reduced to percentage terms, only the top seven have growth rates of more than one per cent per annum, a historically low figure.

Globally, the United States is the country in the world with the most immigrants, around 50 million, four times as many as the next largest recipients (Table 9.3). So America's traditional reputation as a melting pot still has contemporary

© Springer Nature Singapore Pte Ltd. 2020
R. Tiffen et al., *How America Compares*, How the World Compares,
https://doi.org/10.1007/978-981-13-9582-6_9

Table 9.1 Scale of immigration
Foreign-born people as % of total population

Country	2000	2017
Switzerland	22	29
Australia	23	28
New Zealand	17	25
Canada	17	20
Austria	11	19
Sweden	11	18
Belgium	10	17
Ireland	9	17
Germany	13	16
Norway	7	15
United Kingdom	8	14
United States	**11**	**14**
France	10	13
Netherlands	10	13
Denmark	6	11
Italy	4	10
Finland	3	7
Japan	1	2
Mean	*11*	*16*

OECD *Immigration Outlook 2017* and latest figures from OECD *Immigration Outlook 2018*

Table 9.3 Countries with most immigrants
Twenty countries with most immigrants 2017

Country	Millions
United States	**49.8**
Saudi Arabia	12.2
Germany	12.2
Russia	11.7
United Kingdom	8.8
United Arab Emirates	8.3
France	7.9
Canada	7.9
Australia	7.0
Spain	5.9
Italy	5.9
India	5.2
Ukraine	5.0
Turkey	4.9
South Africa	4.0
Kazakhstan	3.6
Thailand	3.6
Pakistan	3.4
Jordan	3.2
Kuwait	3.1

United Nations Department of Economic and social Affairs/Population division *International Migration Report 2017*

Table 9.2 Immigration and population growth
Growth per 1000 population, 2015
Total, natural growth and growth through immigration

Country	Total	Natural	Net migration
Ireland	20.5	7.6	12.9
New Zealand	17.3	6.0	11.3
Australia	13.6	6.2	7.4
Austria	13.2	0.2	13.0
Germany	12.0	−2.3	14.3
Switzerland	10.8	2.3	8.5
Sweden	10.6	2.4	8.1
Canada	8.6	3.5	5.1
Norway	8.5	3.5	5.0
Denmark	8.4	1.0	7.4
United States	**8.4**	**5.2**	**3.2**
United Kingdom	7.8	2.7	5.1
Belgium	6.5	1.0	5.5
Netherlands	4.6	1.4	3.2
France	4.1	3.1	1.0
Finland	2.8	0.5	2.3
Italy	−2.1	−2.7	.5
Mean	*9.2*	*2.4*	*6.7*

No data on Japan
OECD *Immigration Outlook 2017* and latest figures from OECD *Immigration Outlook 2018*

Table 9.4 Countries with highest emigration
Twenty countries of origin of most international migrants, 2017

Country	Millions
India	16.6
Mexico	13.0
Russia	10.6
China	10.0
Bangladesh	7.5
Syria	6.9
Pakistan	6.0
Ukraine	5.9
Philippines	5.7
United Kingdom	4.9
Afghanistan	4.8
Poland	4.7
Indonesia	4.2
Germany	4.2
Kazakhstan	4.1
Palestine	3.8
Romania	3.6
Turkey	3.4
Egypt	3.4
Italy	3.0

United Nations Department of Economic and social Affairs/Population division *International Migration Report 2017*

resonance. While the United States has more immigrants than the other affluent, stable democracies, proportionally, as Table 9.1 shows, in 2017 it was in the bottom half of these 18 countries. One notable feature of the table is that in every single country, the proportion of foreign-born people increased over these 17 years. In some countries, the rise has been very substantial. Now, in only two countries, Finland and Japan are the proportions of foreign-born less than one in ten.

9.2 Settlement of Immigrants

While immigration has increased greatly in a more globalised world, immigrants are often still stepping into an uncertain future. There are variations in how well they settle in their countries of destination and how welcoming those countries are. Often migrants who leave their country of birth in search of a better future can become a relatively deprived group in their new societies. As these tables show, the variations are considerable.

Different countries have had long-standing attitudes towards immigration. The United States, Canada, Australia and New Zealand, which all began their modern history as British settler colonies, are sometimes labelled settlement countries. They have seen immigration as part of their nation-building strategies and have offered migrants relatively good prospects for long-term successful settlement. Some such as Britain, France and the Netherlands have been long-standing destinations especially for people from their former colonies. Others such as Germany, as its manufacturing increased enormously in the post-war decades, were interested in having 'guest workers' to meet immediate labour shortages.

To some extent, these differences are evident in the plight of immigrants. Table 9.5 shows that overall female immigrants have the highest unemployment rate. However, the countries vary in both how high their total unemployment is and on how much difference there is between groups. In the United States, Australia, New Zealand, Canada and Britain, immigrant males actually have a lower unemployment rate than native-born males. The unemployment rate for female migrants is always higher than their native-born counterparts, although again, the difference is minimal in Australia and the United States.

In several European countries, however, male and female migrants have markedly higher unemployment rates, and this is true of the countries with the worst unemployment. In Italy, France and Belgium, the figures suggest the danger of a deprived underclass forming. The gap between native-born and foreign-born unemployment rates in the Scandinavian countries is at least partly explained by the large number of migrants admitted on humanitarian grounds in recent years to these countries.

Just as conditions of close to full employment make it easier for newcomers to adapt and find jobs, so the relative poverty rate in societies overall affects the immigrant experience. In Table 9.6, some of the countries which did best in Table 9.5—the United States, Canada and Australia—are at the upper end of inequality and have the highest relative poverty rates for their domestically born populations. The migrant poverty rate is not markedly greater than domestic, but all fall in the bottom half of the table. In some European countries, the relative poverty rate for immigrants is more than double what it is for the native-born. Belgium is the outlier with the rate being treble.

Table 9.5 Unemployment

Unemployment rates among native-born and foreign-born males and females, 2014

Country	Female native-born	Female foreign-born	Male native-born	Male foreign-born
Australia	6.1	6.6	6.3	5.6
United States	**6.1**	**6.6**	**6.8**	**5.1**
Germany	4.2	7.4	4.8	8.3
New Zealand	6.5	7.5	5.3	5.2
United Kingdom	5.5	8.2	6.6	6.1
Norway	2.5	8.3	3.2	7.6
Switzerland	3.3	8.3	3.4	7.1
Canada	5.9	8.4	7.5	7.4
Austria	4.5	9.5	4.8	10.8
Netherlands	5.9	11.8	6.3	12.2
Ireland	8.6	12.7	13.0	14.2
Denmark	6.0	13.9	6.0	10.8
France	8.8	15.7	9.3	16.4
Sweden	5.9	16.2	6.6	16.6
Belgium	6.5	16.3	7.2	18.7
Finland	7.5	17.1	9.1	16.5
Italy	13.3	17.4	11.6	15.6
Mean	6.3	11.3	6.9	10.8

No data on Japan
OECD *Indicators of Immigrant Integration 2015: Settling In*

Tables 9.6 Poverty

Relative poverty rates (60% or below of median equivalised income), %, 2012, in households with immigrants or native-born

Country	Immigrant	Native	Ratio
Germany	20.8	15.4	1.4
Ireland	21.4	15.9	1.3
Switzerland	23.9	14.9	1.6
New Zealand	25.3	18.7	1.4
Norway	25.5	11.2	2.3
Netherlands	25.7	10.2	2.5
United Kingdom	26.1	16.2	1.6
Sweden	26.8	15.4	1.7
Austria	27.6	13.9	2.0
Australia	29.2	21.5	1.4
Canada	30.1	21.6	1.4
France	30.4	12.5	2.4
Denmark	31.6	14.1	2.2
Italy	35.2	18.7	1.9
United States	**37.3**	**23.4**	**1.6**
Finland	38.1	14.9	2.6
Belgium	39.1	13.0	3.0
Mean	29.1	16.0	1.9

No data on Japan
OECD *Indicators of Immigrant Integration 2015: Settling In*

Table 9.7 Adult literacy

Adult literacy scores 2012 in each group and percentage with low to basic literacy

Country	Native-born	Foreign-born native language speaker	Foreign-born foreign language speaker	Native-born low performers %	Foreign-born native speakers low performers %	Foreign-born foreign speakers low performers %
Australia	285	289	256	11	10	27
Canada	280	269	250	13	19	31
Ireland	268	274	249	17	12	28
UK	275	269	245	14	22	35
Norway	284	283	242	9	14	37
Finland	291	301	240	8	3	36
Netherlands	290	267	239	8	24	40
Austria	274	279	237	12	14	39
Germany	275	257	236	14	24	42
Denmark	276	273	232	12	15	42
Sweden	290	277	230	7	9	47
USA	**275**	**266**	**230**	**14**	**21**	**47**
Italy	253	248	223	26	22	48
Belgium	279	279	221	13	13	52
France	268	243	221	18	34	50
Mean	277	272	237	13	17	40

No data on Japan, New Zealand or Switzerland

OECD *Indicators of Immigrant Integration 2015: Settling In*

Literacy is important for people's ability to function effectively. In 2012, the OECD conducted a large and expensive study of adult literacy (see Sect. 7.8). The literacy scores reported are on a scale of 0–500, and six groups or levels of competence distinguished. The first three columns of Table 9.7 give the mean scores, while the final three columns give the proportions in the bottom two groups (classed as Level One and Below Level One). These groups would find it hard to participate in many of the tasks required in a complex society. Where high proportions are found in the final column of the table, there is the danger that those people will feel excluded from the larger society.

It is clear that as soon as we wish to make more precise analyses that we need to move beyond a simple binary of native-born and foreign-born. This table makes a critical distinction between immigrants who already speak the native language and those who don't. Unsurprisingly, the former are very close to the native-born in their literacy levels. Such distinctions could go further, for example, taking account of the relative proportions coming from economically less developed countries.

While socio-economic integration is basic, political integration—and the security and status that go with citizenship—is also important. Table 9.8 looks only at those immigrants who have been residing in their new country for ten or more years. The top two countries for percentage of the population born overseas (Table 9.1), Australia and Switzerland, have

Table 9.8 Citizenship

% of immigrants residing in country 10+ years, 2012–13, who have been naturalised as citizens

Country	% naturalised
Canada	92
Sweden	84
Australia	83
Netherlands	78
Norway	72
Finland	66
United Kingdom	66
Belgium	62
France	62
Germany	61
United States	**60**
Ireland	56
Austria	53
Denmark	50
Switzerland	45
Italy	37
Mean	64

No data on Japan, New Zealand

OECD *Indicators of Immigrant Integration 2015: Settling In*

very different profiles here, where Switzerland and Italy are the only two countries where less than half of these long-term immigrants have been naturalised. The United States, perhaps surprisingly, is just below the mean.

9.3 Refugees

In 1951, the United Nations adopted the Convention relating to the Status of Refugees, which has been further refined since.[1] Many countries embraced the need to care for refugees in the aftermath of the Holocaust suffered by the Jews under Nazi Germany and with hundreds of thousands fleeing communist rule in Eastern Europe.

A refugee is defined as any person who owing to a well-founded fear of being persecuted on the basis of race, religion or nationality is outside their country and cannot return because of that fear. The United Nations High Commission for Refugees also seeks to help two other main groups. One group is asylum seekers, people who have fled their home country and apply for asylum in the country where they now are, whose refugee status has not yet been decided. The other group is internally displaced persons, individuals forced to flee from their home, but remaining within that country's borders. This group also includes those fleeing from natural disasters.

Since the UN's adoption of the convention, the nature of refugees has changed—from being principally a European phenomenon to one occurring mainly in the Third World. Moreover, the number of refugees is on a scale that no one envisaged in 1951.

Table 9.9 shows that in 20 years to 2016, the number of people of concern to the UNHCR more than trebled. The table also shows the composition of the three main categories—the percentages do not sum to 100 because the other smaller categories are not included. In 2006, for the first time, internally displaced persons comprised a larger group than refugees, and in 2016 were double their number. The country with the largest number of internally displaced persons is Colombia, where Civil War has raged intermittently for many years.

As can be seen in both Tables 9.10 and 9.11 fleeing from war and armed conflict is the most important factor in producing refugees. Syria had a pre-war population of 22 million, and in 2015 almost 5 million refugees left the country with another six and a half million displaced within its borders. The longer-running wars in Afghanistan and Iraq are still causing considerable disruption for their populations. The human side of these conflicts only occasionally receives attention in the Western news media. It should particularly be remembered that half of all refugees are children.

Outside the Middle East, the wars in northern and central Africa—often receiving little attention in the West—are generating large numbers of displaced peoples. Eight of the 16 countries which generated the most refugees were in North or Central Africa.

Most refugees simply flee to the closest destination where they think they will be safe and often do so in very large groups and often then live in specially constructed camps. These arrivals and the urgent settlement problems they bring are often a strain for the receiving country, especially when these countries are themselves not rich. In fact, 84% of refugees are in developing countries. Turkey and Pakistan have been the largest recipients of people escaping from wars. The Democratic Republic of the Congo figures in Tables 9.10, 9.11 and 9.12 showing how the conflicts in central Africa are not respecters of national boundaries.

The case in Table 9.11 which is least due to armed conflict and is rather a dramatic case of ethnic persecution is the treatment of the Rohingyas in Myanmar. The violence of the Burmese army against them has driven many into Bangladesh and resulted in an unknown number of deaths.

When examining the plight of refugees and asylum seekers the starkest statistic is that of the 16.1 million

Table 9.9 World totals of refugees

Year	Total persons of concern (millions)	Refugees %	Asylum seekers %	Internally displaced persons %
1997	20.0	60	5	23
2006	32.9	30	2	39
2016	67.7	25	4	54

OECD *Indicators of Immigrant Integration 2015: Settling In*
United Nations High Commission for Refugees *Statistical Yearbook 2015*
Older figures also draw on UNHCR *The UNHCR 2007 Statistical Yearbook 2006;* UNHCR *Refugees and Others of Concern to UNHCR 1999 Statistical Overview* (Geneva, July 2000)

Table 9.10 Internally displaced persons
Countries with more than one million internally displaced persons receiving UNHCR assistance, end 2015

Country	Number (millions)
Colombia	6.94
Syria	6.57
Iraq	4.40
Sudan	3.22
Yemen	2.53
Nigeria	2.15
South Sudan	1.69
Democratic Republic of the Congo	1.56
Afghanistan	1.17
Pakistan	1.15
Somalia	1.13

United Nations High Commission for Refugees *Statistical Yearbook 2015*

---

[1] Also draws on Refugee Council (Australia) UNHCR Global Trends 2015—How Australia compares with the world (Sydney, June 20, 2016); 2017 figures are from the *OECD Immigration Outlook 2018*.

Table 9.11 National origins of refugees
Countries from which more than a quarter of a million refugees have fled, end 2015

Country	Thousands
Syria	4873
Afghanistan	2666
Somalia	1123
South Sudan	779
Sudan	627
Democratic Republic of the Congo	541
Central African Republic	471
Myanmar	452
Eritrea	407
Colombia	340
Ukraine	321
Vietnam	313
Pakistan	298
Burundi	293
Rwanda	286
Iraq	264

United Nations High Commission for Refugees *Statistical Yearbook 2015*

Table 9.12 Refugees' country of asylum
Countries with most refugees, end 2015

Country	Thousands
Turkey	2541
Pakistan	1561
Lebanon	1070
Iran	979
Ethiopia	736
Jordan	664
Kenya	554
Uganda	477
Democratic Republic of the Congo	383
Chad	370

United Nations High Commission for Refugees *Statistical Yearbook 2015*

refugees under the UNHCR's mandate, at the end of 2015 just 107,000 resettlement places had been offered, representing a tiny 0.66% of the total. Some countries have a consistent record of accepting some refugees. As Table 9.14 shows, for several countries—the USA, Canada, Australia, New Zealand, Finland, Norway and the Netherlands—humanitarian reasons for admission comprised eight to 12% of their immigrant intake, and for most of these countries, this has been consistently the case for some years. But this international resettlement is not keeping pace (and as a total solution cannot keep pace) with the scale of the problem. Financial support for the UNHCR's activities is thus crucial, and the United States is the largest single donor, although the total international support falls short of what is needed.

Table 9.13 Asylum applications
Average per annum for each period, thousands

Country	Average 1980s	Average 1990s	Average 2003–07	Average 2012–14	2016	2017
United States	39.6	89.8	55.2	76.4	262.0	329.8
Germany	70.5	188.0	31.1	115.4	722.4	198.3
Italy	4.3	9.0	11.4	35.4	122.1	126.6
France	28.5	29.7	45.6	58.0	77.9	91.1
Canada	17.4	27.7	25.7	14.4	23.8	50.5
Australia	1.3	9.3	3.6	12.0	27.6	35.2
United Kingdom	4.5	37.4	37.5	29.6	38.4	33.3
Austria	12.8	13.0	20.9	20.0	40.0	22.2
Sweden	15.5	24.6	26.5	57.5	22.4	22.2
Japan	0.1	0.1	0.6	3.5	10.9	19.3
Switzerland	10.0	28.3	13.2	22.3	25.9	16.6
Netherlands	5.5	32.2	11.4	15.0	18.4	16.1
Belgium	4.7	18.0	14.2	14.7	14.7	14.0
Finland	0.0	1.8	2.9	3.0	5.3	4.3
Norway	2.4	5.4	8.2	11.4	3.2	3.4
Denmark	4.8	11.2	2.8	9.3	6.2	3.1
Ireland	–	1.8	5.1	1.0	2.2	2.9
New Zealand	–	1.1	0.5	0.2	0.4	0.6
Mean	*13.9*	*29.3*	*17.6*	*27.7*	*79.1*	*55.0*

United Nations High Commission for Refugees *Statistical Yearbook 2015*
Older figures also draw on UNHCR *Asylum Level and Trends in Industrialized Countries, 2007* (Geneva, March 18, 2008)

9.4 Asylum Seekers

As Table 9.9 on the previous page indicates, asylum seekers have always been a very small proportion of the total refugee problem, but they present a much more vexed political issue in many Western countries.[2]

The phrase 'asylum seekers' strictly refers to those whose refugee status has not yet been determined, but the fact that they are applying to stay in the country to which they have already travelled means they are a more confronting presence. Rather than simply crossing the closest border to find safety, they have sometimes travelled a very considerable distance, many seeking not just momentary safety, but a country where they can start a new life.

A combination of prosperity and proximity seems to account for the destinations asylum seekers go. The major sources of asylum seekers in the United States are from El Salvador, Venezuela and Guatemala, its own region, while those in Germany are drawn principally from Syria, Iraq and Afghanistan.

Table 9.13 also shows how the number of asylum seekers in these countries has grown, with the number in 2016 being almost six times the average annual rate in the 1980s. Again numbers rise and fall with the conflicts in adjoining regions. In particular, the wars accompanying the break-up of the former Yugoslavia caused a large number of asylum seekers to move into other European countries, with most going to Germany. Then, there was a substantial fall-off in the early 2000s.

But the war in Syria brought a new surge into Europe. After the peak year of 2016, where there was a total of 1,423,800 new asylum seekers in these 18 countries, in 2017 there was a fall to 989.5 thousand. This is still much higher than a few years earlier. Moreover, the trend wasn't universal, while Germany saw a sharp drop, in other parts of the world, less directly affected by conflicts in the Middle East, such as the United States, Canada and Australia, the number rose.

Asylum seekers are less easily ignored than the refugees who only go to the closest neighbouring country. But in addition, partly because they go so far, and because often they travel as small family and friendship groups, they are sometimes charged with being economic migrants, rather than refugees, especially because they often seek asylum in the most prosperous countries. Moreover, sometimes they enlist the aid of 'people smugglers', and so their plight becomes confounded with the quantitatively much bigger issue of illegal immigration. If they enter without normal permissions, they provoke concerns about countries' ability to enforce border sovereignty. This all comes on top of the considerable anti-immigrant sentiment already existing in some countries.

The longer journey of the asylum seekers has its own perils. In 2015, more than 5700 would-be migrants died or went missing during their journeys. More than 3770 of these are presumed to have drowned in the Mediterranean.

The increased urgency of issues surrounding refugees and asylum seekers is one of two factors that have reshaped the patterns of immigration intake. The other one as Table 9.14 shows is the contemporary importance of free movement between countries. This is particularly pertinent to the countries of the European Union, which allows people to go where they think opportunities might be greater. In seven countries, this comprises more than half the immigrant intake. This is the primary reason why in most European countries the migrant stock is so much greater in 2015 than in 2000 (Table 9.1).

Traditionally, the greatest number of immigrants came for family reasons, and that is still the case in the United States, Canada, Australia and New Zealand. These settlement countries, more than most others, have also long had a humanitarian component of immigrants, although their intakes are not sensitive to the scale of the external problem, but rather to their own established policies. In recent years,

Table 9.14 Types of migrant intake
2013 data

Country	Total intake (000s)	% Free movement	% Work	% Family	% Humanitarian
United States	990	0	8	74	12
Germany	469	76	5	12	7
United Kingdom	291	34	30	22	7
France	260	37	10	40	5
Canada	259	0	25	63	12
Australia	254	16	24	50	8
Italy	246	32	30	33	4
Switzerland	136	78	2	16	4
Netherlands	106	62	9	20	9
Sweden	87	25	4	37	33
Austria	65	78	2	16	4
Belgium	60	45	13	37	5
Norway	60	63	6	20	11
Japan	57	0	44	36	0
Denmark	52	53	15	17	7
New Zealand	44	8	23	61	8
Ireland	40	57	7	35	0
Finland	24	43	5	37	13
Mean		39	15	35	8

Family includes both families accompanying those coming for work and other family reunions. The small 'other' category has been omitted, so some rows sum to slightly less than 100
OECD Factbook 2016

---

[2]Also draws on Michelle Krupa and Bethlehem Feleke 'The US is on track to admit the fewest number of refugees since the resettlement program began' CNN 29-6-2018.

several European countries have expanded this part of their immigration intake, most dramatically Sweden, which, in 2013, took 33% of its immigrants for humanitarian reasons.

In contrast, under President Trump, the United States slashed the number of refugees it admitted. Since 1975, America has taken in more than three million refugees, more than any other country. In 2018, though it was projected to only admit just over 20,000 refugees, the lowest since modern policies began in 1980, and around one quarter the number admitted in 2016.

10 Gender

10.1 Women and Work

Tables 10.1 and 10.2 show contrasting trends in male and female labour force participation. While the male participation rate showed a substantial decline over this half century, down 11 percentage points for the 18 countries overall, female labour participation showed a dramatic increase, up 26 percentage points. Whereas the average female participation rate of these 18 affluent democracies was almost exactly half the male rate in the 1960s, by 2016 it was just 10 percentage points behind, or seven-eighths the male rate. The labour force participation rate is the proportion of the population of working age (15–64 years) that participates in the labour force either by working or actively seeking work.

In the 1960s, ten of the countries had male participation rates of 90% or more (remembering some labour force participants may be older than the working-age parameters, which explains how Switzerland had a participation rate above 100%), and the others were all in excess of 80%. By 2016, no country had a male participation rate as high as 90, and six had rates below 80, with Italy and Belgium having the lowest. However, since 2000, the male participation rate has stabilised.

Table 10.2 shows strong growth in female labour participation in all the selected countries. The most dramatic rise was in the Netherlands, which was the laggard in the field in the 1960s and now ranks near the top. It rose from 27 to 75%. The female rank ordering shows similarities and differences from the male rate. Switzerland, Sweden and Denmark are near the top in both, while Belgium and Italy are in the rear in both. Japan has the biggest contrast, second in Table 10.1 but 13th and below the mean in Table 10.2. The United States was somewhat below average in both tables. The American female participation rate was above average in the 1960s, but has since increased less than many others, and it actually dropped slightly in the twenty-first century.

Changing parental attitudes towards girls' entitlement to an education, rising educational attainment, stronger career aspirations, the financial pressures of family life and the gradual erosion of official and unofficial prejudice against women have all led to increasing female participation in paid employment.

Tables 10.3 and 10.4 give some support to the old adage that a 'woman's work is never done'. They are measures of the total amount of work—both paid and unpaid—men and women report that they do each day. The male and female minutes per day are broadly similar, with the mean for women being slightly higher.

However, the contrasts between how those totals are reached are substantial. In every country, men report doing more minutes of paid work than women, but also in every country women report doing more minutes of unpaid work than men. Similarly, in every country, males report spending more time on paid than unpaid work. In contrast, in 14 of 18 countries, women report they spend more time on unpaid work. In the four other countries, the difference is quite small.

The contrast is starkest among Japanese males who have the longest duration of paid work and the shortest of unpaid work—both by a very considerable distance. Indeed, Japanese males report spending twice as long in their paid work each day than do the bottom ranking French males, while the male mean for unpaid work is more than double what the Japanese do.

Three countries have a total of more than 500 minutes daily for total female work, but while Canada and Austria are fairly high on both measures, Italian women are in the bottom quarter on paid work, but have the highest figure for minutes of unpaid work, just ahead of Australian women. Norwegian and Swiss women report the least time spent on unpaid work, while Danish and Australian males report the most.

Remember that this is self-reported data, and it is simply a measure of time spent, and not of productivity or efficiency. However, the growing participation of women in the labour force does not seem to have been matched by recent figures in the amount of unpaid work, suggesting that some differences in gender roles remain considerable.

Table 10.1 Male labour force participation
Males in the labour force as % of males aged 15–64

Country	1960s	1980s	2000	2016
Switzerland	105	95	89	88
Japan	90	88	85	85
New Zealand	92	86	83	85
Netherlands	93	78	83	84
Sweden	91	86	82	84
United Kingdom	96	88	84	83
Denmark	95	88	84	83
Australia	94	86	82	82
Germany	93	82	79	82
Canada	88	85	82	82
Austria	89	81	80	81
Norway	90	87	85	80
United States	**87**	**85**	**84**	**79**
Finland	86	82	78	78
Ireland	98	85	80	78
France	89	78	74	76
Italy	88	79	74	75
Belgium	85	75	74	72
Mean	*92*	*84*	*81*	*81*

OECD *The Pursuit of Gender Equality* 2017

Table 10.3 Males paid and unpaid work
Males—minutes of paid and unpaid work per day

Country	Paid	Unpaid	Total
Japan	471	62	533
Canada	341	160	501
Austria	365	135	500
Netherlands	354	133	487
New Zealand	338	141	479
Australia	304	172	476
Switzerland	322	154	476
Ireland	344	129	473
United States	**322**	**149**	**471**
Norway	292	162	454
Italy	349	104	453
Denmark	260	186	446
Germany	282	164	445
United Kingdom	297	141	438
Belgium	266	151	416
Finland	249	159	408
France	233	143	376
Mean	*317*	*144*	*461*

No data on Sweden in Tables 10.3 and 10.4
OECD *The Pursuit of Gender Equality* 2017

Table 10.2 Female labour force participation
Females in the labour force as % of females aged 15–64

Country	1960s	1980s	2000	2016
Sweden	56	78	76	80
Switzerland	52	57	72	80
Denmark	53	75	76	77
Norway	39	68	77	76
Netherlands	27	43	65	75
New Zealand	35	53	67	75
Canada	40	62	70	74
Finland	63	73	72	74
Germany	49	53	63	74
United Kingdom	49	61	69	73
Austria	51	51	62	72
Australia	46	55	65	72
Japan	56	57	60	68
France	47	56	62	68
United States	**46**	**64**	**71**	**67**
Ireland	35	39	56	64
Belgium	39	49	56	63
Italy	34	41	46	55
Mean	*46*	*57*	*66*	*72*

OECD *The Pursuit of Gender Equality* 2017

Table 10.4 Females paid and unpaid work
Females—minutes of paid and unpaid work per day

Country	Paid	Unpaid	Total
Canada	267	254	521
Austria	249	269	518
Italy	197	315	513
Japan	206	299	506
Ireland	197	296	493
United States	**242**	**242**	**484**
Australia	172	311	483
Switzerland	269	207	475
New Zealand	205	264	469
Netherlands	205	254	460
United Kingdom	197	258	454
Germany	181	269	450
Finland	210	232	442
Norway	228	211	440
Denmark	195	243	437
Belgium	189	245	434
France	172	233	405
Mean	*211*	*259*	*470*

OECD *The Pursuit of Gender Equality* 2017

10.2 Gender and Education

Changing gender roles are clearest in education. In the past, at each level of educational attainment, males out-numbered females, but now the balance has swung the other way and at an increasing rate. In Table 10.5, the gap in the youngest cohort between males and females graduating with tertiary degrees was relatively small in 2000. On average, the female percentage was already greater, although in five countries the proportion of males still exceeded females. Over the next 15 years, the mean female graduation rate increased 16 points while the male rate increased only nine points. Not one of the 18 countries any longer had a higher proportion of male graduates. In 14 countries, 49% or more of females in this young cohort are graduates, but this is only true in Canada and Japan among males. The United States is close to the 2016 mean for both sexes, although in neither sex did it rise by as much as most others after 2000.

The trend towards a female majority has been edging up the education ladder—from completing secondary school to university undergraduate level and now towards the number of Ph.Ds. Other OECD data shows that in 2014 women comprised 47% of Ph.D. graduates across these countries. Apart from Japan, where just 30% of Ph.D. graduates are female, the other countries are clustered between 42 and 53%. The United States is one of several countries which are around 50-50.

The increasing number of female graduates has been accompanied by an increasing number of female professionals. In 1980, across these 18 countries, just one in six doctors were female. Thirty-five years later, it was more than four in ten, around two and a half times as many (Table 10.6). By 2015, more than half of all doctors are women in Finland and the Netherlands, with the other Scandinavian countries close behind. As is often the case in gender differences, Japan is considerably behind the western democracies. Perhaps more surprisingly, in each of the years, the United States ranks the second last. This is in contrast to its position in the other tables on this page and raises the question of why medicine has remained more of a masculine preserve than other professions in America.

Another long-running concern was that females were concentrated in some types of jobs. Table 10.7 shows the share of female graduates in science, technology, engineering and mathematics (STEM) degrees. A majority of graduates is male in all countries except Italy. This may reflect the relatively low proportion of young people graduating in Italy (11%). Among males in the 25–34-year-old cohort, the Italian graduation rate is just half the mean of the other countries. The United States is part of a group of five countries where females comprise more than 40% of STEM graduates.

Possibly the most male-concentrated contemporary profession in these countries is IT specialists. Just 1.4% of female employees work in this area, while the rate among male workers is more than four times as great (6.7%). The United States has a relatively high number of people working

Table 10.5 Gender and tertiary degrees
Share of young people with tertiary degrees by gender
% 25–34-year-old males and females with tertiary degrees

Country	Males 2000	Males 2015	Females 2000	Females 2015
Canada	45	50	56	68
Japan	46	58	49	61
Ireland	45	46	50	58
Norway	30	40	40	57
Australia	29	43	38	54
Denmark	25	36	34	54
Sweden	34	39	39	54
United Kingdom	30	46	29	53
United States	**36**	**42**	**42**	**51**
Belgium	33	37	39	50
Netherlands	27	41	26	50
Switzerland	35	47	17	50
Finland	30	33	46	49
France	32	40	37	49
New Zealand	26	35	31	43
Austria	16	36	14	42
Germany	23	29	20	31
Italy	10	19	13	31
Mean	*31*	*40*	*34*	*50*

OECD *The Pursuit of Gender Equality* 2017

Table 10.6 Female doctors
Female doctors as % of total

Country	1980	2000	2015
Finland	33	50	58
Netherlands	20	35	53
Denmark	20	36	49
Norway	17	34	48
Sweden	22	40	48
Austria	21	37	47
United Kingdom	20	35	46
Germany	22	36	46
France	21	37	44
New Zealand	16	33	44
Ireland	–	37	43
Canada	15	31	42
Italy	17	30	41
Belgium	15	28	41
Switzerland	17	29	41
Australia	19	30	40
United States	**11**	**25**	**35**
Japan	10	14	20
Mean	*19*	*33*	*43*

OECD *The Pursuit of Gender Equality* 2017

Table 10.7 Women with science and technology degrees
Female Share of Science, Technology, Engineering and Mathematics (STEM) graduates (2015)

Country	%
Italy	53
United Kingdom	46
Canada	45
Finland	43
United States	**40**
Sweden	40
New Zealand	39
Germany	38
France	38
Australia	37
Ireland	37
Denmark	36
Austria	34
Norway	33
Switzerland	32
Belgium	29
Netherlands	27
Japan	25
Mean	37

OECD *The Pursuit of Gender Equality* 2017

Table 10.8 Gender and IT specialists
IT specialists as % of all male and female workers 2014

Country	Male	Female	Gap
Finland	9.8	2.2	7.6
Sweden	8.3	2.0	6.3
Canada	7.1	2.0	5.1
United States	**6.0**	**1.9**	**4.1**
Ireland	6.7	1.7	5.0
United Kingdom	7.6	1.5	6.1
Denmark	6.7	1.4	5.3
Australia	5.8	1.4	4.4
Switzerland	8.4	1.2	7.2
Norway	6.7	1.2	5.5
Belgium	6.3	1.1	5.2
Netherlands	7.1	1.0	6.1
Germany	5.8	1.0	4.8
France	4.6	0.9	3.7
Italy	4.1	0.8	3.3
Austria	5.6	0.7	4.9
Mean	*6.7*	*1.4*	*5.3*

No data on Japan and New Zealand
OECD *The Pursuit of Gender Equality* 2017

as IT specialists, just a little behind Finland, Sweden and Canada, and has a smaller rate of difference between males and females than these countries Table 10.8.

Both in IT and in the proportion of STEM graduates, the United States is a relative leader in allowing females to move into traditionally male domains. It sits around the middle in the proportion of female graduates, but is a laggard in the number of female doctors.

10.3 Glass Ceilings and Equity Issues

There is a substantial earnings gap between men and women, but its dimensions and causes need to be precisely delineated. Other OECD data shows that in annual labour income, there is a 40% gap across these 18 countries. However, this pays no regard, for example, to the much greater proportion of women working part-time. Table 10.9 offers a more exact comparison, looking at the gap between the median pay of full-time employees. This shows a much narrower but still substantial gap of 13.5% overall.

Some countries are consistent on different measures of gender equity—Japan is usually near the bottom; the Scandinavian countries near the top. However, others bounce around. For example, Belgium and Italy (and to a lesser extent France) rank low on women's participation in the labour force (Table 10.2), but at the top on the closeness of the median pay for each sex, showing that the somewhat lower proportion of women working full-time are closer to men in their income. The United States ranks the second last on this measure.

Table 10.10 captures the current flux in women's status and opportunities. Female participation has increased so that in 2015 half the central government employees in these 18

Table 10.9 Median pay of males and females
Difference between median male and female earnings of full-time employees divided by male median earnings

Country	2010	2015
Belgium	4.6	3.4
Italy	9.9	5.6
Denmark	8.9	5.8
New Zealand	7.0	6.1
Norway	8.1	7.1
France	9.1	9.9
Australia	14.0	13.0
Sweden	14.3	13.4
Netherlands	17.9	14.1
Ireland	12.8	14.4
Switzerland	20.1	16.9
Austria	19.2	17.0
Germany	16.8	17.1
United Kingdom	19.2	17.1
Finland	18.9	18.1
Canada	19.0	18.6
United States	**18.8**	**18.9**
Japan	28.7	25.7
Mean	*14.9*	*13.5*

OECD *Employment Outlook* 2017

10.3 Glass Ceilings and Equity Issues

Table 10.10 Female public servants
Female % of central government employees; and % central government employees in senior positions 2015

Country	% central government employees	% of senior positions
Sweden	58	44
Norway	55	43
Canada	55	40
Australia	58	37
United Kingdom	54	37
Finland	58	34
United States	**43**	**34**
Italy	52	33
France	59	32
Austria	45	29
Ireland	60	29
Netherlands	44	28
Denmark	53	22
Belgium	52	21
Switzerland	31	15
Japan	18	3
Mean	50	30

No data on Germany or New Zealand
OECD *The Pursuit of Gender Equality* 2017

Table 10.11 Females in managerial employment
Female % managerial employment and gap compared with their % of labour force

Country	% 2016	Gap
United States	**43.4**	**3**
Sweden	39.5	8
Australia	36.2	10
Norway	36.0	11
Canada	35.5	12
United Kingdom	35.4	11
Switzerland	35.2	11
Ireland	34.3	11
Finland	33.3	15
Belgium	32.6	14
France	31.7	16
Austria	29.7	17
Germany	29.3	17
Denmark	26.9	20
Italy	26.6	16
Netherlands	26.0	20
Japan	12.4	31
Mean	32.0	14.3

No data on New Zealand
OECD *The Pursuit of Gender Equality* 2017

Table 10.12 Females on company boards
% of female seats on boards of directors of publicly listed companies

Country	% 2016
Norway	41
France	37
Sweden	36
Finland	30
Italy	30
Netherlands	28
Belgium	27
Denmark	27
Germany	27
United Kingdom	27
Australia	23
New Zealand	23
Austria	20
Canada	19
United States	**16**
Ireland	16
Switzerland	13
Japan	3
Mean	25

OECD *The Pursuit of Gender Equality* 2017

countries were women. However, only three in ten of senior positions were occupied by women. Japan comes a distant last in both columns, while Sweden and Norway are at the top or close to the top in both columns. The United States is below the mean in the proportion of female public servants, but above average on those in senior ranks.

This picture is consistent with Table 10.11, where the United States has the highest proportion of females in managerial employment, and where their proportion is closest to their overall numbers in the workforce.

The English-speaking countries are near the top in proportions of women in management. But conversely, in Table 10.12—the proportion of female directors of publicly listed companies—the English-speaking countries are all in the bottom half of the table. Here West European, and especially Scandinavian, countries rank the highest. Membership of company boards is much more subject to networks and patronage than promotion to managerial positions, and this overall percentage is several points lower than the public sector managerial figure.

The rising proportion of female doctors and of public servants in general suggests that women have progressed most rapidly where the criteria are more meritocratic and less quickly where subjective considerations are more important. So barriers were broken first in education, then in the public sector and professions, and more slowly in the private sector.

10.4 Women in Public Life

The extent to which women were marginalised in politics in previous decades is shown in the first column in Table 10.13, where, as late as 1975, only one in twelve

Table 10.13 Female members of legislatures
Women members of lower houses of parliament or congress as % of total

Country	1975	1995	2017
Sweden	21	40	44
Finland	23	34	42
Norway	16	39	40
Belgium	7	12	39
Denmark	16	33	37
Germany	6	26	37
Netherlands	9	31	37
Switzerland	8	18	32
Austria	8	23	31
Italy	4	15	31
New Zealand	5	21	31
United Kingdom	4	10	30
Australia	0	10	29
Canada	3	18	26
France	2	6	26
Ireland	3	13	22
United States	4	11	19
Japan	1	3	10
Mean	*8*	*20*	*31*

Later years from *Pursuit of Gender Equality*; earlier from Inter-Parliamentary Union data

Table 10.14 Female cabinet ministers
Women cabinet ministers as % of total

Country	1994	2000	2017
France	7	38	53
Canada	14	24	52
Sweden	30	55	52
Denmark	29	45	43
Finland	39	44	39
New Zealand	8	44	39
Netherlands	31	31	38
Norway	35	42	37
Germany	16	36	33
United Kingdom	9	33	31
Switzerland	17	29	29
Italy	12	18	28
Ireland	16	19	27
Australia	13	20	24
Austria	16	31	23
Belgium	11	19	23
United States	14	32	17
Japan	6	6	16
Mean	*18*	*31*	*33*

Later years from *Pursuit of Gender Equality*; earlier from Inter-Parliamentary Union data

members of legislatures were women. Even the Scandinavian countries, usually the most advanced on gender issues, only had one in five. Since then numbers have grown rapidly, and by 2017, the overall percentage was four times as big as in 1975 (31:8). However, in none of these democracies has the proportion yet reached a 50–50 split.

There is considerable variation between countries, with the highest, Sweden, in 2017 being double or more the three lowest—Ireland, the United States and Japan. Japan is again the laggard on an issue of gender equality. It is perhaps more surprising that among these 18 democracies, the United States is the second lowest, with just one in five members of the House of Representatives being women.

With each election, numbers can fluctuate, but there is no doubt that the trend is towards more female representatives. That trend is not present in this century in numbers of cabinet members (Table 10.14). The overall percentage is only slightly higher than it was at the turn of the century. With much smaller numbers involved, percentages fluctuate more dramatically, and there are almost as many declines as there are increases. For example, the American figure has dropped precipitately, with far fewer female members of the cabinet under Trump than there was under Bill Clinton in 2000. In three countries in 2017—France, Canada and Sweden—more than half of cabinet members were females, while in Japan and the USA the figure was only about one in six.

In eight of the 18 democracies, including the United States, there is yet to be a female head of government. Indeed, the United States ranks bottom or the second last on each of these three measures of women's participation in public life (Table 10.15).

The country which has had the greatest number of heads of government is Switzerland, although this is a by-product of that country's particular political system. Government is much more collegial than in any other democracy, de-emphasising individual leadership in favour of the cabinet as a whole. Moreover, the president holds office only for one year, although that person may become president again at a later time. The succession is very influenced by seniority. Switzerland has had seven female presidents.

In the two semi-presidential systems—Finland and France—both the president and prime minister can be considered the head of government—president elected directly by the public, prime minister, appointed by the president, having normally been elected by their party. Finland has had one female president and two female prime ministers. Finnish President Tarja Halonen, who served for 12 years, is the second longest serving female head of government. France has had one female prime minister, although for less than one year, but has never had a female president.

The first female prime minister, among these 18 democracies, was Margaret Thatcher in the UK, and she enjoyed the third-longest tenure among them. The female leader with the longest tenure is the still-serving German Chancellor Angela Merkel. Helen Clark of New Zealand is the fourth, and in three separate tenures, Norway's Gro Harlem Brundtland fifth.

Table 10.15 Female heads of government

Country	Year	Title	Name	Tenure
Austria			Nil	
Belgium			Nil	
Ireland			Nil	
Italy			Nil	
Japan			Nil	
Netherlands			Nil	
Sweden			Nil	
United States			**Nil**	
Australia	2010	PM	Julia Gillard	3 y, 3 d
Canada	1993	PM	Kim Campbell	132 d
Denmark	2011	PM	Helle Thorning-Schmidt	3 y, 268 d
Finland	2000	Pres	Tarja Halonen	12 y
Finland	2003	PM	Anneli Jaatteenmaki	68 d
Finland	2010	PM	Mari Kiviniemi	1 y
France	1991	PM	Edith Cresson	323 d
Germany	2005	PM	Angela Merkel	12 y+
New Zealand	1997	PM	Jenny Shipley	2 y
New Zealand	1999	PM	Helen Clark	8 y, 350 d
New Zealand	2017	PM	Jacinda Ardern	+
Norway	1981	PM	Gro Harlem Brundtland	252 d
Norway	1986	PM	Gro Harlem Brundtland	3 y, 160 d
Norway	1990	PM	Gro Harlem Brundtland	5 y, 357 d
Norway	2013	PM	Erna Solberg	4 y, 127 d
Switzerland	1999	Pres	Ruth Dreifuss	1 y
Switzerland	2007	Pres	Micheline Calmy-Rey	1 y
Switzerland	2010	Pres	Doris Leuthard	1 y
Switzerland	2011	Pres	Micheline Calmy-Rey	1 y
Switzerland	2012	Pres	Eveline Widmer-Schlumpf	1 y
Switzerland	2016	Pres	Simonetta Sommaruga	1 y
Switzerland	2017	Pres	Doris Leuthard	1 y
United Kingdom	1979	PM	Margaret Thatcher	11 y, 208 d
United Kingdom	2016	PM	Theresa May	1 y+

+ means person still in office in early 2018; y = years d = days
Wikipedia, and national sources

This list of female heads of government provides a very mixed group of conservatives and liberals, electoral successes and electoral failures, and it would be hard for a political observer of any persuasion to think they are consistently superior or inferior to their male peers.

10.5 Global Gender Gap

There have been many attempts to capture gender inequality and female disadvantage in a single measure. One of the earliest was from the United Nations Development Program (UNDP), which adapted its Human Development Index (HDI) to create a Gender Development Index (GDI). As described in Chap. 3, the HDI was developed to go beyond crude aggregate measures of national income to gauge human well-being in society. It added life expectancy and educational achievements to its economic indicator.

It has since extended this into a Gender Development Index, which measures the differences in male and female HDI. It should be stressed that this is a measure of the gap between the sexes rather than the levels. Thus, a high score on this does not reflect women's life chances that come from living in a more educated or affluent society, but simply their chances relative to men in that country. There are 19 countries scoring 1000 or higher where females are doing better than males (and 170 where it is less than 1000). One that scores more than 1000 is Russia, but it is instructive to examine why. While Russian men have a much higher income than Russian women, and almost equal education levels, the key to Russia's high score is the large gap in life expectancy. The life expectancy at birth of Russian women is 76.8 years, but for men it is only 65.6 years. Poor life expectancy for men is hardly the most promising key to women's progress.

The UNDP also constructed a gender inequality index, which combines inequalities between men and women in three dimensions: reproductive health (maternal mortality; adolescent birth rate), empowerment (female share of seats in the legislature) and the labour market (some secondary schooling and labour force participation). The problem here is another common one with composite measures. It is not clear that more information is gained rather than lost by combining such disparate elements. (The two on the reproductive health are crucial to female well-being but are not a measure of gender inequality.)

Rather, in Table 10.16, we have chosen to use the latest edition of the Global Gender Gap produced by the World Economic Forum. Its score is as a decimal place where 1 would equal parity, and the decimal score can be expressed as a percentage of how much the gender gap has been overcome. The table reports the top 37 scoring countries, all the selected democracies and the bottom five scoring countries. This scale was chosen because it is based on comprehensive, diligent and transparent research.

It is also chosen because it is well-established (first compiled in 2006) and so changes can be traced. In its report on the Gender Gap in 2017, the average for the 144 countries was 68%. All the top ten countries have now crossed the threshold of closing more than 80% of their gender gap. But progress is slow. Of the 142 countries covered in the 2016 and 2017 reports, 82 improved their score while 60 went backwards. On current trends, the WEF estimates it would take 100 years for the 106 countries covered since 2006 to close the gender gap.

In some ways, more interesting than the total Gender Gap Index are the four dimensions on which it is based, calculated from 15 variables. On two of the dimensions, the gender gap globally has almost closed. On health outcomes, 96% of the gap has closed, and in educational attainments, 95% has closed. The big differences are in economic participation (only 58% of the gap closed) and political empowerment (23%).

The low ranking of the United States is surprising. America does very well on gender equity in educational attainment, rating near the top of all the countries. The variables that tear it down are, surprisingly, healthy life expectancy and, less surprisingly, political empowerment. The various measures on economic participation and opportunity are mixed but overall the USA is ranked 19th.

The ordering of countries in the table has several surprises. While the Scandinavian countries are grouped near the top, there are also countries from Africa, South America and Eastern Europe with high ratings. Important Asian countries, such as China (ranked 100), India (108), Japan (114) and South Korea (118) rank lower than they do in many other global indicators. The most predictable perhaps is that Islamic countries tend to rate lower, as, also, do countries racked by internal conflict.

Table 10.16 Global gender gap
World Economic Forum Gender Gap Index 2017
Global rankings for top 37 countries, and selected others, scores from 0 to 1 (equity)

Country	Rank	Score
Iceland	1	0.878
Norway	2	0.830
Finland	3	0.823
Rwanda	4	0.822
Sweden	5	0.816
Nicaragua	6	0.814
Slovenia	7	0.805
Ireland	8	0.794
New Zealand	9	0.791
Philippines	10	0.790
France	11	0.778
Germany	12	0.778
Namibia	13	0.777
Denmark	14	0.776
United Kingdom	15	0.770
Canada	16	0.769
Bolivia	17	0.758
Bulgaria	18	0.756
South Africa	19	0.756
Latvia	20	0.756
Switzerland	21	0.755
Burundi	22	0.755
Barbados	23	0.750
Spain	24	0.746
Cuba	25	0.745
Belarus	26	0.744
Bahamas	27	0.743
Lithuania	28	0.742
Mozambique	29	0.741
Moldova	30	0.740
Belgium	31	0.739
Netherlands	32	0.737
Portugal	33	0.734
Argentina	34	0.732
Australia	35	0.731
Colombia	36	0.731
Estonia	37	0.731
United States	**49**	**0.718**
Austria	57	0.709
Italy	82	0.692
Japan	114	0.657
Iran	140	0.583
Chad	141	0.575
Syria	142	0.568
Pakistan	143	0.546
Yemen	144	0.516

World Economic Forum *The Global Gender Gap 2017*

International Relations

11.1 Military Spending and Foreign Aid

The United States government will spend an estimated $7 trillion in 2018, making it the world's largest economic entity.[1] In the international arena, it exercises enormous power as an aid donor and as a buyer and seller of weapons. While there has been much speculation about the relative decline of the USA, among wealthy democracies there is still no other country that comes close to American spending for geopolitical purposes, even if the EU is taken as a single body.

In absolute terms, the United States is by far the world's largest donor of overseas direct aid, spending about $2.8 billion in 2017. But relative to gross national income (GNI) it is the smallest donor among these 18 affluent democracies (Table 11.3). In the 1970s, the UN General Assembly established a target of 0.7% GNI for ODA from developed countries; only a few Scandinavian countries regularly meet and exceed this target, though others such as Germany and the UK have steadily moved towards it. The OECD set a less ambitious goal of 0.3%, which a third of these countries do not reach.

Nonetheless, Americans believe that foreign aid takes up a far larger portion of the US budget than it actually does. A 2014 poll by the Kaiser Family Foundation found fewer than five per cent of respondents correctly estimated foreign aid as less than one per cent of US government spending, while the average respondent gave an estimate of 31%. This replicates other studies, going back decades, showing that the public grossly overestimates how much is spent on foreign aid. Social scientists have long hypothesised that this misperception dampens already precarious support for foreign aid among the American public, and 59% of Americans think they spend too much on foreign aid.

The United States is the undisputed world leader in military spending. With a defence budget of around $700 billion in 2018, it regularly outspends the next ten largest military spenders combined.

As we see in Table 5.6, it devotes a greater share of government spending to the military than any of the other selected countries. While military expenditure was 8.8% of government spending in 2017—down in recent years because of the budget 'sequester' negotiated by Congress in 2013—the Congressional Budget Office states one-sixth of all *federal* spending goes to national defence. The Department of Defense has 3.2 million employees, making it the world's largest employer according to *Forbes* magazine (China's People's Liberation Army is the second largest, with 2.3 million, while Walmart and McDonalds are third and fourth, with 1.9 million and 1.7 million employees, respectively).

Military expenditure in the United States is currently just over 3% of GDP (Table 11.1), which is large for a wealthy democracy, but dwarfed by several Middle Eastern states (Saudi Arabia spends more than 10% of its GDP on the military). The United States regularly criticises its NATO allies for not spending enough on their militaries, criticism which has intensified under President Donald Trump, who has increased the US defence budget. Only a handful of NATO countries meet the agreed spending target of two per cent of GDP.

Measured as a share of national income, the current spending is in stark contrast to the Cold War period. In 1970, during the Vietnam War, the United States was spending 7.9% of GDP on the military, and these 18 countries averaged 3.0%. The end of the Cold War brought a considerable peace dividend, as shown by the 1997 figures in the table. However, after 9/11 and military involvements in Afghanistan and Iraq, American spending in relation to GDP rose again. Several of the countries near the bottom of the table have gone in the other direction.

The United States also possesses the world's largest arms industry (Table 11.2). Russia comes second, having sold

---

[1]Also draws on earlier data on military spending from Rodney Tiffen and Ross Gittins *How Australia Compares* (Cambridge UP, 2009).

Table 11.1 Military expenditure

Military expenditure as percentage of GDP, 1997–2017

Country	1997	2007	2017
United States[a]	**3.2**	**3.8**	**3.1**
France[a]	2.8	2.3	2.3
Australia	1.9	1.8	2.0
UK[a]	2.3	2.2	1.8
Norway[a]	2.0	1.5	1.6
Italy[a]	1.8	1.6	1.5
Finland	1.5	1.3	1.4
Canada[a]	1.2	1.2	1.3
Denmark[a]	1.6	1.3	1.2
Germany[a]	1.5	1.2	1.2
Netherlands[a]	1.7	1.4	1.2
New Zealand	1.7	1.2	1.2
Sweden	2.0	1.3	1.0
Belgium[a]	1.5	1.1	0.9
Japan	0.9	0.9	0.9
Austria	1.0	0.9	0.7
Switzerland	1.2	0.7	0.7
Ireland	0.9	0.5	0.4
Mean	*1.7*	*1.5*	*1.4*

SIPRI Military Expenditure Database https://www.sipri.org/databases/milex

[a]NATO member

Table 11.2 Arms trade

Exports and imports of weapons (US$ millions) 2013–17

Country	Exports	Imports
United States	**50,062**	**2930**
France	9706	275
Germany	8469	442
United Kingdom	6952	2260
Italy	3590	2043
Netherlands	3101	556
Switzerland	1322	106
Sweden	1256	237
Canada	1095	1470
Norway	862	749
Australia	469	5558
Finland	313	1110
Belgium	97	211
Austria	91	29
Denmark	89	435
Ireland	39	130
New Zealand	17	200
Japan	2	1805

SIPRI Military Expenditure Database https://www.sipri.org/databases/milex

Table 11.3 Foreign aid

Net overseas development assistance donated, 1997, 2007 and 2017 2017 money (in 2015 US$ millions)

Country	1997	2007	2017	$
Sweden	0.79	0.94	1.01	5380
Norway	0.84	0.95	0.99	3943
Denmark	0.97	0.81	0.72	2314
UK	0.26	0.36	0.69	18,425
Germany	0.28	0.37	0.66	23,844
Netherlands	0.81	0.81	0.60	4822
Switzerland	0.32	0.37	0.46	3083
Belgium	0.31	0.43	0.45	2111
France	0.44	0.38	0.43	11,057
Finland	0.32	0.39	0.41	1024
Austria	0.24	0.50	0.30	1188
Ireland	0.32	0.55	0.30	783
Italy	0.11	0.19	0.29	5605
Canada	0.34	0.29	0.26	4090
Australia	0.27	0.32	0.23	2761
Japan	0.21	0.17	0.23	11,864
New Zealand	0.26	0.27	0.23	417
United States	**0.09**	**0.16**	**0.18**	**34,638**
Mean	*0.40*	*0.46*	*0.47*	

OECD *Development Assistance Report 2018*

around $32 billion in weapons in the last five years, to the USA's $50 billion. Since 1976, all foreign arms sales have gone through the Department of Defense. Continuing congressional approval for spending on massive weapons systems such as Lockheed's F-35 Fighter Jet (projected to have an ultimate cost of $1.2 trillion) is often contingent on the promise of billions in export sales to allies. American allies are themselves well represented in the ranks of the world's biggest arms dealers, with France, Germany, the UK and the Netherlands all in the top ten arms exporters from 2013 to 2017 (Table 11.2).

11.2 America's International Standing

The Pew Global Attitudes Project yearly surveys are the richest source of data on attitudes towards the USA. In it, respondents are asked their attitude towards America by choosing from the following statement: 'Please tell me if you have a very favorable, somewhat favorable, somewhat unfavorable or very unfavorable opinion of the United States'. Respondents are asked to judge an entire nation as if it were a monolithic entity in the same manner as they would an individual political leader or party. While this may be overly simple, the evidence reported in Table 11.4 on changing attitudes to America in 23 countries during different stages of three presidencies gives excellent insights.

The table reports the percentages in each country saying they had an unfavourable view of the USA. In 2002, after the 9/11 terrorist attacks, America received widespread public sympathy, especially among Western democracies. The major exception to this was in some, but not all, majority Muslim countries.

11.2 America's International Standing

Table 11.4 International attitudes to America
% in each country saying they had an *unfavourable* view of the USA

Country	2002 Bush post 9/11	2004 Bush post-Iraq	2008 Late Bush	2010 Early Obama	2016 Late Obama	2017 Trump
Western democracies						
Australia	–	38	48	–	34	48
Canada	27	34	42	28	30	51
France	34	62	57	26	31	52
Germany	35	59	66	35	38	62
Italy	23	38	38	22	23	31
Netherlands	–	54	–	–	29	59
Spain	–	55	55	28	26	60
Sweden	–	–	49	–	28	51
United Kingdom	16	34	37	24	26	40
Majority Muslim						
Egypt	–	69	75	82	85	–
Indonesia	–	57	53	34	26	–
Jordan	75	93	79	79	83	82
Lebanon	59	71	49	47	60	64
Pakistan	69	60	63	68	62	–
Palestinian ter.	–	98	86	82	70	–
Turkey	54	83	77	74	58	79
Other Asian						
Japan	26	–	48	32	23	39
South Korea	44	50	28	18	14	23
China	–	53	48	37	44	–
Americas						
Argentina	49	–	62	41	43	44
Brazil	–	–	–	29	23	35
Mexico	25	–	44	35	29	65
Other						
Israel	–	20	20	28	18	18
Kenya	15	–	11	3	19	26
Poland	11	23	24	19	16	15
Russia	33	55	48	33	81	52
Means						
Western democracies	*27*	*47*	*49*	*28*	*29*	*49*
Majority Muslim	*64*	*76*	*69*	*67*	*63*	*75*
Total	**37**	**55**	**50**	**39**	**39**	**47**

Data for each year or if no survey conducted from the adjacent year
Collated from many Pew Research studies of global opinion: http://www.pewglobal.org/database/indicator/1/survey/19/response/Unfavorable/

Bush's decision to go to war in Iraq had a dramatic negative impact on global opinion on the USA. Attitudes became more unfavourable in every nation surveyed, except for Pakistan. Most dramatically, unfavourable opinion leapt from 34 to 62% in France and 35 to 59% in Germany. The decisions by President Chirac and Chancellor Schröder not to join the American coalition of the willing in Iraq appear to have had strong popular support in their countries. America's unfavourability in the Middle East (except for Israel) was extremely high in the wake of the Iraq War, with 98% of respondents in the Palestinian territories and 93% in Jordan having a negative attitude towards America.

Little in general changed in global attitudes to the USA from 2004 to 2008. The table means indicate broad stability. Opinion became notably more negative in Australia (38% up to 48%) as opposition hardened to the war in Iraq. In a few countries, negative opinion declined, particularly South Korea, where it almost halved, from 50 to 28%. American efforts in the six-party talks and North Korea demonstrating its nuclear capacities with an underground test on 9 October 2006 probably account for this change in attitudes.

The election of Barack Obama improved attitudes towards the USA in 20 of 23 countries, all except for Israel, Egypt and Pakistan. It brought unfavourability ratings back to where they had been in 2002. In Western Europe, negative sentiment nearly halved in several countries. Opinion in Muslim majority countries towards the USA during the Obama presidency was somewhat more favourable than during the Bush era. However, several countries went in the other direction with Egypt particularly becoming less favourably disposed. Not surprisingly, in Indonesia, where Obama had spent part of his childhood, negative opinion dropped substantially. This widespread improvement in attitudes to America broadly lasted into the late Obama period.

Donald Trump's presidency did not enjoy a honeymoon in international opinion. Unfavourable opinion in both Western democracies and majority Muslim countries increased substantially with Spain and Germany showing the biggest jumps. Not surprisingly after Trump's claims that he would make Mexico pay for a border wall that would stop it sending its criminals and 'rapists' to America, opinion hardened from 29% unfavourable in 2016 to 65% in 2017.

The table shows broad movements in attitudes to the United States, but the importance of bilateral factors is also evident. During the Bush and Obama presidencies, Pakistani opinion often ran counter to the dominant trends. With Pakistan, there is evidence that American foreign policy behaviour mattered more than who the US president was. US aid to Pakistan in the wake of the deadly 2005 Azad Kashmir earthquake probably improved attitudes towards the USA, whereas Obama's use of military drones in Pakistani territory probably worsened them.

Another anomaly in the Obama period is Russia, where unfavourable opinion jumped from 33 to 81%. The US response to Russia's annexing of Crimea in 2014 accounts for this change. Similarly, Russia went against the generally more negative response to Trump's presidency, with unfavourable opinion going down to 52%.

Overall, these surveys do not suggest a pervasive anti-Americanism. Rather, the ups and downs suggest who the Americans elect as their president and what the USA does in the world matter a lot in influencing the attitudes of non-Americans.

11.3 Terrorism

The 11 September 2001 attack on the Twin Towers in New York, which killed 2996 people, is the most infamous terrorist incident in history and made terrorism an urgent issue throughout the democratic world. However, Table 11.5 shows terrorism was prevalent both before and after it. And a comparison of Tables 11.6 and 11.7 shows the toll of terrorism is much less in the stable democracies than in countries with significant civil conflicts.

Table 11.5 Deaths from terrorism
Total fatalities from terrorist attacks each year

Year	Total
1996	6966
1997	10,924
1998	4688
1999	3393
2000	4403
2001	7729
2002	4805
2003	3317
2004	5743
2005	6631
2006	9380
2007	12,824
2008	9157
2009	9273
2010	7827
2011	8246
2012	15,497
2013	22,273
2014	44,490
2015	38,853
2016	34,871
2017	26,445

The National Consortium for the Study of Terrorism and Responses to Terrorism (START), based at the University of Maryland
START *Global Terrorism in 2017, Background report*, published August 2018

Table 11.6 Countries most impacted by terrorism
Total fatalities 2014–2017

Country	Total
Iraq	41,533
Afghanistan	23,864
Nigeria	17,310
Syria	12,072
Somalia	6531
Pakistan	6210
Yemen	6006
Egypt	2658
Libya	2306
India	1809
Turkey	1757

The National Consortium for the Study of Terrorism and Responses to Terrorism (START), based at the University of Maryland
START *Global Terrorism in 2017, Background report*, published August 2018

11.3 Terrorism

Table 11.7 Terrorist fatalities in the selected democracies
Total number killed in terrorist attacks 2014–2017

Country	Total
France	265
United States	**243**
United Kingdom	46
Belgium	42
Germany	29
Japan	19
Canada	14
Australia	10
Sweden	9
Denmark	3
Austria	2
Finland	2
Ireland	2
New Zealand	2
Italy	1
Netherlands	1
Norway	0
Switzerland	0

The National Consortium for the Study of Terrorism and Responses to Terrorism (START), based at the University of Maryland
START *Global Terrorism in 2017, Background report*, published August 2018

The National Consortium for the Study of Terrorism and Responses to Terrorism (START) based in the University of Maryland has painstakingly compiled systematic data on terrorism over several decades, and it is their data on which these tables are based.

According to START, in 2017 there were 10,900 terrorist attacks around the world which killed more than 26,400 people, which includes 8075 perpetrators and 18,448 victims.

Table 11.5 shows that around the world in the 22 years from 1996 to 2017, a total of 297,735 people were killed in terrorist attacks. The numbers jump around from year to year depending on individual conflicts and incidents. However, the last six years in the table show a big increase. More people died from terrorism in these last six years than in the previous 16. 2014 was the peak year, and the three years since have seen some decline, but the number of deaths is still well above earlier levels.

Of all the deaths from terrorism in the world between 2014 and 2017, more than half came from four countries and around five-eighths come from the 11 most affected countries, listed in Table 11.6. Countries with the highest number of battle-related deaths also have the highest levels of deaths from terrorism. Iraq and Afghanistan are the two countries suffering most from terrorism, and these figures are the legacy of the wars in which these countries were caught up. Those wars also exacerbated other conflicts in the region, which in turn have fanned the growth of terrorism. In the contemporary world, the major perpetrators of terrorism are Muslim, but equally Muslims are the most numerous victims. (While these countries are the deadliest sites for terrorist activity, it should also be remembered that 77 countries recorded at least one death from terrorism in 2016.)

The deadliest terrorist group in the world today is the Islamic State of Iraq and the Levant (ISIL). It gained traction in the years after the allied overthrow of Saddam Hussein and is militarily active in Iraq and Syria, where it has lost considerable ground in recent years. These reverses have not diminished its international terrorist involvements. ISIL was behind the deadliest terrorist attack in French history, the coordinated attacks on concert, restaurant and sport facilities in Paris in November 2015 which killed 130 and injured 413 people.

Targets and methods keep changing. Terrorist attacks provoke counter-actions by authorities, so for example, while explosives on airplanes were deadly in the 1970s and '80s, improved security since has made this less prevalent. In recent years, in several countries, there has been the use of vehicles to attack pedestrians. The single worst incident was in Nice, on Bastille Day 2015, a 19 ton truck was deliberately driven into crowds, with 86 people killed and 434 injured. Authorities have started to place bollards to make such attacks more difficult.

Since 2001, terrorism has been a major concern in Western democracies. Table 11.7 shows that in the four years 2014–17, these countries had a combined total of 690 deaths from terrorism, a minute fraction of the world total, although a tragedy for those killed and their loved ones.

There is a different pattern in politically stable countries with strong institutions. It seems that a higher proportion of intended attacks are foiled by the authorities, and there are probably more 'lone wolf' attacks, where the perpetrator may give allegiance to a group, but is not organisationally linked to them. Such attacks tend to be less deadly. Between 2012 and 2016, there were 27,000 terrorist attacks around the world that did not result in a single fatality.

Some have pointed out that there is a greater chance of dying from falling off a ladder than from terrorism. This is true but misleading. Deaths from terrorism would be much higher except for the authorities' preventative actions. Moreover, the essence of terrorism is to produce a psychological and political impact far out of proportion to the physical damage. It is thus often designed to attack normal life, to injure innocent victims and to disrupt major social events.

11.4 Globalisation

Globalisation is a much-used but ill-defined term. It captures an essential aspect of the contemporary world—that countries are more interconnected than they used to be, and that developments in transport and communication have facilitated this interconnectedness. People, information, capital, goods and services cross borders far more, and far more easily, than they used to.

In recent decades, there have been many attempts to measure globalisation. The KOF (Swiss Economic Institute) Index of Globalisation is the most important. It is the most cited measure, having been used in more than 100 studies. Its most recent report—published in 2018, covering data up to 2015—covers 185 countries. It has a range of zero to 100 (least to most globalised), and Table 11.8 lists the top 40 ranked countries.

The KOF says that the level of globalisation fell slightly in 2015. Worldwide it increased rapidly between 1990 and 2007, but has risen only slightly since the Great Recession. The fall in 2015 was the first since 1975.

Like nearly all other indicators, the KOF Index conceives of globalisation as multidimensional. It weights the economic, social and political dimensions equally. Its new version is comprised of 42 variables.

Globalisation is sometimes a deliberate policy and other times a by-product of other developments or of a country's nature. For example, in economic globalisation small contiguous countries, which are EU members, such as the Netherlands and Belgium, tend to score highly—although the term globalisation is a misnomer to the extent that these countries interact a lot with a few neighbouring countries, rather than with all areas of the globe.

Conversely, one variable the KOF uses to measure social globalisation is the number of airports hosting international flights a country has. But this reflects geography as much as involvement in international travel. The United States is always going to seem more global than the Netherlands on this measure.

Two other measures which have attracted considerable criticism are the number of McDonald's outlets and IKEA shops as indicators of cultural globalisation. Whatever one's feelings about these two companies, this seems to equate cultural globalisation with cultural homogeneity.

The measure of political globalisation includes such features as the number of embassies present in a country, the country's participation in UN peacekeeping operations, their membership in international organisations and multilateral treaties. On this measure, Ireland and New Zealand rank very low (Table 11.9). This reflects that they are small countries and many countries choose to cover them diplomatically from embassies in London and Canberra,

Table 11.8 Globalisation
Scores and rankings of top 40 countries in KOF Globalisation Index 2018

Country	Rank	Score
Belgium	1	90.47
Netherlands	2	90.24
Switzerland	3	89.70
Sweden	4	88.05
Austria	5	87.91
Denmark	6	87.85
France	7	87.34
United Kingdom	8	87.23
Germany	9	86.89
Finland	10	85.98
Norway	11	85.81
Hungary	12	84.20
Ireland	13	83.53
Canada	14	83.45
Czech Republic	15	83.41
Spain	16	83.31
Portugal	17	82.21
Italy	18	82.15
Luxembourg	19	82.00
Estonia	20	81.97
Slovak Republic	21	80.74
Greece	22	80.31
Singapore	23	80.01
United States	**24**	**79.95**
Slovenia	25	79.76
Bulgaria	26	79.52
Australia	27	79.29
Malaysia	28	79.28
Croatia	29	79.04
Lithuania	30	78.78
Poland	31	78.72
New Zealand	32	78.00
Romania	33	77.88
Malta	34	77.51
Japan	35	77.30
Korea, Rep.	36	76.67
Israel	37	75.73
Cyprus	38	75.60
Latvia	39	75.42
Serbia	40	75.28

Gygli, Savina, Florian Haelg and Jan-Egbert Sturm 'The KOF Globalisation Index—Revisited' (2018, Working paper No. 439) KOF Swiss Economic Institute
KOF globalisation database

respectively. Both have very small armed forces and rarely participate in UN peacekeeping. Do these things make them less global? In contrast to this measure, China ranks 14th in the world, reflecting its importance to other countries. Does this make China more 'global' than New Zealand in its outlook?

11.4 Globalisation

Globalisation tends to be much higher in richer countries than in poorer countries. They have the greater resources and capacities to participate internationally. It may be that especially for poorer countries globalisation increases vulnerability as well as increases opportunities. All the selected affluent democracies rank in the top 35 of the KOF's 185 countries. Indeed, the top 11 places are filled by several of these countries (Table 11.8), but with the United States, Australia, New Zealand and Japan ranking somewhat lower, although all within the top fifth.

Perhaps, the most notable aspect of Table 11.9 is how much the rankings change between the three columns. Moreover, if we knew the scores on all the sub-measures, we would probably find even more variation.

In all composite measures, there are issues of weighting. But the issues here are even more basic. Is a coherent and meaningful index of globalisation possible? When we read in Table 11.8 that the United States is just below Singapore and just above Slovenia is it telling us anything meaningful, something that tells us how these various nations are likely to behave, or about the quality of life for their citizens?

The KOF has undertaken an immense research task, gathering authoritative data on their 42 variables on almost 200 countries. Important conceptual questions remain, however. Perhaps in this case, more information is lost than gained by seeking to reduce all the various elements into a single measure. The term globalisation conjures several dimensions—interdependence, openness, cosmopolitanism. It may be more informative to see how the many elements interact with each other rather than to combine them.

Table 11.9 Components of globalisation

From KOF Globalisation Index, ranked according to total rank in Table 11.8

Country	Economic rank	Political rank	Social rank
Belgium	4	8	10
Netherlands	3	6	19
Switzerland	9	9	3
Sweden	15	7	13
Austria	14	10	8
Denmark	12	18	4
France	24	2	17
United Kingdom	23	5	6
Germany	26	3	15
Finland	19	19	11
Norway	29	27	1
Ireland	6	67	5
Canada	43	15	9
Italy	44	1	39
United States	**63**	**11**	**29**
Australia	65	26	20
New Zealand	42	65	7
Japan	62	25	42

Gygli, Savina, Florian Haelg and Jan-Egbert Sturm 'The KOF Globalisation Index—Revisited' (2018, Working paper No. 439) KOF Swiss Economic Institute
KOF globalisation database

Environment

12.1 Biodiversity

Environmental issues do not always lend themselves to comparative, quantitative summary.[1] Every country has its own natural endowments and problems bestowed by its unique geography. Sometimes comparative measures are merely charting these different geographic-cum-economic inheritances rather than any meaningful difference in environmental performance or quality. Similarly many environmental problems are primarily local—the effluent produced by a neighbourhood factory or the destruction of a particular urban heritage in the name of development. National summary measures cannot capture these local impacts.

Tables 12.1 and 12.2 firstly reflect the selected countries' natural endowments. Australia and the United States have the most species of mammals and birds, with Canada and Japan also high in both tables. The countries with the smallest areas tend to be near the bottom. Counting species as if they are all of the same value like a unit of currency is a crude measure, but does give some clue about countries' biodiversity.

The American non-profit environmental organisation, Conservation International, identified 17 megadiverse countries which harbour a high number of species and also many endemic species (i.e. not found in other countries). Several are in tropical and subtropical regions, including some with relatively small areas (e.g. Papua New Guinea and Ecuador). The two largest in area and covering the most diverse terrains and temperature zones—and the only two among the 18 selected democracies—are the USA and Australia.

With economic development and population growth, many ecosystems have been degraded, biodiversity-rich areas are declining and wildlife is increasingly threatened. In North America and Europe, farmland and forest birds have declined by nearly 30% in 40 years. In 2018, the World Wide Fund for Nature (WWF) reported that mammals, birds, fish and reptiles had declined by 60% since 1970. The two tables show that in these 18 countries, one in five mammal species and one in four bird species are under threat, either with extinction in the wild in the immediate future or at high risk in the medium-term future.

Table 12.3 charts the land cover in these countries, and there is a very rough correlation between threatened species and the percentage of urban land. In this table, land classed as 'bare area' is inhospitable to human activity, while 'other vegetation' is also quite sparse. It seems the higher the proportions of these two, the lower the population density (see Table 1.9).

Many forests are threatened by degradation, fragmentation and conversion to other uses. A common response to the pressures on the natural habitat has been to set aside protected areas. The two oldest national parks in the world are the Tobago Main Ridge Forest Reserve (established 1776) and the Bogd Khan Uul Mountain in Mongolia (1778). The first in the developed world was Yellowstone National Park, proclaimed in 1872. Late in the nineteenth century, Australia, New Zealand and Canada also established their first national parks. Canada established Parks Canada in 1911 becoming the world's first national service dedicated to protecting and presenting natural and historical treasures, followed five years later by President Woodrow Wilson creating the National Park Service.

While the wish to preserve nature in national parks has a long history, especially in the New World democracies, recently it has taken on added force. Across these 18 countries, the area covered by national parks in 2018 was more than five times the area set aside in 1960. In total area, as Table 12.4 shows, Australia, the United States and Canada have by far the largest area devoted to national parks, but as a proportion of total area, Germany leads the way.

A protected area is defined by the International Union for the Conservation of Nature (IUCN) as a clearly defined geographic space, recognised, dedicated and managed, through

---

[1] Damian Carrington 'Humanity has wiped out 60% of animal populations since 1970, report finds' *Guardian* 30-10-2018.

Table 12.1 Mammals and threatened species

Country	Number of known species in country	Percentage under threat 2017
United States	**453**	**17**
Australia	402	27
Canada	209	25
Japan	160	21
Italy	126	18
France	125	14
United Kingdom	101	–
Austria	101	27
Germany	93	34
Norway	89	19
Belgium	84	21
Switzerland	83	36
Finland	75	9
Denmark	67	16
New Zealand	65	–
Sweden	65	22
Ireland	57	2
Netherlands	53	21
Mean	–	21

OECD Environment Statistics database

Tables 12.2 Birds and threatened species

Country	Number of known species in country	Percentage under threat 2017
United States	**831**	**12**
Australia	790	17
Japan	700	14
Ireland	478	27
Canada	461	19
France	391	27
United Kingdom	272	41
Italy	267	28
Germany	264	36
Norway	264	17
Sweden	257	20
New Zealand	254	–
Finland	248	35
Austria	242	27
Denmark	209	16
Switzerland	205	35
Belgium	198	28
Netherlands	168	24
Mean	–	25

OECD Environment Statistics database

Table 12.3 Land cover
% of total land by various types of cover

Country	Forest	Grassland	Other vegetation	Wetlands	Bare area	Cropland	Urban
Belgium	17.8	13.8	4.2	0.3	0.6	36.4	26.9
Netherlands	6.4	29.9	3.8	2.0	9.3	28.4	20.3
Germany	26.8	8.2	3.9	0.5	1.4	46.1	13.0
United Kingdom	6.0	41.8	10.0	5.2	2.8	24.4	9.8
Switzerland	32.7	18.9	7.8	0.1	13.2	18.7	8.6
Italy	25.6	2.3	12.7	0.1	3.0	48.2	8.2
Denmark	9.0	1.6	2.3	2.0	4.8	72.6	7.8
Austria	48.6	11.0	7.0	0.3	3.5	23.5	6.3
Japan	64.5	0.1	20.4	0.1	2.8	6.4	5.8
France	33.1	16.0	5.8	0.6	1.5	37.6	5.5
Ireland	2.4	65.2	7.9	13.0	3.7	5.4	2.4
United States	**24.3**	**27.0**	**26.2**	**3.3**	**4.5**	**12.9**	**1.9**
Sweden	63.0	0.1	12.0	7.7	8.0	7.6	1.7
Finland	67.7	0.0	7.9	8.0	7.8	7.1	1.6
New Zealand	30.7	16.6	7.7	0.4	7.0	36.7	0.9
Norway	38.5	0.0	37.5	8.5	11.5	3.1	0.9
Australia	8.8	14.4	64.6	1.4	6.0	4.6	0.2
Canada	39.2	3.3	29.6	4.2	19.7	3.8	0.2

OECD Green Growth Indicators

12.1 Biodiversity

Table 12.4 Protected areas

Country	Total sq km 2018	Percentage of total area 2018	Percentage of forests under sustainable management
Germany	134,595	38	68
New Zealand	88,134	33	11
Austria	23,932	29	51
United Kingdom	69,681	29	44
France	141,233	26	31
Belgium	7141	23	43
Italy	64,938	22	9
Japan	81,288	21	1
Australia	1,487,571	19	9
Denmark	7791	18	71
Norway	55,586	17	76
Finland	49,937	15	94
Sweden	66,314	15	69
Ireland	9908	14	55
United States	**1,227,703**	**13**	**16**
Netherlands	3984	11	41
Canada	960,318	10	26
Switzerland	4095	10	87
Mean	*249,119*	*20*	*45*

OECD Environment Statistics database, and forest management from *OECD Green Growth Indicators*

legal or other effective means, to achieve the long-term conservation of nature, or of culturally valued assets.

Short of declaring a full-scale national park, it is often crucial that economic activities in forest areas be conducted in a sustainable manner. Several countries have adopted sustainability principles, agreed by forest stewardship committees and independently certified. Their share of forests under sustainable management certification has been increasing, with the Scandinavian countries, Germany and Switzerland most devoted to combining economic activities and sustaining the forests.

Over many decades, human development—population growth and increasing economic activity—has threatened biodiversity prompting a growing awareness of the problems. The battle between these competing considerations will continue indefinitely into the future.

12.2 Global Warming

Some environmental issues are purely local in scope, but others are global.[2] The issue of global warming, if left unaddressed, is the greatest long-term threat to current

Table 12.5 Global temperature anomalies

Temperature anomaly is °C different from 1951 to 1980 mean

Decade	Temperature anomaly (°C)	Change from previous decade (°C)
1880s	−0.274	–
1890s	−0.254	+0.020
1900s	−0.259	−0.005
1910s	−0.276	−0.017
1920s	−0.175	+0.101
1930s	−0.043	+0.132
1940s	+0.035	+0.078
1950s	−0.020	−0.055
1960s	−0.014	+0.006
1970s	−0.001	+0.013
1980s	+0.176	+0.177
1990s	+0.313	+0.137
2000s	+0.513	+0.200
2010s	+0.728	+0.215

Data for 2010–2019 decade is not yet complete

Hannah Richie and Max Roser 'CO_2 and other Greenhouse Gas Emissions' *Our World in Data*. (Reproduced in Wikipedia)

patterns of social and economic life, not only in the selected countries but throughout the world. The tables in this section capture some of the key elements.

Table 12.5 shows the global temperature each decade from the 1880s until the present. It looks at departures from the 1951–1980 period and the difference in temperature from the

---

[2]Robert Glasser 'The Cascading Impacts of Climate Change' *Australian Outlook* July 31, 2018; 'NASA's James Hansen: Data proves global warming is causing crazy weather' *Inhabitat* July 8 2012.

previous decade. For the last half century, each decade has been hotter than the previous one. The latest decade so far is 0.73 °C above that norm. The five warmest years on record have all come in the 2010s and the ten hottest all since 1998.

Global warming is attributed to the greenhouse effect, a shorthand description for the way carbon dioxide and other gases form a blanket, which stops some of the Sun's heat escaping from the earth, so making the planet warmer. Greenhouse gases (GHG) are important in sustaining a habitable temperature for the planet: if there were no GHGs, our planet would be too cold for life as we know it. Equally, as they increase, the temperature is rising.

Table 12.6 shows the increasing amount of carbon dioxide in the atmosphere. Since the Industrial Revolution energy-driven consumption of fossil fuels has led to a rapid increase in CO_2 emissions. Carbon dioxide levels are higher than at any point in at least the past 800,000 years. The last time atmospheric CO_2 amounts were this high was more than three million years ago, when the temperatures were 2–3 °C higher than now, and sea levels were 15–25 m higher. If global energy demand continues to grow and be met mostly with fossil fuels, atmospheric carbon dioxide is likely to exceed 900 ppm by the end of the century.

Table 12.7 shows that the emission of greenhouse gases is still rising, almost 50% greater in 2014 than in 1990. Although carbon dioxide is the most important, altogether there are six greenhouse gases. In order to look at the totality of their impact, the measure of carbon dioxide equivalents (CO_{2e}) has been constructed. One tonne of methane, for example, has the same effect as 21 tonnes of CO_2, so one tonne of methane has the warming effect of 21 CO_{2e}. The major sources for methane and nitrogen dioxide are agriculture. The table shows that in these years, the others rose only slightly, while carbon dioxide emissions increased substantially.

Table 12.8 shows that in the 42 years between 1970 and 2012, carbon dioxide emissions more than doubled. The proportion coming from transport remained about the same, while that from manufacturing and construction declined. The source which continues to grow most is from electricity generation.

As global emissions keep increasing, their consequences will become more severe, and there is the danger of passing tipping points where the environmental damage cannot be reversed. We are dealing with complex, interacting systems, so there are many competing predictions of how this will be manifested.

Although this is a global issue, the impacts at regional level will vary: droughts in some areas, but more rain in others, more wildfires in areas prone to them. Some predict fewer hurricanes, but more severe ones. Many predict that the greater energy in the system will lead to more extreme weather events. NASA climatologist James Hansen pointed out that 'extreme heat events' used to be rare. They covered less than one per cent of the earth's surface between 1951 and 1980, but now cover about 10% of the land area.

Oceans, which cover 71% of the earth's surface, have acted as a major carbon sink: from 1994 to 2010, approximately 27% of the carbon dioxide released was taken up by the oceans, acidifying the upper layers and raising their temperature. The impacts on marine life—especially when combined with over-fishing and increasing pollution such as plastics—may be dire. The destruction of coral reefs is one likely consequence.

Perhaps the greatest area of speculation is how climate change will lead to rising sea levels. A frequently cited scenario involves the melting of polar ice caps, resulting in the dumping of freshwater into the ocean and raised sea levels. Such rises threaten low-lying Pacific Islands, densely populated coastal regions as in Nigeria and Bangladesh, and some cities (e.g. Miami). Coastal ecosystems will experience more storm surges.

Table 12.6 Atmospheric carbon dioxide
Global average atmospheric carbon dioxide (CO_2 parts per million (ppm))

Year	Carbon dioxide
To 1850	280
1970	328
2017	405

Rebecca Lindsey 'Climate change: Atmospheric Carbon Dioxide' NOAA *Climate.gov*

Table 12.7 Global greenhouse gas emissions
Greenhouse gas emissions (GHG) gigatons (Gt) in carbon dioxide equivalents (CO_{2e})

	1990	2000	2014
Total GHG	**34**	**37**	**49**
Carbon dioxide (CO_2)	25.0	27.0	37.0
Methane (CH_4)	6.3	6.4	7.5
Nitrogen dioxide (N_2O)	2.6	2.6	3.0
Fluoride gases	0.3	0.4	0.9

World Resources Institute (*CAIT* Climate Access Indicators Tool) CAIT Country Greenhouse Gas Emissions Data

Table 12.8 Global carbon dioxide emissions
Total carbon dioxide emissions (metric tons) (Mtoe) and its major sources (%)

Year	Total	Electricity/ heating (%)	Manufacturing/ construction (%)	Transport (%)
1970	14,531	31	26	20
1990	21,713	39	21	21
2012	33,845	44	19	21

Other, more minor sources not included; 1970 major sources % are from 1971
World Resources Institute (*CAIT* Climate Access Indicators Tool) CAIT Country Greenhouse Gas Emissions Data

12.3 Greenhouse Gas Emissions

Most policy issues involve reactions to already-manifest problems, but global warming involves the anticipation of a problem, whose adverse consequences will damage future generations more than the present one.[3] Furthermore, the measures needed to combat it have immediate costs, while their benefits are in the avoidance of future catastrophes—not the most promising scenario for immediate, decisive action.

In addition, global warming is a uniquely global issue. It can only be addressed by concerted international action, but the tables on the opposite page suggest how difficult this will be to achieve. A crucial problem is balancing reductions in emissions with maintaining and enhancing living standards. Poorer countries, such as the leading emitters listed in the table, are not going to agree to an argument that they must forever remain at a lesser stage of economic development than richer ones.

Historically, the cumulative emissions from the European countries and the USA have contributed most to the growth in greenhouse gases. This was recognised in the Kyoto Protocol of 1998, where only the developed countries committed to reducing emissions. In all future international agreements, however, all countries were to be included.

Table 12.9 shows that eight of the 12 countries with the highest emissions now are from the developing world. China now far surpasses the United States as the biggest emitter, the two together producing around one-third of the planet's emissions. Of the 12 leading countries, nine increased their total emissions between 1990 and 2014.

Major European countries—such as Germany, Britain, France and Italy—have moved most decisively towards reducing emissions, and the table demonstrates the effectiveness of EU policies in this direction. Other reductions are less policy directed. Russia's reduction reflects the deindustrialisation of the economy following the end of the Soviet Union and its subsidising of heavy industry. Australia's figure reflects that 1990 was an exceptional year in terms of land clearing, and its reduction is wholly due to that declining—its emissions from energy, for example, have increased substantially.

It is misleading to only look at total emissions, where the size of a country's population and economy is the central factor, without also looking at CO_{2e} emissions per person.

---

[3]Isobel Thompson 'Donald Trump still doesn't believe in climate change' *VF* January 29, 2018; Lisa Friedman '"I don't know that it's man-made," Trump says of climate change. It is.' *NYT* October 15, 2018; Coral Davenport and Lisa Friedman 'How Trump is ensuring that greenhouse gas emissions will rise' *NYT* November 26 2018.

Table 12.9 Major greenhouse gas emitters
Metric megatons (Mt) of carbon dioxide equivalents (CO_{2e}) per year
Leading 13 countries plus selected democracies

Country	Total 1990	Total 2000	Total 2014	Change 1990–2014
China	2800	4200	12,000	+++
United States	**5600**	**6400**	**6300**	**+**
India	1100	1600	3200	+++
Indonesia	1300	1300	2470	+++
Russia	3200	2300	2030	--
Brazil	1400	1600	1400	=
Japan	1100	1200	1320	+
Canada	640	720	870	++
Germany	1100	920	817	--
Iran	250	440	801	+++
Mexico	450	610	729	+++
South Korea	260	480	632	+++
Australia	580	550	530	–
United Kingdom	730	640	494	--
Italy	460	490	369	--
France	470	470	334	--
Netherlands	200	210	181	–
Belgium	130	130	100	–
Austria	63	66	70	+
Finland	49	48	65	+
New Zealand	43	49	60	+
Ireland	51	65	58	+
Denmark	67	67	48	--
Sweden	48	47	47	=
Switzerland	50	49	46	–
Norway	31	33	25	–

World Resources Institute (*CAIT* Climate Access Indicators Tool)
CAIT Country Greenhouse Gas Emissions Data

Table 12.10 produces a very different rank ordering from Table 12.9. By far the highest emitters per capita are Canada, Australia and the United States. Many of the European countries have per capita emissions that are less than half these three. So also do six of the eight countries included in the list of the heaviest national emitters. The average American produces more than double the tons of CO_{2e} compared to the average Chinese and almost eight times that of the average Indian. According to the OECD, its member countries average 9.6 tonnes per person compared with 3.4 tonnes in the rest of the world.

Table 12.11 presents a more encouraging view. In every single one of the economically advanced democracies and in the eight other high-emitting countries, carbon dioxide emissions are becoming decoupled from economic growth. In both groups, the CO_{2e} emissions per million dollars of GDP in 2014 were less than half what they had been in 2000. Some of this is due to the strengthening of climate policies, and some to the changing patterns of energy consumption and other market trends.

Table 12.10 National greenhouse gas emissions per person
CO_{2e} metric tons per person

Country	2000	2014
(a) Selected democracies		
Sweden	5.3	4.8
Norway	7.3	4.9
France	7.8	5.0
Switzerland	6.9	5.6
Italy	8.6	6.1
United Kingdom	10.8	7.6
Austria	8.2	8.2
Denmark	12.6	8.6
Belgium	13.0	9.4
Germany	11.2	10.1
Japan	9.5	10.4
Netherlands	13.0	10.8
Finland	9.2	12.0
Ireland	17.0	12.6
New Zealand	12.8	13.4
United States	**22.7**	**19.8**
Australia	30.7	22.3
Canada	23.4	24.4
Mean	12.8	10.9
(b) Other highest emitting countries		
India	1.6	2.5
Mexico	6.0	5.9
Brazil	9.2	6.7
China	3.3	8.5
Indonesia	6.2	9.7
Iran	6.7	10.2
South Korea	10.1	12.5
Russia	15.4	14.1
Mean	7.3	8.8

World Resources Institute (*CAIT* Climate Access Indicators Tool) CAIT Country Greenhouse Gas Emissions Data

Table 12.11 National greenhouse gas emissions and the economy
CO_{2e} per million $ of GDP

Country	2000 GDP	2014 GDP
(a) Selected democracies		
Norway	190	50
Switzerland	180	66
Sweden	180	82
France	350	120
Denmark	410	140
Austria	330	160
United Kingdom	390	160
Italy	430	170
Belgium	560	200
Germany	470	210
Netherlands	500	210
Ireland	650	230
Finland	380	240
Japan	250	270
New Zealand	940	300
Australia	1400	360
United States	**620**	**360**
Canada	970	480
Mean	511	212
(b) Other highest emitting countries		
South Korea	850	450
Brazil	2400	550
Mexico	890	560
Russia	8700	980
China	3400	1100
India	3500	1600
Iran	4000	1900
Indonesia	8000	2800
Mean	3968	1243

World Resources Institute (*CAIT* Climate Access Indicators Tool) CAIT Country Greenhouse Gas Emissions Data

Nevertheless, the dominant picture from these tables is bleak. Greenhouse gas emissions are still rising in many countries, with only Western Europe providing a clear counter-trend. There was renewed hope when in December 2015, 195 countries signed the Paris Climate Change Agreement and pledged to keep the increase in global average temperatures to below 2 °C and if possible to 1.5 °C, with each country making its own promises.

Such international agreements are always fragile, and under President Trump, the United States withdrew, saying —without detail—it was a terrible deal for the USA. The Paris Agreement would have led to 'lost jobs, lower wages, shuttered factories and vastly diminished economic production', he said.

As a presidential candidate, his position was that climate change was a hoax created by and for the Chinese to make the USA uncompetitive. He told an interviewer in January 2018 there is cooling and there is heating. In October 2018, he said that he acknowledged that 'something's changing', but thought 'it will change back again' and did not think the increasing temperatures were man-made. In November 2018, the American Government's four yearly National Climate Assessment, consisting of 1656 pages, was published. Trump simply responded 'I don't believe it'.

12.4 Energy

Energy generation is itself a major part of the economy but is also pivotal to other economic and social activities, and it can have huge impacts on the environment in air pollution, in the production of greenhouse gases and in the depletion of non-renewable resources.

Table 12.12 shows that total energy use for the whole world increased substantially in the 25 years between 1990 and 2015. The two principal uses of this energy are

12.4 Energy

Table 12.12 World energy totals and sources
Total primary energy supply (TPES) by source (%)
Unit: Mtoe (million tonnes of oil equivalent)

Source	1990 %	2000 %	2015 %
Coal	25	23	30
Natural gas	19	21	15
Nuclear	6	7	5
Hydro	2	2	3
Geothermal, solar, etc.	0	1	2
Biofuels and waste	10	10	10
Primary and secondary oil	37	36	34
Total	8773	10,034	12,669

IEA World Energy Balances 2018

electricity generation and transport. The International Energy Agency (IEA), taking a longer period, observed that between 1971 and 2013 the world's total primary energy supply more than doubled. This equates to a compound growth rate of 2.2% per year. Over the same period, the world population grew by 1.5% per annum and its GDP by 3.0% per annum.

Table 12.13 shows the primary energy supply per person in 2014. The six heaviest users are three Nordic countries where one suspects heating is a major component, and the United States, Canada and Australia, where road transport per person is greatest (as well as heating in Canada).

On a per-person basis, most of the selected countries reduced their energy usage, by an average of six per cent, which is in contrast to the decades from 1976 to 2006, when energy supply went up by about 20% for each person, reflecting continuing growth in domestic usage and motor transport.

Table 12.12 shows broad constancy in the world's sources of energy between 1990 and 2015. Coal and oil are the biggest sources in all years, while natural gas shows more volatility.

Perhaps the greatest message from Table 12.14 is the variety of sources of energy in the selected countries, some of this stemming from natural inheritances. The United States, Germany and Australia all had strong domestic reserves of coal, and in them, it still constitutes at least one-fifth of their primary energy supply. However, in half, the countries' solid fossil fuels now constitute less than one-tenth of their energy supply.

Renewables and waste include hydropower, plus solar and wind power. The countries with the highest reliance on these have strong supplies of hydropower. Increasingly, although from a very low base, other renewables are becoming more important. Globally, geothermal and solar crept up from one to two per cent, and hydro from two to three—still very minor shares, but edging up.

There is a great divergence between the countries in the degree to which they have embraced nuclear energy. In the 1970s, France was its great champion, and it is still the leading country among the selected democracies. At the time, many thought nuclear power was the wave of the future, but in recent decades, it has gone into reverse, because of both cost and safety issues.

Table 12.13 Energy intensity
Total primary energy supply (TPES) per capita 2014

Country	2014	Percentage of change since 2000
Italy	2.4	−16
Ireland	2.8	−19
United Kingdom	2.8	−19
Denmark	2.9	−10
Switzerland	3.1	−4
Japan	3.5	−13
Austria	3.8	33
France	3.8	−8
Germany	3.8	−6
Netherlands	4.3	0
New Zealand	4.6	−6
Belgium	4.8	−12
Sweden	4.8	−7
Australia	5.5	−4
Norway	6.2	12
Finland	6.3	−5
United States	**6.9**	**−14**
Canada	7.2	−13
Mean	4.4	−6

OECD Environment at a Glance 2015

Table 12.14 Structure of primary energy supply
Percentage of total, 2014

Country	Solid fossil fuels	Oil	Gas	Nuclear	Renewables and waste
Switzerland	1	37	10	28	24
Norway	3	39	16	0	43
Sweden	4	24	2	35	35
France	4	28	13	46	9
Belgium	6	45	24	17	8
New Zealand	7	32	22	0	39
Canada	7	30	33	11	18
Italy	9	36	36	0	19
Austria	10	36	20	0	34
Netherlands	13	40	40	1	6
Finland	15	27	8	19	32
Denmark	16	36	17	0	31
Ireland	16	47	30	0	8
United Kingdom	17	33	34	9	7
United States	**20**	**36**	**28**	**10**	**7**
Germany	25	33	21	8	12
Japan	27	44	24	0	5
Australia	34	35	25	0	7
Mean	13	35	22	10	19

OECD Environment at a Glance 2015

Between 2000 and 2010, nuclear power globally declined not only proportionally but in absolute terms, the only source of energy to do that when energy generation itself is still expanding. Table 12.14 shows that in 2014 there were eight countries where nuclear energy's contribution was zero. Seven of them have never had any, but the eighth is Japan. Before the earthquake and tsunami created such damage at the Fukushima Nuclear Power Plant in March 2011, 30% of Japan's electricity came from nuclear power, with plans to increase it further. After initially vowing to abandon nuclear energy, the government has been moving towards reviving at least some of its previous capacity. Belgium, Germany and Switzerland have also decided to phase out nuclear power.

12.5 Policies and Pollution

Environmental problems are overwhelmingly externalities—the consequence of an industrial or commercial activity which affects other parties without this being reflected in market prices. In other words, these problems need public intervention because markets alone are unlikely to produce a solution.

There are many environmental challenges facing affluent democracies, but the greatest is addressing the ultimate externality—climate change. The Paris Agreement makes clear the need to decarbonise economies, and the OECD thinks that pricing carbon emissions is the most effective way to move to carbon-neutral growth. Embedding an effective carbon price changes market calculations. Within the new environment which more properly takes account of externalities, each emitter has an incentive to rationally pursue their self-interest by finding ways to cut emissions. So, putting a price on carbon emissions decentralises abatement decisions.

Table 12.15 shows what percentage of each country's emissions is taxed at or above what the OECD regards as the minimum rate that will have any impact, namely 30 Euro (around $US33) a tonne. The first column shows that only one-third of carbon emissions are taxed at this rate across the 18 selected democracies. The range is great, with just two countries—Switzerland and Norway—taxing more than half their emissions, and with the top half of the table all filled by European countries. At the other extreme is the United States where only three per cent of emissions are taxed at the minimum effective rate.

The second data column has a rank ordering close to the first. This shows the gap between the carbon price and the cost of emissions, and so the extent to which polluters are not paying for the damage from carbon emissions. The lower

Table 12.15 Carbon pricing
Percentage of total emissions priced at or above EUR30 per tonne
Carbon pricing gap at EUR30

Country	Percentage of total emissions priced	Carbon pricing gap
Switzerland	70	27
Norway	61	34
United Kingdom	49	42
Finland	42	53
France	42	41
Italy	40	46
Netherlands	38	43
Ireland	36	42
Austria	34	51
Denmark	32	52
Sweden	25	63
Belgium	23	65
Japan	21	69
Australia	20	79
New Zealand	20	76
Germany	19	53
Canada	16	65
United States	**3**	**75**
Mean	33	54

OECD Effective Carbon Rates 2018

the figure, the greater is a country's readiness for the low-carbon economy, and its long-term competitiveness. Again Switzerland leads the way, while Australia, New Zealand and the United States are the laggards.

The OECD notes that the pricing gap varies substantially between the sectors. It is lowest in road transport, at 21%, although a lot of this arose for other reasons—aiming to reduce traffic congestion, air pollution or oil consumption for balance of trade reasons. The gap is greatest in electricity generation.

Table 12.16 looks more generally at environmentally related taxes, including taxes on energy products for transport and for stationary purposes (e.g. electricity and fossil fuels); motor vehicles and transport (one-off sales, or recurrent taxes on registration or road use); and waste management among others. These are a means for governments to shape relative prices, to provide market signals that influence the behaviour of producers and consumers and recoup costs of environmental policies more generally.

Environmental taxes remain very small compared to labour taxes, and the table shows they actually decreased as a share of national income in the two decades between 1995 and 2014, even as various environmental issues became

12.5 Policies and Pollution

Table 12.16 Environmentally related taxes
Percentage of GDP

Country	1995	2014
Denmark	4.3	4.1
Italy	3.2	3.9
Netherlands	3.2	3.3
Austria	2.6	2.9
Finland	3.0	2.9
United Kingdom	2.7	2.3
Ireland	2.9	2.2
Sweden	2.8	2.2
Norway	3.4	2.1
Belgium	2.5	2.0
France	2.4	2.0
Germany	2.3	2.0
Australia	2.6	1.9
Switzerland	1.8	1.8
Japan	1.7	1.5
New Zealand	1.7	1.3
Canada	1.7	1.2
United States	**1.1**	**0.7**
Mean	2.5	2.2

Table 12.17 Municipal waste
Waste per person, 2013

Country	Waste per person (kg/cap)	Percentage change (2000–2013)	Final private expenditure (US$)
Japan	354	−18	19
Belgium	438	−8	20
Sweden	458	7	20
Italy	484	−5	17
Finland	493	−2	19
United Kingdom	494	−14	27
Norway	501	37	28
Netherlands	525	−12	18
France	530	3	19
Austria	580	8	21
Ireland	587	−20	17
Germany	614	−4	22
New Zealand	626	−27	15
Australia	647	−7	26
Switzerland	712	8	25
United States	**725**	**−7**	**34**
Denmark	751	10	18
Mean	560	−2	22

No data on Canada
OECD Environment at a Glance 2015

more acute. Perhaps the main message from the table is how small these taxes are everywhere, but when examining differences between them, again the West European countries are at the top, and the United States (and Canada and New Zealand) at the bottom.

Waste is a by-product of nearly all human activities. Even in ancient cities, the hygienic and efficient disposal of waste was a major problem. With the scale of contemporary metropolises, industrial production, and affluent consumer lifestyles, waste disposal and pollution control have become expensive and contentious policy issues.

Table 12.17 shows a surprisingly large range in the amount of waste generated per person in the selected countries, with the United States producing the second most on a per-person basis. Most of the countries are reducing the amount of waste produced per person, with Denmark, Switzerland and Norway being notable exceptions. Waste disposal is more expensive in the United States than any of the countries, reflecting cost structures as well as volume.

As the problem of waste disposal has grown with larger populations and greater affluence, there has been more concern about disposing of garbage more efficiently. Table 12.18 shows the treatment of waste products. The first column covers the percentage of waste which is recycled or composted. At the other extreme is where it is simply buried as landfill. New Zealand has moved the least towards processing their waste, but the other New World democracies also simply bury more than half their waste, in contrast to several European countries and Japan, for whom this has now become negligible.

Table 12.18 Disposal and treatment of waste
Percentage of each means of disposal, 2013

Country	Material recovery	Incineration with or without energy recovery	Landfill
Germany	65	35	0
Switzerland	51	49	0
Belgium	55	44	1
Netherlands	50	49	1
Sweden	50	50	1
Japan	19	78	1
Denmark	44	54	2
Norway	39	57	2
Austria	58	35	4
Finland	33	42	25
France	38	34	28
United Kingdom	43	21	34
Italy	41	21	38
Ireland	40	18	42
United States	**35**	**12**	**54**
Australia	41	1	58
Canada	24	4	72
New Zealand	0	0	100
Mean	40	33	26

Material recovery includes recycling and composting
OECD Environment at a Glance 2015

12.6 Environmental Performance and Health

In several chapters of this book, we see the wish of organisations to construct a single scoreboard to chart progress or make comparisons—such as on globalisation, liveability of cities and gender to name a few. The Environmental Performance Index (EPI) does this here, and like some of the others is based on a massive and high-quality research enterprise.

The tenth EPI Report in 2018 ranks 180 countries on 24 performance indicators. The Yale Center for Environmental Law and Policy and the Columbia Center for International Earth Science Information Network are the principal drivers of the report, which was built on the best available data from international research entities.

Like some other indices, it makes each indicator into a scale between zero and 100 before joining them all—with various weightings—into a single index. It has two principal sub-components—environmental health (which contributes 40% of the total score) and ecosystem vitality (60%) (Table 12.19).

The index shows that more affluent countries are better able to address environmental issues, although at every income level, some countries achieve scores that exceed their peer nations at similar stages of economic development.

The leading countries in the index—Switzerland, France and Denmark—are all affluent democracies. All the 18 selected democracies are in the global top 30. The lowest ranking country among these 18 is the United States, ranked 27th. America's total score is dragged down by poor performance in areas such as deforestation and greenhouse gas emissions.

A closer look at the two sub-components reveals a strong contrast. These affluent democracies have largely succeeded in addressing issues of environmental health. Their water supply, sanitation, waste disposal and control of air pollution are all among the world's best. All of them score higher on environmental health than on ecosystem vitality, where their urban and economic development often has adverse environmental impacts. The best performing countries, such as Switzerland, exhibit not only long-standing commitments to protecting public health, but to preserving natural resources, and decoupling greenhouse gas emissions from economic activity. The United States scores well on environmental health, but among the lowest on ecosystem vitality.

One of the principal environmental health threats is from air pollution, and here the difference between the developed and developing world is particularly pronounced. The World Health Organisation says that 4.2 million deaths a year are caused by ambient (outdoor) air pollution. It estimates that one quarter of all deaths from cardiovascular diseases are caused by air pollution, and that exposure to airborne pollution is the fourth leading cause of premature death globally.

Table 12.19 Environmental performance index
0–100 where 100 = best
Top 30 (of 180) countries plus selected others

Country	Global rank	EPI score	Environmental health	Ecosystem vitality
Switzerland	1	87.4	93.6	83.3
France	2	84.0	95.7	76.1
Denmark	3	81.6	98.2	70.5
Malta	4	80.9	93.8	72.3
Sweden	5	80.5	94.4	71.2
United Kingdom	6	79.9	96.0	69.1
Luxembourg	7	79.1	95.1	68.5
Austria	8	79.0	86.4	74.0
Ireland	9	78.8	95.9	67.3
Finland	10	78.6	99.4	64.8
Iceland	11	78.6	98.4	65.3
Spain	12	78.4	94.2	67.9
Germany	13	78.4	88.7	71.5
Norway	14	77.5	97.9	63.9
Belgium	15	77.4	89.4	69.4
Italy	16	77.0	85.9	71.0
New Zealand	17	76.0	96.0	62.6
Netherlands	18	75.5	92.3	64.3
Israel	19	75.0	94.1	62.3
Japan	20	74.7	93.0	62.5
Australia	21	74.1	98.0	58.2
Greece	22	73.6	91.0	62.0
Taiwan	23	72.8	69.9	74.8
Cyprus	24	72.6	88.0	62.4
Canada	25	72.2	97.5	55.3
Portugal	26	71.9	90.5	59.5
United States	**27**	**71.2**	**93.9**	**56.0**
Slovakia	28	70.6	63.9	75.1
Lithuania	29	69.3	72.6	67.2
Bulgaria	30	67.9	69.6	66.7
Selected others				
Russia	52	63.8	75.5	56.0
South Korea	60	62.3	73.3	55.0
China	120	50.7	31.7	63.4
India	177	30.6	9.3	44.7

World Economic Forum *Environmental Performance Index*

The key issue here is exposure to fine particulate matter ($PM_{2.5}$), which can penetrate the lung, leading to higher incidences of cardiovascular and respiratory disease. These particulates may include heavy metals and toxic organic substances. Particulate matter can be a complex mixture of solid and liquid particles of organic and inorganic substances suspended in the air. Small particulates of less than PM_{10} can penetrate deep into the respiratory tract causing significant health damage. Fine particulates less than $PM_{2.5}$ penetrate deeper and are even more toxic. Emissions from transport, industry, electricity generation, agriculture and domestic household sources are the main contributors to outdoor pollution.

12.6 Environmental Performance and Health

Table 12.20 Air pollution
% of population exposed to outdoor PM$_{2.5}$

Country	1998	2015
Norway	8.2	4.4
New Zealand	6.8	5.0
Australia	7.1	5.2
Finland	9.9	6.0
Ireland	9.7	6.7
Sweden	13.0	7.0
Canada	10.9	7.7
Denmark	15.4	10.6
United Kingdom	15.2	10.7
United States	**18.1**	**10.9**
Switzerland	14.1	12.5
France	15.7	12.7
Germany	18.5	14.3
Belgium	21.5	14.9
Netherlands	21.4	15.1
Japan	14.5	15.5
Austria	15.9	15.7
Italy	19.2	20.0
Mean	*14.2*	*10.8*

OECD Green Growth Indicators 2017

Table 12.21 Worst air pollution
Worst 10 countries globally for acute exposure to ambient PM$_{2.5}$ concentrations

Country	Index
Thailand	37
Democratic Republic of the Congo	36
Republic of the Congo	32
Singapore	31
Tajikistan	28
Pakistan	20
China	12
India	2
Bangladesh	0
Nepal	0

World Economic Forum *Environmental Performance Index*

The two Tables 12.20 and 12.21 present data on air pollution in different ways. Table 12.20 shows the proportion of the population in the selected democracies exposed to dangerous levels of particulate matter. In the 17 years between 1998 and 2015, the mean for the 18 democracies declined by a quarter. The United States is now around the mean, thanks to being one of the most dramatic improvers.

Table 12.21, from the EPI, has converted such exposure into an index where 100 is the best and zero is the worst. When expressed in this way, six of the democracies (Australia, Finland, Ireland, New Zealand, Norway and Sweden) actually score 100 on this measure, and the mean for these countries is 93, which is what America scores. The two bottom scoring countries are Austria (81) and Italy (75).

In contrast, Table 12.21 presents the ten countries with the worst population exposure to fine particulate matter. The bottom five have scores of 20 or less and include the relatively dynamic economies of China and South Asia. Their economic dynamism has so far exacerbated the health threats from air pollution.

The authors of the EPI conclude that 'the world has entered a new era of data-driven environmental policy-making'. Unfortunately, the tables on this and previous pages do not give great support for that optimism.

Science, Technology and the Digital Revolution

13.1 Inputs

As the industrial society is superseded by the post-industrial society, the ability to create, distribute and exploit knowledge is increasingly central to a country's competitive advantage and rising standard of living. So, investing in these areas is important for innovation, job creation and continuing economic growth.

Table 13.1 shows that across the 18 countries, the amount spent on research and development has been growing more quickly than national income. Even more emphatically, Table 13.2 shows that the number of researchers employed has been growing considerably faster than the labour force as a whole, comprising more than double the proportion in 2015 as in 1985. Researchers are defined broadly as professionals engaged in the conception and creation of new knowledge, products and processes.

The United States is just above the mean in proportion of R and D spending and just below on the proportion of researchers employed, but in absolute size, it is by far the most important country. More than any other country (and the EU as a whole), it is the centre of research activities in the contemporary world.

As would be expected, the rankings in Tables 13.1 and 13.2 are broadly similar, although there are some inconsistencies. In both tables, Japan, Sweden and Finland rank highly. Similarly, Italy and New Zealand rank near the bottom in both, as do to a lesser extent Canada and Australia. Japan, Switzerland, Austria and Finland increased their commitment most in the first table, while Italy and New Zealand barely moved. Ireland and the United Kingdom have not increased the proportion of GDP but have substantially increased the number of researchers. Ireland's failure to increase the proportion of GDP is probably a reflection of its recent spectacular economic growth.

In all 18 countries, at least half the research and development funding is supplied by business. The six countries where the business share is smallest—New Zealand, Canada, Norway, Italy, the Netherlands and Australia—all rank in the bottom half and all but Australia in the bottom third of spending on R and D relative to GDP. Similarly, the seven countries where business supplies the greatest support relative to government all rank highly in Table 13.1, except for Ireland. This suggests that it is more the attitudes of business than of governments that drives the relative research effort (Table 13.3).

Table 13.1 Research and development
% of GDP devoted to R&D

Country	1985	1995	2005	2015
Switzerland	2.6	2.6	2.9	3.4
Japan	2.6	2.7	3.3	3.3
Sweden	2.8	3.3	3.9	3.3
Austria	1.2	1.5	2.4	3.1
Denmark	1.2	1.8	2.5	3.0
Finland	1.5	2.3	3.5	2.9
Germany	2.6	2.2	2.5	2.9
United States	**2.8**	**2.5**	**2.6**	**2.8**
Belgium	1.6	1.7	1.9	2.5
France	2.2	2.3	2.1	2.2
Australia	1.1	1.6	1.8	2.1
Netherlands	2.0	2.0	1.7	2.0
Norway	1.5	1.7	1.5	1.9
Canada	1.4	1.7	2.0	1.7
United Kingdom	2.2	2.0	1.8	1.7
Ireland	0.8	1.3	1.3	1.5
Italy	1.1	1.0	1.1	1.3
New Zealand	–	1.0	1.2	1.3
Mean	*1.8*	*1.9*	*2.2*	*2.4*

First three columns from *OECD Science, Technology and Industry Scoreboard 2007. Innovation and Performance in the Global Economy* (2007). Final column from *OECD Science, Technology and Industry Scoreboard 2017. The Digital Transformation*

Table 13.2 Researchers
Researchers per 1000 employees

Country	1985	1995	2005	2015
Denmark	3.3	6.1	10.2	15.0
Finland	4.1	8.2	16.5	15.0
Sweden	5.0	8.2	12.5	13.6
Belgium	4.1	6.0	7.6	12.0
Norway	4.8	7.5	9.3	11.1
Ireland	2.5	4.5	5.9	10.8
Japan	6.3	8.3	11.0	10.0
Austria	2.1	3.9	6.8	9.9
France	4.7	6.7	8.0	9.8
United Kingdom	4.9	5.2	5.5	9.2
United States	**7.3**	**8.1**	**9.7**	**9.1**
Australia	4.3	7.1	8.5	9.0
Germany	5.3	6.2	7.0	9.0
Canada	4.4	6.4	7.7	8.8
Netherlands	4.3	4.8	4.5	8.8
Switzerland	4.2	5.5	6.1	8.8
New Zealand	–	4.7	10.2	7.9
Italy	2.9	3.5	2.9	4.9
Mean	*4.4*	*6.2*	*8.3*	*10.2*

First three columns from *OECD Science, Technology and Industry Scoreboard 2007. Innovation and Performance in the Global Economy* (2007). Final column from *OECD Science, Technology and Industry Scoreboard 2017. The Digital Transformation*

Table 13.3 Business research and development
Business R and D as % of all R and D

Country	2005	2015
Japan	76	79
Belgium	68	72
United States	**69**	**72**
Austria	70	71
Ireland	66	71
Switzerland	74	71
Sweden	73	70
Germany	69	69
Finland	71	67
United Kingdom	61	66
France	62	65
Denmark	68	64
Australia	54	56
Netherlands	53	56
Italy	50	55
Norway	54	54
Canada	56	53
New Zealand	42	50
Mean	*63*	*64*

OECD *Science, Technology and Industry Scoreboard 2017. The Digital Transformation*

13.2 Outputs

Investment is important, but it is only one factor leading to innovation.[1] Cornell University, the leading French business school, INSEAD and the World Intellectual Property Organisation have constructed an Innovation Index. In 2018, its 11th edition scored 126 countries based on 57 variables. Apart from countries' investment in research and technology, it includes the political and regulatory environment; the business environment; national infrastructure; human capital and creative outputs.

As always in the construction of such an over-arching index, there can be issues to do with what is included and with the relative weighting of different factors. However, the extent to which a particular national environment encourages innovation clearly needs to be multi-dimensional.

The 18 selected democracies all score highly—Singapore is the only other country in the top ten. The lowest ranking of these countries, by a considerable margin, is Italy (ranked 31st globally) and Belgium second lowest (25th).

Switzerland leads this table and ranks near the top also on the other tables on this page. The United States also rates highly.

---

[1] Also draws on Jay Shambaugh et al. 'Eleven Facts about Innovation and Patents' The Hamilton Project, Brookings, December 2017.

13.2 Outputs

Table 13.4 Global innovation index
2018 Index (0–100, where 100 is highest)

Country	Global rank	Score
Switzerland	1	68.4
Netherlands	2	63.3
Sweden	3	63.1
United Kingdom	4	60.1
United States	**6**	**59.8**
Finland	7	59.6
Denmark	8	58.4
Germany	9	58.0
Ireland	10	57.2
Japan	13	55.0
France	16	54.4
Canada	18	53.0
Norway	19	52.6
Australia	20	52.0
Austria	21	51.3
New Zealand	22	51.3
Belgium	25	50.5
Italy	31	46.3
D18 Mean		*56.4*
Global Median (126 countries)		*33.8*

Cornell University, INSEAD, and WIPO (2018) *The Global Innovation Index: Energizing the World with Innovation* (Ithaca, Fontainebleau and Geneva)

Table 13.5 Intellectual property receipts
IP receipts as % total trade 2016

Country	2016%
United States	**5.0**
Japan	5.0
Switzerland	4.4
Netherlands	4.2
Sweden	3.4
Finland	3.2
Ireland	2.6
France	2.1
United Kingdom	2.0
Denmark	1.5
Germany	1.2
Belgium	0.9
Canada	0.9
Italy	0.6
New Zealand	0.6
Austria	0.5
Australia	0.3
Norway	0.3
Mean	*2.2*

Cornell University, INSEAD, and WIPO (2018) *The Global Innovation Index: Energizing the World with Innovation* (Ithaca, Fontainebleau and Geneva)

Table 13.6 High-tech exports
% total trade 2016

Country	% 2016
France	14.3
Switzerland	14.1
Germany	13.9
Japan	12.6
Ireland	11.9
Netherlands	11.8
Austria	11.5
Belgium	10.4
United Kingdom	9.8
Sweden	8.8
United States	**7.2**
Denmark	6.6
Italy	5.8
Canada	5.4
Finland	4.7
Norway	3.5
Australia	2.2
New Zealand	1.4
Mean	*8.7*

Cornell University, INSEAD, and WIPO (2018) *The Global Innovation Index: Energizing the World with Innovation* (Ithaca, Fontainebleau and Geneva)

Patents are one tangible measure of inventive activity that has potential commercial value, and as individuals and companies have become more conscious of the importance of intellectual property, and as in nearly all phases of economic and social life, there is more emphasis on innovation, patent activity has increased. The US Patent Office receives six times as many patent applications as it did in 1980.

While national governments have had national patent offices for well over a century, the registering of them internationally and international agreements to observe them have increased over recent generations. The OECD has developed the measure of triadic patent families defined as a set of patents taken at the European Patent Office, the Japan Patent Office and the US Patent and Trademark Office that protect the same invention. This improves the international comparability of patent activity by eliminating the influence of national home office 'advantage'. Patents included in the triadic family are typical of higher value, as patentees only expend the extra cost and effort of registering transnationally if they think it is worthwhile.

Table 13.7 examines countries' triadic patent activity in relation to population, showing that it increased by around 20% overall between 1995 and 2005. Japan and Switzerland, both above 100 per million population, were clearly the top two countries.

In absolute volume of triadic patents issued worldwide in 2015, Japan was the leader with 31%, the US second with 27%, while the EU had 24%. As might be expected from their pre-eminence in total patents, Japan and the United States are the leaders in intellectual property receipts (Table 13.5), while Switzerland with its heavy relative involvement is third.

Table 13.7 Patents
Triadic patents per million population

Country	1995	2005	2013
Switzerland	102	107	148
Japan	75	119	126
Germany	58	76	68
Sweden	76	72	67
Denmark	35	41	65
Austria	27	37	59
Netherlands	46	73	55
United States	**45**	**55**	**46**
Finland	60	50	44
Belgium	36	32	42
France	32	39	39
United Kingdom	26	26	28
Norway	20	24	24
Canada	13	25	16
Ireland	8	14	16
Australia	12	20	13
Italy	11	12	12
New Zealand	6	16	11
Mean	*38*	*47*	*49*

First two columns from *OECD Science, Technology and Industry Scoreboard 2007. Innovation and Performance in the Global Economy* (2007). Final column from *OECD Factbook* (2016)

High-tech exports are an indicator of the technological sophistication of manufacturing in a country. They include aerospace, computers and office machines, electronics and telecommunications, pharmaceutical and chemical products. Switzerland and Japan maintain their prominence, while France and Germany, around the middle of other tables, come to the fore as well. The measure is a percentage of total trade, and while the American figure is just below the mean, lower than would be expected from the previous tables, this may reflect more its all-round trading strength, rather than any lack in high-tech manufacturing.

In all three tables, Norway, Australia, Canada, New Zealand and Italy are in the bottom third. They are regularly technology followers rather than innovators. This may be a rational strategy. While often there are first-mover advantages with innovations, there are also, as Thorstein Veblen wrote about the rise of Imperial Germany, advantages of being second. Others can go through the teething problems, and face the up-front risks and costs, and no country can be a pioneer in all areas. But these countries also run the danger of becoming branch office economies and not keeping up with the dynamism of evolving economies.

This is not an option for a world leader such as the United States. While America ranks highly in all these tables, its pre-eminence is not as great as it was. It was one of the few countries to drop in the number of triadic patents filed between 2005 and 2013, possibly a blip rather than a precursor to relative decline.

13.3 The Digital Revolution

If we compare life in the advanced democracies today with three or four decades earlier, the rapid diffusion of digital technologies has transformed what people take for granted, and it is all but impossible to imagine life now without them.[2]

The first was personal computers (PCs), which changed the way most people work, increasing productivity and convenience. So, it may be surprising to recall just how recent their invention and spread has been. They began in a small way in the early 1980s, but take-up was relatively slow. In 1990, there was one personal computer for every ten people in the selected countries—one for every five in America, then the leading country for PCs. By 2005, there were almost two PCs for every three people—including business and home computers. By this time, the United States was still well above the mean but had dropped to fifth. Italy and Belgium were the clear laggards with less than four PCs for every ten people. Now personal computers are so ubiquitous, so greatly outnumbering people, that the OECD has stopped producing data in this way.

When looking at the growth of personal computers, it should also be remembered that their capacity in 1988 was only a fraction of what it was by 2018. It is a remarkable story of decreasing price and increasing power. The range of tasks for which people use PCs has increased, and it is the means by which most people connect to the other great popular digital innovation of recent times—the Internet.

There are few more rapid social changes than the spread of personal computers, but Table 13.8 describes one. The cellular mobile telephone went from novelty to ubiquity in 20 years. In 1985, mobile services were only commonly used in the Nordic countries, and in the selected countries overall there were only three mobile phones for every 1000 people. By 2017, mobile phones outnumber people in all the selected countries except Canada.

Mobile phone technology developed in Scandinavia, and for a long time, those countries were the world leaders in its use. Then, in the early 1990s, the next phase of rapid adoption came in the English-speaking world. In the late 1990s, the most dramatic growth was in some European countries—Italy, Austria and Ireland—which were relatively late adopters of the technology, but which now rank among the leaders.

The growth of the next innovation—the Internet—is just as dramatic. The very idea of the Internet was unimaginable for most people before the mid-1990s. According to

---
[2]Data on number of personal computers can be found in Rodney Tiffen and Ross Gittins *How Australia Compares* (2nd ed., Cambridge University Press, 2009).

13.3 The Digital Revolution

Table 13.8 Mobile telephones
Number per 100 population

Country	1985	1995	2005	2017
Austria	0	5	106	171
Italy	0	7	123	143
New Zealand	0	10	88	136
Finland	1	20	100	133
Japan	0	9	75	133
Switzerland	0	6	94	133
Germany	–	5	96	129
Sweden	1	23	101	125
Denmark	1	16	100	122
United States	**0**	**13**	**71**	**122**
Netherlands	0	4	97	121
United Kingdom	0	10	110	120
Australia	0	12	91	113
Norway	2	23	103	108
France	0	2	79	106
Belgium	0	2	92	105
Ireland	0	4	103	103
Canada	0	9	53	86
Mean	0	10	93	123

First three columns International Telecommunication Union *Yearbook of Statistics 2008, Telecommunication Services 1997–2006* (Geneva, ITU, 2008). Last column is from World Bank World Development Indicators

Table 13.9 Internet users
Per 100 population

Country	1995	2005	2016
Japan	2	67	98
Denmark	4	77	97
Norway	6	80	97
United Kingdom	2	66	95
Finland	14	73	94
Netherlands	7	79	93
Sweden	5	81	93
Germany	2	65	90
Switzerland	4	70	90
Australia	3	63	88
Canada	4	68	88
Belgium	1	58	87
France	2	43	86
Austria	2	55	84
New Zealand	5	64	84
Ireland	1	37	82
United States	**9**	**69**	**79**
Italy	1	48	69
Mean	4	65	88

First three columns International Telecommunication Union *Yearbook of Statistics 2008, Telecommunication Services 1997–2006* (Geneva, ITU, 2008). Final column: OECD *Science, Technology and Industry Scoreboard 2017. The Digital Transformation*

Table 13.9, in 1995 only one person in 25 used the Internet; a decade later two in three did, and 20 years later almost nine in ten did. It has transformed the way in which people seek information and entertainment and communicate with each other. Table 13.9 shows a clustering at the top, with Italy a clear laggard. Perhaps surprisingly, the United States ranks second bottom on the table, despite being above the mean in 2005.

The most recent of these digital revolutions has been the growth of mobile internet access so that people on their mobile phones and devices such as Ipads can access data wherever they have telephone or wireless reception (Table 13.10). As late as 2010 only just under half the population had such access; six years later, 100% did (that number is skewed upwards by multiple devices and subscriptions).

As use of the Internet grew, and expectations about what it should deliver kept rising, the initial access through dial-up devices was seen as too slow and limited. Broadband access, faster and always connected, became the norm. In the 12 years covered by Table 13.11, households with broadband access grew from around one in three to 17 in 20. In some European countries—densely populated countries with small areas—the figure is well over 90%.

Table 13.10 Mobile internet penetration
Total (data and/or voice) per 100 people

Country	2010	2016
New Zealand	76	152
Germany	31	147
Australia	56	129
United States	**61**	**126**
France	64	123
United Kingdom	84	122
Switzerland	39	104
Japan	45	100
Denmark	44	98
Sweden	65	96
Italy	44	90
Netherlands	38	88
Norway	38	88
Austria	33	87
Ireland	36	80
Finland	26	77
Canada	30	69
Belgium	10	66
Mean	45	102

OECD *Science, Technology and Industry Scoreboard 2017. The Digital Transformation*

Table 13.11 Households with broadband Internet access
%

Country	2005	2017
Netherlands	54	98
Norway	41	94
Finland	36	93
Sweden	40	93
United Kingdom	32	93
Denmark	51	92
Germany	23	92
Switzerland	53	90
Austria	23	88
Ireland	7	88
Belgium	41	84
Canada	50	80
France	30	79
Italy	13	79
Australia	28	77
United States	**51**	**77**
Japan	42	65
Mean	*36*	*86*

No data on New Zealand; LAY for Japan, Australia, Canada is 2010–2012
OECD Telecommunications Database

Again the United States, in 2005, was one of the four leading countries for households with broadband, but by 2017 had dropped back to equal second last.

In several tables, a similar trajectory occurs: the United States is an early adopter of new technologies; is prominent in the growth of innovations; but then the diffusion of those technologies reaches a limit, well before they become universally used, and stabilizing at a lower rate of take-up than in some other countries.

13.4 Digital Divides

With the diffusion of any new technology, there is often concern about the gap between the haves and have nots. In the case of digital technology, it threatened to become one of information rich versus information poor. As the diffusion of some of these technologies comes close to universal, however, the concern with digital divides may dissipate somewhat.

Not surprisingly in new technologies, there is a considerable gap between young and old. Table 13.12 shows that in every country except the United States 90% or more of 16–24-year olds are using the Internet. Indeed in 14 countries, the figure is 97% or higher. On average across the 18 countries, around three in four 55–74-year olds use the Internet, so there is a gap of around 24% between the two age cohorts. Among older people, the United States is close to the mean.

These figures are from 2016. One suspects the gap would have been greater in 2006 and will be smaller by 2026. People in the post 55 age groups will have increasingly started using the Internet when they were younger and still likely to be more receptive to new possibilities.

Although the means are broadly similar for Tables 13.12 and 13.13, it may be that the gap between tertiary educated and those with low educational attainment will be harder to

Table 13.12 Internet usage by age groups
% 2016

Country	16–24-year olds	55–74-year olds
Denmark	100	92
Norway	100	92
Sweden	92	91
Netherlands	97	87
United Kingdom	100	85
Finland	100	84
Japan	99	77
Germany	99	74
Australia	98	73
Switzerland	100	72
Belgium	98	71
United States	**85**	**71**
New Zealand	93	70
France	97	69
Austria	99	63
Ireland	97	56
Canada	99	48
Italy	90	42
Mean	*97*	*73*

OECD *Science, Technology and Industry Scoreboard 2017. The Digital Transformation*

Table 13.13 Internet usage and education
% 2016

Country	Low educational level	Tertiary educated
Denmark	95	100
Finland	87	99
Netherlands	83	99
Norway	95	99
United Kingdom	78	99
Belgium	71	98
France	68	98
Austria	62	97
Germany	81	97
Switzerland	76	97
Australia	69	96
Ireland	55	95
Sweden	83	95
Italy	48	92
New Zealand	–	92
United States	**59**	**88**
Mean	*74*	*96*

No data on Canada or Japan

13.4 Digital Divides

Table 13.14 Urban and rural broadband
% households with broadband

Country	Urban 2010	Rural 2010	Urban 2016	Rural 2016
New Zealand	87	79	96	95
United Kingdom	68	71	93	94
Netherlands	79	78	96	93
Denmark	81	76	92	91
Germany	76	70	90	88
Finland	75	73	91	87
Switzerland	77	80	90	85
Sweden	85	79	90	84
Belgium	73	62	83	83
Austria	63	61	85	83
Ireland	59	50	88	81
France	63	51	80	78
Italy	47	41	78	72
United States	**68**	**57**	**73**	**64**
Mean	71	66	87	84

No data on Australia, Canada, Japan or Norway
OECD *Science, Technology and Industry Scoreboard 2017. The Digital Transformation*

close. (It should be remembered that educational levels correlate with age.) Among those with tertiary education, more than 90% use the Internet, except in America where it is 88%. In six European countries, more than 80% of those with a low educational level use the Internet. However, there is much more of a spread between the 18 countries—in Italy, Ireland and the United States, it is less than 60%.

Part of the reason for the digital divide lay in unequal access to the infrastructure. Table 13.14 shows the percentage of households with broadband access in urban and rural areas. In both 2010 and 2016, a greater proportion of urban households than rural households had such access, but across the 14 countries on which we have data, the gap had almost disappeared, down to three points.

All countries improved in both urban and rural areas across the six years, and by 2016 in several countries, there was basically no difference in broadband access. In seven of 14 countries, the gap was 2% or less. The gap was biggest, and rural access least, in Italy and the United States: Italy had a gap of six points, with 72% of rural households having access; the US had a gap of nine points, with only 64% of rural households having access. Italy is often a technological laggard. The American figure is more surprising and may reflect that the construction of infrastructure there is more in commercial hands than in many other countries, and many rural areas are not regarded as markets likely to be profitable.

To conclude on a hopeful note, it is likely that the digital divide is narrowing rather than widening, and it will be interesting to see where it stands in a decade's time.

13.5 Online and Automated Activities

The rise of the Internet means that many activities and transactions can now be performed digitally rather than in person. In theory, this provides users with greater convenience and possibilities.

E-government or Government 2.0 are grander titles than the reality so far deserves, but more and more interactions between citizens and governments can be done online. Information about government services and regulations is increasingly available over the Internet, while citizens can make payments over the Internet, submit their tax returns, and complete bureaucratic forms, for example, to do with starting a new business. Educational institutions increasingly allow students to complete programs online.

For E-government services to be effective, certain conditions must be met. The first is access, and there can be ongoing issues of inclusion for the old, non-native language speakers, and others. Quality of design and ease of use are clearly critical. Trust is another pre-requisite. Citizens must be confident that this will not be a means of undue surveillance over them and that systems are secure.

Table 13.15 is taken from a United Nations survey on e-government around the world, and this is one of the indices they constructed. Great Britain tops the table, and the other English-speaking countries, apart from Ireland, are also concentrated the top half. It is likely that in this area,

Table 13.15 E-government
Government Online Index 2016 (100 = highest)

Country	Index
United Kingdom	100
Australia	98
Canada	96
Finland	94
France	94
New Zealand	94
Netherlands	93
United States	**93**
Austria	91
Japan	88
Sweden	88
Italy	87
Germany	84
Ireland	81
Norway	80
Denmark	78
Belgium	71
Switzerland	60
Mean	87

Cornell University, INSEAD, and WIPO (2018) *The Global Innovation Index: Energizing the World with Innovation* (Ithaca, Fontainebleau and Geneva)

Table 13.16 Online purchases

% who made an online purchase in the last year

Country	All 2006	All 2016	Age 55–74 2016	Age 16–24 2016
United Kingdom	79	87	79	88
Denmark	76	84	74	91
Germany	73	82	69	81
Sweden	71	80	68	79
Netherlands	74	79	64	84
Norway	76	79	61	87
France	70	75	62	78
Switzerland	70	74	61	76
Finland	68	72	44	80
Ireland	52	71	42	67
United States	**70**	**70**	**67**	**62**
Austria	57	68	47	82
New Zealand	–	68	–	59
Belgium	49	65	50	68
Australia	70	63	48	63
Canada	52	57	–	52
Japan	63	54	–	–
Italy	27	41	29	44
Mean	*64*	*70*	*58*	*73*

OECD *Science, Technology and Industry Scoreboard 2017. The Digital Transformation*

Table 13.17 Generic top-level domains

Per thousand population 15–69-year old, 2016

Country	gTLDs
United States	**100**
Netherlands	77
Canada	76
Australia	63
Ireland	62
United Kingdom	61
Switzerland	60
Germany	55
New Zealand	53
Norway	51
Denmark	48
Sweden	43
France	41
Austria	37
Finland	29
Belgium	24
Italy	23
Japan	16
Mean	*51*

Cornell University, INSEAD, and WIPO (2018) *The Global Innovation Index: Energizing the World with Innovation* (Ithaca, Fontainebleau and Geneva)

rankings can change relatively quickly, when governments opt to make a concerted effort. Some countries, such as Switzerland, Denmark and Germany, that generally rank well on IT measures, are currently near the bottom.

Table 13.16 gives data on what percentage of people in each country made an online purchase in the last year. In 2016, across the 18 countries, 70% of people did. Italy is again the laggard. The low Japanese figure perhaps reflects that country's emphasis on the direct relationship between seller and buyer. Britain and a range of countries from north-western Europe top the table. As might be expected younger people are more likely to have made an online purchase than older people—although, uniquely and seemingly inexplicably, not in the United States.

Perhaps, the most surprising aspect of the table is that there was an increase of only 6% in the purchases in the decade from 2006 to 2016. Some countries increased substantially, but a few went backwards and the United States was stable. Perhaps, a level of resistance for some reason has been reached—fear of fraud or theft, or worry about the quality of goods or some such. While there have been forecasts of how online shopping will take the world by storm, and that department stores and other physical shops are feeling its impact, it will be interesting to see how much this figure changes over the next decade. It may be that there will still be substantial proportions who do not partake, but that those who do will use it increasingly frequently.

Generic top-level domains are labels, such as .com, .net, .org, .gov and several others, which are controlled by the governing authority, the Internet Assigned Numbers Authority. Table 13.17 gives the number of top-level domains per thousand population, aged 15–69. It can be taken as one proxy indicator of the vigour of Internet activity, as organisations and businesses seek to establish the Internet presence. America clearly tops the list and is double the mean of the others. The other English-speaking countries all rank highly.

Computerisation has changed how many jobs are done, and no doubt introduced many labour-saving efficiencies in large organisations. Another aspect of computerisation is automation, and whether robots can replace humans in some tasks. So far, as Table 13.18 shows robots have made a very limited impact. Japan, perhaps because of its concern about its ageing labour force wedded to the country's technological sophistication, clearly leads the way, but only in the four top countries is there as much as one robot for every 100 workers. In New Zealand and Ireland, it is one robot for every 1000 workers.

No doubt technological change will keep transforming the nature of work, but the fear that robots will replace humans on any large scale so far seems exaggerated.

13.5 Online and Automated Activities

Table 13.18 Robots

Country	Robots per 1000 workers 2015
Japan	28.0
Germany	14.5
Sweden	10.5
United States	**10.5**
Denmark	8.6
Belgium	8.3
Italy	8.0
France	7.0
Austria	6.8
Finland	6.2
Netherlands	4.6
United Kingdom	4.2
Australia	2.7
Norway	2.4
Canada	1.8
Ireland	1.1
New Zealand	1.0
Mean	*7.4*

No data on Switzerland

OECD *Science, Technology and Industry Scoreboard 2017. The Digital Transformation*

Media

14.1 Newspapers and Online News

While, after Gutenberg's invention of the printing press, the book has some claim to be the first mass medium, it was the newspaper, which from the eighteenth century on became central to political life and to the development of democracy.[1] But this first mass news medium is now in sharp decline. Table 14.1 shows the proportion of people buying newspapers in these 18 democracies in 2014 is essentially half what it was in 1980.

Moreover the rate of decline, in the first 14 years of this century was much sharper than in the last 20 years of the twentieth century. In these 14 years, every one of the countries had a substantial decline. Previously, the two countries with the highest rates of newspaper circulation—Japan and Norway—had withstood the trend, but now they are also experiencing it.

The relative standing of the countries in Table 14.1 has only changed slightly. Newspapers have been and continue to be most popular in Japan and the countries of north-western Europe. France and Italy have always been near the bottom. If anything the decline has been sharpest in some English-speaking democracies, especially Britain and Australia.

These circulation falls only hint at the industry's crisis. Advertising revenue has followed circulation revenue down, as has employment. In 2012, the Newspaper Association of America found newspapers were only reclaiming $1 in digital advertising revenue for every $25 of lost print advertising revenue. In 2016, the US Bureau of Labor Statistics reported that newspaper jobs were down from nearly 458,000 in 1990 to about 183,000 in March 2016, a fall of almost 60%.

As print sales decline, and will continue to decline, the question is whether online news sources will fill the gap in informing the public. The international Pew survey in 2018 found that on average in the selected countries for which there was data more than half the population claimed that they used the Internet every day to look for news (Table 14.2). Several newspapers have claimed that their readerships are now greater than they ever were because of their online presence. This takes no account of how thoroughly these readers are absorbing the news. Nor as we shall explore in Table 14.4 does it relate to the ability of these news outlets to monetize their readership.

Apart from the migration from print to online, the other issue has been the growing role of the Internet and social media in diffusing news. As Table 14.2 shows, in most of the countries between 34 and 42% of the population say they consult social networking sites for news. The United States tops this tightly clustered group. In Japan and Germany, the figure is substantially lower.

By far the most important social medium used as a news source is Facebook. The data in Tables 14.3 and 14.4 is from the Reuters Institute Digital News Report, based on large samples in many countries and coordinated by the Reuters Institute for the Study of Journalism at Oxford University. While Germany and Japan again trail the others in Table 14.3, it shows the Italians have embraced Facebook news more than the other democracies.

Table 14.4 shows, unsurprisingly, that the proportions saying they paid to get online news is much smaller than the proportion saying they had used the Internet for news, on average about one quarter the figure in Table 14.2. As with the purchase of newspapers, the Scandinavian countries rank near the top. For a very, very few globally recognized brands, the digital age brings new and profitable possibilities. The *New York Times* now has 2.9 million digital-only subscribers, out of a total circulation of 3.8 million.

However, the table points to the problem for most news organisations in the Internet age. To employ large numbers of journalists, news organisations need to monetize their digital presence, but they seem to be finding a public reluctant to pay.

---

[1] Also draws on Roy Greenslade 'Almost 60% of US newspaper jobs vanish in 26 years' *Guardian* June 6, 2016; Rick Edmonds 'Newspapers get $1 in new digital ad revenue for every $25 in print ad revenue lost' *Poynter* September 10, 2012.

Table 14.1 Newspaper circulation
Daily newspapers sold per 1000 population

Country	1980	2000	2014
Japan	567	577	359
Norway	463	573	300
Finland	505	443	282
Sweden	528	464	243
Switzerland	393	365	218
Austria	351	309	209
Germany	–	289	202
Netherlands	326	279	170
United Kingdom	417	320	154
Denmark	366	279	136
United States	**270**	**197**	**127**
Belgium	232	153	116
New Zealand	334	201	115
Canada	221	166	114
Ireland	229	151	106
France	192	142	99
Australia	323	162	87
Italy	101	110	53
Mean	*342*	*288*	*172*

1980 from UNESCO *Statistical Yearbook 1999*; 2000 from Euromonitor Global Market Information Database (no longer available); 2014 from World Association of Newspapers *World Press Trends*

Table 14.2 Use of internet and social media for news
% reporting they consult each for news at least daily, 2018

Country	Internet	Social networking sites
Sweden	70	40
Netherlands	65	35
Australia	61	41
Canada	59	42
United States	**59**	**39**
Japan	55	20
United Kingdom	54	36
France	50	36
Germany	46	21
Italy	45	34
Mean	*56*	*34*

Other countries not included in survey
Amy Mitchell et al. 'Publics globally want unbiased news coverage, but are divided on whether their news media deliver' Pew Research Center, January 2018

Table 14.3 Facebook as a news source
% saying they used Facebook as a news source in the last week, 2017

Country	%
Italy	51
Australia	41
France	41
Norway	40
Belgium	39
United States	**39**
Canada	38
Ireland	38
Sweden	36
Denmark	34
Finland	33
Switzerland	33
Austria	30
Netherlands	29
United Kingdom	27
Germany	24
Japan	9
Mean	*34*

No data on New Zealand
Nic Newman et al. *Reuters Institute Digital News Report 2018*

Table 14.4 Paying for online news
% who have paid to get online news in the last year, 2018

Country	%
Norway	30
Sweden	26
Australia	20
Finland	18
United States	**16**
Denmark	15
Belgium	14
Netherlands	13
Italy	12
Switzerland	12
France	11
Ireland	11
Japan	10
Canada	9
Austria	8
Germany	8
United Kingdom	7
Mean	*14*

No data on New Zealand
Nic Newman et al. *Reuters Institute Digital News Report 2018*

14.2 Television and Public Broadcasting

In none of the selected countries did broadcasting (first radio and later television) develop as just another industry where market forces could reign. Whereas in none of the countries is there any government-owned newspaper, only in America was there no publicly owned television channel. Public ownership was the norm, partly because of technological necessity. Almost everywhere television began as a terrestrial analog service, meaning there was a limited spectrum on which it could be transmitted. Now it is also delivered through satellite and cable systems, nearly all of which are digital. So where scarcity once ruled, now there is an abundance of available channels. The average American household can receive more than 100. The early arguments about the scarcity of the spectrum are a long way in the past.

But public intervention also rose from the cultural peculiarities and political power of broadcasting. There was an almost universal belief that a free market could not operate in TV—that it would produce rubbish—with no standards, no local content, no quality drama, no children's programmes, no quality news or current affairs. And last, but not least, no profits.

By 1970 (Table 14.5), television had been available in most of the countries for one to two decades. Twelve were still public service monopolies. Britain and Finland had begun that way but since added commercial services. Australia, Japan and Canada had commercial services almost from the beginning, and in the first two, there had always been more commercial than public channels. Only in America did television originate without a public broadcaster.

The American Public Broadcasting Service (PBS) is distinctive. It developed rather later than commercial television in the USA. In some ways, being a non-profit organisation, it was more like an association of community broadcasters rather than a conventional public service broadcaster. It has never received government funding on a scale that would allow it to be a serious competitor to the commercial networks. Although it has the smallest proportionate audience in the table, it is still held in some esteem, consistently seen as the most trusted TV network in polls.

The simplest definition of a public service broadcaster is that it is owned by the government. But as the table shows, there is considerable variation beyond this. The most obvious difference is the relative generosity of government funding. Five European countries had the equivalent of more than $US100 annual public funding per head. For seven countries, including Japan and Australia, as well as some European ones, public funding constitutes more than 80% of their funding.

Table 14.5 Television and public broadcasting

First column summarises each country's television system, 1970; the next three refer to the role of the public broadcaster

Country	System 1970	Per capita public funding 2011 (US$)	Public share of total funding 2012	Audience share 2012
Austria	Public	92	55	35
Belgium	Public	68	69	26
Denmark	Public	116	57	66
France	Public	68	80	25
Germany	Public	124	86	43
Ireland	Public	53	52	30
Italy	Public	38	57	43
Netherlands	Public	–	79	24
New Zealand	Public	21	29	62
Norway	Public	180	96	41
Sweden	Public	117	95	31
Switzerland	Public	164	71	30
Canada	Mixed–public	33	63	6
Finland	Mixed–public	108	97	42
United Kingdom	Mixed–public	97	61	54
Australia	Mixed–comm'l	53	81	18
Japan	Mixed–comm'l	67	98	20
United States	**Commercial**	**3**	**33**	**2**
Mean		83	79	33

Constructed from Rodney Benson et al. 'Public Media Autonomy and Accountability: Best and Worst Policy Practices in 12 Leading Democracies' *International Journal of Communication* 11 (2017), 1–22; Nordicity Analysis of Government Support for Public Broadcasting and Other Culture in Canada' (CBC/Radio-Canada, October 2013); Ingmar Rovekamp 'Public Service Broadcasting in an International Companion' DICE Report 3/2014; McKinsey and Company *Public Service Broadcasters Around the World* (1999)

These figures show some big changes since 1970. New Zealand's broadcaster is still publicly owned, but receives the least public money apart from the PBS, and is centrally dependent on advertising revenue. It therefore functions more like a commercial than a public service broadcaster. The next most poorly funded public broadcaster, the Canadian Broadcasting Corporation, has become fairly marginal in that country's TV viewing, with just a 6% audience share.

In the multichannel television environment, nearly all channels have seen their audience shares decline compared to a decade or two earlier. However, data published by the European Audio-Visual Observatory suggest that in several European countries, if anything, the growth of channels available has been more threatening to the audience share of the major free to air commercial networks than to the public broadcasters.

The attraction of public broadcasting is that it will allow programming beyond normal commercial incentives of securing the biggest audience at the minimum cost. There are two central potential problems with it though. There is no objective formula for how much funding they should receive, and in practice, this is only very tangentially related to performance or audience sentiment. The second is the danger of government interference. There is no ranking of public broadcasters in terms of their independence.

The most successful public broadcasters—those in Britain, Sweden, Denmark, Germany—successfully combined substantial audience share with distinctive programming and political independence. In many of these countries, the public broadcaster is the most trusted source of news.

Table 14.6 Average television viewing time
Average household viewing time, hours per day, in each year

Country	2005	2011
United States	**8.2**	**8.5**
Italy	4.1	4.2
Canada	3.1	4.1
United Kingdom	3.0	4.0
Japan	3.7	3.8
Germany	–	3.5
France	–	3.4
New Zealand	2.7	3.4
Denmark	3.0	3.3
Australia	3.2	3.2
Ireland	2.6	3.2
Netherlands	–	3.1
Finland	2.8	3.0
Norway	–	3.0
Belgium	3.8	2.9
Austria	2.8	2.8
Switzerland	2.5	2.5
Sweden	2.4	2.0
Mean	*3.4*	*3.6*

OECD *Communications Outlook 2007* and OECD *Communications Outlook 2013*

With all the attractions of the Internet, one might have guessed that the amount of time spent viewing television would have declined, but Table 14.6 finds that on average it has remained essentially the same in 2011 as in 2005. America, as in all such comparative surveys of television watching, is again the world champion on this measure.

14.3 Worlds of Journalism

By far the most extensive comparative survey of journalists is the Worlds of Journalism Study, coordinated by Thomas Hanitzsch of the University of Munich and Folker Hanusch of the University of Vienna. The second wave of the study carried out between 2012 and 2016 surveyed journalists in 67 countries, with a total sample of 27,500, with an average sample size of 400–500 in each. The third wave will begin in 2020.

The very wide-ranging questionnaire explored journalists' views of journalism's identity, how in each country it functioned as an institution and its relationship with the larger society. It examined their perceptions of influences on their work, their ideas about journalistic ethics, and about the changing nature of the news media.

The survey has been conducted across all continents, in very different cultures, in societies at different stages of economic development and under a variety of political systems. Our interest here is limited to our 18 stable, affluent democracies. As might be expected in countries with long-established traditions of independent media these journalists share many attitudes. They all claim considerable editorial autonomy; they share a commitment to reporting things as they are and do not see their role as supporting government policy. They share the belief that journalists should always adhere to codes of professional ethics.

The tables on the opposite page present some interesting contrasts however. It should be remembered here that in these results we focus only on national differences. Researchers in the study itself will further look at differences between, for example, television and newspaper journalists, or public versus commercial broadcasting journalists, or quality versus popular newspaper journalists.

Journalists were asked about the relative importance of various of their roles on a scale between one not important and five very important. On this compressed scale, Table 14.7 shows fairly strong differences between the countries on journalists seeing their role as letting people express their views. Being a forum for debate and so reflecting and promoting civil society is much more important to journalists in Sweden and the United States and much less important to those in Japan and Germany. The other English-speaking democracies also see it as important, with the notable exception of Britain. Britain has a much stronger

Table 14.7 Journalists' opinions on letting people express their views

Rated from 1 (not at all important) to 5 (very important)

Country	Mean
Sweden	4.4
United States	**4.2**
France	4.0
New Zealand	4.0
Australia	3.9
Canada	3.9
Finland	3.8
Italy	3.8
Ireland	3.7
Norway	3.7
Netherlands	3.6
Belgium	3.5
Denmark	3.5
Switzerland	3.5
Austria	3.4
United Kingdom	3.4
Germany	3.3
Japan	2.8
Mean	*3.7*

Worlds of Journalism Study: http://www.worldsofjournalism.org/

Table 14.8 Journalists' views on changes in journalism's ethical standards

% saying strengthened or weakened, with % saying no change omitted

Country	Strengthened	Weakened
Japan	60	14
United Kingdom	50	29
Norway	48	22
Ireland	35	39
Finland	33	30
France	28	36
Austria	27	37
Belgium	27	26
Canada	24	34
Switzerland	21	37
Italy	18	66
Sweden	18	32
Australia	17	42
Netherlands	17	50
United States	**17**	**45**
New Zealand	15	60
Germany	14	47
Mean	*27*	*38*

No data on Denmark
Worlds of Journalism Study: http://www.worldsofjournalism.org/

tabloid newspaper tradition than the others, and perhaps the difference stems from that.

Table 14.8 shows that in four countries, journalists think that ethical standards have been strengthened in recent times; indeed in three of these (Japan, the United Kingdom and Norway) emphatic majorities have this opinion. In a few countries opinion is evenly divided, but in most journalists perceive a decline in ethical standards, and in several opinion is very lop-sided: −48 in Italy; −45 in New Zealand; −37 in the Netherlands; −34 in Germany; −28 in the United States; and −25 in Australia.

These are dramatic contrasts. The survey in Britain followed some years after a scandal involving the tabloid *News of the World* and phone hacking, and an exhaustive inquiry under Lord Leveson. There is not a single event that might similarly explain the change in Japan and Norway. Perhaps in those countries that show marked decline journalists think that news organisations' financial problems have made them more willing to cut corners or pursue dubious stunts.

Tables 14.9 and 14.10 provide an interesting contrast. In every country, and by a very substantial margin, journalists think that journalism's place in society has declined, that it is accorded less credibility. The United States is typical—four times as many journalists think its credibility has decreased as think it has increased.

On the other hand, in several but far from all countries, majorities think the relevance of journalism has increased. This belief in the continuing importance of their profession is strongest in the United States, with the other English-speaking countries clustered behind it. This suggests that their commitment to what they see as the social value and proper role of their profession is as strong as ever. On the other hand, in the four countries at the bottom of the table—Italy, Switzerland, France and Austria—a clear majority of journalists think journalism has become less relevant. It is hard to know what sentiment informs this opinion—possibly a declining sense of

Table 14.9 Journalists' views on the changing credibility of journalism

% saying increased or decreased, with % saying no change omitted

Country	Increased	Decreased
Norway	19	43
Canada	15	56
Japan	14	57
Ireland	13	54
Sweden	13	48
United States	**13**	**53**
Belgium	11	58
Finland	11	55
Germany	10	64
New Zealand	9	68
United Kingdom	9	66
Australia	8	55
Netherlands	8	56
France	7	80
Austria	6	65
Italy	6	81
Switzerland	6	68
Mean	*10*	*60*

No data on Denmark
Worlds of Journalism Study: http://www.worldsofjournalism.org/

Table 14.10 Journalists' views on journalism's relevance
% saying increased or decreased, with % saying no change omitted

Country	Increased	Decreased
United States	**52**	**22**
Canada	51	21
Australia	46	18
United Kingdom	37	22
Ireland	36	27
Finland	33	24
Belgium	31	24
New Zealand	31	36
Norway	31	25
Germany	30	37
Sweden	29	32
Japan	27	26
Netherlands	26	26
Austria	21	41
France	19	53
Switzerland	17	40
Italy	14	65
Mean	*31*	*32*

No data on Denmark
Worlds of Journalism Study: http://www.worldsofjournalism.org/

Table 14.11 How news organisations cover political issues
% from Pew public opinion survey, 2017

Country	Very and somewhat well	Of those not supporting governing party	Among supporters of governing party	Gap
Netherlands	74	–	–	–
Canada	73	67	86	19
Germany	72	62	80	18
Sweden	66	58	82	24
Japan	55	–	–	–
United Kingdom	52	49	61	12
Australia	48	51	42	−9
France	47	46	55	9
United States	**47**	**55**	**21**	**−34**
Italy	36	34	51	17

Would you say news organisations are doing this very well, somewhat well, not too well or not well at all: reporting the different positions on political issues fairly
Amy Mitchell et al. 'Publics globally want unbiased news coverage, but are divided on whether their news media deliver' Pew Research Center, January 2018

the potential for journalists to influence developments in the age of fragmented audiences and social media.

14.4 Public Responses and Attitudes

In Table 14.9, it was clear that journalists felt their position in society has deteriorated in recent years. The tables on this page outline some public attitudes. Although they present only contemporary rather than trend data, they do not offer great reassurance about the public's judgement of journalistic performance.

The international Pew Study on attitudes to the news media asked several questions about media performance. On some, such as covering the big stories, they were judged positively. Table 14.11 gives the results on a task central to democratic debate—the reporting of different positions on political issues. Here, there is a more mixed evaluation, with several countries grouped around 50% thinking the news media did this well or very well. Three countries—the Netherlands, Canada and Germany—have substantially more satisfied publics than the others. The United States ranks second bottom, ahead only of Italy in the countries on which we have data.

America is also distinctive in another way. In all the other countries, except Australia, those supporting the governing party rate the news media more highly on this than those who do not support the governing party. Perhaps there is a general tendency for supporters of the incumbents to be more satisfied although that would be a leap from the slender evidence of a small group of countries surveyed at a particular moment. To be more certain, we would have to see similar data after there have been changes of government.

In contrast, in the United States the partisan gap is the highest, double the mean of the others. And supporters of the governing party, the Republicans, are less than half as likely to endorse the news media on this than Democrats (21:55). The apparent dissatisfaction of Republicans with how issues are covered needs further exploration.

The other two tables come from the annual Reuters Institute surveys on digital news. Table 14.12 reports the findings from a question phrased in very general terms about trusting most news most of the time. It does not distinguish between different media, or different news organisations, or different types of stories. The question thus taps general sentiments towards the media. About half the countries are clustered between 46 and 51% endorsing the view that media can be generally trusted. Finland is the clear leader in endorsing the trustworthiness of its media, and again, as in the previous table, the Dutch, Canadian and German publics have relatively high opinions of their media. Again the three countries at the bottom of Table 14.11—Italy, the United States and France—are at the bottom of this one, having under 40% endorsing the general trustworthiness of the news.

Table 14.13 reports on the phrase that has become so frequently invoked in recent years—fake news. The first thing to notice is that far more people are concerned about the possibility of fake news on the Internet than think they have been exposed to it, by a factor of three to one across the 17 countries.

14.4 Public Responses and Attitudes

Table 14.12 Trust in media
% agreeing that you can trust most news most of the time, 2017

Country	%
Finland	62
Netherlands	51
Denmark	50
Germany	50
Canada	49
Norway	49
Belgium	48
Ireland	46
Switzerland	46
Austria	45
Japan	43
United Kingdom	43
Australia	42
Sweden	42
Italy	39
United States	**38**
France	30
Mean	45

No data on New Zealand
Nic Newman et al. *Reuters Institute Digital News Report 2017*

Table 14.13 Fake news
% saying they had been exposed to completely made-up news in the last week, and % saying they were concerned about what is real and what is fake on the Internet, 2017

Country	Exposed	Concerned
Denmark	9	36
Germany	9	37
Netherlands	10	30
Switzerland	13	47
Belgium	13	46
Austria	14	38
Norway	14	41
United Kingdom	15	58
France	16	62
Ireland	17	57
Japan	17	48
Canada	19	60
Finland	20	55
Sweden	22	49
Australia	25	65
Italy	25	51
United States	**31**	**64**
Mean	17	50

No data on New Zealand
Nic Newman et al. *Reuters Institute Digital News Report 2018* and Sora Park et al. *Digital News Report: Australia 2018* (News and Media Research Centre, University of Canberra)

The second is that there is considerable variation between countries. Just one in eleven Danes and Germans think they have recently been exposed to fake news, compared to one in three Americans. Americans top both columns.

It would be interesting to probe further what those who say they have been exposed to fake news actually experienced. Did they feel they had been deceived by a story, which they then discovered was false? Or were they stories which they immediately discounted as 'fake', and what were the clues that made them do so? Are they sure they were not just writing off news stories they saw as unwelcome?

In the Worlds of Journalism data, the dedication of American journalists to their profession was evident. In this public opinion data, America also stands out, but here because the American public seems more cynical about their media than people in most of the other selected democracies.

14.5 Press Freedom

A free and well-functioning news media is essential to a robust democracy. Two eminent groups have attempted to quantify how well this is achieved in different countries. The Washington-based Freedom House was founded in 1941 to be 'a clear voice for democracy and freedom around the world'. Since 1972, it has published an annual report *Freedom in the World*. Since 1980, it has published its Freedom of the Press Index, looking at media independence and freedom (Table 14.15). More recently, since 2009, it has also published Freedom on the Net.

The majority of its funding comes from the American government, and critics have sometimes charged that its reports reflect an American view, being a harsher critic of left-wing than right-wing dictatorships, for example. No such criticisms are relevant to the table opposite, however.

The Paris-based Reporters Sans Frontieres (RSF) or in English, Reporters Without Borders, founded in 1985, is an advocacy organisation on issues relating to freedom of information and freedom of the press. It performs a valuable role monitoring and publicising the plight of journalists killed or imprisoned as a result of their work. More generally, it campaigns against censorship and attempts at media suppression. It publishes an annual World Press Freedom Index, with its current scoring system in use since 2013 (Table 14.14).

Both organisations have broad networks of experts and informants that help compile their data. Both are concerned with press freedom rather than the quality of the media. Freedom House provides scores and rankings for 199 countries. In an area where so much involves subjective judgements, some reliance on expert opinions is inevitable, although both make the questions as precise as possible. Freedom House's informants address 23 questions covering the legal environment, political environment and economic environment. The RSF Index, on 180 countries, compiles data on pluralism, media independence, the legislative framework, transparency and media infrastructure.

Table 14.14 World press freedom index (RSF)
Score of zero = most free. Top-rating countries with populations > one million

Country	Global rank	Score
Norway	1	7.63
Sweden	2	8.31
Netherlands	3	10.01
Finland	4	10.26
Switzerland	5	11.27
Jamaica	6	11.33
Belgium	7	13.16
New Zealand	8	13.62
Denmark	9	13.99
Costa Rica	10	14.01
Austria	11	14.04
Estonia	12	14.08
Portugal	14	14.17
Germany	15	14.39
Ireland	16	14.59
Canada	18	15.28
Australia	19	15.46
Uruguay	20	15.56
Ghana	23	18.41
Latvia	24	19.63
Cyprus	25	19.85
Namibia	26	20.24
Slovakia	27	20.26
South Africa	28	20.39
Spain	31	20.51
Slovenia	32	21.69
France	33	21.87
Czech Republic	34	21.89
Lithuania	36	22.20
Chile	38	22.69
United Kingdom	40	23.25
Burkina Faso	41	23.33
Taiwan	42	23.36
South Korea	43	23.51
Romania	44	23.65
United States	**45**	**23.73**
Italy	46	24.12
Japan	67	28.64

2018 World Press Freedom Index (RSF) (Reporters without Frontiers)

Table 14.15 Freedom of the press
Freedom House, 2017
Zero = most free. Top-rating countries with populations > one million

Country	Global rank	Score
Norway	1	8
Netherlands	2	11
Sweden	3	11
Belgium	4	12
Denmark	5	12
Finland	6	12
Switzerland	7	13
Costa Rica	13	16
Estonia	14	16
Portugal	17	17
Canada	20	18
Ireland	21	18
Jamaica	23	19
New Zealand	24	19
Germany	25	20
Czech Republic	26	21
Lithuania	27	21
Australia	31	22
Austria	32	22
Cyprus	34	23
Slovenia	36	23
United States	**37**	**23**
Uruguay	38	24
Taiwan	40	25
Trinidad and Tobago	41	25
United Kingdom	42	25
France	44	26
Latvia	46	26
Slovakia	47	26
Japan	50	27
Spain	54	28
Chile	56	29
Mauritius	57	29
Papua New Guinea	58	29
Italy	62	31
Namibia	63	32
Ghana	64	33
Israel	65	33

Freedom House *Freedom of the Press Report 2018*

Both assign scores where 0 is best and 100 worst. In addition to the precise score, both assign general groupings. RSF divides countries in to good (0–15); fairly good (15.01–25); problematic (25.01–35); bad (35.01–55); and very bad (55.01–100). Freedom House ranks countries as free (0–31); partly free (31–60); and not free (61+). Just 13% of the world's population enjoys a free press in its estimation.

Both scales have proved to be broadly reliable: the two scales give broadly similar evaluations, and most countries' scores do not change radically from year to year. Seven of the selected democracies are rated among the most democratic in both lists: Norway, Sweden, Netherlands, Finland, Switzerland, Belgium and Denmark. (Freedom House, in particular, includes several very small countries, not included in the tables opposite, some of which it ranks very highly.)

Similarly among the 18 democracies both rank Italy and Japan lowest, although not in the same order—for RSF Japan is the only selected democracy rated as problematic; for Freedom House Italy is the only one rated only as partly free.

There are only two great inconsistencies. For some unknown reason, Freedom House takes a much more critical view than RSF of Austria (rated 11 by RSF but only 32 by Freedom House and New Zealand (8 and 24, respectively).

In both indices, the United States scores in the 20s, rated 37th in the world by Freedom House, and 45th by RSF. The United Kingdom rates slightly higher; and Australia and Canada somewhat higher again. The relatively low ratings for Britain and America may surprise many, given their long free speech traditions, and especially the solidity of their media institutions. Countries with much less media capacity rate more highly.

The value of a single score is that it allows comparisons between large groups of countries and makes it possible to trace changing scores and rankings over several years. Beyond individual countries, it can help to map global trends. Freedom House concluded that in 2017 'press freedom globally has declined to its lowest levels in 13 years'. The global mean was 46.0 in 2004 but had worsened to 49.4 in 2017.

It is important to differentiate institutions from atmospherics. Since the advent of Donald Trump in the United States, antinews media rhetoric has become much more pronounced and bitter—'enemies of the people', 'fake news'. There is now far more contention surrounding journalists and their work, but so far at least not greater legal constraints on them.

14.6 Cinema and Cultural Industries

After the advent of television, cinema was predicted to go into decline, but it has continued to prosper. Table 14.16 shows that there was a very slight decline in attendance between 2006 and 2017, but overall it was essentially stable. Going to the pictures is still most popular in America, although there was more of a decline there than in most other countries—only Canada was greater. Cinema-going is still twice as popular in the United States as in the bottom eight countries in the table. English-speaking countries fill six of the top seven places on the table, along with France.

As might be expected the United States is also the country where most frequently the films attended were produced in their own country (Table 14.17). Predictably the rankings on the relative importance of national production to some extent reflect a country's population ranking, which determines the size of the home market which can sustain a national film industry. But they also show the importance of language as an effective non-tariff barrier in this industry. The four countries at the bottom of the table are relatively

Table 14.16 Cinema attendance
Average number of visits per person per year

Country	2006	2017
United States	**4.8**	**3.8**
Australia	4.0	3.4
Ireland	–	3.4
New Zealand	–	3.4
France	3.1	3.1
Canada	3.8	2.7
United Kingdom	2.6	2.6
Denmark	2.3	2.2
Norway	2.6	2.2
Netherlands	1.4	2.1
Austria	2.1	1.7
Belgium	2.3	1.7
Sweden	1.7	1.7
Finland	1.3	1.6
Italy	1.8	1.6
Switzerland	2.3	1.6
Germany	1.7	1.5
Japan	1.3	1.4
Mean	2.4	2.3

Focus 2007. World Film Market Trends (European Audiovisual Observatory, Strasbourg, 2007) and *Focus 2018. World Film Market Trends* (European Audiovisual Observatory, Strasbourg, 2018)

Table 14.17 National origin of films
% of films attended produced within the country in each year

Country	2006	2017
United States	**91**	**92**
Japan	53	55
France	45	37
United Kingdom	19	37
Finland	23	27
Germany	26	24
Denmark	25	20
Italy	26	18
Norway	16	18
Sweden	19	17
Netherlands	11	12
Belgium	6	8
Switzerland	10	7
Austria	–	6
Australia	5	4
Canada	4	2
Ireland	–	2
New Zealand	–	2
Mean	25	22

Focus 2007. World Film Market Trends (European Audiovisual Observatory, Strasbourg, 2007) and *Focus 2018. World Film Market Trends* (European Audiovisual Observatory, Strasbourg, 2018)

Table 14.18 Cultural exports
Exports of cultural goods and services as % of total trade 2015

Country	%
United States	**2.3**
United Kingdom	2.2
Belgium	1.7
Austria	1.1
France	1.1
Netherlands	1.1
Sweden	0.9
Finland	0.8
Germany	0.7
Canada	0.6
Denmark	0.6
Australia	0.4
Italy	0.4
New Zealand	0.3
Ireland	0.1
Japan	0.1
Norway	0.1
Mean	*0.9*

No data on Switzerland
Cornell University, INSEAD, and WIPO (2018) *The Global Innovation Index: Energizing the World with Innovation* (Ithaca, Fontainebleau and Geneva)

small English-speaking ones where American and to a lesser extent British films dominate the domestic markets.

Table 14.18 supports the impressions from Table 14.17. The United States and United Kingdom are by some distance the biggest exporters of cultural goods and services as a proportion of their total trade. The smaller English-speaking countries are all in the bottom half of the table. Whereas language acted as a non-tariff barrier to protect the local cinema industries, it is an impediment to many cultural exports, with Japan and Norway at the bottom of the table.

In each of these tables, the United States tops the rankings, showing the strength of its cultural industries both domestically and internationally.

Family

15.1 Marriage

While some indicators are volatile and jump around from year to year, most demographic and social variables tend to be stable and move at glacial speed. Nevertheless, over a period of decades or a generation, changes can be substantial, even revolutionary. It is not an exaggeration to say that family life in the selected countries has been undergoing revolutionary changes in practices, attitudes and expectations. To some extent, these changes are captured in the data in these and the following tables.

Tables 15.1 and 15.2 show that young people are increasingly delaying marriage. For both males and females, over the 34 years from 1980 to 2014, the mean age for first marriage across these 18 countries rose by six years. The average age for males' first marriages remains at three years older than females. The USA and Japan have moved least, so that now the USA has the youngest average age for first marriage among the selected countries. Sweden, Denmark and Norway are among the oldest for both sexes, while the average in Italy has also risen sharply.

The tables on this page reflect two trends—firstly a change in how couples relate to each other but secondly also a change in attitude about whether relationships need to be legalised. There is little evidence that couples begin cohabiting at later ages in the way that they now marry at later ages. The statistics cannot capture any changes in attitudes or expectations. But certainly couples have less urgency in legally sealing their bond through marriage.

The most common way of measuring trends is through what is called crude rates of marriage and divorce, which expresses the numbers of marriages and divorces per 1000 population. These are indeed crude measures. For example, with population aging, there is a smaller proportion of people in the age groups where marriage is most common, so the crude rate would misleadingly suggest a decline in marriage whereas there has simply been a change in the age composition of the population.

A partial solution to these unsatisfactory measures is presented in Tables 15.3 and 15.4, which examines the marital status of men and women aged 35–39 in 1970, and then 40 years later in 2010. It shows the percentage of females who were married has dropped 26 points, while the number still single (who may include those cohabiting) has risen 22 points. Those divorced and separated rose more modestly from 4 to 10%. The percentage of married males has dropped even more sharply, down 30 points across these 18 democracies. Sweden and Norway have shown the sharpest declines, with single males now outnumbering married males in this age group. Their proportion of single males is double that of America, which has the lowest proportion of singles in both males and females.

The change in the percentage of people in their late 30s who are divorced shows much more variation. (The rate for females is higher than for males, but that probably reflects that females tend to marry at somewhat younger ages.) The United States has the highest proportion of divorced and separated among both males and females, and the figure has increased substantially. Several countries which had very low divorce rates in 1970 had a high proportionate increase.

Many explanations have been given for rising divorce rates. However, the starting point must be changes in the legal availability and ease of divorce. It was only in 1995 that a referendum in Ireland removed the constitutional prohibition on divorce in that country, the last country to make it legally possible. Similarly before the increase in women's employment gave them greater financial independence, divorce was not a practical prospect for many women even if the marital relationship was an unhappy or even violent one. It is only after considering the legal and financial practicalities that more emotional factors should be considered.

Divorce does not dent most people's faith in marriage. US Census figures show that 58% of recent American weddings were first marriages for both spouses, but 21% involved both spouses marrying for at least the second time.

Table 15.1 Females' age at first marriage
Average age of females at first marriage

Country	1980	2014
United States	**24**	**27**
Australia	23	28
Belgium	22	29
Japan	26	29
New Zealand	22	29
Netherlands	23	30
Switzerland	25	30
United Kingdom	24	30
Austria	23	31
Finland	24	31
France	23	31
Germany	23	31
Ireland	25	31
Italy	24	31
Denmark	25	32
Norway	24	32
Sweden	26	33
Mean	*24*	*30*

No data on Canada
From OECD *Family database* www.oecd.org/els/family/database.htm

Table 15.2 Males' age at first marriage
Average age of males at first marriage

Country	1980	2014
United States	**26**	**29**
Australia	25	30
New Zealand	25	30
Japan	29	31
Belgium	24	32
United Kingdom	25	32
Austria	26	33
Finland	27	33
France	25	33
Germany	26	33
Ireland	27	33
Netherlands	26	33
Switzerland	30	33
Denmark	27	34
Italy	27	34
Norway	29	34
Sweden	29	36
Mean	*27*	*33*

1980 figures for Norway, Switzerland and USA = 1990
No data on Canada
From OECD *Family database* www.oecd.org/els/family/database.htm

Table 15.3 Females' marital status
Marital status of females, 35–40 years old, 1970, 2010

Country	Married 1970	Married 2010	Single 1970	Single 2010	Divorced 1970	Divorced 2010
Italy	84	70	13	27	1	3
Japan	90	70	6	23	3	7
Switzerland	83	67	11	24	5	8
United States	**83**	**67**	**6**	**16**	**9**	**16**
Australia	89	63	5	23	4	14
Austria	83	63	11	29	4	8
Ireland	82	62	17	32	..	6
Denmark	88	61	7	29	5	10
Belgium	90	59	7	28	2	13
Canada	89	59	7	31	2	10
Netherlands	90	58	8	33	2	9
United Kingdom	89	57	7	32	3	11
Germany	79	56	10	33	10	11
New Zealand	88	56	5	34	3	9
France	87	55	9	37	3	8
Norway	89	52	7	37	3	11
Sweden	85	50	8	40	6	9
Mean	*86*	*60*	*8*	*30*	*4*	*10*

Divorced column includes separated. Small number of widowed people omitted, so rows sum to just less than 100
No data on Finland
United Nations Department of Economic and Social Affairs. Population Division (2013) *World Marriage Data 2012*

15.1 Marriage

Table 15.4 Males' marital status
Marital status of males, 35–40 years old, 1970, 2010

Country	Married 1970	Married 2010	Single 1970	Single 2010	Divorced 1970	Divorced 2010
United States	**86**	**65**	**8**	**23**	**5**	**12**
Japan	94	61	5	36	1	3
Australia	85	59	11	31	4	10
Ireland	71	59	29	37	..	4
Italy	84	58	15	41	1	1
Switzerland	80	58	12	36	8	6
Canada	88	56	10	38	2	6
New Zealand	88	55	8	40	4	5
Denmark	84	54	12	39	4	7
United Kingdom	87	54	12	39	2	8
Austria	85	53	12	41	3	7
Belgium	88	52	10	38	2	9
France	83	50	15	44	2	6
Netherlands	88	50	11	44	1	6
Germany	74	47	18	45	8	8
Norway	84	46	14	47	3	8
Sweden	80	43	16	51	4	6
Mean	*84*	*54*	*13*	*39*	*3*	*7*

Divorced column includes separated
No data on Finland
Small number of widowed people omitted, so rows for each year may sum to just less than 100
United Nations Department of Economic and Social Affairs. Population Division (2013) *World Marriage Data 2012*

Of those currently married, for three quarters (75%) it is their first marriage; for one in five (19%) their second marriage and for one in 20 (5%) their third or later marriage.

15.2 Children

As we saw in Table 1.13 above, women in these economically advanced democracies are bearing fewer children than they did 50 and 100 years ago. Table 15.5 shows that not only are women having fewer children, but they are having them at a later age. In the 45 years from 1970 to 2015, the average at which women bore their first child rose by six years, from 24 to 30. The 18 countries are now closely grouped—in 17 of the 18 countries the average age of mothers at the birth of the first child is between 29 and 31. The exception is the United States which is now the clear leader in younger mothers.

Indeed, the delay in having children is one of the major reasons women are having fewer children. Explaining the trends in birth rates involves many potential factors, but one central consideration is the increased control women have over their own fertility. This is manifested in the dramatic fall in the number of births to adolescent women. Measured against the number of births to 15–19-year-old women per 1000 in that age group (Table 15.6), the rate in 2015 was less than a quarter of what it had been in 1970. Japan always had a very low rate, but now it has been joined by the West

Table 15.5 Mothers' age at birth of first child

Country	1970	2015
United States	**25**	**26**
Austria	25	29
Belgium	24	29
Canada	23	29
Denmark	24	29
Finland	24	29
France	24	29
Norway	24	29
Sweden	26	29
United Kingdom	24	29
Australia	23	30
Germany	24	30
Ireland	25	30
Netherlands	24	30
Italy	25	31
Japan	26	31
New Zealand	23	31
Switzerland	25	31
Mean	24	30

From OECD *Family database* www.oecd.org/els/family/database.htm

Table 15.6 Births to adolescent mothers
Births to 15–19-year-old women per 1000 in age group

Country	1970	2015
Denmark	32	3
Netherlands	23	3
Switzerland	23	3
Japan	4	4
Italy	27	5
Norway	45	5
Sweden	34	5
Finland	32	6
Belgium	31	7
Austria	58	8
Germany	56	8
France	37	9
Ireland	17	9
Canada	42	13
Australia	51	14
United Kingdom	49	14
New Zealand	64	22
United States	**69**	**27**
Mean	*38*	*9*

From OECD *Family database* www.oecd.org/els/family/database.htm

Table 15.7 Living arrangements of children
% of children living with two parents, one parent or some other arrangement, 2015

Country	Two	One	Other
Japan	88	12	1
Switzerland	88	12	0
Italy	87	12	0
Netherlands	87	13	0
Finland	86	13	1
Austria	83	16	1
Germany	83	16	1
Ireland	82	18	0
Australia	81	18	1
Canada	80	19	2
Sweden	80	19	1
France	77	23	1
Norway	77	22	1
United Kingdom	77	23	0
Belgium	76	23	1
Denmark	76	23	1
United States	**69**	**27**	**4**
Mean	*81*	*18*	*1*

No data on New Zealand
From OECD *Family database* www.oecd.org/els/family/database.htm

European countries. The five English-speaking countries have the highest proportion, with New Zealand and the United States by far the highest, although all of these also showed substantial drops.

Table 15.7 shows that four in five children live in households with two parents, but the country with the lowest proportion is the USA, where only seven in ten do. The higher divorce rate impacts on a substantial number of children's living arrangements, although from these statistics alone there is no way of knowing how much this impinges on the quality of their upbringing.

At the individual level, the OECD cites survey evidence showing that majorities of women in many countries would have preferred to have had more children than they did and also aspire to have more than they end up actually having. This is probably in sharp contrast to their grandmothers.

What prevents contemporary families from having more children if the aspiration is still there? Probably several factors interact, and some light is thrown on these in later tables in this chapter. Many people delay having children until they feel they are in a stable, long-term relationship, and if marriage statistics are a guide, this is tending to happen at a later age. Similarly, with higher education qualifications, most young women have their own career aspirations, and juggling progression at work with having a family can pose many difficulties. Similarly, although younger adults are in many ways more affluent than preceding generations, in many countries they are juggling paying mortgages, childcare fees and perhaps university debts. Such financial stress is a powerful contraceptive.

15.3 Households

The demographic and social changes associated with living longer, with the delay in getting married, with increased divorce and with having fewer children, have led to considerable changes in the composition of households. Table 15.8 shows that the long-term downward trend in the size of households is continuing although more recently at a very slow pace. The mean crept down by just 0.2 people over 30 years. All countries have a mean household size of between two and three people, actually between 2.1 and 2.7.

The *New York Times* reported in 2006 that the latest US Census showed that married couples had finally slipped into the minority, comprising just under 50% of households. Adding the first two columns in Table 15.9 shows that in 2015, this was still the case in the USA as well as in Norway and Japan. In other countries, couple-centred households are still in the majority, but only just.

Decades ago, the main household type in these societies became the nuclear rather than the extended family. Larger average household sizes—five or more persons—are still observed across much of Africa and the Middle East. The proportion of households that includes both a child under 15 years of age and an older person aged 60 years or over is highest globally in Senegal at 37% and lowest in the Netherlands at 0.2%.

The more recent trends manifested in Table 15.9 are the increased number of people living alone, and to a lesser

15.3 Households

Table 15.8 Household size
Average number of people living in a household

Country	1985	2015
Ireland	3.2	2.7
New Zealand	2.7	2.7
United Kingdom	2.4	2.6
Australia	2.7	2.5
Italy	2.9	2.4
Japan	3.0	2.4
Austria	2.5	2.3
Belgium	2.4	2.3
Canada	2.6	2.3
France	2.5	2.3
Netherlands	2.3	2.3
United States	**2.7**	**2.3**
Norway	2.2	2.2
Sweden	2.0	2.2
Switzerland	–	2.2
Denmark	2.2	2.1
Finland	2.2	2.1
Germany	2.2	2.1
Mean	2.5	2.3

UN Economic and Social Affairs *Household Size and Composition Around the World 2017*

Table 15.9 Types of household
% of households with each set of living arrangements, 2015

Country	Couples with children	Couples without children	Single Parent	Living Alone	Other
Finland	21	29	6	41	4
Norway	25	23	7	40	5
Denmark	22	28	6	37	6
Germany	21	31	5	37	6
Switzerland	25	31	4	37	3
Austria	23	27	7	36	7
Netherlands	26	31	6	36	2
Sweden	24	28	7	36	5
Belgium	25	28	8	34	5
France	26	28	7	34	5
Japan	17	30	3	34	16
Italy	27	28	5	31	9
United Kingdom	22	28	9	31	10
Canada	26	30	10	28	6
United States	**20**	**28**	**10**	**27**	**15**
Australia	31	26	10	24	9
Ireland	33	24	9	24	10
New Zealand	29	28	11	24	8
Mean	25	28	7	33	7

From OECD *Family database* www.oecd.org/els/family/database.htm

Table 15.10 Partnership and cohabitation
% living with or without partner, and of those with a partner overall % married or cohabiting, 2015

Country	Living without a partner	Living with partner	Married	Cohabiting
Sweden	37	63	44	19
New Zealand	34	66	50	16
Norway	39	61	46	15
France	36	64	49	15
Denmark	36	64	50	14
Netherlands	33	67	53	14
United Kingdom	39	61	48	12
Canada	33	67	54	12
Switzerland	36	64	53	11
Austria	41	59	49	10
Australia	36	64	54	10
Ireland	41	59	50	9
Belgium	38	62	54	9
Germany	37	63	54	9
United States	**41**	**60**	**52**	**7**
Italy	42	58	53	5
Mean	37	63	51	12

No data on Finland or Japan
From OECD *Family database* www.oecd.org/els/family/database.htm

The majority of people (note the percentage has changed from households to people) in these societies still live with a partner, as Table 15.10 shows. The majority of these are married, but almost one quarter as many are cohabiting. The proportion of cohabiting shows large variations between countries. Just one in twenty people in Italy cohabit, but almost one in five Swedes do. Italy, the United States, Ireland and Austria—each with just over two in five people—have the highest proportions living without a partner. This includes those still single, those widowed and those separated or divorced.

15.4 Mothers and Employment

The most far-reaching financial decision any couple makes is whether to have children. The OECD's *Babies and Bosses* volume (2010) cites material from various countries to explore how having children impacts on family finances. An Australian Government report estimated a couple on average income with two children may spend around $400,000 over 20 years, and this does not include indirect costs, such as the need for larger housing, and the impact on the mother's employment.

Another Australian study concluded that for women who have completed secondary education, having one child decreases after-tax lifetime earnings by around $162,000. However, this figure has been decreasing, and the amount will vary with social practices. The same volume reports that

extent the rise of single-parent households. One in three households in these 18 countries now consists of a person living alone. This is mainly, but far from only, among older people. For many, this is a positive choice, but it does raise the potential issue of increased atomization and isolation.

in Nordic countries, mothers at age 45 have earned between 82 and 89% of what non-mothers earned, but at the other extreme in the Netherlands and Germany the same group have only 56–74% of non-mothers' earnings.

The variety is manifested in Table 15.11 which shows the employment rate for all women, for mothers and for mothers of young children. Each of the columns—and the differences between the columns—shows substantial variations. It should be remembered that the table does not control for age, and as Table 10.2 above showed, female labour force participation has been climbing sharply over the decades.

The three Scandinavian countries—Norway, Sweden and Denmark—top each column. They have the highest female employment rate and motherhood makes little difference to employment rates in them. Italy is second bottom on women's general employment rate, but having children only diminishes women's employment very slightly. The three countries where German cultural influence is greatest—Germany, Austria and Switzerland—all have relatively low female employment rates to begin with, and then having young children further lowers employment rates substantially, so that they occupy the bottom three places in the last column. The United States is around the mean on all three measures.

Table 15.11 Women, motherhood and employment
Employment rates of women, 2015 (or LAY)

Country	Female employment Rate	Mothers' employment rate	Mothers with young children employment rate
Norway	84	84	84
Sweden	82	82	78
Denmark	82	83	76
Belgium	77	74	72
Netherlands	62	56	60
Ireland	63	59	59
United States	**67**	**65**	**55**
Italy	55	52	51
United Kingdom	71	65	50
Canada	71	67	49
France	69	66	48
Australia	67	61	47
Finland	73	69	34
Germany	72	65	34
Switzerland	48	36	29
Austria	64	59	26
Mean	*69*	*65*	*53*

No data on Japan or New Zealand
Flynn, Lindsay 'Childcare Markets and Maternal Employment: A Typology' *LIS Working Paper Series No 728*, January 2018 (Luxembourg Income Study)

Table 15.12 Parents and employment
Patterns of employment in couples with children—Full-time (FT), Part-time (PT), etc.

Country	Both FT	One FT; one PT	One FT; one not working	Neither working	Other
Denmark	68	11	16	3	2
Sweden	68	10	14	4	4
Finland	56	7	26	4	8
France	50	15	24	6	5
Belgium	47	22	20	6	5
United States	**45**	**13**	**35**	**4**	**3**
Ireland	32	22	28	9	9
New Zealand	32	27	32	5	3
Austria	31	40	21	4	5
United Kingdom	31	31	24	5	8
Italy	30	18	38	9	6
Germany	25	40	27	4	4
Australia	23	34	29	6	8
Netherlands	21	51	20	4	5
Mean	*40*	*24*	*25*	*5*	*5*

No data on Canada, Japan, Norway or Switzerland
From OECD *Family database* www.oecd.org/els/family/database.htm

In Table 15.12, the OECD examines the employment patterns of couples with children. It has data only on 14 of the 18 countries and does not control for the age of children. The largest group of couples, on average four in ten, has both parents working. Then there are two almost equally sized groups, with one spouse working full-time and other part-time, and the other with one working full-time and the other not working at all. It seems that in many countries part-time work is a good solution for meeting the financial, career and childcare challenges of parenthood. The relative lack of a parent working part-time is one reason why Italy and the USA have the highest rates of one parent not working at all.

Table 15.13 compares the incomes in each country of different family types. It takes the average income of a household of two adults, with one working and no children as 100. The most disadvantaged group by this measure are single-parent households, whose average income, across the 18 countries, is just over two-thirds (68) of the comparison group. There is considerable variation with Denmark the highest (92) and Japan the lowest (45). Single parent families also do relatively poorly in the United States, which comes in second bottom at 60.

The middle column shows that families with one child and only one adult working earn substantially less than the comparison group. The group which does best is those where both parents work. The countries at the bottom are those which have fewest employment opportunities for mothers.

The OECD does not give contemporary data for a key comparison group. Their data in the 1990s showed that the most affluent family type in all these societies was, not

Table 15.13 Income levels of different family types
Relative income in each country where average income of household of two adults, one working, no children = 100

Country	Single adult, at least one child	Two adults, one working, one child	Two adults, two working, child
Denmark	92	87	133
Australia	76	87	124
Ireland	68	83	123
Canada	69	76	121
Belgium	77	78	119
New Zealand	76	83	119
Italy	68	63	115
Netherlands	70	82	113
Norway	70	76	111
Finland	74	74	110
United States	**60**	**75**	**108**
Sweden	64	74	105
United Kingdom	61	73	105
Germany	69	86	102
France	63	72	99
Japan	45	88	96
Austria	65	67	94
Mean	68	78	112

No data on Switzerland
From OECD *Family database* www.oecd.org/els/family/database.htm

surprisingly, two adults with no children. On average, they had around a quarter more disposable income than families consisting of two adults with children.

This all suggests that if governments are serious about raising the birth rate, the single most important thing they can do is make it easier for families, women in particular, to combine parenthood and work. The tables on the next pages address some aspects of what makes this more or less feasible.

15.5 Family Policy

Governments have discovered family policy. Even though as Table 5.1 showed, government spending as a proportion of GDP has slightly declined since the 1990s, in the OECD as a whole spending on family policy increased from 1.6% of GDP in 1980 to 2.2% in 2003. Table 15.15 shows that in these 18 countries public spending on families is still inching up at very slightly more than the pace of economic growth.

Family spending includes only public support that is exclusively for families, such as child payments and allowances, parental leave benefits and childcare support. Other types of spending such as health and housing support are of benefit to families but that is not their primary purpose, so they are not included in this category.

Table 15.14 examines the most basic legislative policy for encouraging childbirth, maternity leave. Maternity leave provisions were slow to develop in English-speaking countries, because the traditional view was that mothers did not and ought not to work. In contrast, Norwegian women had the right to maternity leave before they had the right to vote. As female labour force participation increased in nearly all the selected countries, the demands for maternity leave also increased. Over the decades, firstly the right to return to the mother's previous position was guaranteed, while periods of unpaid and paid leave have gradually been increased.

Table 15.14 Parental leave
Weeks of paid maternity and paternity leave 2016

Country	Maternity	Paternity
United Kingdom	39.0	2.0
Ireland	26.0	0.0
Italy	21.7	0.4
Denmark	18.0	2.0
New Zealand	18.0	0.0
Finland	17.5	3.0
Canada	17.0	0.0
Austria	16.0	0.0
France	16.0	2.0
Netherlands	16.0	0.4
Belgium	15.0	2.0
Germany	14.0	0.0
Japan	14.0	0.0
Switzerland	14.0	0.0
Norway	13.0	0.0
Sweden	12.9	1.4
Australia	6.0	2.0
United States	**0.0**	**0.0**
Mean	16.3	0.8

From OECD *Family database* www.oecd.org/els/family/database.htm

Table 15.15 Public expenditure on families
Total public expenditure on families as % GDP

Country	2001	2013
United Kingdom	2.7	4.0
Denmark	3.5	3.7
France	3.6	3.7
Sweden	2.9	3.6
Ireland	2.3	3.4
Belgium	3.0	3.3
Finland	2.8	3.2
Norway	3.2	3.1
Germany	2.9	3.0
Australia	3.0	2.8
New Zealand	2.6	2.8
Austria	2.7	2.6
Italy	–	2.0
Switzerland	–	2.0
Netherlands	1.7	1.8
Japan	1.1	1.5
Canada	1.1	1.4
United States	**1.5**	**1.1**
Mean	2.5	2.7

From OECD *Family database* www.oecd.org/els/family/database.htm

The table offers only skeletal data on nationally legislated parental leave provisions. The variety of public policies defies simple summary. There are almost infinite formulas of paid and unpaid, or fractional pay for different periods, which mothers may be eligible for, as well as differing provisions for fathers and the right to make choices about who takes parental leave. Moreover, different groups often have different rights, in federations varying between states, or with different private corporations having different conditions. In some countries, employers have to contribute—although the formulas for doing so differ—but in most government is the major contributor.

Nevertheless, the differences between countries are substantial. The United Kingdom is now the most generous, as it was in Table 15.15. The United States stands out as the only country which has no legally binding or publicly financed parental leave at all.

Public spending on early childhood education and care has been climbing in nearly all these countries. Table 15.16 shows that the United States, Ireland, Belgium and Australia were still not spending almost any public money in this area in 1990, but all countries now do, and in six of these 18 it is now more than one per cent of GDP. Section 7.7 above explores the educational reasons why governments and families are investing more in this area.

The USA was again the laggard in this area in 2013 as it was in parental leave and in total public spending on family policies. This may be a consequence of the American emphasis on low-taxing, low-spending governments, and in particular its lesser tendency to engage in social spending.

Table 15.16 Public spending on early childhood education and care % GDP

Country	1990	2000	2013
Sweden	1.91	1.00	1.64
Denmark	1.27	1.37	1.36
France	0.64	1.19	1.27
Norway	0.64	0.69	1.25
Finland	1.09	0.93	1.11
New Zealand	0.01	0.58	1.00
Belgium	0.00	0.49	0.78
United Kingdom	–	0.68	0.76
Netherlands	–	0.33	0.69
Australia	0.06	0.38	0.61
Germany	0.26	0.33	0.58
Italy	0.15	0.48	0.54
Ireland	0.00	0.22	0.52
Austria	0.22	0.27	0.49
Japan	0.19	0.30	0.37
United States	**0.00**	**0.39**	**0.35**
Mean	*0.46*	*0.60*	*0.83*

No data on Canada or Switzerland
From OECD *Family database* www.oecd.org/els/family/database.htm

Table 15.17 Public spending on family benefits % GDP, 2013

Country	Total	Cash	Services	Tax Breaks
United Kingdom	4.0	2.4	1.4	0.2
Denmark	3.7	1.4	2.2	0.0
France	3.7	1.6	1.4	0.7
Sweden	3.6	1.5	2.2	0.0
Ireland	3.4	2.4	0.9	0.1
Belgium	3.3	1.8	1.0	0.5
Finland	3.2	1.5	1.7	0.0
Norway	3.1	1.2	1.8	0.1
Germany	3.0	1.1	1.1	0.9
Australia	2.8	1.9	0.9	0.0
New Zealand	2.8	1.7	1.1	0.0
Austria	2.6	1.9	0.7	0.0
Italy	2.0	0.8	0.7	0.6
Switzerland	2.0	1.2	0.4	0.5
Netherlands	1.8	0.7	0.7	0.5
Japan	1.5	0.8	0.5	0.2
Canada	1.4	1.0	0.2	0.2
United States	**1.1**	**0.1**	**0.6**	**0.4**
Mean	*2.7*	*1.4*	*1.1*	*0.3*

From OECD *Family database* www.oecd.org/els/family/database.htm

Giving families financial assistance—either through child allowances or through tax concessions—has been universal among these countries, although the means and rationales have varied greatly over time and between countries. Table 15.17 has three components—the provision of services, the giving of cash benefits to eligible recipients and the granting of tax breaks of various kinds. Level is more important than type of support, but countries have their own characteristic mixes. The Nordic countries stress the provision of services, cash is most important in Britain and Ireland, and tax breaks are relatively important in the USA.

Spending on family policies is probably popular with the public, many of whom can see its tangible impacts. Moreover, governments are likely to act in order to address the aging society and to meet the wishes of prospective parents, wanting to have babies, but aware of the financial costs and the developmental needs of young children.

15.6 Childcare and Early Education

'Today's rising generation is the first in which a majority are spending a large part of early childhood in some form of out-of-home childcare. At the same time, neuroscientific research is demonstrating that loving, stable, secure, and stimulating relationships with caregivers in the earliest months and years of life are critical for every aspect of a child's development'. It may be that, as the old axiom puts it, it takes a village to raise a child, but in the contemporary urban environment with nuclear families, much of the village's work, as this quote from UNICEF's Innocenti Research Centre puts it succinctly, is now done by institutions.

If parents want to maintain their material standard of living, for most it will be necessary for the mother to enter into paid employment. Central to this decision, and to their quality of life as parents of young children, will be the availability of affordable and high-quality childcare. It is a policy area which has become increasingly important on the political agenda.

Table 15.18 examines the differing costs of childcare, using what proportion it would consume of the post-tax income of a couple close to the median income. Interestingly, there was quite a bit of movement in both directions between 2004 and 2016. Some governments were probably responding to the need for budget austerity—and so childcare became markedly more expensive in the United Kingdom and Finland. Austria moved radically in the other direction.

The relative commitment of public funds affects the accessibility and the affordability of childcare for parents. To some extent, we see that countries that committed the most public funds in Table 15.16 on the previous page—such as the Scandinavian countries—have the most affordable childcare in Table 15.18. The countries fall into three broad groups. In six countries, the typical fee for two children attending full-time is less than ten per cent of these parents' post-tax income. In another four countries, it is under 20%, but in the remaining eight, including the United States,

Table 15.18 Costs of childcare
% of after-tax income, for two children, for couples with one parent on median income and other at 67% of median income

Country	2004	2016
Austria	18.4	2.6
Sweden	6.6	3.9
Germany	6.1	4.7
Norway	11.9	5.3
Denmark	10.2	9.1
France	16.7	9.8
Belgium	14.0	11.4
Japan	18.4	15.2
Finland	6.9	17.9
Australia	19.0	19.8
Canada	20.1	21.0
Netherlands	24.5	21.3
United States	**22.7**	**22.5**
Ireland	33.9	26.1
Switzerland	26.6	26.3
New Zealand	25.5	29.1
United Kingdom	27.2	40.8
Mean	*18.2*	*16.9*

No data on Italy in either year
OECD *The Pursuit of Gender Equality* (2017)

Table 15.19 Participation of young children in childcare
Participation rates in formal childcare of 0–2 year olds 2014

Country	%
Denmark	65
Netherlands	56
Belgium	55
Norway	52
France	52
Sweden	47
New Zealand	42
Switzerland	38
Ireland	35
United Kingdom	34
Germany	32
Australia	32
Japan	31
United States	**28**
Finland	28
Italy	24
Austria	19
Mean	*40*

No data on Canada
OECD *The Pursuit of Gender Equality* (2017)

childcare for two children would consume at least one in five dollars of their post-tax income.

Table 15.19 looks at the childcare participation rate of children from birth to two years old. Presumably, this would be higher among one to two year olds than among younger infants. Austria is at the bottom of the table, perhaps helping to explain why in Table 15.18 it recently raised its subsidies so much. The national variations are considerable. Countries from north-west Europe (with the exception of Finland) have the highest rates. The United States percentage is below the mean.

Most work days are considerably longer than school hours, raising the issue for parents about how to cover the gap. Apart from personal, informal solutions that people may find, school-based care before or after school is a good option for many. The range in Table 15.20 is even larger than the differences in childcare in Table 15.19. A majority of primary school-aged children in Denmark and Sweden go to such arrangements, while less than one in twelve children in America and Ireland do.

A distinction needs to be made between childcare and pre-school education. The latter is limited to organised, centre-based programs designed to foster learning and emotional and social development in children for three until compulsory school age. In many European countries, compulsory primary schooling does not begin until six years of age, but a far greater proportion in many countries attend pre-school.

As the initial quotation from the UNICEF Innocenti Research Centre stressed, scientific research is stressing the

Table 15.20 Out of school care
% 6–11 year olds attending institution-based care outside school hours 2014

Country	%
Denmark	68
Sweden	59
Belgium	43
Norway	35
Switzerland	24
Austria	23
Netherlands	20
France	19
United Kingdom	19
Japan	17
Finland	15
Australia	12
Germany	11
Italy	11
Ireland	8
United States	**7**
Mean	*24*

No data on Canada or New Zealand
OECD *The Pursuit of Gender Equality* (2017)

importance of relationships and environments in children's early years in their intellectual and emotional development. It is highly probable that these issues will continue to gain importance in coming decades.

15.7 Abortion

While political contention continues with undiminished intensity in the United States, it is instructive to look beyond immediate controversies to trends in the incidence and availability of abortions in America and globally. Three trends are central: the rate of abortions has been declining substantially in most countries, although more dramatically in developed than developing countries; access to legal abortions has increased in several countries; and to a considerable, although not yet sufficient, extent abortions are becoming safer for the women undergoing them.

The data on the opposite page comes from the Guttmacher Institute which assiduously documents trends around the world in the availability, safety and incidence of abortions. Since the 2018 referendum when Ireland voted to make abortion legal, all of our selected 18 democracies fall towards the permissive end of Guttmacher's six-point scale on the legal availability of abortions.

For most countries in the world, official data is not available, and so independent estimates of the number of abortions need to be made. This is particularly the case in countries where abortion is not legally available, and in

Table 15.21 Abortion
Abortions per 1000 women aged 15–49, 2010–2014

Country	
Switzerland	5
Belgium	8
Finland	8
Netherlands	8
Denmark	12
New Zealand	12
Norway	12
United Kingdom	13
United States	**13**
France	15
Sweden	18
Mean	*11*

No data on Australia, Austria, Canada, Germany, Ireland, Japan
Susheela Singh et al. *Abortion Worldwide 2017. Uneven Progress and Unequal Access* (Guttmacher Institute)

Third World countries where official statistical systems are not as fully developed.

On the best data available the Guttmacher Institute estimates that in the 20 years between 1990–94 and 2010–14 the global abortion rate for women in the relevant age group dropped from 40 per 1000 to 35 per 1000 (Table 15.22). The drop in developed countries was dramatic, down to around 60% of what it had been 20 years earlier. The drop was sharpest in Eastern Europe (88–42), thanks to the much

Table 15.22 Global abortion trends
Abortions per 1000 women aged 15–44

Regions	1990–94	2010–14
World	40	35
Developed Countries	46	27
Developing countries	39	37
North America	25	17
Northern Europe	22	18
Western Europe	13	18
Oceania	20	19
Southern Europe	38	26
Western Africa	28	31
Central America	27	33
East Africa	32	34
Middle Africa	32	35
Southern Africa	32	35
Southeast Asia	46	35
Western Asia	46	35
Eastern Asia	44	36
South and Central Asia	36	37
Northern Africa	40	38
Eastern Europe	88	42
South America	43	47
Caribbean	60	65

Gilda Sedgh et al. 'Abortion incidence between 1990 and 2014: global, regional, and subregional levels and trends' *The Lancet* V388, July 16, 2016

15.7 Abortion

greater ease of obtaining contraception in the post-communist era. It was also substantial in North America and Southern Europe.

Table 15.21 only has data on 12 of the selected democracies, as the others do not have official authoritative data available. In the most recent period, 2010–14, all these countries have fewer than 20 abortions per 1000 women in the relevant age group. The United States is close to the mean for these countries. According to an article in the *New York Times*, the abortion rate in the United States now is half what it was in 1981, and three-quarters of abortions are among poor and low-income women.

Developing countries show much more variation, with several regions showing an increase in abortion rates over the two decades. This was particularly the case in the Caribbean, and Central and South America (Table 15.22).

The Guttmacher Institute also compiles data on the safety of abortions, with three categories: safe—takes place using a safe method and is done by an appropriately trained provider; least safe if neither of these conditions apply, and a middle category, partly safe, if one of the two applies. Table 15.23 gives the data for safe and least safe, and partly safe can be calculated by adding the two columns together and subtracting from 100.

The table shows stark variations. Through Europe, North America and Eastern Asia, the percentage of least safe abortions is zero (i.e. less than 0.5%). But in Africa, except for Southern Africa, the proportion is alarmingly high, with the worst being in Middle Africa. The Caribbean and Central America have the next highest rates of least safe abortions.

It has been estimated that globally 13% of all women's deaths during pregnancy and childbirth are due to abortions. These deaths are concentrated in poor countries and countries where abortion is illegal. The Guttmacher Institute has concluded that making abortion illegal does not reduce the number of abortions, but sharply increases their danger, as women are driven to clandestine and unsafe procedures. Rural, poor women are the most likely to experience complications.

The vast majority of abortions result from unintended pregnancies. The estimated unintended pregnancy rate in developed countries is 45 per 1000 women in the relevant age group (down from 64 two decades earlier), and in developing countries, 65 (down from 77). Globally 56% of unintended pregnancies end in abortion. Clearly, the best way to reduce abortion rates is not to make it illegal but to make contraception more widely available.

In America, almost uniquely in the world, abortion remains a totemic issue of political conflict. However, technology is changing the social realities over which the political debates rage, as better contraception is developed, and more widely used. Moreover, medication abortions, taking drugs to secure a termination rather than undergoing a surgical procedure, are now possible in the first ten weeks of pregnancy, and increasingly used in richer countries.

Table 15.23 Safety of abortions
Safe Abortions 2010–2014, % of all abortions

Regions	Safe	Least safe
World	55	15
Developed Countries	88	0
Developing countries	51	16
North America	99	0
Northern Europe	98	0
Western Europe	94	0
Southern Europe	91	0
Eastern Asia	89	0
Eastern Europe	86	0
Southern Africa	74	7
Oceania	66	26
Southeast Asia	60	14
Western Asia	52	12
South and Central Asia	42	13
Northern Africa	29	44
Caribbean	25	25
South America	25	12
East Africa	24	47
Central America	18	30
Western Africa	15	52
Middle Africa	12	69

Lifestyles and Consumption

16.1 Housing

Home ownership has long been a central aspiration of many people in these affluent democracies. It offers financial security from instabilities in the rental market and also a personal security and satisfaction in owning one's own home. It is also the central financial investment that many families make.

Home ownership is much easier where land is relatively cheap so, as Table 16.1 shows; in 1960, it was highest in the four New World democracies, and for different reasons in Japan. As early as 1911, half of Australians owned their home, a figure that was reached in Britain only in the 1970s. Home ownership also tends to be higher in rural areas than in major cities. In 1960, Japan topped the table and its declining rate over the next 50 years reflects its increasing urbanisation. Many families owned their small village homes, but their children could not afford to buy real estate in Tokyo.

The countries show considerable divergence and contrasting trajectories in the decades since. The four New World democracies—despite their substantial economic growth in the intervening half-century—have broadly plateaued. Home ownership in 2012 was only slightly higher than in 1960. Ireland, Britain and Italy show the biggest leaps since 1960.

For the 18 countries overall, home ownership did not increase between 2000 and 2012. In some, the percentage edged up, but in just as many it was stable or decreased. Has, for whatever reason, home ownership reached its broad upper limit in many of these countries?

In all countries, then, as Table 16.2 shows, a substantial proportion of the population lives in rental accommodation. Younger people who may eventually go on to own their home form a large part of this group, but many people, especially from poorer socio-economic groups, will always rent. Thus, the cost and quality and security of rental accommodation are of general concern and also a welfare issue for younger and poorer groups. The largest proportions of private renters are in Germany, Switzerland and Japan, and anecdotal evidence suggests that the rental market works fairly satisfactorily in those countries.

Publicly provided rental accommodation comprises less than 10% of the dwelling stock in 10 of the 18 countries and seems to serve a largely residual function in those countries for the poorest or most vulnerable. In several countries—most notably the Netherlands—there is a much larger social rental sector, and there is debate about whether this substantial presence also improves the quality and cost of the private housing markets.

Table 16.3 shows a central reason why the proportion of home ownership has not risen more in some countries. For each country, an index of 100 shows its long-term house price in relation to income. The relative cost of housing has trended in sharply contrasting ways in the selected countries. In the four countries at the top—New Zealand, Sweden, Australia and Canada—housing prices are by historical standards very expensive and still were rising. Apart from other possible factors, these are all countries with relatively high rates of immigration, which is probably increasing demand.

In contrast, the United States reached a relative peak in 2007 but then the recession of 2008 produced a sharp drop in property prices, and a decade later they were not anywhere back near the 2007 level in relation to incomes. Japan, with its stable and ageing population, has by far the lowest current house prices in relation to income by long-term standards.

One factor that should not have made housing more expensive is the size of dwellings. Table 16.4 showed this did not change between 2005 and 2015. This shows a considerable variation, with Italians having the smallest houses, and Canada, the United States, New Zealand and Australia the largest. People in those four countries have substantially larger dwellings than most Europeans.

Table 16.1 Home ownership
Home ownership as a % of all households

Country	1960	2000	2012
Ireland	60	78	80
Italy	45	70	71
Australia	63	69	70
United Kingdom	42	69	70
Belgium	50	74	68
Canada	66	64	68
United States	**64**	**65**	**68**
New Zealand	69	71	67
Norway	53	59	63
Austria	38	57	59
Finland	57	67	59
France	41	55	57
Netherlands	29	51	57
Sweden	36	60	56
Denmark	43	53	49
Germany	29	43	43
Japan	71	60	36
Switzerland	34	30	35
Mean	49	61	60

1960 data is from Francis G Castles *Comparative Public Policy. Patterns of Post-War Transformation* (Cheltenham, UK, Edward Elgar, 1998) p. 251; figures for 2000 or nearest available year from Girouard, N. et al. (2006) 'Recent House Price Developments: The Role of Fundamentals' OECD Economics Department Working Papers No 475; for 2012 from *OECD Economic Survey: Luxembourg 2012*

Table 16.3 House price to income ratio
Long-term average for each country = 100

Country	2000	2007	2017
New Zealand	84	129	161
Sweden	88	121	154
Australia	91	124	153
Canada	84	116	152
Belgium	90	128	139
Norway	96	125	135
Austria	97	87	129
United Kingdom	83	137	129
Netherlands	118	143	124
France	79	132	122
Denmark	105	152	119
Ireland	117	154	111
Switzerland	76	83	104
United States	**94**	**112**	**98**
Italy	85	118	97
Finland	96	106	96
Germany	94	78	87
Japan	98	75	76
Mean	93	118	121

OECD Economic Outlook 2018 Vo.1 1

Table 16.2 Housing and dwelling stock
% people living in each type, 2012

Country	Owner	Private rental	Public rental	Other
Ireland	80	10	11	0
Italy	71	15	5	9
Australia	70	24	5	1
United Kingdom	70	13	17	0
Belgium	68	24	7	1
Canada	68	32	0	0
United States	**68**	**26**	**5**	**1**
New Zealand	67	28	6	0
Norway	63	19	4	14
Austria	59	20	21	0
Finland	59	14	16	11
France	57	22	18	3
Netherlands	57	8	35	0
Sweden	56	23	21	0
Denmark	49	17	21	13
Germany	43	49	8	0
Japan	36	61	0	3
Switzerland	35	57	1	8
Mean	60	26	11	4

OECD Economic Survey: Luxembourg 2012

Table 16.4 Rooms per person
The average number of rooms in a dwelling divided by the number of persons living there. (Excludes, e.g., bathroom, toilet, garage, kitchenette)

Country	2005–10	2011–15
Canada	2.6	2.5
New Zealand	2.3	2.4
United States	**2.3**	**2.4**
Australia	2.3	2.3
Belgium	2.2	2.2
Ireland	2.0	2.1
Netherlands	2.0	2.0
Norway	2.0	2.0
United Kingdom	1.8	2.0
Denmark	1.9	1.9
Finland	1.9	1.9
Japan	1.8	1.9
Switzerland	1.8	1.9
France	1.7	1.8
Germany	1.7	1.8
Sweden	1.8	1.7
Austria	1.7	1.6
Italy	1.4	1.4
Mean	2.0	2.0

OECD How's Life 2017

16.2 Food

The intake of energy in food and drink is measured in calories, or more normally in thousands of calories, kilocalories (kcals). In general, the balance between food intake and activity is the key to weight stability, gain or loss—although individual metabolisms vary in how these relate.

Dietary advice, for example from the National Health Service in the UK, often says that with normal activity a balanced diet of 2500 kcals for a man and 2000 kcals for a woman will leave weight as stable. The amounts indicated in Table 16.5 show that the people in the selected countries would find this dietary advice overly restrictive. The average per-person consumption across the 18 countries in 2013 was 3412 kcal.

The rank ordering in this table shows a rough correlation with the tables on obesity in Table 6.28 above. Perhaps, though, the concern with weight gain is having more impact: between 1970 and 2000, average calorie intake was still rising; in the next 13 years, the 18 nation mean barely moved. In 12 of the countries, calorie intake was either stable or falling. This includes the United States, which had the highest average calorie intake in 2000, but declined somewhat in the following 13 years, so that now it has been passed by Austria and Belgium.

The Western countries are fairly closely clustered, all falling within plus or minus about 300 kcals of the mean. Nevertheless the gap between the leader Austria and the lowest Western country, New Zealand is still a substantial 631 kcals. The notable exception is Japan, probably not coincidentally the country with the highest life expectancy. Japan is also an extreme outlier in the next two tables—the average per-person consumption of fat and sugar.

The data on fat, in Table 16.6, shares some of the characteristics of total food intake. After increasing in the previous 30 years, it remained broadly stable in the next 13. The same three countries with the greatest calorie intake—Austria, the United States and Belgium—top the list on fat also. There is a greater range here and greater variety—several countries were still substantially increasing their fat intake—most notably Australia and Finland, while Ireland and the Netherlands had cut theirs sharply.

The figures on sugar show quite a different ranking from those on fat. The United States emerges as having the sweetest tooth, but New Zealand and Denmark—in the bottom half on fat—move up considerably, and Switzerland is high on both. France is among the highest on fat but among the lowest on sugar (Table 16.7).

Perhaps as troubling as what is eaten is what is not eaten. Table 16.8 involves self-reported data on eating fruit and vegetables daily. This is not about total amounts consumed, but frequency of eating them, and then only on one measure of frequency—daily or not.

Nevertheless, the data shows that Australia and New Zealand lead the way on fruit, and those two with the United States are the highest on daily consuming vegetables. On this measure, Germany, the Netherlands and Finland should all be increasing their fruit and vegetables to achieve a more balanced diet.

Table 16.5 Total food consumption
Kilocalories per capita per day

Country	1970	2000	2013
Austria	3232	3726	3768
Belgium	3095	3709	3733
United States	**3026**	**3755**	**3682**
Ireland	3444	3727	3600
Italy	3422	3668	3579
Germany	3147	3336	3499
Canada	2936	3506	3494
Norway	3022	3378	3485
France	3302	3605	3482
United Kingdom	3327	3362	3424
Switzerland	3478	3440	3391
Finland	3129	3151	3368
Denmark	3158	3313	3367
Australia	3239	2991	3276
Netherlands	3022	3265	3228
Sweden	2877	3099	3179
New Zealand	2953	3173	3137
Japan	2716	2899	2726
Mean	3140	3395	3412

OECD Health data and *OECD Health at a Glance 2017*

Table 16.6 Consumption of fat
Grammes per capita per day

Country	1970	2000	2013
Japan	55	90	87
New Zealand	114	114	116
Ireland	125	140	126
Netherlands	132	146	126
Sweden	117	123	130
Denmark	141	134	135
United Kingdom	144	141	138
Finland	124	123	140
Germany	127	143	142
Canada	114	148	147
Norway	132	139	149
Australia	117	130	151
Switzerland	149	150	154
Italy	111	154	155
France	126	170	159
Belgium	128	162	162
United States	**120**	**154**	**162**
Austria	125	159	170
Mean	122	140	142

OECD Health data and *OECD Health at a Glance 2017*

Table 16.7 Consumption of sugar
Total kilos per capita per annum

Country	2000	2013
Japan	29	27
Finland	39	32
Italy	31	32
France	40	39
United Kingdom	37	41
Sweden	47	42
Norway	46	44
Austria	47	45
Netherlands	46	45
Australia	45	46
Ireland	44	46
Canada	51	48
Germany	42	49
Belgium	55	52
Denmark	54	56
New Zealand	57	59
Switzerland	55	60
United States	**69**	**64**
Mean	*46*	*46*

OECD Health data and *OECD Health at a Glance 2017*

Table 16.8 Eating fruit and vegetables daily
% saying they do

Country	Fruit	Vegetables
Australia	95	99
New Zealand	81	95
Italy	76	61
Canada	69	75
United Kingdom	63	66
Switzerland	62	69
Sweden	59	68
United States	**58**	**92**
Austria	56	48
France	55	58
Ireland	55	67
Belgium	54	78
Norway	54	55
Denmark	53	44
Germany	47	34
Netherlands	43	29
Finland	32	40
Mean	*60*	*63*

No data on Japan
OECD Health data and *OECD Health at a Glance 2017*

16.3 Alcohol

Detailed international figures, from the OECD and others, suggest that in the English-speaking democracies and some others alcohol consumption trended steadily upward in the decades after World War II until 1980, but then started to decline. One can only speculate on the reasons for this, but it is plausible that in the decades of growing affluence following World War II, increasing alcohol consumption was part of the rewards people reaped. However from the 1970s and 1980s onward, there has been a greater sense of the health and social costs of over-consumption, and perhaps, this has increasingly tempered alcohol drinking habits.

Table 16.9 shows that the litres of alcohol consumed per person across these 18 countries was roughly the same in 2000 as in 1970, and then declined by around 10% in the next 15 years. Some of the very high early figures (e.g. France and Italy) may not be reliable, but the overall pattern is clear.

The rankings at the top of the table probably reinforce popular views about which countries imbibe the most alcohol. Perhaps, more surprising are the most abstemious countries: Norway, Sweden, Japan and Italy. The United States is below the mean, although not by as much as it was in earlier years.

There are marked differences among the selected countries in their preference for different types of alcoholic drinks. Table 16.10 gives proportions of the three main types of alcohol consumed within each country. In other words, although Germany and Norway drink similar proportions of beer, because their total alcohol intake is so different, the average German drinks twice as much alcohol as the average Norwegian. (Some countries sum to less than 100 because other alcoholic beverages are not included.)

Table 16.9 Alcohol consumption
Total alcohol, per capita, litres per annum

Country	1970	2000	2015
Germany	13.4	12.9	12.0
France	20.4	13.9	11.9
Austria	13.9	13.2	11.4
Ireland	7.0	14.2	10.7
Belgium	11.7	11.3	10.4
Australia	11.6	10.2	9.7
Switzerland	14.2	11.2	9.5
United Kingdom	9.5	10.4	9.5
Denmark	8.6	13.1	9.3
United States	**7.1**	**8.3**	**8.8**
New Zealand	9.8	8.9	8.7
Finland	5.8	8.6	8.5
Canada	8.8	7.6	8.1
Netherlands	7.8	10.1	8.0
Japan	6.1	8.6	7.2
Sweden	7.2	6.2	7.2
Italy	17.8	9.8	7.1
Norway	4.7	5.7	6.0
Mean	*10.3*	*10.2*	*9.1*

OECD Health data and *OECD Health at a Glance 2017*

16.3 Alcohol

Table 16.10 Types of alcohol consumed
% total alcohol intake, approx. 2013

Country	Spirits	Beer	Wine
Japan	52	19	4
United States	**33**	**50**	**17**
Canada	27	51	22
Finland	24	46	18
France	23	19	56
United Kingdom	22	37	34
Germany	19	54	28
Ireland	19	48	26
Norway	19	44	35
Switzerland	18	32	49
Netherlands	17	47	36
New Zealand	15	38	34
Sweden	15	37	47
Austria	14	50	36
Belgium	14	49	36
Denmark	14	38	48
Australia	13	44	37
Italy	12	23	66
Mean	*21*	*40*	*35*

Hannah Ritchie and Max Roser 'Alcohol Consumption', April 2018, Published online at OurWorldInData.org

Table 16.11 Heavy drinking
Heavy drinking session in last month, 2010

Country	%
Italy	6
New Zealand	6
Netherlands	7
Australia	13
Norway	14
Germany	16
Switzerland	21
Canada	23
Japan	25
United States	**25**
France	31
Denmark	32
United Kingdom	33
Sweden	35
Belgium	42
Ireland	48
Austria	52
Finland	54
Mean	*27*

Hannah Ritchie and Max Roser 'Alcohol Consumption', April 2018, Published online at OurWorldInData.org

Japan ranks highest on spirits due to the popularity there of sake and whisky. America ranks second. The United States is the only one of these democracies ever to make all alcohol illegal. The Prohibition Era, lasting from 1921 to 1933, had several unintended consequences: firstly, it fuelled an illegal boot-legging industry and the growth of organised crime; secondly, it contributed to increased police corruption; and thirdly, and still of relevance, it increased the relative popularity of spirits, because spirits provided a high concentration of alcohol in a small volume, and so were the easiest to conceal.

Beer is the most popular alcoholic drink in most of these countries, but is less popular than wine in France and Italy, and to a lesser extent in Switzerland, Sweden and Denmark. Wine is still very much a minority taste in Japan, while the United States and Canada also consume proportionately less wine than the other countries.

The problems stemming from alcohol are not revealed by figures on average per-person intake. Rather, taken in excess, alcohol is associated with severe health problems, dependency and anti-social behaviour.

Alcohol has its worst impacts when drunk during binge drinking. Table 16.11 has data on (self-reported) heavy drinking sessions. A heavy drinking episode is here defined as the percentage of alcohol drinkers who had more than six standard alcohol drinks in a single session. Of course, some would have involved much more.

The table shows great variation. In three countries, less than ten per cent of drinkers have had heavy drinking sessions in the last month, while in three others around half the alcohol drinkers have done so. The rankings here show only a very rough correspondence with those in the table on total consumption of alcohol. The two countries with the greatest alcohol intake—France and Germany—are around the middle of this table, while the normally abstemious Finns and Swedes seem prone to engaging in occasional heavy drinking episodes. Ireland and Austria are high in both tables; the United States just below the mean in both.

Perhaps the most tragic aspect of drinking alcohol is its role in car accidents. Table 16.12 gives the proportion of traffic fatalities in which alcohol played at least a contributing

Table 16.12 Alcohol consumption and traffic fatalities
% traffic fatalities in which alcohol is implicated

Country	%
Japan	6
Austria	7
Germany	9
Ireland	16
Switzerland	16
Norway	17
Netherlands	19
Sweden	19
Finland	22
Belgium	25
Italy	25
France	29
Australia	30
New Zealand	31
United States	**31**
Canada	34
Mean	*21*

No data on Denmark or United Kingdom
Hannah Ritchie and Max Roser 'Alcohol Consumption', April 2018, Published online at OurWorldInData.org

role. America, Canada, Australia and New Zealand all have a catastrophic percentage of 30 or higher. On the other hand, three of the four heaviest alcohol consuming nations—Austria, Germany and Ireland—fill three of the four lowest places on this table. This suggests that it is not alcohol per se that is the problem but its lethal combination with driving cars. Although all four of the worst countries have already taken several measures to reduce the road toll associated with drink driving, clearly more must be done.

16.4 Eating and Drinking Habits

Across these 18 countries as a whole, people now drink ten times as much coffee as tea. Coffee consumption (measured in kilograms per person) grew across the countries in the 15 years between 2002 and 2017 (Table 16.13), while tea consumption remained stable (Table 16.14).

Coffee consumption is higher in Europe than in the English-speaking countries and Japan. These countries drink less, but they showed the largest increases across the 15 year period. Among European countries, there is a strong correlation between colder climates and greater coffee consumption. Finns, Norwegians and Danes drink the most, while Italians, Germans and French people drink about half as much as the Finns.

Tea drinking is most popular in Ireland (where its consumption is still increasing), in Britain, Australia, New Zealand and Japan. It did not catch on to the same extent in

Table 16.13 Drinking coffee
Annual per capita consumption (kg)

Country	2002	2017
Finland	10.1	12.0
Norway	10.7	9.9
Denmark	9.7	8.7
Netherlands	7.1	8.4
Sweden	7.8	8.2
Switzerland	7.0	7.9
Belgium	5.0	6.8
Canada	2.4	6.2
Austria	5.5	5.9
Italy	3.2	5.8
Germany	5.7	5.5
France	3.9	5.1
United States	**3.0**	**4.2**
New Zealand	0.9	3.7
Ireland	0.7	3.5
Japan	1.4	3.3
Australia	2.0	3.0
United Kingdom	1.2	2.8
Mean	*4.9*	*6.2*

First column is from Global Market Information Database (GMID), published by Euromonitor. No longer available online. Last column is from Oliver Smith 'Mapped: The countries that drink the most coffee' *The Telegraph* 1-10-2017, from International Coffee Organisation

Table 16.14 Drinking tea
Annual per capita consumption (kg)

Country	2002	2016
Ireland	1.5	2.2
United Kingdom	2.3	1.9
New Zealand	1.0	1.2
Japan	0.9	1.0
Australia	0.8	0.8
Netherlands	0.8	0.8
Germany	0.7	0.7
Canada	0.2	0.5
Switzerland	0.4	0.4
Norway	0.4	0.3
Sweden	0.4	0.3
Austria	0.3	0.3
Finland	0.3	0.2
Denmark	0.2	0.2
France	0.2	0.2
United States	**0.2**	**0.2**
Belgium	0.1	0.1
Italy	0.1	0.1
Mean	*0.6*	*0.6*

First column is from Global Market Information Database (GMID), published by Euromonitor. No longer available online. Last column is from Wikipedia 'List of countries by tea consumption per capita', using data from Statista and Quartz

16.4 Eating and Drinking Habits

Table 16.15 Eating meat
Kilograms per person per year

Country	1970	2000	2013
Australia	105	111	116
United States	**106**	**122**	**115**
New Zealand	104	93	101
Austria	76	99	91
Canada	95	101	91
Netherlands	60	90	90
France	87	100	87
Ireland	72	95	87
Germany	77	83	86
Italy	55	89	84
Denmark	56	70	82
Sweden	53	69	82
United Kingdom	73	77	82
Finland	45	66	78
Switzerland	71	72	72
Norway	40	61	71
Belgium	77	81	70
Japan	18	45	50
Mean	*71*	*85*	*85*

Hannah Ritchie and Max Roser 'Meat and Seafood Production and Consumption' August 2017. Published online at OurWorldInData.org

Table 16.16 Eating fish and seafood
Kilograms per capita per year

Country	1970	2000	2013
Norway	43	50	52
Japan	60	67	49
Finland	22	31	36
France	20	31	34
Sweden	29	28	32
Australia	13	22	26
Belgium	18	24	25
Italy	14	23	25
New Zealand	16	23	25
Canada	14	24	23
Denmark	21	22	23
Ireland	11	24	22
Netherlands	13	22	22
United Kingdom	21	20	21
United States	**15**	**22**	**21**
Switzerland	10	16	18
Austria	8	10	14
Germany	12	13	13
Mean	*20*	*26*	*27*

Hannah Ritchie and Max Roser 'Meat and Seafood Production and Consumption' August 2017. Published online at OurWorldInData.org

England's North American colonies. The fact that Americans only drink on average 0.2 kg of tea a year might be the ultimate triumph of the Boston Tea Party. In contrast to coffee, in 14 countries tea consumption is either stable or declining.

Australia, the United States, New Zealand and Canada (plus Austria) tend to be the most carnivorous countries. As with alcohol, it may be with meat that there was some learning that there can be too much of a good thing. The 18 nation mean rose from 71 to 85 kilos per person up to 2000, but has been stable since, although individual countries are moving in both directions. Japan has by far the lowest meat consumption, although it almost trebled between 1970 and 2013.

Like meat, consumption of fish and seafood saw a substantial rise in the 30 years to 2000, but broad stability since. The two countries which have traditionally had strong seafood diets—Norway and Japan—are at the top of Table 16.16, with Finland and Sweden always high, and France climbing most rapidly. The landlocked countries of Austria and Switzerland have always been near the bottom, although perhaps German tastes also play a part, as that country's consumption has barely changed since 1970. Fish consumption continues to be below average in the United States and United Kingdom (Table 16.15).

While the relative health virtues of seafood, as opposed to meat, have been emphasised in recent decades, that advice arrived at the wrong moment economically. The oceans have been fished more intensively than ever, and the quality of the catch has been declining as its price has been rising. Indeed, global aquaculture production now exceeds the wild fishery catch. Perhaps it is the increasing price of seafood that accounts for Japan's sharp decline in consumption between 2000 and 2013.

In these countries, consumption patterns might have had their origins in the relative costs and availability of different foods and are then solidified into national cuisines and tastes. But as trade becomes more efficient, more options are available at reasonable prices. So, the tables in this section have evidence both of some growing convergence in taste and also of the persistence of ingrained habits.

16.5 Urban Mobility and Transport

Cities are shaped by their history and geography.[1] The final column of Table 16.17 gives the built-up area per person in each country. In an indirect way, this is a proxy measure for urban sprawl. Australia and the United States, which we saw in Table 16.4 tend to have larger houses, also have the largest built-up areas per person, where historically at least, land was cheaper. In contrast, the countries at the bottom of the table tend to have higher population densities, or more of their inhabitants living in a few large, geographically concentrated cities. The resulting urban environment then affects

---

[1] Also draws on *Top10Hell* 'Top ten countries with most bicycles per capita' published March 14 2011.

Table 16.17 Urban sprawl
Built-up areas in square kilometres (km^2) and in square metres (m^2) per person 2014

Country	% land	m^2 per person
Australia	0.15	497
United States	**1.63**	**472**
Belgium	15.37	417
Denmark	4.96	374
Norway	0.59	361
France	4.25	361
Austria	3.51	345
Netherlands	16.96	345
Germany	7.62	334
New Zealand	0.53	313
Canada	0.14	306
Switzerland	5.82	289
Italy	5.48	267
Ireland	1.62	240
United Kingdom	5.89	223
Japan	7.36	213
Sweden	0.48	208
Finland	0.27	156
Mean	*4.59*	*318*

OECD Green Growth Indicators

Table 16.18 Commuting time
Travelling time to work (minutes)

Country	Minutes
Sweden	18
Finland	21
United States	**21**
Italy	22
United Kingdom	22
Denmark	23
France	23
Ireland	23
New Zealand	23
Australia	25
Belgium	27
Germany	27
Netherlands	28
Austria	29
Norway	29
Canada	30
Japan	40
Mean	*25*

No data on Switzerland
OECD How's Life 2017

the behaviour of their inhabitants, especially their transport patterns.

Table 16.18 gives the average commuting time to work. This is a crude measure because there are huge variations within each country. Commuting time in New York would be very different to that in a small town in Arkansas, for example. The figures are a good guide to the relative compactness and ease of transport in Sweden and Finland and the long commuting times in Japan, especially Tokyo.

Dispersed populations tend to be more reliant on cars for transport. Table 16.19 shows that the four New World democracies are the leading car owners among the selected countries. America's love affair with the car is evident—there are now nine cars for every ten people.

One notable aspect of this table is that while car ownership rose substantially between 1995 and 2006, on balance it did not in the years to 2017, when the picture is much more mixed. The place of the car in the top four countries is undiminished, and a few others (Finland and Denmark) had strong rises. But in ten countries the rate of car ownership declined—after decades of consistent increases. The reasons for this watershed can only be guessed at: denser urban living, impatience with traffic congestion, high petrol prices and/or the ageing society.

Although comprehensive, systematic data was not available for all 18 countries, it seems, in contrast, that bicycle ownership and commuting by bicycle are on the rise in several countries. In the Netherlands in 2012, there were 99 bikes for every 100 people, while in Denmark the figure was 80 for every 100. One-quarter of Dutch people commuted to work by bicycle, and in Copenhagen, the average travelling speed for cyclists was 16 km per hour while for cars it was 27 km per hour.

Table 16.19 Cars
Road motor vehicles per 1000 population

Country	1995	2006	2017
United States	**771**	**755**	**910**
New Zealand	658	735	774
Australia	603	659	740
Canada	565	590	662
Italy	573	666	625
Finland	427	534	604
Japan	537	612	591
Germany	540	592	555
Austria	543	547	550
Switzerland	498	573	539
Norway	474	562	506
Belgium	487	540	503
Denmark	386	451	492
Netherlands	430	495	481
France	520	595	479
Sweden	447	512	477
United Kingdom	428	538	469
Ireland	318	433	439
Mean	*511*	*577*	*578*

First columns are from *OECD Factbook 2008* Quality of Life—Road motor vehicles and road fatalities; final column from Wikipedia 'List of countries by vehicles per capita', based on World Bank data

As noted above, national figures are a fairly crude guide to transport in countries, because of the large contrasts between city and country. The International Union for Public Transport (UITP), based in Brussels, has compiled detailed data on 63 cities, and Table 16.20 offers data for several cities from the selected countries. Only two American cities —Chicago and Portland—are in their data set.

As was noted in Sect. 1.3, estimates of city sizes should be taken with some caution. It should also be noted that the number of cars per person in cities is usually smaller than in provincial and rural areas. All these cities have lower rates of car ownership than their country's national figure given in Table 16.19. Moreover, smaller cities tend to have higher car ownership than larger cities in the same country: Chicago's rate is 391 compared to Portland's 840; London's is 307 compared to Birmingham's 450; Sydney's rate is 500 compared to Brisbane's 624, Stockholm's 389 to Gothenburg's 453.

The final column gives the total kilometres each inhabitant travels by public transport per year. Tokyo-ites are the leading commuters, travelling 5684 km, pa, while the next three cities—Rome, Stockholm and London—are around half that. The Canadian, Australian and American cities are all near the bottom of the table. Brisbane and Portland are the bottom two. The average Portland resident travels less than one-tenth the distance by public transport than the average Tokyo dweller does.

16.6 Most Liveable Cities

The scoreboard syndrome—the wish to reduce social complexity and the quality of living to a single score—perhaps reaches its peak in the league tables of most liveable cities. The two most widely cited ones are those compiled annually by the Economist Intelligence Unit (EIU) and Mercer Consulting. Table 16.21 lists the top 50 cities in the EIU's ranking and gives Mercer's ranking for the same cities.

The EIU ranked 140 cities, giving a score from 0 to 100 for most liveable. Mercer ranked 215 cities. Again a higher score indicates more liveable, but it assigns New York a score of 100 and then ranks others in relation to it.

In neither list do American cities rank highly. The EIU has 11, but with nine of these ranked between 37 and 50, and none in the top 20. Honolulu (23) and Pittsburgh (32) rank highest. Mercer has seven, with San Francisco (30) the highest. New York (45) and Philadelphia (50) are in Mercer's top 50 not in the EIU's.

In contrast, Australia and Canada both have three in the EIU's top ten. Japan has two, but one of these, Osaka, is ranked three by the EIU, but does not figure in Mercer's top 50. Nine of the EIU's top 50 do not make it into Mercer's. Only four of the EIU's top ten are in Mercer's top ten.

It is evident that the two organisations have somewhat different ideas about what constitutes quality living.

Both methodologies involve taking a considerable range of criteria—the EIU 30 and Mercer 39, and assigning scores to them. Both consider aspects of personal safety from crime and political unrest, healthcare and sanitation considerations, the economic environment, aspects of residential, transport and communications infrastructure, education, and then culture and entertainment.

As in all composite indicators, many will find the weighting of factors arbitrary or problematic, but in this case the scoring of individual components is also problematic. The great bulk of the EIU's 30 criteria involve judgements by their staff rather than objective measures. Nor is there any allowance that people may value different things, that one person's idea of unbearable humidity may be another's warm and balmy.

These two, and other such rankings, attract publicity when they are published, with local news media seizing on how their own city is faring. However, much of the publicity is based upon a false premise. Mercer explicitly says that its central purpose is 'to judge whether an expatriate is entitled

Table 16.20 Cities and public transport
Cars = Passenger cars per thousand inhabitants
Public transport = Total public transport vehicle kilometres travelled per inhabitant, 2012

City	Population (million)	Cars	Public transport
Tokyo	37.24	329	5684
Rome	2.91	641	2856
Stockholm	2.13	389	2842
London	8.31	307	2841
Munich	1.44	452	2825
Paris	11.98	414	2497
Copenhagen	1.69	360	2246
Hamburg	3.33	452	2196
Zurich	1.41	484	2189
Oslo	1.17	450	2091
Brussels	1.16	441	2046
Berlin	3.38	339	1968
Helsinki	1.17	391	1909
Vienna	1.74	390	1733
Gothenburg	1.60	453	1536
Vancouver	2.41	439	1222
Sydney	4.68	500	1155
Montreal	3.77	573	1140
Birmingham	2.76	450	1084
Geneva	0.47	467	1017
Chicago	**8.29**	**391**	**802**
Dublin	1.80	396	730
Brisbane	2.88	624	721
Portland	**1.49**	**840**	**514**

UITP Advancing Public Transport 'Mobility in Cities Database' www.uitp.org Brussels

Table 16.21 Most liveable city
EIU = Global Rank in the Economist Intelligence Unit's list 2018
Mercer = Global Rank in the Mercer Quality of Living Survey 2017

City	EIU	Mercer
Vienna	1	1
Melbourne	2	=16
Osaka	3	–
Calgary	4	33
Sydney	5	=10
Vancouver	6	5
Tokyo	=7	=50
Toronto	=7	=16
Copenhagen	9	9
Adelaide	10	29
Zurich	11	2
Auckland	=12	=3
Frankfurt	=12	7
Geneva	=14	8
Perth	=14	=21
Helsinki	16	32
Amsterdam	17	12
Hamburg	18	19
Montreal	=19	=21
Paris	=19	39
Berlin	21	13
Brisbane	22	37
Honolulu	**23**	**36**
Luxembourg	24	18
Munich	25	=3
Wellington	26	15
Oslo	27	=25
Dusseldorf	28	6
Brussels	29	27
Barcelona	=30	43
Lyon	=30	40
Pittsburgh	**=32**	–
Stockholm	=32	=23
Budapest	34	–
Hong Kong	=35	–
Manchester	=35	–
Singapore	=37	=25
Washington DC	**=37**	**48**
Madrid	=39	49
Minneapolis	**=39**	–
Dublin	41	34
Boston	**42**	**35**
Reykjavik	43	–
Chicago	**=44**	**47**
Miami	**=44**	–
Milan	=46	42
Seattle	**=46**	**44**
London	48	41
San Francisco	**49**	**=30**
Atlanta	**=50**	–
Los Angeles	**=50**	–

Mark Abadi 'The 50 Most Liveable Cities in the World in 2018' *Business Insider* August 29, 2018; 'Mercer Quality of Living Survey' Wikipedia; Economist Intelligence Unit *The Global Liveability Report 2017*

to a hardship allowance'. The EIU claims that its index has a broad range of uses from benchmarking perceptions of levels of development to assigning hardship allowances as part of expatriate relocation packages. It quantifies the challenges that might be presented to an individual's lifestyle in a given location, and depending on the score, it is recommended whether or not a premium should be paid to expatriate employees in these cities.

Both measures have some skew towards what is wanted by affluent expatriates (such as private schools and private health facilities) and towards the international connectivity of the cities. Some of these may be less relevant to native inhabitants.

But what does it mean that, for example, Singapore and Washington DC got the same score? Surely knowing the very different routes by which they achieved the score is more important. It is a worthwhile exercise to consider the different elements that affect people's quality of life in cities, even if these most common scoreboards have more entertainment than analytical value.

A. T. Kearney is a leading management consulting firm with global reach. Since 2008, it has done regular rankings of what it considers the world's most important cities. Cities, it says, 'are ecosystems for businesses and innovation'. The Global Cities Index (Table 16.22) is based on 27 metrics relating to business activity, human capital, information exchange, cultural experience and political engagement. The Global Cities Outlook evaluates a city's potential and likely future influence.

Perhaps the outstanding difference between Index and Outlook is the apparent decline of Asia. Tokyo drops from 4 to 23 and Singapore from 6 to 11. The other Asian cities drop right out of the 25: Hong Kong, Beijing, Seoul and Shanghai. There is some turnover of European cities, while several North American ones—Vancouver, Atlanta, and Houston—enter, and San Francisco leaps from 23rd to first place. This would seem a very American imaginary of where future influence will lie.

16.7 Happiness and Social Capital

The *World Happiness Report* is published by the United Nations Sustainable Development Solutions Network and edited by John Helliwell, Richard Layard and Jeffrey Sachs. Its centrepiece datum is polling conducted by the Gallup World Poll, and based on the question devised many decades ago by social psychologist Hadley Cantril:

> Please imagine a ladder with steps numbered from zero at the bottom to ten at the top. Suppose we say that the top of the ladder represents the best possible life for you and the bottom of the ladder represents the worst possible life for you.

Table 16.22 Global cities index
Index = AT Kearney top 25 cities globally 2017
Outlook = likely to be in future

City	Index rank	Outlook rank
New York	1	2
London	2	4
Paris	3	3
Tokyo	4	23
Hong Kong	5	–
Singapore	6	11
Chicago	7	15
Los Angeles	8	25
Beijing	9	–
Washington DC	10	19
Brussels	11	–
Seoul	12	–
Madrid	13	–
Berlin	14	18
Melbourne	15	6
Toronto	16	20
Sydney	17	13
Moscow	18	10
Shanghai	19	–
Vienna	20	–
Boston	21	5
Amsterdam	22	16
San Francisco	23	1
Barcelona	24	–
Istanbul	25	–

A.T. Kearney *Global Cities 2017: Leaders in a World of Disruptive Innovation*

If the top step is 10 and the bottom step is 0, on which step of the ladder do you feel you personally stand at the present time?

The results for the 18 selected democracies in the 2017 report are in Table 16.23. There is broad reliability in the national results from year to year. However, as can be seen the top countries are closely grouped, and in different years, Norway, Finland, Denmark and Switzerland have all scored highest. Those countries' mean scores (and also Iceland's) are consistently close to 7.5. There is next a group that consistently scores close to 7.3: the Netherlands, Canada, New Zealand, Australia and Sweden. The United States is just below the mean. Italy and Japan are at the bottom.

A national mean score of course does not explore the great ranges within each country. Moreover, a single measure on a ten point scale can only begin to capture the various cultural and emotional aspects of social life.

Nevertheless, especially when carried out regularly over such a large group of nations over several years, the happiness score does reveal interesting differences. The analysts in the *World Happiness Report* argue that six variables are most associated with the happiness scores: income, healthy life expectancy, social support, freedom, trust and generosity.

The other two tables relate to the last two of these. Trust is an important ingredient in social life. Trust in social institutions is one aspect; here (Table 16.24) the results of a generalised question about interpersonal trust are reported.

Table 16.23 Happiness
Cantril's ladder of life satisfaction (10 = highest)

Country	Global rank	Score
Norway	1	7.537
Denmark	2	7.522
Switzerland	4	7.494
Finland	5	7.469
Netherlands	6	7.377
Canada	7	7.316
New Zealand	8	7.314
Australia	9	7.284
Sweden	10	7.284
Austria	13	7.006
United States	**14**	**6.993**
Ireland	15	6.977
Germany	16	6.951
Belgium	17	6.891
United Kingdom	19	6.714
France	31	6.442
Italy	48	5.964
Japan	51	5.920
Mean		7.025

John Helliwell, Richard Layard and Jeffrey D. Sachs (eds) *World Happiness Report 2017*

Table 16.24 Trust in other people
% agreeing people can generally be trusted, LAY 2009–2016

Country	%
Netherlands	66
Sweden	64
Finland	58
New Zealand	56
Australia	54
Switzerland	49
Germany	42
Canada	41
United States	**38**
Japan	36
United Kingdom	30
Italy	28
France	19
Mean	45

No data on Austria, Belgium, Denmark, Ireland and Norway
Esteban Ortiz-Ospina and Max Roser (2018)—"Trust". Published online at OurWorldInData.org

Table 16.25 Volunteering
% of working-age population who declared they volunteered at least once a month through an organisation, 2012

Country	%
United States	**30**
New Zealand	29
Norway	28
Netherlands	27
Canada	26
Denmark	24
Germany	23
Austria	22
Australia	21
Finland	21
Belgium	20
Ireland	20
Sweden	19
United Kingdom	18
France	15
Italy	13
Japan	11
Mean	*21*

No data on Switzerland
OECD How's Life 2017

The commonly used question is to ask people whether they agree that 'most people can be trusted'. It taps a very general disposition, and how it relates to actual trusting behaviours cannot be assumed. Nevertheless, the broad differences between countries are consistent over time. Here, the Dutch and the Swedes are the most trusting; the Americans just below the mean; and the French by far the most mistrustful.

The final Table (16.25) looks at self-reported volunteer activity in an organisation. Such engagement with civic life is one indicator of social cohesion and an emotional investment in the community. There is a considerable range, with the top ranking United States having three times as many volunteers as the Japanese. This reflects an American tradition of engagement in voluntary organisations.

Crime and Social Problems

17.1 Measuring Crime Trends

Crime and Social Problems is probably the chapter in this book where the capacity of statistics to capture reality is most problematic.[1] Official crime statistics are always haunted by the 'dark figure'—the gap between the official and the actual rates of crime. The dark figure has two main sources, either that crime is not reported to the police or that reported crime is not recorded. Neither is constant over time. It used to be the case, for example, that very serious offences such as sexual assaults, domestic violence and child abuse were not reported because the victim felt powerless to achieve justice or feared the police process that would follow. One suspects, and hopes, that the proportion of such offences reported now has increased substantially.

Even after a report is made, police have some discretion about whether and how it is recorded. Ulterior bureaucratic-political motives may enter—either deflating the rate of unsolved crimes to make themselves look more effective or inflating it in order to plead for extra resources. More importantly, the recorded rate reflects not just the incidence of offences, but the levels and patterns of policing, especially in some areas, such as drug and public order offences.

The inherent problems are magnified when we aim to compare different jurisdictions. While homicide, for example, will have a broadly common definition, others such as assault and types of robbery differ greatly. Even on the apparently simple task of comparing the number of police officers, differing definitions make the figures all but meaningless. British criminologists Gordon Barclay and Cynthia Tavares found that the country with the highest number of police officers in relation to population, Italy (550 officers per 100,000 people) had around three times as many as the lowest country, Finland (158), with the United States close to the mean with 224. The differences seem at least partly due to countries at the top including as 'police' several categories of regulatory and enforcement officials that other nations do not.

One partial solution to how useless official figures are in comparing crime rates is to measure trends in each country's crime rate against its own past. Table 17.1 does this, showing that in most countries the official crime rate fell between 2008 and 2013. America's fall was the second sharpest of these countries.

A better solution, but one that depends on large scale international cooperation and funding, is to look not at official statistics, but at the public experience and perception of crime. This approach involves taking large, broadly representative samples of the public, and asking them the same questions, thus over-riding differences and inaccuracies in official data. It does rely on the accuracy of the sampling and the willingness of respondents to participate.

The International Crime Victims Survey (ICVS) coordinated five waves of surveys—1989, 1992, 1996, 2000 and 2004–2005—to collect systematic comparative data on the experience of crime. Participation was uneven especially in the earlier waves, and sadly the project has not been continued. The ICVS data in Table 17.2 has three notable aspects. Firstly, the number claiming to have experienced crime in the previous year is considerably higher than the official crime rates would suggest. This is partly because as that survey also found only around half the people who experience a crime report it to police.

Secondly, the table suggests a downward trend in crime across these 18 democracies. Thirdly—in contrast to some tables later in this chapter—America falls around the middle of the table, suggesting that its crime rate was not substantially out of line with other economically advanced democracies.

---

[1] Also draws on United Nations Office on Drugs and Crime International Statistics on Crime (Helsinki, European Institute for Crime Prevention and Control, 2010).Gordon Barclay and Cynthia Tavares 'International comparisons of criminal justice statistics 2001' UK Home Office Issue 12/03 24 October 2003. www.csdp.org/research/hosb1203.pdf.

© Springer Nature Singapore Pte Ltd. 2020
R. Tiffen et al., *How America Compares*, How the World Compares,
https://doi.org/10.1007/978-981-13-9582-6_17

Table 17.1 Change in the crime rate
Persons brought into formal contact with the police or criminal justice system
Trend from 2008 to 2013, where 2008 rate is 100
A score <100 means the crime rate decreased

Country	Score
Netherlands	66
Japan	77
United States	**77**
New Zealand	84
Canada	86
Sweden	87
Finland	88
France	92
Germany	94
Belgium	96
Norway	101
Austria	107
Italy	108
Australia	112
Mean	*91*

No data on Denmark, Ireland, Switzerland or the United Kingdom
OECD *Society at a Glance 2016*

Table 17.2 Changing incidence of crime
% saying they had been a victim of any one of ten crimes in the previous year

Country	1992 (or EAY)	2000	2004
Japan	–	11.9	9.9
Austria	–	13.9	11.6
France	16.4	17.2	12.0
Italy	20.3	–	12.6
Finland	17.2	16.6	12.7
Germany	16.6	–	13.1
Norway	13.4	–	15.8
Sweden	18.7	22.6	16.1
Canada	24.0	20.5	17.2
Australia	24.0	25.2	17.3
United States	**22.2**	**17.6**	**17.5**
Belgium	15.2	17.5	17.7
Switzerland	13.0	15.6	18.1
Denmark	–	20.6	18.8
Netherlands	25.7	20.2	19.7
United Kingdom	15.0	21.6	21.0
New Zealand	25.7	–	21.5
Ireland	–	–	21.9
Mean	*19.1*	*18.5*	*16.4*

Jan van Dijk, John van Kesteren, Paul Smit *Criminal Victimisation in International Perspective. Key Findings from the 2004–2005 ICVS and EU ICS* (WODC, 2007, The Hague)
For France, Germany and Norway 1992 figure is from 1989 survey wave; Austria's 2000 figure is from 1996

Both Tables 17.1 and 17.2 suggest there has been some fall in the crime rate. This may come as a surprise. Partly this is because media coverage concentrates on individual crimes,

Table 17.3 Public fear of Burglary
% of population thinking a burglary in the next year is likely or very likely
And % who experienced a burglary in the previous 12 months, 2004

Country	Expect	Experienced
Finland	13	0.8
Denmark	14	2.7
United States	**16**	**2.5**
Sweden	17	0.7
Netherlands	18	1.3
Austria	21	0.9
Norway	21	1.2
Germany	23	0.9
Canada	25	2.0
Switzerland	26	1.6
Belgium	33	1.8
Ireland	33	2.3
United Kingdom	34	3.3
Australia	36	2.5
New Zealand	36	3.2
France	38	1.6
Italy	43	2.1
Japan	48	0.9
Mean	*28*	*1.8*

Jan van Dijk, John van Kesteren, Paul Smit *Criminal Victimisation in International Perspective. Key Findings from the 2004–2005 ICVS and EU ICS* (WODC, 2007, The Hague)
For France, Germany and Norway 1992 figure is from 1989 survey wave; Austria's 2000 figure is from 1996

with the most dramatic and awful being the most newsworthy. In contrast, crime *rates* figure in the news only rarely.

Moreover, public perceptions tend to dwell on the negative, as is shown by the telling contrast between the two columns in Table 17.3. The first column offers the proportion thinking a burglary of their home is likely or very likely in the next year, while column two reports the proportion who had experienced a burglary in the previous 12 months. While the overall average has 28% who think a burglary is likely in the next year, less than 2% had experienced such an event in the past year. In other words, there is far more apprehension of burglary than direct experience of it.

17.2 Homicides and Firearms

Table 17.4 shows that the homicide rate over 55 years in the selected democracies countries followed a parabolic figure, with the rate steadily worsening until the early 1990s and then improving for the next two decades.[2] The 2015 figures

---
[2]Also draws on Martin Maximino 'Active Shooters' *Journalist's Resource, Shorenstein Center* February 11, 2015; Adam Lankford 'Public Mass Shooters and Firearms: A Cross-National Study of 171 Countries' *Violence and Victims* V31, No 2, 2016.

17.2 Homicides and Firearms

Table 17.4 Homicides
Number of intentional homicides per 100,000 population

Country	1960	1980	2000	2015
Japan	1.9	0.9	0.6	0.3
Austria	1.2	1.2	1.0	0.5
Ireland	0.1	0.8	0.1	0.6
Netherlands	0.3	0.8	1.1	0.6
Norway	0.4	1.1	1.1	0.6
Switzerland	0.6	1.0	1.0	0.7
Germany	0.9	1.2	1.2	0.8
Italy	1.3	1.9	1.3	0.8
New Zealand	1.0	1.3	1.3	0.9
United Kingdom	0.5	1.0	1.7	0.9
Australia	1.5	1.9	1.9	1.0
Denmark	0.5	1.3	1.0	1.0
Sweden	0.6	1.2	1.1	1.1
Finland	3.0	3.0	2.9	1.6
France	1.6	1.0	1.8	1.6
Canada	1.4	2.0	1.6	1.7
Belgium	0.6	1.5	2.1	1.9
United States	**5.0**	**10.2**	**5.5**	**4.9**
Mean	1.2	1.9	1.6	1.2

First two columns from OECD *Health Data*; last two columns from World Bank *Development Indicators*

were almost the same as for 1960. In the United States in 2016, there were 17,250 murders but that is still well below the rate at its peak in the 1980s and 1990s. Of course the timing and trends vary somewhat between countries, but perhaps what is more notable is the similarity between their trends.

Table 17.4 demonstrates the extremely high homicide rate in America compared with the other democracies, five times the average of the others. Twelve countries had a homicide rate of one person per 100,000 or less in 2015, and nearly all these countries are on a downward trend. Despite sharing in the overall decline in homicide rates, the United States is still an extreme outlier in the homicide rate.

Table 17.5 concentrates on gun-related deaths. It therefore omits non-gun homicides and non-gun suicides. In 1961, the earliest year the FBI collated such data, just over half the murders in America were committed with a firearm. By 2015, the figure was over 70%.

The outstanding feature of the table is just how much gun ownership and gun-related deaths vary between the countries, and what an outlier the United States is. In America, there is basically one gun per person. In Japan, there is less than one gun for every 100 people. Similarly, for every gun-related death in Japan per 100,000 people, there are more than 100 in the United States. There is a broad but far from perfect correlation between the prevalence of guns in a country and the incidence of gun-related deaths. This suggests that the spread of guns in society is a central contributor to the rate of gun-related deaths, but not the only factor.

Another feature is that the rate of gun-related deaths from suicide in the 18 countries is about four times as great as those from homicide. In almost every country, gun-related suicide

Table 17.5 Gun-related deaths
Rate per 100,000 population, 2015 or nearest available year

Country	Total	Homicides	Suicides	Unintentional	Guns (per 100 people)
Japan	0.06	0.00	0.04	0.01	0.6
United Kingdom	0.23	0.06	0.15	0.00	2.8
Netherlands	0.58	0.29	0.28	0.01	3.9
Ireland	0.80	0.25	0.28	0.08	3.9
Australia	0.93	0.16	0.76	0.01	13.7
Germany	1.01	0.07	0.84	0.01	30.3
New Zealand	1.07	0.11	0.84	0.05	30.0
Denmark	1.28	0.22	1.09	0.04	12.0
Italy	1.31	0.35	0.87	0.09	11.9
Sweden	1.47	0.19	1.20	0.06	31.6
Norway	1.75	0.10	1.63	0.02	31.3
Belgium	1.82	0.33	1.33	0.02	17.2
Canada	1.97	0.38	1.52	0.05	30.8
Austria	2.63	0.10	2.43	0.01	30.4
France	2.83	0.21	2.16	0.04	31.2
Switzerland	3.01	0.21	2.74	0.04	24.5
Finland	3.25	0.32	2.94	0.02	27.5
United States	**10.50**	**3.50**	**6.69**	**0.18**	**101.1**
Mean	2.03	0.38	1.54	0.04	24.1

Wikipedia List of countries by firearm-related death rates, accessed March 2018. The gun data draws particularly from gunpolicy.org, an organization based at Sydney University School of Public Health, and from causes of death data compiled by the WHO and OECD

deaths out number gun-related homicide deaths. In countries with high gun ownership and a high gun-related death toll—Finland, Switzerland, France and Austria—their position owes much more to the high suicide than to the high homicide rate. In Finland, for example, the ratio is 9:1 gun-related suicides to homicides. In America, the contrast is not as stark, but it is still almost double. After the Australian government introduced gun reform following a massacre in 1996, both the homicide and suicide rates dropped sharply. Over the next several years, gun-related homicides declined from 77.4 to 52.8 and gun-related suicides from 446 per year to 239.

A grim statistic is that with the profusion of guns the risk of being killed in a gun-related accident also increases. The risk of dying in a gun-related accident in the United States is actually higher than the gun-related homicide rate in seven of the other countries.

These statistics do not exhaust the harm done by guns. In the figures, the group Gun Violence has collated, in 2017, there were 15,580 gun-related deaths in the United States, but there were also twice that number of gun-related injuries—31,178.

It should also be pointed out that the table only refers to guns in general. It is likely that Americans have more handguns and more automatic and semi-automatic weapons than people in other democracies.

Mass shootings, often defined as events in which four or more people, excluding the shooter, are killed, are more common in the USA than elsewhere. Professor Adam Lankford's research shows that between 1966 and 2012, other countries averaged a total of 1.7 mass shootings. The United States had 90. Four others reached double figures: the Philippines 18, Russia 15, Yemen 11 and France 10. The United States with just under five per cent of the world's population accounted for 31% of the mass shooting incidents.

17.3 Law and Justice

An independent judicial system operating with integrity, fairness and effectiveness is central to a well-functioning democracy. These are not ideals which are easily quantified or compared internationally. Fortunately, two groups have rigorously applied themselves to the task.

The World Justice Project (WJP), based in Washington but with members across the world, each year constructs the WJP Rule of Law Index. In 2017, it covered 113 countries and was based on household surveys with a combined sample of 110,000 people plus 3000 expert surveys in those 113 countries. The surveys aim to see how each country's legal system works from the experience and perspective of ordinary people.

Table 17.6 gives the results according to the 16 countries' score and global rank. (There is no data for Ireland and Switzerland.) The most fundamental point is how high these

Table 17.6 The rule of law (1)
WJP Scale, 0–1, where 1 is best, 2017

Country	Score	Global ranking
Denmark	0.89	1
Norway	0.89	2
Finland	0.87	3
Sweden	0.86	4
Netherlands	0.85	5
Germany	0.83	6
New Zealand	0.83	7
Austria	0.81	8
Canada	0.81	9
Australia	0.81	10
United Kingdom	0.81	11
Japan	0.79	14
Belgium	0.77	15
France	0.74	18
United States	**0.73**	**19**
Italy	0.65	31

No data on Ireland or Switzerland
World Justice Project *Rule of Law Index 2017–2018*

stable democracies figure in the global rankings. Eleven of the selected countries fill the top 11 positions globally, and the only one not in the top 20 is Italy, ranked 31st. The global median country is Macedonia, ranked 57 globally, with a score of 0.53.

The WJP calculates eight factors and 44 sub-factors in reaching its overall score. The first four generally refer to whether the law imposes limits on the exercise of power by the state and private entities. The second four refer to whether people are protected from violence and crime and whether they have access to dispute settlement procedures.

The eight factors are (1) constraints on government powers; (2) absence of corruption; (3) open government; (4) fundamental rights; (5) order and security; (6) regulatory enforcement; (7) civil justice; and (8) criminal justice. The rankings on the eight components are also revealing. For example, Singapore and Hong Kong rank very highly on some measures, such as the absence of corruption and order and security, but much less well on constraints on government power and fundamental rights. Among the 16 democracies, the lowest ranking factor is most often order and security, reflecting that their crime rates are sometimes quite high.

The Sustainable Governance Indicators (SGI) are compiled by the Bertelsmann Stiftung, which looks at sustainable policy performance and governance capacities in 41 OECD and EU countries. It assembled 100 international experts to evaluate 16 fields of policy performance; four aspects of democracy; and 12 aspects of governance.

17.3 Law and Justice

Table 17.7 Rule of law (2)
SGI Scale 1–10, where 10 is best, 2017

Country	Rule of law
Denmark	9.8
New Zealand	9.5
Sweden	9.5
Norway	9.3
Germany	9.0
Australia	8.3
Austria	8.3
Finland	8.3
Switzerland	8.3
Belgium	8.0
Canada	7.8
Ireland	7.8
United States	**7.8**
United Kingdom	7.5
Italy	7.3
Netherlands	7.0
France	6.5
Japan	4.8

Sustainable Governance Indicators *SGI 2017 Survey* (Bertelsmann Stiftung)
http://www.sgi-network.org/2017/

Table 17.8 Safe living conditions
SGI scale 1–10, where 10 = safest, 2017

Country	Score
Japan	8.4
Norway	8.2
Switzerland	8.2
Finland	8.0
Austria	7.8
New Zealand	7.8
Australia	7.5
United Kingdom	7.5
Denmark	7.3
Germany	7.3
Ireland	7.3
Canada	7.2
Netherlands	7.1
Italy	6.9
Sweden	6.9
Belgium	6.2
France	5.4
United States	**4.2**

Sustainable Governance Indicators *SGI 2017 Survey* (Bertelsmann Stiftung)
http://www.sgi-network.org/2017/

The two most relevant here are their indicators for rule of law and for safe living.

SGI's rule of law indicator has four components: legal certainty; judicial review; appointment of justices; and corruption prevention. Because it emphasises different aspects than the WJP, the rankings in Table 17.7 are rather different from 17.6. Most of the same countries are in the top half of both tables, but there is more movement of rankings in the bottom countries. The United States does considerably better, partly because it is ranked relatively highly on the appointment of justices, whereas Japan, which does not rank particularly highly on any of the SGI components, is by far the lowest on this one.

Table 17.8, safe living, compiles data that addresses the question of how effectively internal security policy protects a country's citizens. The indicator combines homicide and theft rates, as well as confidence in the police. The United States lags on this indicator, especially because of its high homicide rate, and above average theft rate, although its confidence in police is above average. Japan tops this table, having been 16th in the SGI rule of law table.

When the public is polled about their confidence in their legal system, the countries of northwest Europe are at the top. Table 17.9 shows that in only two countries—Italy and the USA—do fewer than half the public express confidence in the legal system. Interestingly, over these nine years, the percentage in most countries was stable or increasing, the 18-country mean increasing slightly. Only the bottom two,

Table 17.9 Citizens' confidence in the legal system
% expressing confidence

Country	2007	2016
Denmark	84	82
Norway	79	82
Switzerland	73	81
Finland	77	75
Germany	51	70
Ireland	65	70
New Zealand	48	69
Sweden	68	69
Austria	74	68
Japan	53	68
Netherlands	65	66
United Kingdom	55	63
Canada	60	62
Australia	49	58
Belgium	52	53
France	48	53
United States	**55**	**43**
Italy	39	24
Mean	61	64

OECD *Government at a Glance 2017*

Italy and the USA, showed a sharp downward slide. There does not seem to be any obvious factor why Americans' confidence in their legal system dropped by twelve points in these years, and it may owe more to a changing political culture rather than developments in the legal system.

17.4 Imprisonment and Capital Punishment

Among these 18 democracies, the United States is clearly the outlier both in imprisonment rates and in numbers executed.[3]

Whereas the crime rate generally fell in the selected countries from the early 1990s on, imprisonment rates increased. This may reflect increasingly punitive attitudes, although the imprisonment rate is a product of several factors—the rate at which people are arrested, the seriousness of their offences, the rate at which they are convicted (and remanded in custody before that), as well as the proportion of the convicted given a prison sentence and the average length of the term imposed. In the selected countries, as Table 17.10 shows, the imprisonment rate kept rising until 2010, since when it has plateaued or dropped slightly.

The imprisonment rates show enormous variation. The United States imprisons more than four times as many people as the other 17 countries. Interestingly, the next four places on the table are also taken by English-speaking countries. Possibly, this reflects American influence on their political cultures. The imprisonment rates in Britain, Australia and New Zealand show sharp rises over the decades. Only one non-English-speaking country has an imprisonment rate more than 100. Japan and the Nordic countries have the lowest rates.

According to scholar, Marie Gottschalk, American incarceration practices were not exceptional for most of the twentieth century. Until 1970, it had a rate higher, but not remarkably higher, than other Western countries. From then on, its imprisonment rates escalated far more sharply than any other country's. In 2010, 7.3 million US adults were in prison or had been to prison. Between 1980 and 2010, the adult male population that had spent time in prison jumped from 1.79 to 5.55%. For African-American males, the figure jumped from 5.76 to 15.14%.

The cost of such a large imprisonment rate is a contributing reason why in Table 5.6 the United States spends the highest proportion of the government budget on public order and safety.

Amnesty International reports that more than two-thirds of the countries in the world have abolished the death penalty in law or practice. As Table 17.11 shows, 16 of the selected democracies have abolished it. The two countries still practising execution are the United States and Japan. None of the other 16 countries has executed anyone for at least 40 years. Ironically, the last execution among them occurred in France in 1977, the year that the United States resumed exercising the death penalty.

The US Supreme Court ruled in 1976 that executions were allowable under the US Constitution, which forbids cruel and unusual punishment. From 1977 to 2005, 1000

Table 17.10 Imprisonment
Prisoners per 100,000 population

Country	1982	1992	2010	2016
Japan	46	36	57	47
Sweden	55	63	74	55
Finland	99	65	61	57
Denmark	62	66	71	61
Netherlands	32	49	92	69
Norway	46	58	74	71
Germany	80	71	85	76
Ireland	–	61	94	82
Switzerland	–	79	79	84
Italy	62	81	112	86
Austria	–	87	102	95
France	59	84	99	99
Belgium	64	71	97	105
Canada	107	123	117	106
United Kingdom	91	91	152	146
Australia	46	89	135	152
New Zealand	84	119	198	202
United States	**301**	**505**	**731**	**698**
Mean	*82*	*100*	*135*	*127*

OECD *Society at a Glance 2016*

Table 17.11 Capital punishment

Country	Does country retain death penalty?	Year abolished for ordinary crimes	Year of last execution
Sweden	No	1921	1910
Finland	No	1949	1944
Switzerland	No	1942	1944
Italy	No	1947	1947
Norway	No	1905	1948
Germany[a]	No	1949	1949
Austria	No	1950	1950
Belgium	No	1996	1950
Denmark	No	1933	1950
Netherlands	No	1870	1952
Ireland	No	1990	1954
New Zealand	No	1989	1957
Canada	No	1976	1962
United Kingdom	No	1973	1964
Australia	No	1985	1967
France	No	1981	1977
Japan	Yes	–	–
United States	**Yes**	–	–

Country	Number executed 2016	Number sentenced to death 2016	Number under sentence of death end 2016
Japan	3	3	141
United States	**20**	**32**	**2832**

[a]West Germany abolished death penalty in 1949; East Germany in 1987
Amnesty International *Death Sentences and Executions 2016* (London, Amnesty International, 2017) and earlier editions

---

[3]Also draws on David Trilling Shorenstein Center December 1, 2017.

people were executed. The peak was in 1999 with 98 executions, and since then, it has trended downwards, with 20 being executed in 2016.

According to Amnesty International, China carried out at least 1000 executions in 2016, but its secrecy means the exact number is not known. Of known executions in 2016, Iran performed 567, Saudi Arabia 154, Pakistan 87 and Egypt 44. The means of execution varied considerably: lethal injection, hanging, shooting and, in Saudi Arabia, beheading. Some executions in Iran and North Korea were conducted publicly.

A somewhat bizarre aspect of the two democracies that retain the death penalty is that they now sentence far more people to death than they actually execute. In America at the end of 2016, there were 2832 people on death row.

17.5 Suicide

Although it receives far less media and political attention, each year suicide claims almost ten times as many victims in the selected countries as does homicide.[4] Table 17.12 shows that across these 18 countries in 2015, 11.8 people in every 100,000 died from committing suicide, while Table 17.4 showed that 1.2 per 100,000 were homicide victims.

Suicide is perhaps the most individualistic of all behaviours, so it is not surprising that it does not always show strong patterning. Countries have moved in opposite directions and at different times.

Although the movement is not as dramatic as in the homicide rate—the 18 nation mean moving in a fairly small range over the 55 years covering in the table—it does show a steady decline from its 1980 peak. Five countries had rates higher than 20 in 1980, but none does in 2015. The greatest drops have been in Denmark (29.2 down to 10.6) and Switzerland (23.8 down to 12.2).

The figures for 2015 show a clustering of ten countries with rates between 10.5 and 12.5. Italy and the United Kingdom have the lowest rates, as they do for many of the previous decades. Japan has the highest, and it is consistently at or near the top. Similarly, the four European countries above it—Belgium, France, Finland and Austria—have all tended to be consistently higher than the mean. Ireland began with the lowest rate, but has edged up to now be about average.

None of the patterns which sometimes explain the clustering of countries on other phenomena correlates well with suicide. Catholic Italy has the lowest rate, but Catholic Belgium and Austria have among the highest, while Catholic

Table 17.12 Suicide
Suicides per 100,000 people

Country	1960	1970	1980	1990	2000	2015
Italy	6.2	5.6	6.7	6.5	5.8	6.3
United Kingdom	9.7	7.3	8.1	7.4	6.4	7.5
Netherlands	7.3	8.5	9.9	8.7	8.2	10.5
Norway	6.2	8.1	11.9	14.4	11.6	10.5
Denmark	19.7	20.4	29.2	20.5	11.4	10.6
Germany	17.5	20.2	18.5	14.5	11.0	10.8
Canada	8.8	12.4	13.9	12.0	10.8	10.9
Ireland	3.0	1.9	7.1	10.1	11.8	10.9
Sweden	15.9	20.4	17.7	15.0	10.9	11.7
Australia	11.3	13.3	11.2	12.5	11.8	12.2
Switzerland	18.6	18.2	23.8	19.1	16.2	12.2
New Zealand	10.7	10.7	11.3	13.4	12.0	12.5
United States	**11.4**	**12.3**	**11.6**	**11.9**	**9.8**	**13.5**
Austria	21.2	23.0	23.7	20.5	16.8	13.9
Finland	21.6	21.4	24.1	27.8	20.4	14.1
France	15.0	14.7	17.9	17.7	15.6	14.3
Belgium	13.3	15.1	20.2	16.6	–	16.1
Japan	25.1	17.4	17.9	14.5	19.1	17.6
Mean	12.4	13.9	15.8	14.6	12.3	11.8

OECD *Health at a Glance 2017*

Ireland is in the middle. Nordic Finland has the second highest rate, but the other three Scandinavian countries are in the lower half of the table. The English-speaking countries are spread throughout the table, with Britain having the second lowest rate.

The United States was consistently below the mean until the year 2000, but between 2000 and 2015, its rate showed the greatest increase, and now it is above the mean. The *Economist* notes that in contrast to most OECD countries, in America, the number of suicides has been rising by about 1000 a year every year since 2003. In 2016, there were 45,000 suicides in America: 23,000 of them by gun, 11,700 by hanging and 5300 by overdose. Suicide is now the tenth-leading cause of death in America and the second-leading cause among those aged 15–34.

All societies have marked consistent differences between different groups. In particular, males commit suicide at around three times the rate of females. In America now, white men commit suicide at nearly three times the rate of black, Hispanic and Asian men. In the United States, suicide rates in rural areas are higher than in large cities: 11.9 per 100,000 people in large metropolitan areas; 14.9 in smaller cities and towns; and 17.3 in rural areas.

In most countries, suicide rates are higher in older than younger people. Table 17.13 shows that rates among adolescents are in most of the selected countries lower than the overall rate. The dramatic exception is New Zealand, which has a markedly higher suicide rate among teenagers, and one which has become substantially worse. Norway and Finland which had high suicide rates among teenagers in earlier decades both improved substantially leading up to 2015.

---
[4] Also draws on the *Economist* 'Self-destructing' March 31 2018 and Center for Disease Control Press Release 'Americans in rural areas more likely to die by suicide' October 5, 2017.

Table 17.13 Teenage suicides
Suicides by adolescents, per 100,000, for each year

Country	1990	2000	2015
Italy	2.5	2.7	2.0
United Kingdom	3.7	4.0	3.3
Norway	12.7	13.6	3.4
France	5.7	5.4	3.7
Netherlands	4.4	4.6	4.1
Denmark	4.9	6.8	4.8
Germany	5.8	5.9	4.8
Sweden	6.2	7.3	6.4
Belgium	6.2	9.5	6.8
Switzerland	11.0	8.4	7.0
Japan	3.8	6.4	7.3
Ireland	6.5	12.4	7.6
Australia	10.8	10.1	8.8
United States	**11.1**	**8.0**	**8.9**
Austria	10.5	12.4	9.0
Finland	23.1	13.9	9.0
Canada	12.1	10.8	10.3
New Zealand	15.1	15.4	24.1
Mean	*8.7*	*8.8*	*7.3*

OECD *Family database* www.oecd.org/els/family/database.htm

Table 17.14 Motor vehicle deaths
Fatalities per 100,000 population

Country	1960	1970	1980	1990	2000	2010	2015
Norway	8.6	15.0	9.1	7.8	7.6	4.3	2.3
Sweden	14.4	16.5	10.5	9.1	6.7	2.8	2.7
United Kingdom	14.3	14.2	12.1	9.4	6.1	3.0	2.8
Denmark	17.1	24.2	13.5	12.3	9.3	4.6	3.1
Switzerland	22.0	26.1	18.5	13.9	8.3	4.2	3.1
Ireland	9.0	16.6	17.9	13.6	11.0	4.7	3.5
Netherlands	17.6	24.8	13.7	8.8	7.3	3.9	3.7
Japan	15.9	22.5	11.4	11.8	8.2	4.6	3.8
Germany	25.6	32.2	20.3	13.6	9.1	4.5	4.3
Finland	18.1	23.7	11.4	13.0	7.7	5.1	4.9
Australia	28.1	32.8	24.6	13.7	9.5	6.1	5.1
Canada	21.8	25.0	22.1	14.3	9.5	6.6	5.2
France	18.1	23.2	20.4	19.8	13.7	6.4	5.4
Austria	27.6	33.3	25.5	20.4	12.2	6.6	5.6
Italy	17.8	24.3	19.2	12.6	12.4	7.0	5.6
Belgium	19.2	29.8	24.9	19.9	14.4	7.7	6.5
New Zealand	16.5	24.2	19.8	21.4	12.0	8.6	6.9
United States	**22.6**	**27.0**	**22.4**	**17.9**	**14.9**	**10.7**	**10.9**
Mean	*18.6*	*24.2*	*17.6*	*14.4*	*10.0*	*5.6*	*4.7*

www.oecd.data.org/roadaccidents

These figures about differing and changing rates pose more questions than answers. For example, while Japan has consistently been among the countries with the highest suicide rate, as Table 17.12 shows, it has also shown more volatility than most. Sometimes this rise may be due to increased economic stresses, but there are also cultural factors. There is more idea of an 'honourable' suicide in Japan, but in addition, it is a country that allows fewer 'second chances' than some others. According to the *Economist*, 'Japanese society rarely lets people bounce back from the perceived shame of failure or bankruptcy'.

Each suicide is an individual tragedy, and reducing the rate should be a policy priority. One solution would be reducing the number using guns. The *Economist* notes that 83% of attempted suicides by gun are successful, compared with 61% of hangings and just 15% of drug overdoses. According to a Harvard study, only one in ten people who survive a suicide attempt go on to kill themselves later.

17.6 Motor Vehicle Deaths

The figures in Table 17.14 show what a terrible toll car accidents claim in the selected countries, but also what a policy success has been achieved in this area.[5] Especially because of the age structure of its victims—concentrated among young people, particularly young males—car accidents remain an important cause of premature death. For the individuals and families involved, it is a great tragedy. Nevertheless, the table also shows how much progress has been made and how a series of measures has dramatically reduced the road toll in all the countries.

As cars became more widely affordable in the decades after World War II, the deaths from car accidents rose enormously. In all the selected countries, the road toll seemed to mount inexorably in the post-World War II decades and increased by more than a quarter between 1960 and 1970.

Since then, however, there has been a consistent and steady improvement, providing testimony to the capacity of well-directed policies to ameliorate the problem. In all but one of the countries, there was an increase in the road toll between 1960 and 1970, and in all but one, there was a decrease between 1970 and 1980. The 18-country mean rose by a third in the 1960s, but then it declined by an even bigger margin in the 1970s. It is particularly impressive that in every one of the periods since in the table, the number of road deaths has decreased substantially, even in the five years to 2015.

To varying degrees in different countries, the arsenal of changes has included: improved car design; compulsory wearing of seat belts; improved road design, including the identification of 'black spots'; reductions in speed limits; a much stricter approach to driving under the influence of alcohol, including random testing; and improved driver education. The improvement is more remarkable, because

---

[5]Earlier OECD data on traffic injuries can be found in Rodney Tiffen and Ross Gittins *How Australia Compares* (2nd ed, 2009). See also David Leonhardt *New York Times*, January 24, 2018.

the density of car ownership and the distances travelled in them have continued to increase.

Although all of the countries have reduced their rate substantially in recent decades, they have done so to different degrees. The most successful have been Britain and the Scandinavian countries. The least successful are New Zealand and America. Although it was not always thus, the smaller, densely populated European countries and Japan now have the lowest road tolls.

Perhaps it is the nature of the driving in America and New Zealand—with higher speeds in rural areas—that is the reason for them not continuing to improve as much as the others. However, the relatively high American figure may also lie in the uneven observance of the successful policy measures, which are overwhelmingly a state rather than federal responsibility. David Leonhardt, in the New York Times, has pointed out that half of the American fatalities in vehicle crashes were not wearing seat belts.

The casualties from traffic accidents are not only in the fatalities, but also in the injuries suffered. Injuries range enormously—from the permanently incapacitated to the temporarily inconvenienced. In very round figures, however, for every road traffic fatality, there are at least 50 others suffering injuries.

Religion

18.1 Religion

The United States has often been regarded as an anomaly among wealthy democracies because of its high levels of religiosity. While large majorities in other historically Christian countries may profess a belief in God or membership of a Christian church, the United States is unusual in its intensity of religious practice. The US Constitution, like several others, strictly separates church and state, but religion is nonetheless highly visible in its politics. Candidates for public office nearly always identify with a religion, and the divide between religious conservatives and religious liberals has become a central one in cultural and political life.

There are many plausible explanations for this exceptional American religiosity, from the religious foundations of the colonies to the competitive nature of the free religious 'marketplace' to the lower levels of existential security among poorer Americans.

Recently, there has been a new vigorous debate about whether the United States is still such a religious outlier. The most recent survey data from the Pew Foundation shows that more than 20% of Americans now identify as having 'no religion', a number comparable to other wealthy democracies, and that this number is growing rapidly. Some conservative religious commentators have warned that the United States is in danger of becoming another 'secular country', while this possibility has been celebrated by more secular-minded people who lament the continuing grip of religion on American culture and politics.

Discerning the reach and power of religion is difficult. For example, religious conservatives undoubtedly played a major role in electing President Donald Trump in 2016, with a record 81% of white evangelical Christians voting for Trump. Though he has consistently lived up to his policy promises to Christians, Trump himself is one of the least pious candidates for the presidency in recent memory, and some have interpreted evangelicals' embrace of him as the ultimate triumph of secular culture.

Social scientists who study religion identify three components of religious life that must be understood—belief, behaviour and belonging. Survey data about religion can be perilous, especially when it is limited to just one of the three. Social desirability bias—which means that respondents say what they think the interviewer wants to hear—means they may overstate their level of religious practice in the same way they overstate their propensity to vote or to exercise.

Distinguishing the three components is important: respondents may feel they belong to a religious group, but have little belief and never attend services. Or they may have idiosyncratic personal beliefs and practices that they don't reveal (e.g. superstitions that their churches warn against, but which sit quite comfortably alongside religion in their own lives). For these reasons, there is often little consistency between different surveys when it comes to religion, especially when comparing between the categories of belief, belonging and behaviour. Sometimes, their response may reflect their religious tradition rather than their current beliefs or practices. For example, while 87% of Norwegians identify themselves as Christians, just 53% say they believe in God.

The figures from *Brill's Encyclopedia of Religion* (Table 18.1) show that America has a somewhat more pluralistic religious tradition than some other countries. It is only in the United States and Canada that there are more than one per cent identifying as Jewish. Islam has become more important in some European countries, but has not yet reached 10% in any. The table omits other religions with Hinduism and Buddhism having a few per cent in some countries, probably due to immigration from Asia. In Japan, the combined figure for people professing Buddhism and Shintoism, sometimes embracing both, adds up to over 80%.

`While all these countries, apart from Japan, have strong Christian traditions, they differ in the mixes. The four Scandinavian countries were overwhelmingly Protestant, with a very small Catholic presence. These four now figure as the most secular on most measures. Five countries—Ireland, Italy, Belgium, Austria and France—were overwhelmingly

Table 18.1 Religious affiliation
Percentage of population professing different religions

Country	Christian	Muslim	Jewish	Agnostic/atheist
Ireland	92	–	–	6
Norway	87	5	–	6
Denmark	81	5	–	13
Finland	79	1	–	19
United States	**78**	**1**	**2**	**15**
Switzerland	77	6	–	16
Italy	77	5	–	17
Austria	73	7	–	20
United Kingdom	70	6	–	21
Canada	68	3	1	21
Belgium	67	7	–	25
Germany	67	6	–	26
France	65	9	–	24
Australia	64	3	–	25
Sweden	60	8	–	30
Netherlands	60	7	–	31
New Zealand	58	2	–	34
Japan	2	–	–	13
Mean	*68*	*5*	*0.2*	*20*

Other religions omitted, so percentages do not sum to 100
Mean < 0.5% in country
Brill's Dictionary of Religion Online

Table 18.2 Attending religious services
How often do you attend religious services?

Country	Once a week or more	Less than once a week	Never or almost never
Ireland	44	42	14
United States	**33**	**36**	**30**
Italy	31	56	11
Canada	25	42	34
United Kingdom	17	36	46
Austria	16	52	32
Australia	14	33	52
New Zealand	14	36	48
Switzerland	13	56	32
Netherlands	11	35	53
Belgium	10	37	53
Germany	10	54	34
France	8	32	60
Finland	7	68	25
Norway	5	54	41
Sweden	4	39	56
Denmark	3	63	33
Japan	2	86	10
Mean	*14*	*48*	*37*

Data from the World Values Survey Wave 6, 2010–2014; World Values Survey Wave 5, 2005–2009; and European Values Survey Wave 4, 2004–2008. LAY for each country

Table 18.3 Belief in God
Do you believe in God?

Country	Yes	No	No answer/don't know
United States	**88**	**11**	**1**
Ireland	87	8	5
Italy	84	9	8
Austria	72	19	9
Switzerland	69	22	9
Australia	64	34	2
Germany	63	34	3
United Kingdom	61	29	10
Belgium	59	32	2
Denmark	59	34	7
New Zealand	57	24	19
Finland	56	24	20
Norway	53	44	3
France	52	44	5
Netherlands	48	52	1
Japan	41	28	31
Sweden	41	50	8
Mean	*62*	*29*	*8*

No data on Canada
Data from the World Values Survey Wave 6, 2010–2014; World Values Survey Wave 5, 2005–2009; and European Values Survey Wave 4, 2004–2008. LAY for each country

Catholic. These now vary, but Ireland and Italy still figure as among the most religious. The other countries, including the United States, had more of a mix of Catholic and Protestant.

The tables do confirm a picture of America's relative religiosity. The United States has the highest levels of professing belief in God (Table 18.3) and the second highest percentage (after Ireland) of attending religious services weekly or more often (Table 18.2).

GPSR Compliance

The European Union's (EU) General Product Safety Regulation (GPSR) is a set of rules that requires consumer products to be safe and our obligations to ensure this.

If you have any concerns about our products, you can contact us on

ProductSafety@springernature.com

In case Publisher is established outside the EU, the EU authorized representative is:

Springer Nature Customer Service Center GmbH
Europaplatz 3
69115 Heidelberg, Germany

www.ingramcontent.com/pod-product-compliance
Lightning Source LLC
LaVergne TN
LVHW080249260326
834688LV00042BA/1187